BETWEEN RELIGION AND RATIONALITY

BETWEEN RELIGION AND RATIONALITY

ESSAYS IN RUSSIAN LITERATURE
AND CULTURE

Joseph Frank

PRINCETON UNIVERSITY PRESS

PRINCETON AND OXFORD

COPYRIGHT © 2010 BY JOSEPH FRANK

PUBLISHED BY PRINCETON UNIVERSITY PRESS,
41 WILLIAM STREET, PRINCETON, NEW JERSEY 08540
REQUESTS FOR PERMISSION TO REPRODUCE MATERIAL FROM THIS WORK
SHOULD BE SENT TO PERMISSIONS, PRINCETON UNIVERSITY PRESS

IN THE UNITED KINGDOM: PRINCETON UNIVERSITY PRESS,
6 OXFORD STREET, WOODSTOCK, OXFORDSHIRE OX20 1TW
ALL RIGHTS RESERVED

LIBRARY OF CONGRESS CATALOGING-IN-PUBLICATION DATA
FRANK, JOSEPH, 1918–
BETWEEN RELIGION AND RATIONALITY : ESSAYS IN RUSSIAN
LITERATURE AND CULTURE / JOSEPH FRANK.
P. CM.
INCLUDES INDEX.
ISBN 978-0-691-14256-2 (CLOTH : ALK. PAPER)
ISBN (PBK. : ALK. PAPER) 978-0-691-14566-2
1. RUSSIAN LITERATURE—19TH CENTURY—HISTORY AND
CRITICISM. 2. AUTHORS, RUSSIAN—19TH CENTURY—HISTORY
AND CRITICISM. 3. DOSTOYEVSKY, FYODOR, 1821–1881—RELIGION.
4. DOSTOYEVSKY, FYODOR, 1821–1881—PHILOSOPHY. 5. RELIGION
AND LITERATURE—RUSSIA. 6. PHILOSOPHY IN LITERATURE.
7. RUSSIA—INTELLECTUAL LIFE—1801–1917. I. TITLE.
PG3012.F73 2010
891.709'003—DC22   2009043863

BRITISH LIBRARY CATALOGING-IN-PUBLICATION DATA IS AVAILABLE
THIS BOOK HAS BEEN COMPOSED IN GALLIARD

PRINTED ON ACID-FREE PAPER. ∞

PRESS.PRINCETON.EDU
PRINTED IN THE UNITED STATES OF AMERICA
1 3 5 7 9 10 8 6 4 2

CONTENTS

INTRODUCTION 1

PART I. CLASSICS

ONE
Poor Folk and *House of the Dead* 9

TWO
The Idiot 29

THREE
Demons 46

FOUR
War and Peace 64

PART II. THE RUSSIAN TRADITION

FIVE
Natasha's Dance: A Cultural History of Russia 87

SIX
A Life of Pushkin 107

SEVEN
Oblomov and Goncharov 118

EIGHT
Lydia Ginzburg, *On Psychological Prose* 129

NINE
Richard Pipes, *Russian Conservatism and Its Critics* 143

PART III. THE DOSTOEVSKIAN ORBIT

TEN
Dostoevsky and Anti-Semitism 159

ELEVEN
In Search of Dostoevsky 173

TWELVE
Arkady Kovner   185

THIRTEEN
J. M. Coetzee, *The Master of Petersburg*   196

FOURTEEN
Dostoevsky and Evil   204

PART IV. TWENTIETH-CENTURY ISSUES

FIFTEEN
Anton Chekhov   219

SIXTEEN
The Triumph of Abram Tertz   230

SEVENTEEN
D. S. Mirsky   249

EIGHTEEN
Vladimir Nabokov: *Lectures on Literature*   261

INDEX   287

BETWEEN RELIGION AND RATIONALITY

INTRODUCTION

THE PRESENT VOLUME is composed of essays and reviews largely written over the years when I was working on the five volumes I devoted to studying Dostoevsky and his times. Such incidental pieces were of course conditioned by my concern with that key figure in Russian literature, but it is impossible to write about Dostoevsky without dealing with many others as well, and especially his great rival Tolstoy. Moreover, since my aim was to approach Dostoevsky not primarily as a biographical personality but as a writer whose work in effect provided "a condensed history of 19th century Russian culture"[1] (seen of course from his own idiosyncratic point of view), it was necessary to range over a much larger area than merely the details of his existence could provide. In my view, Dostoevsky's stories, novels, and journalism essentially responded to the moral-philosophical and moral-religious issues raised by the evolution of radical ideology during his lifetime (positively in his works of the 1840s, negatively, as its most devastating critic, beginning in the 1860s). It was thus necessary to become acquainted with his entire social-cultural context, and I kept an eye out for various books as they appeared that dealt with one or another facet of this broader horizon. Some of these works did not concern Dostoevsky directly but dealt with problems of Russian culture that formed the essential background of his creations. I have added to this collection a piece on Vladimir Nabokov's *Lectures on Literature*, which, although not dealing with Russian works except indirectly, is too fascinating to be eliminated for this external reason. It was, after all, written by a Russian author.

The title I have given this volume, *Between Religion and Rationality*, also indicates a general sense of what distinguishes the thematics of the Russian novel from those of other literary traditions. The distinctiveness of the Russian novel was noted at the end of the nineteenth century by the unjustly neglected figure of the Vicomte Eugene Melchior de Vogüé, whose book, *The Russian Novel* (1866), first brought this body of work to worldwide attention. The vicomte, himself a minor man of letters and later novelist, was stationed in the French Embassy at Petersburg for several years. He was one of the few foreign diplomats who made an effort to learn the Russian language and, marrying into the highest strata of Russian society, gained entrance to the court circles surrounding Alexander II. He was also personally acquainted with Turgenev and Dostoevsky (much

---

[1] Joseph Frank, *Dostoevsky: The Mantle of the Prophet* (Princeton: Princeton University Press, 2002), xiii.

more with the former than the latter) and became intimately familiar with Russian history and culture as well. After the publication of his book, sales of the few Russian novels already translated into French shot up like skyrockets, and a whole new translation industry was created to make others available to the reading public. Vogüé's book, written in an expressively personal style filled with firsthand impressions of Russian life, the Russian landscape, and the authors he had met, was translated everywhere and had the same results elsewhere as in France.

Writing in the context of a French Naturalism dominated by the pessimism and determinism of Flaubert and Zola, and whose end result as he saw it was *Bouvard et Pecuchet*, what impressed Vogüé most was the Russian refusal to accept such moral nihilism as their final word. The most important Russian novelists, as he accurately presented them, all came out of the so-called Natural School, whose ancestors were Gogol's novel *Dead Souls* and his novella *The Overcoat* (the latter so important for Dostoevsky's *Poor Folk*). Their images of life did not spare the sordid and the degrading, but what Vogüé admired in the Russians was a much broader view of humanity than was apparent in his own literature. "In going through their strangest books," he writes (and many Russian novels now considered masterpieces, such as *The Brothers Karamazov*, were still "strange" to his French classical tastes), "one senses a regulatory book in their neighborhood, a venerable volume that occupies a place of honor in the Imperial Library of Petersburg, the Ostromir Evangel of Novgorod (1056)."[2] It was this volume, dating from the early centuries of Christianity in Russia, that represented for him the source and spirit of much of the later literature that followed.

For Vogüé, the attraction of the Russian novel stemmed from its refusal to submit to a world in which the latest discoveries (or theories) of science took precedence over the age-old injunctions of Christian morality. It was only in the English novel of the time, as both Vogüé and other French critics suggested, that one could find anything comparable to the Russian. Indeed, he remarks that "despite my definitive taste for Turgenev and Tolstoy, I perhaps prefer that enchantress Mary Evans"[3] (George Eliot's real name), whose novels like *Adam Bede* and *Silas Marner* gave voice to the morality of English Protestantism. The novels of Dickens as well are filled with those overt Christian sentiments that Vogüé finds so lacking in his own literature. But while the nineteenth-century English novel may portray the difficulties of its characters to live up to the prescriptions of Christian morality, one does not find in it the same depiction of the struggle

---

[2] Eugène-Melchior de Vogüé, *The Russian Novel*, trans. H. A. Sawyer (London: Chapman and Hall, 1913), 18.
[3] Ibid., 15.

with the source of that morality itself, the Christian faith. Religion in the English novel is simply part of the social background, as one can see in the novels of Jane Austen or, a bit later, in Trollope's *Barchester Towers*. There is nothing in English to compete with Dostoevsky's remarkable attempt in *The Idiot* to dramatize the dilemmas of "a perfectly beautiful man"[4] modeled on the image of Christ.

Certainly one reason is that, before the eighteenth century, there was very little that could be called "the Russian novel." The genre previously had been represented almost exclusively by the hagiographic lives of saints, by the translation of a few Byzantine and Hellenistic romances, and, centuries later, by the imitation of Western models. The history of Russian culture contained nothing comparable to the efforts made since the Renaissance in Europe, inspiring its literature, to reconcile the Christian ethos with the demands of secular life, a process that has been superbly traced in that classic of modern criticism, Erich Auerbach's *Mimesis*. Russian literary realism, as Auerbach remarks, began very late, only during the second half of the nineteenth century, and is "based on a Christian and traditionally patriarchical concept of the creaturely dignity of every human individual regardless of social rank and position, and hence ... is fundamentally related rather to old-Christian than to modern occidental realism."[5] Russian literature thus took off at a relatively late stage, and it took some time before, instead of being merely imitative, it was capable of adapting these imported, unfamiliar forms to Russian realities.

The first important writer who really did so was Pushkin, and his irresistible narrative poem *Eugene Onegin* has often been called the first great Russian novel. No Russian writer was more familiar with European literature; but it is typical that his appealing heroine Tatyana, the origin of a whole line of similar female figures, ends by an act of self-sacrifice to a marriage vow. There is nothing specifically religious about her decision, but it is linked in the poem with the effect on her sensibility of her peasant nanny, whose values were those of a Russian religious tradition steeped in reverence for the self-sacrifice of Christ. The effect of such peasant religiosity on the Western-educated upper classes can also be seen in such a figure as Platon Karataev in *War and Peace*, whose serene acceptance of the vagaries of his life persuades Tolstoy's hero Pierre Bezuhov to accept all the harrowing incidents of his fate with tranquility and even with joy. Nor should one forget Konstantin Levin in *Anna Karenina*, whose life is transformed by hearing peasants speak of God as he is mowing hay in their midst.

---

[4] Fyodor Dostoevsky, *Polnoe Sobraniie Sochinenii*, ed. and ann. G. M. Fridlender et al., 30 vols. (Leningrad, 1972–1990), 28/bk. 2:241; December 31, 1867/January 12, 1868.

[5] Erich Auerbach, *Mimesis: The Representation of Reality in Western Literature* (Princeton: Princeton University Press, 2003), 521.

These are only several examples of the manner in which the disintegrating effects of the imposed Western culture assimilated by the educated upper class in Russia come into conflict with, and ultimately give way to, the religious sensibility absorbed from the omnipresent peasant world. It was Dostoevsky, as already suggested, whose great novels contain the most explicit expression of this clash. Dostoevsky dramatizes it in an incomparable fashion by depicting the various doctrines then in vogue to transform and (presumably) to improve a society dominated by social injustice and glaring inequality. His genius consisted in his consummate ability to depict the moral-psychological consequences of such ideas on his major characters—their struggle with, as it were, their Russian conscience—and to raise such struggles to the level of high tragedy. Despite the brilliance and originality of Mikhail Bakhtin, it has always seemed to me that Vyacheslav Ivanov's characterization of Dostoevsky's works as "novel-tragedies" came closer to their effect on the reader than Mikhail Bakhtin's emphasis on their "dialogism"—the competing clash of ideas and attitudes taking place between (as well as within) his characters. The harried circumstances of Dostoevsky's life, including his four years in a prison camp, also allowed him to portray such conflicts ranging through both the heights and depths of the Russian social order.

The "ideological" nature of the Russian novel, the manner in which its characters discuss and dispute as well as embody the reigning social theories of the day, has often been noted. Usually, this feature is attributed to the strictness of Russian censorship, the lack of any public venue where such issues could be safely disputed; and certainly this was an important factor. But a deeper reason could be the novelty of such ideas suddenly intruding on a world totally unprepared to receive them by any period of transition and compromise, such as had been worked out in European literature for several centuries. Russians themselves have often noted that the "radical" ideas of the West, when they came to Russia, were immediately driven to their most extreme consequences; they were not merely theories to be discussed, as was largely the case in other countries, but plans to be put into action. The greatest work inspired by this tendency is of course Dostoevsky's *Demons*.

Not all these incidental pieces deal directly with this perennial Russian problem, but it hovers in the background of Russian culture as a whole and keeps appearing and reappearing as an essential aspect of the Russian moral-cultural psyche. Chekhov, for example, wrote, "I can only regard with bewilderment an educated man who is also religious."[6] But then, in his beautiful story *The Student*, he portrays how two peasant women weep

---

[6] Anton Chekhov, *Polnoe Sobraniie Sochinenii i Pisem*, 30 vols. (Moscow: Nauka, 1974–1983); *Pisma*, 11:234; July 12, 1903.

on hearing a recital of Peter's betrayal of Christ; and the seminary student addressing them, whose faith itself is shown to be questionable, realizes to what extent these emotions are still alive among the common people after nineteen hundred years. Also, there is the unforgettable scene in Andrey Sinyavsky's study of Russian religion of his encounter with the *Raskol* (Old Believers) in his prison camp, who meet secretly at night in the boiler room to recite *The Apocalypse*, each of them having memorized a chapter.

To what extent this problematic of Russian culture will continue to exist amidst the transformations that have taken place since the rise and fall of Soviet communism can remain a matter of speculation only. But since it managed to survive the attempt of the ex-seminary student Stalin to stamp it out entirely, and flourishes once again in the relative religious freedom prevailing since the collapse of the Soviet system, one may assume that it is still destined for a long life.

I should like to express my gratitude to my teaching assistant at Stanford, Irina M. Erman, for her invaluable aid in locating the sources of quotations and references in my articles, as well as obtaining permission for their republication.

PART I

CLASSICS

ONE

POOR FOLK AND *HOUSE OF THE DEAD*

IF ONE WERE ASKED to select two books of Dostoevsky that represented the variety and range of his literary talent, no better choice could be made than *The House of the Dead* and *Poor Folk*. Dostoevsky is best known for his larger and later novels such as *Crime and Punishment*, *Demons*, and *The Brothers Karamazov*, while an influential critical tradition views him primarily as the unsurpassed chronicler of the moral-psychological dilemmas of the alienated, refractory urban intelligentsia. Once he became more widely known outside of Russia, this latter aspect of his work has had the greatest influence on later writers; but it represents much too limited a perspective on the full scope of his creations.

To be sure, there are elements of the later Dostoevsky in *Poor Folk*, with its vivid depiction of the St. Petersburg background and its first embryonic sketch of intelligentsia types. Its main character, though, is not a member of this group at all and anything but rebellious. He is a humble, socially and emotionally downtrodden clerk in the vast Russian bureaucracy of St. Petersburg, frightened to death at his temerity in questioning, even in thought, the supreme virtues of the God-ordained order in which he lives.

House of the Dead, on the other hand, stands alone in the Dostoevsky corpus as an unprecedented depiction, the first in Russian literature, of the prison gulags of the vast tsarist empire. Dostoevsky's initial readers were shocked by the conditions of life he described, but we have since learned from Solzhenitsyn's *Gulag Archipelago* that these were relatively humane compared to their successors under the Bolsheviks. The book also contains a gallery of Russian peasant-types and sketches of Russian peasant life that equal those of Turgenev and Tolstoy, both of whom admired the book (Tolstoy thought it the best work Dostoevsky had ever written). Such peasant-types are depicted only fleetingly in the major novels; but they were by no means outside his artistic purview.

These two books are thus miles apart in theme and artistic treatment.[1] The first initiates Dostoevsky's exploration of guilt-ridden characters; the

---

Introduction to *The House of the Dead and Poor Folk*, copyright © 2004 by Joseph Frank, originally published in a slightly different form in 2004 in the Barnes and Noble Classics edition of *The House of the Dead and Poor Folk* by Fyodor Dostoyevsky.

[1] For informative studies of *Poor Folk* and *House of the Dead*, see K. Mochulsky, *Dostoevsky*, trans. Michael A. Minihan (Princeton, 1967), chaps. 2 and 9.

second demonstrates his ability as an objective reporter and observer of a new social milieu. But there is one thing they have in common: both opened the path to fame (if not to fortune) for their author. *Poor Folk* brought him into the forefront of the Russian literary scene at the age of twenty-four, and for a brief period he was, quite literally, the talk of the town.

House of the Dead, on the other hand, was begun when he was thirty-nine, having returned to Russia after serving a prison sentence in Siberia and being absent from the literary scene for ten years. His first creations at this time, the novellas *Uncle's Dream* and *A Friend of the Family*, were received quite tepidly, and it was generally felt that his talent had not survived his exile. His prison memoirs, however, convinced even his detractors that they had been mistaken. These memoirs created a sensation by opening up a world hitherto concealed from the Russian reader. For the first time, the outcast criminal inhabitants of this hidden universe, generally looked down upon as little better than subhuman, were treated with respect and even occasionally with sympathy. Dostoevsky made no effort to conceal their sometimes horrendous crimes; but he saw them as sentient human beings whose behavior deserved to be understood if not pardoned.

Two

Poor Folk is Dostoevsky's first novel, and the story of its creation, as well as its reception, has become famous in the annals of Russian literature.[2] Both Feodor Dostoevsky and his older brother Mikhail had made up their minds as adolescents to pursue a literary career. Both, however, obeyed the wishes of their father to study to become military engineers, and Dostoevsky was still taking advanced courses, though living independently, in the years just preceding his literary début. Even before leaving home for their studies, he and Mikhail had steeped themselves in the literature of their time. Indeed, the admiration of the youthful Feodor for Pushkin was so great that, on hearing of the poet's death in a duel (1837), he told his family that if he had not already been wearing mourning for his mother, he would have done so in memory of the poet. One of the very last speeches he made in his life was a panegyric of Pushkin as equal, if not superior, to the greatest writers of European literature.

---

[2] Joseph Frank, *Dostoevsky, The Seeds of Revolt, 1821–1849* (Princeton, 1976), chap. 11, contains a lengthier discussion of *Poor Folk* than is given here. See also Victor Terras, *The Young Dostoevsky, 1846–1869* (The Hague, 1969), chaps. 1–3, which does not include a special section on *Poor Folk* but informatively analyzes the work from various points of view.

Dostoevsky came to maturity during a transition period of Russian culture, a moment when it was evolving from the metaphysical and fantastic motifs of German Romanticism toward the more down-to-earth social thematics of the French. His letters to Mikhail are thus filled with references to writers of both types. E.T.A. Hoffmann enjoyed a tremendous vogue at this time in Russia, and in 1838 Feodor writes that he had read "all of Hoffmann in Russian and German."[3] He continued to admire this Romantic fabulist and in 1861 wrote an article declaring him superior to Edgar Allen Poe. But he was enthusiastically proclaiming at the same time that "Balzac is great. His characters are the creations of universal mind!"[4] Dostoevsky's first publication, as a matter of fact, was a translation of Balzac's *Eugénie Grandet* undertaken at the end of 1843 to supplement his income.

If Balzac was important for Dostoevsky, of perhaps even greater significance was Victor Hugo, who in one of his poems spoke of himself as having "pleaded for those who are the lowest and the most miserable."[5] In a letter of 1840, Dostoevsky declared Hugo's Christian social Romanticism to be as momentous for the modern world as Homer had been for the ancient; and Hugo's social Christian radicalism left a permanent imprint on his own ideological views. One of Hugo's works, *Le dernier jour d'un condamne* (*The Last Day of a Condemned Man*) is the diary of someone awaiting execution for an unspecified crime—an intensely moving, and still very relevant, anguished outcry against capital punishment. Dostoevsky knew it by heart; and when he believed he was going to be executed himself, phrases from it returned to his mind. Traces of its effect can also be found throughout his novels.

In the early 1840s, the most prestigious literary genre was still that of Romantic tragedy, with Russians like Pushkin (*Boris Godunov*) following in the footsteps of Shakespeare, Schiller, and Hugo. It is thus no surprise that Dostoevsky's first try at literary composition should have been in this genre. In 1841 he read to friends parts of two dramas, *Mary Stuart* and *Boris Godunov*, which alas have not survived. But the titles are enough to show the range of his literary ambition, which did not hesitate to measure itself against the greatest. Romantic drama, however, was already losing its appeal for the younger generation, and Dostoevsky's own evolution followed the literary trend.

The new vogue turned to the social thematics of French Romanticism, as well as to the prose forms that had been developed there, among them the so-called physiological sketch, intended to portray the feel and texture

---

[3] Feodor Dostoevsky, *Pisma*, ed. and ann. A. S. Dolinin, 4 vols. (Moscow, 1928–1959), 1:47; August 9, 1838. Subsequently referred to as *Pisma*.

[4] Ibid.

[5] Victor Hugo, *Oeuvres Complètes* (Paris, 1882), 6:91

of ordinary life. One of the dominating figures of Russian literature, the impassioned and fiery critic Vissarion Belinsky, had become converted to French Utopian socialism in 1841 and immediately began to urge Russian writers to follow the French example. Gogol's *Dead Souls* had been published in 1842, and the *Petersburg Tales*, including *The Overcoat*, in 1843. Belinsky interpreted Gogol very freely as having pioneered the down-to-earth and socially conscious depiction of Russian life that he wished to encourage; and in 1843, as a memoirist tells us, Dostoevsky "was particularly fond of reading Gogol, and loved to declaim pages of *Dead Souls* by heart."[6]

Dostoevsky did not immediately surrender the idea of writing for the stage, but now he refers to a work called *The Jew Yankel* (a character in Gogol's novel, *Taras Bulba*), which indicates a shift to a less elevated subject. Whether such a work was ever written remains in doubt; but in the early fall of 1844 he tells Mikhail he is working on "a rather original novel"[7] that he hopes will bring in four hundred rubles. This is the first reference to *Poor Folk*, which he planned to send to Belinsky's journal *Notes of the Fatherland*. The manuscript, however, reached its destination by a much more original route.

Three

Dostoevsky was then sharing a flat with D. V. Grigorovich, himself a burgeoning writer, and read him the completed work. Grigorovich was so impressed that he took the manuscript to N. A. Nekrasov, destined to become a famous poet and already an active literary editor. Both were so overcome that they rushed to Dostoevsky's apartment at four in the morning—it was a Petersburg "white night"—to congratulate him on his accomplishment. They belonged to a group of young writers who, clustered around Belinsky, were known as his *pléiade*; and Nekrasov brought him the manuscript the next day. Belinsky's reaction is best described in the words of P. V. Annenkov, an important critic and cultural commentator, who visited him two days later. "You see this manuscript?" he said. "I haven't been able to tear myself away from it for almost two days now. It's a novel by a beginner, a new talent ... but his novel reveals such secrets of life and character in Russia as no one before even dreamed of ... it's the first attempt at a social novel we've had."[8]

---

[6] A. S. Dolinin (ed.), *F. M. Dostoevsky v Vospominaniakh Sovremmennikov*, 2 vols. (Moscow, 1964), 1:114. Subsequently referred to as *DVS*.

[7] *Pisma*, 1:73; September 30, 1844.

[8] P. V. Annenkov, *The Extraordinary Decade*, trans. Irwin Titunik (Ann Arbor, 1968), 150.

Belinsky's enthusiasm is quite understandable because, as Dostoevsky wrote to Mikhail shortly after joining the *pléiade* himself, he "seriously sees in me *a public proof* and justification of his opinions."[9] The critic had called for the Russians to follow the French, and to depict lower-class Russian life in all its varieties (a famous sketch by Grigorovich, used by Dostoevsky in *Poor Folk*, was devoted to organ-grinders). But emphasis in such works was placed on the description of externals, on photographic accuracy (the sketches were also called "daguerrotypes" and accompanied by illustrations), rather than on imaginative penetration and inner identification with the people involved. Also, even when an author collected sketches in a volume, they were not united by any sort of narrative continuity. Dostoevsky created the first Russian social novel by fusing such physiological sketches into a story about two lonely souls struggling to keep afloat in the treacherous sea of St. Petersburg life.

Dostoevsky is once supposed to have said (though the source has never been located, and the remark is sometimes attributed to Turgenev) that all of Russian literature emerged from Gogol's *The Overcoat*. Whether or not Dostoevsky ever uttered such a thought, there is no doubt that the dictum applies to *Poor Folk*. Indeed, the reference to Gogol illustrates a more important general point. There has been a strong tendency, especially in Western criticism, to focus on Dostoevsky's quite sensational biography in seeking to explore the sources of his work; but such sources are as much literary and social-cultural as purely personal. Whatever happened in his life was invariably assimilated and interpreted in terms of such a larger context. To understand his work, it is thus necessary to keep this surrounding ideological framework constantly in mind.

In *Poor Folk*, we find the influence not only of Gogol but also of Nikolay Karamzin, a dominating literary figure of the time, the title of whose story, *Poor Liza*, would immediately come to the mind of the Russian reader. Both works depict the sad fate of the lower classes (a peasant flower-girl in Karamzin, seduced and abandoned by a noble lover), but Dostoevsky's tone is far grittier than Karamzin's idyllic-sentimental treatment. Parodies are also included in *Poor Folk* of Romantic historical novels, and reference is made to the latest vogue for "physiological sketches." Of most importance is the relation of *Poor Folk* to two stories, Pushkin's *The Stationmaster* and Gogol's *The Overcoat*, both of which are read by Dostoevsky's main character, Makar Devushkin. The first, like *Poor Liza*, again dwells on the misfortunes of the humble and the defenseless when confronted with their betters; and Makar sees his own sad fate prefigured in that of the hapless stationmaster. Gogol's story, however, drives him into a rage; and a good way to approach *Poor Folk* is to examine the reason for such indignation.

---

[9] *Pisma*, 1:82; October 8, 1845.

The Overcoat is very far from embodying the plea for social justice that Belinsky was now advocating, though it does contain one passage in which such an appeal is made. The story, however, is as much a caricature of the main figure, who bears the implicitly scatological name of Akaky Akakievich, as it is a call for a more benevolent attitude toward those of his inferior status. Gogol's story takes its place in a long line in which such characters—lower-level copyists and clerks in the St. Petersburg bureaucracy—were the butt of comic anecdotes; and his own treatment is no different. Akaky is a human cipher, perfectly happy to grind away at his routine task and incapable of assuming any other; the narrator views him with the same relentless mockery that Akaky experiences at the hands of his office-mates. But at one point a younger clerk rebukes the others for mercilessly tormenting their helpless victim and reminds them that he is, after all, "their brother." Akaky's life is temporarily enriched when he acquires a new overcoat (hence the title), which becomes for him the equivalent of a loved object. A few days later it is stolen as he is walking home during the night. Unceremoniously evicted when he shows up at the home of an official of his district to appeal for aid, he dies shortly afterwards.

Four

Dostoevsky's *Poor Folk* turns this story inside out, as it were, by adopting the form of the sentimental epistolary novel. His two main characters write letters to each other, and we thus become aware of everything through *their* reactions and responses rather than through the superclious remarks of a narrator. Makar Devushkin is a middle-aged copying clerk like Akaky, and his correspondent is Varvara Dobreselova, a young girl barely out of her teens. They are related in some distant fashion, and Makar is trying to protect her from the wiles of a procuress who, in the guise of a friend of the family, has already succeeded in selling her once to a wealthy libertine. Devushkin is timidly in love with Varvara himself, but the difference in their ages, if nothing else, makes any such relation impossible; what she feels for him is friendly affection and gratitude, nothing more.

Both are tender, lonely, fragile souls, whose solicitude for each other brings a ray of warmth into their otherwise bleak lives; but their innocent little idyll is soon ended by the pressure of the sordid forces against which they struggle. Devushkin reduces himself to abject poverty for the sake of Varvara, and he suffers agonies of humiliation, which he tries to conceal, as he sinks lower and lower in the social scale. Finally, Varvara's violator shows up again and churlishly offers her marriage—not out of remorse or even desire but because he wishes to engender an heir to disinherit a nephew. The hopelessness of her position, and the chance to reestablish her social situation, compel Varvara to accept a loveless union with a callous mate and a harsh life in the Russian provinces.

This simple storyline is surrounded with a number of accessories that enlarge it into a true social novel. Inserted among the earlier letters is Varvara's diary, which introduces the classic contrast between the happiness and innocence of rustic childhood and the dangers and corruptions of the city. In these pages we catch a glimpse of a succession of penniless girls who have suffered the same fate as Varvara, or who, under the guise of beneficence, are being prepared for it by the sinister procuress Anna Feodorovna. The same insert-diary also contains the portrait of the gravely ill tubercular student young Pokrovsky, a devotee of Pushkin, who is Dostoevsky's first delineation of the new young intellectual, a *raznochinets* (someone with no official rank or status), eventually to evolve into Raskolnikov. As Varvara's informal tutor and intellectual mentor, he stirs her first romantic feelings. Pokrovsky is the illegitimate son of Bykov, the same landowner who raped Varvara, by another of Anna Feodorovna's "protegées"; the latter was then married off to a hopelessly drunken ex-clerk who gave the young man his name.

The relation of the pseudo-father, old Pokrovsky, to his educated son, whose cultural attainments he admires to the point of idolatry, symbolize as well the aspirations of Makar Devushkin himself to rise to a higher social-cultural status than the one in which he is placed. The funeral of young Pokrovsky, with the older one running after the carriage in a pouring rain as books fall out of his pockets, rivals Dickens in its tragicomic pathos. Belinsky remarked that it was impossible not to laugh at old Pokrovsky; "but if he does not touch you deeply at the same time you are laughing ... do not speak of this to anyone, so that some Pokrovsky, a buffoon and a drunkard, will not have to blush for you as a human being."[10] Another narrative line involves the Gorshkov family, the father an ex-clerk come from the provinces to clear himself of a charge; they live in such heart-rending poverty that even the impoverished Devushkin cannot resist giving them twenty kopeks to buy some food.

All these narrative strands interweave to build up an image of the same unavailing struggle to keep afloat humanly in the face of crushing circumstances. Everywhere poverty and humiliation, the exploitation of the weak and the helpless by the rich, powerful, and unscrupulous—all this in the midst of crowded St. Petersburg slum life, with its nauseating odors and debris-littered dwellings. Describing his own quarters, Devushkin writes: "On every landing there are boxes, broken chairs and cupboards, rags hung out, windows broken, tubs stand around full of all sorts of dirt and litter, eggshells and the refuse of fish; there is a horrid smell ... in fact it's

---

[10] Belinsky's article is reprinted in *F. M. Dostoevsky v Russkoi Kritike* (Moscow, 1956), 16.

not nice."[11] Dostoevsky's use of anticlimax here conveys the slightly risible (but nonetheless touching and moving) quality of Devushkin as a person. Yet amidst all this squalor, there are treasures of emotive responsiveness and moral sensitivity that appear in the most unlikely figures—unlikely, at least, from the point of view of previous Russian literature.[12]

Poor Folk combines these local-color aspects of the physiological sketches with a new and unerring insight into the tortures of the humiliated sensibility. "Poor people are touchy—that's in the nature of things," Devushkin explains to Varvara. "I felt that even in the past. The poor man is exacting; he takes a different view of God's world and looks askance at every passerby and turns a troubled gaze about him and looks at every word, wondering whether people are not talking about him, whether they are saying that he is ugly, speculating about what he would feel exactly," etc. (374). This "different view of God's world," the world as seen from below rather than above, constitutes the major innovation of Dostoevsky vis-à-vis Gogol. The situations and the psychology of *Poor Folk* thus speak for themselves against class pride and class prejudice; but the book also contains a much more outspoken protest, even though cast in terms of an easily comprehended "allegory."

Five

Makar Devushkin is by no means an uncomplicated character, and he undergoes a distinct evolution. In his early letters, he accepts his lowly place in life without a murmur of protest, even taking pride in performing his unassuming task as conscientiously as he can. He is perfectly content to live in the world as he finds it, although refusing to accept the condescending image of himself that he knows exists in the eyes of his social superiors. All the same, he at first unquestioningly accepts the rightness and justness of the social order in which he lives; but this instinctive faith is severely shaken by his inability to protect and provide for Varvara.

At the very lowest point of Devushkin's misery—hounded by his landlady, insulted by the boardinghouse slavies, and tormented by his ragged appearance—he loses heart entirely and takes to drink. But this is also the moment when a faint spark of rebellion flares even in his docile breast.

---

[11] Fyodor Dostoevsky, *The House of the Dead and Poor Folk*, trans. Constance Garnett (New York: Barnes and Noble Classics, 2004), 317. Subsequent references to this edition are cited in parentheses in the text.

[12] In a stimulating analysis, Robert L. Belknap shows that Dostoevsky did not always value suffering simply for its own sake. "The Didactic Plot: The Lesson about Suffering in *Poor Folk*," in *Critical Essays on Dostoevsky*, ed. Robin Feuer Miller (Boston, 1986), 30–39.

Walking along one of the fashionable Petersburg streets just after leaving the dreary slums in which he lives, he suddenly begins to wonder why he and Varvara should be condemned to poverty and misery. And he guiltily finds himself protesting ("I know that it's wrong to think like that, that it's free-thinking") against a world in which some people are just born to wealth, "while another begins life in an orphan asylum.... And you know it often happens that Ivan the fool is favored by fortune" (396). Such notions are an attack on the entire structure of his own hierarchical society; and he goes even further by proclaiming the distinctly Utopian socialist idea that the humblest worker is more worthy of respect, because he is more useful, than any wealthy, idle social parasite.

Devushkin's timid revolt against social injustice is embodied in his vision of an apartment house, on whose ground floor lives a poor shoemaker, whose only concern is the "boots" that he makes to feed his family. "His children are crying, his wife is hungry"; why should he not think only of "boots"? But elsewhere in the same building there is "a wealthy man in his gilded apartments," and he also thinks of "boots, that is, boots in a different manner, in a different sense, but still boots. "Why is there not someone to tell him to stop "thinking of nothing but yourself, living for nothing but yourself.... Look about you, can't you see some object more noble to worry about than your boots?" (399–400). Such a plea for the wealthy to concern themselves with the plight of the less fortunate obviously has Christian overtones; and if we are to define Dostoevsky's political beliefs at all in this period, it would be as a Christian socialist.

The same motif is dramatized in another scene, but given more than a material significance, when Devushkin is summoned to appear before his civil service superior because of some minor error. His terror and tatterdemilion garments so move the kind-hearted general that he gives Devushkin a hundred rubles. Refusing to allow the grateful clerk to kiss his hand, he also gives him an egalitarian handshake instead; and this respect for his human dignity takes on more importance for Devushkin than the money. "I swear that however cast down I was and afflicted in the bitterest days of our misfortune ... I swear that the hundred rubles is not as much to me as that His Excellency deigned to shake hands with me, a straw, a worthless drunkard" (405–6). This tension between the psychological and spiritual, on the one hand, and the economic and material, on the other, will run through all of Dostoevsky's later work and eventually receive its unsurpassed expression in the Legend of the Grand Inquisitor.

Another motif timidly broached in *Poor Folk*, and which also anticipates the later Dostoevsky, occurs as Varvara is preparing to leave after marriage. She has placed her fate, she says, in God's "holy, inscrutable power" (415), and Devushkin can only agree. "Of course everything is according to God's will; that is so, that certainly must be so, that is, it certainly must be God's will in this; and the Providence of the Heavenly Creator is blessed, of course, and inscrutable.... Only Varinka, how can it be so soon? ... I ... will be left alone" (415–16). Devushkin's despairingly stumbling efforts to reconcile a belief in God's wisdom and goodness with the tragedy of his own life, and implicitly of human life in general, clearly foreshadow the anguished reflections of many other Dostoevsky characters assailed by the same conundrum.

Six

The French Utopian socialists by whom Dostoevsky was influenced, and particularly those of the Christian variety, were not advocates of violence or revolution; they believed it possible to change the world by demonstrating the benefits of their precepts. One may well wonder, therefore, why Dostoevsky and all the other members of the discussion group to which he belonged (the Petrashevsky circle) were arrested in the spring of 1849. One reason is that the wave of revolution that swept through Europe in 1848 had frightened Tsar Nicholas I. Although the Petrashevtsi as a whole were guilty of nothing more than talk that might be considered subversive, and which they had carried on undisturbed for several years, this was enough now for the tsar to order them hauled in. It was once generally accepted in Dostoevsky scholarship that, like most of the others, he had been an innocent victim of a despotic tyrant; and various theories have been offered as to why, in later life, he seemed to have accepted his condemnation with relative equanimity.

In fact, however, as we now know, he was far from being as innocent as long believed. The Petrashevsky circle as a whole never made any attempt to conceal their meetings or discussions; but Dostoevsky belonged to a small secret group *within* the larger circle whose aim was to foment a revolution against serfdom. The seven members of this small group managed to conceal its existence from the commission of army officers appointed to investigate the activities of the circle as a whole. But why should a Christian socialist like Dostoevsky have participated in such a conspiracy?

The answer is probably that he hated serfdom with every bone in his body, and his seething revulsion against it was openly expressed the few times that he spoke at the larger group gatherings. Also, he may well have believed (though this is only inferential) that his father had been murdered by the serfs on their country property. This may help to explain why he agreed to become a member of this activist subgroup and even acted as a recruiting agent. A friend he visited recalled Dostoevsky (in a document first published in 1922) sitting in his nightshirt "like a dying Socrates"[13] unsuccessfully trying to persuade him to join. Dostoevsky thus lived all his life with the knowledge that he had once himself been a secret revolutionary conspirator, and his masterful depiction of the psychology of such characters can be attributed to this personal experience.

After his arrest, he was held in solitary confinement for a year and a half, questioned repeatedly (his caste status as a Russian nobleman precluded any physical mistreatment), and finally underwent the ordeal of a mock execution. He believed for about a half hour that he had been sentenced to be shot but then learned his true sentence—four years in a labor camp, and then service in the Russian Army. This mock execution was undoubtedly one of the most crucial experiences of his life. It was then, while he was standing in the shadow of death, that the religious question so timidly adumbrated in *Poor Folk* began to take on the supreme importance it assumed in the later work. It also conditioned him to open his eyes and his sensibility to the manner in which the Christian ethos had penetrated—or so he came to believe—to the depths of the personality even of the most ignorant and illiterate Russian peasant-convicts among whom he was now condemned to live.

After serving out his prison term, Dostoevsky began life in relative freedom as a private in the army, and then, with the help of influential friends in Petersburg, was promoted to officer. This promotion gave him the privilege of eventually being able to resign and once more take up his literary career. As already mentioned, he produced two novellas while still in Siberia, but his major work of this time, *House of the Dead*, was written after his return. Dostoevsky had thought of such a work earlier and mentions it in a letter in 1859 to his brother Mikhail while still traveling back to the capital. "These *Notes from the House of the Dead*," he tells him, "have now taken shape in my mind.... My figure will disappear. These are the notes of an unknown; but I guarantee their interest. There will be the serious and the gloomy and the humorous and peasant conversation with a particular convict coloring ... recorded by me *on the spot* [Dostoevsky had secretly kept a notebook in the camp, although this was forbidden] and the depiction of characters *unheard of* previously in literature ... and finally, the most important, my name."[14] So that while Dostoevsky himself will presumably disappear (he becomes only the editor of a manuscript left by a minor official who supposedly had murdered his wife), in fact everyone will be aware that the editor is talking about himself. Indeed, there

---

[13] Letter from Maikov to Viskovatov, 1885, in Peter Sekinin (ed.), The Dostoevsky Archive: Firsthand Accounts of the Novelist from Contemporaries, Memoirs and Rare Periodicals (Jefferson: McFarland, 1997), 79.

[14] *Pisma*, 2:605; October 9, 1859.

are several indications in the text that, unlike the common-law offenses of the peasant-convicts, the author has been sent to Siberia for a political crime.

Dostoevsky and Mikhail were planning to bring out a new journal *Vremya* (*Time*) in 1860, a period of relative liberalization of the press. Most of the book was published there in monthly installments, and it contributed greatly to the success of the magazine. The first several chapters, however, were published in another, rather obscure periodical. Dostoevsky was worried that his aim of opening the gates of the prison-camp world to public inspection would never pass the censorship; and he decided to allow another editor to explore the lay of the land.

His first installment was published without a hitch, but the second ran into trouble—of a kind that often turns the history of tsarist censorship into a black comedy. Far from objecting, as might have been expected, that the portrayal of prison conditions was too harsh to be permitted, the censors feared that peasants might be tempted to *commit* crimes just to enjoy the amenities of prison life that Dostoevsky portrayed. This objection was overcome by the consideration that the largely illiterate peasants were hardly likely to read the book; and Dostoevsky also wrote a supplement, not included in the final text, explaining that, even if one lived in paradise, "the moral torture" of loss of freedom would make camp life ultimately unbearable.

Seven

House of the Dead appears to be, on the surface, an extremely simple book.[15] It contains the memoirs of Dostoevsky's years in the prison camp, and for the readers of his time it brought to public scrutiny a whole world hitherto concealed from their gaze. Here was a gallery of peasant-criminals, most of whom had committed at least one murder, and about whom nobody else had ever written with such intimate knowledge. The aim of the work was to reveal their lives and their psychology, depicted, so far as possible, from their own point of view. Dostoevsky was in a unique position to accomplish this task because his sentence had placed him, unlike other members of his class, on the same social level as the peasant-convicts (actually on a level of inferiority, since they were better able to perform the physical tasks

---

[15] Joseph Frank, *Dostoevsky: The Years of Ordeal, 1850–1859* (Princeton, 1983), chaps. 6–11, deals with *House of the Dead* primarily from a biographical point of view. Frank, *Dostoevsky: The Stir of Liberation, 1860–1865* (Princeton, 1986), chap. 15, discusses the work from a literary point of view. Robert Louis Jackson, *The Art of Dostoevsky* (Princeton, 1981), chaps. 1–5, contains penetrating discussions of various aspects of *House of the Dead*.

assigned). They thus behaved with him unrestrainedly, as would not have been possible in nonprison conditions, where the class distinction would have governed their conduct and their words.

For the first time the Russian reader was presented with a peasant world possessing its own norms and values, and which Dostoevsky depicts primarily through sketches of the utterances, actions, and behavior of its inhabitants. The book unleashed a huge debate in the Russian press about the conditions it described, and some of the senselessly cruel regulations it brought to light were angrily challenged. Dostoevsky also stressed that there were different motivations for a crime such as murder (sometimes it was sordid; sometimes it was self-defense), even though both were inexplicably punished with the same sentence; and such considerations led to widespread discussion of Russian legal anomalies. What predominated in the reaction to the book was a recognition of the author's "humanism." Dostoevsky, it was felt, had succeeded in "redeeming" a whole class of criminals and outcasts (not all, to be sure, but the vast majority), and, as it were, returning them to the human fold. No attempt was made to lessen their misdeeds or to sentimentalize over their fate. But instead of being seen as aberrant monsters, they were shown rather as human beings whose often desperate crimes could be understood as responses to understandably tormenting situations.

For present-day readers, the impact of Dostoevsky's book in its own time is of less interest than what it reveals about the author himself. As I have said, he made superficial efforts to conceal his own presence by inventing a fictitious narrator, and his focus is on the world he is portraying rather than directly on himself. But in his *Diary of a Writer* (1873), Dostoevsky spoke of these years as having brought about "the regeneration of my convictions,"[16] that is, the convictions he had held before his arrest and imprisonment. These were now abandoned—though the process was by no means instantaneous—and replaced by those to which he remained faithful for the remainder of his life. Without approaching this change of heart and mind directly, *House of the Dead* can nonetheless, if read with sufficient care, help us to understand the transformation brought about by his prison years in Dostoevsky's ideas and values.

One such transformation involved the relation between the upper educated class and the people. We now know he had believed in the possibility of fomenting a revolution among the peasantry—a revolution led and guided by upper-class superiors like himself. No such hope could continue to exist, however, after the events portrayed in the chapter "The Complaint." Here Dostoevsky describes how he attempted to join a pro-

---

[16] F. M. Dostoevsky, *Diary of a Writer,* trans. and ann. Boris Brasol (Salt Lake City: Peregrine Smith Books, 1979), 152.

test organized by the peasant-convicts against the miserable rations they were being fed; but they forcibly led him away to the kitchen where the nonpeasant-convicts, and others who had refused to join the strike, were gathered. "I had never before been so insulted in prison," he writes, even though he depicts his daily humiliation on other grounds, "and this time I felt it very bitterly" (265). These quotidian offenses to his dignity were only incidental and personal; but here his rejection cut to the core of what had been a deeply held conviction.

When he questioned a friendly prisoner about this incident, asking why he had not been able to join in with them "as comrades," the peasant-convict replied in perplexity: "But ... but how can you be our comrades?" (270). The gap between the peasants and others was so great, not only in status but in mentality, that "even though [the ex-nobles] have been deprived of all the privileges of caste ... [the others] do not recognize them as comrades. This happens even without any conscious prejudice, but simply, in all sincerity, unconsciously" (32). The very notion of them acting together thus proved to be completely delusory; and never afterwards would Dostoevsky believe that the Russian peasantry would respond to any call of revolution issuing from the intelligentsia. Indeed, such calls were often uttered in a vocabulary whose terms the peasants could not even understand; and he would continue to maintain that the greatest social problem of Russia, whatever the economic or political situation, was to bridge the yawning gap of incomprehension between the peasantry and the educated class.

Also, Dostoevsky's view of the peasantry itself underwent an extremely significant evolution. A work like *Poor Folk*, with its sympathy and pity for the lower classes (even if not the peasantry) would indicate that Dostoevsky shared the Christian socialist view of their moral superiority to their betters. In a letter to his brother Mikhail, written just before departing for exile, he remarked that he was not being sent to a jungle but would be with other beings like himself, perhaps even better than himself. Nothing was more shocking and upsetting for him than to find, in the prison camp, a world that could only be labeled as one of moral horror. The peasant-convicts stole from each other incessantly, and Dostoevsky was not spared; every form of vice was available, including female and male prostitution; drunken quarrels were a daily occurrence; and cruel beatings among the convicts themselves were very frequent. Dostoevsky's image of this world is painted in appalling colors. "Noise, uproar, laughter, swearing, the clank of chains, smoke and grime, shaven heads, branded faces, ragged clothes, *everything degraded and defiled*" (14). Dostoevsky sometimes fled to the hospital, even though not ill and despite the risk of infection, where friendly doctors allowed him to stay. "I was fleeing from the prison. Life was unbearable there, more unbearable than the hospital, *morally unbearable*" (214).

Nonetheless, after a certain amount of time, Dostoevsky's revulsion against the prisoners and their world began to be altered by other impressions. For one thing, the more he learned about the circumstances in which many of their crimes had been committed, the more he could see that they were often a response to unbearable oppression or mistreatment. Moreover, what impressed him very deeply was that, whatever their crimes, the peasants unconditionally accepted the traditional Christian morality that condemned their behavior. Indeed, it was only because this morality exercised its effect that the pandemonium of the ordinary prison environment was replaced, even if only momentarily, by a less revolting atmosphere.

At Christmas, for example, gifts for the prisoners were sent by the lower classes of the town, and these were divided evenly by the convicts themselves with no quarreling at all. The effect of the holy day was enough to stem the incessant thievery and brutal brawling. At Easter, the convicts were relieved of work and went to church two or three times a day. They "prayed very earnestly, and every one brought his poor farthing to the church every time to buy a candle or to put it in the collection.... When, with the chalice in his hands the priest read the words ' ... accept me, O Lord, even as the thief,' almost all of them bowed down to the ground with the clanking of chains, apparently applying the words literally to themselves" (230). However much they may have violated Christ's commandments, their reverence for such injunctions did not diminish, and these continued to remain the standard by which they judged their own behavior. One of Dostoevsky's most fervent convictions was that—unlike, as he believed, the European proletariat—the Russian people would never attempt to justify, or refuse to acknowledge, their violations of the moral law.

What occurred to Dostoevsky at this time is best depicted in a sketch, "The Peasant Marey," that curiously enough he wrote seventeen years later and published in his *Diary of a Writer* (1876–1877).[17] Here he returns to reminisce about his prison years; and though the sketch is not included in his memoirs, it symbolically condenses the lengthier internal development that occurred during this time. It is placed in Easter week, when the convicts, after their brief moment of piety, had returned to their usual rowdiness and unruliness. "Disgraceful, hideous songs; card games ... a few convicts, already beaten half to death ... knives had already been drawn a few times" (425). To escape this repulsive spectacle, Dostoevsky walks outside and meets an educated Polish convict, also a political prisoner, who says to him in French: "I hate these bandits" (267). The Pole obviously intuited that Dostoevsky was harboring much the same revulsion against his barbarous fellow countrymen.

---

[17] See Robert Louis Jackson, "The Triple Vision: 'The Peasant Marey,' " in *Critical Essays on Dostoevsky*, ed. Robin Feuer Miller (Boston, 1986), 177–88.

Dostoevsky then returns to his bunk bed and recalls an episode from his childhood. Walking alone in a forest, where his mother had warned him that wolves might be wandering, he thought he heard a cry that a wolf was roaming in the vicinity. Frightened, he ran to one of his father's serf-peasants named Marey, plowing in a field. The gray-haired Marey assured the terrified child that no cry had been uttered and, calming him with the tenderness of "a mother," blessed him with the sign of the cross and sent him home. This spontaneous kindness on the part of an enserfed peasant, with every reason to abhor his master and his family, suddenly resurfaced in Dostoevsky's memory, transforming his entire attitude toward the peasant world around him as he pondered its meaning. "I suddenly felt I regard these unfortunates in an entirely different way and that suddenly, through some sort of miracle, the former hatred and anger in my heart had vanished.... This disgraced peasant, with shaven head and brand marks on his face, drunk and roaring out his hoarse, drunken song—why he might also be that very same Marey; I cannot peer into his heart, after all" (430). Dostoevsky was thus capable both of acknowledging the abhorrent aspects of peasant behavior and of seeking—and finding, as he persuaded himself—the redeeming Christian features lying concealed beneath the repellent surface.

By contrast, at the very same time that the peasant-convicts were thus metamorphosing into "Marey," Dostoevsky could not find a single redeeming feature in an upper-class convict named Aristov. He had been sent to prison for having falsely denounced others to the authorities as political subversives in exchange for payment to finance a life of debauchery. In prison, he served as a spy on his fellow inmates for the sadistic major in charge of the camp. He was clever, good-looking, well educated, and for Dostoevsky "the most revolting example of the depths to which a man can sink and degenerate and the extent to which he can destroy all moral feeling in himself without difficulty or repentance" (78). Far better the instinctive Christianity of the peasants, whatever *their* crimes, than Aristov's self-satisfied and gloating pleasure in his own ignominy! In *Crime and Punishment*, the name of Aristov is first given to the character who became Svidrigailov; and Dostoevsky's later declaration that, morally speaking, the people had nothing to learn from the educated class may well be traced to such a recollection.

Eight

There can be no doubt that one aspect of Dostoevsky's "regeneration of his convictions" referred to this change in his former condescendingly upper-class attitude toward the peasantry. But there is another, much deeper feature of this "regeneration" that can be detected in *House of the Dead*, and which involves his own most fundamental religious idea-feelings. It was long thought that Dostoevsky became converted to atheism in the 1840s, and that, under the stress of his mock execution and the ordeal of the prison camp, he returned to a belief in God and to fidelity to God's anointed, the tsar. Matters are not so simple, however, and there is no evidence that he ever lost his faith in the existence of God and the divinity of Christ, though he was thoroughly familiar with all the arguments being made against them by such thinkers as Ludwig Feuerbach and D. F. Strauss. But he remained a Christian socialist, whose ideal was to embody the law of love preached by a divine Christ into the daily life of his own society.

However, the ordeal of the mock execution had brought him face to face with eternity, and observations in the prison camp had also revealed to him the power of the irrational in the human psyche. The convicts sometimes acted in the most irrational and even self-destructive ways simply to give themselves a sense of freedom; and they were often sustained by the most delusory hopes about the betterment of their conditions. Without such hope, indeed, Dostoevsky concluded that they would have gone berserk (some of them did). "When he has lost all hope, all object in life," Dostoevsky writes, "man becomes a monster in his misery" (257–58).

Such observations are not specifically applied to religion, but there is one striking passage in the book that, if extended a bit, gives us a revelatory glimpse into the transformation of Dostoevsky's own faith as a result of his prison years. Noting that the prisoners resented the forced labor they were required to perform, he yet remarks that it was not intolerable because it made sense and could be seen to serve a useful purpose. But what if they were required to perform perfectly useless tasks? What if they "had to pour water from one vessel to another and back, over and over again, to pound sand, to move a heap of earth from one place to another and back again—I believe the convict would hang himself in a few days or would commit a thousand crimes, preferring rather to die than to endure such humiliation, shame and torture" (26). (Nothing of this sort, to be sure, happened in Dostoevsky's camp; but his conclusion can be supported by evidence gathered from Nazi work camps during the Second World War.)

What does this have to do with the question of religious faith? The answer is that, if we transpose the terms of this passage slightly, its religious-metaphysical implications become self-evident. Not to believe in God and immortality, for the Dostoevsky who emerged from the prison camp, is to be condemned to live in an ultimately senseless universe—analogous to that of the prisoners performing a useless task. The result, as he said himself, was that a thousand crimes would be committed to escape such humiliating degradation; or those condemned to such a fate would destroy themselves.

The characters in his great novels (all written after *House of the Dead*), who have lost or renounced their faith, consequently behave in this fashion—they commit crimes or take their own lives. And while their motives are more complicated than in Dostoevsky's thought-experiment, the psychological root of their behavior is much the same—the Christian moral laws of their universe have become senseless for them, and they have become monsters in their misery. The world of the post-Siberian Dostoevsky is thus no longer limited to applying the Christian law of love to earthly life, or rather, this problematic is now broadened and enriched by an excruciatingly heightened awareness of the importance of its linkage with the ultimate religious and supernatural sources of the Christian faith.

Nine

House of the Dead is thus a superb job of reportage, opening up a whole new world for the Russian reader, as well as a providing a penetrating glimpse into Dostoevsky's inner development. As a work, however, it seems at first sight to be more or less a collection of scenes and sketches, fascinating in their own right but given unity only by a common location. In fact, though, the book is very carefully constructed to correspond indirectly, by the manner in which its material is organized and arranged, with the inner process of Dostoevsky's encounter with, and assimilation of, this strange new world.

In part 1, the first six chapters depict his disorienting perceptions and the initial shock of contact ("First Impressions"), which then move on to the depiction of individual characters ("Petrov, Isaiah Fomich, Baklushin"). In part 2 the chapters are held together externally ("The Hospital") or by loose general groupings ("Prison Animals," "Comrades"). The narrator, whose surprised and startled reactions were quite prominent earlier, fades into the background as he merges into the everyday life of the community.

Dostoevsky's handling of time is particularly subtle and anticipates the experiments of our own day in correlating the shape of the narrative to accord with subjective experience. Time literally comes to a stop in the early chapters as the narrator concentrates on the novelty of the unfamiliar environment into which he has been thrown. More than a hundred pages are devoted to his first month; but the years then pass by unobtrusively as he becomes accustomed to camp routine, though time comes into prominence thematically as the end of his sentence nears. (The narrator received a ten-year sentence, but Dostoevsky had been given only four.)

House of the Dead is nominally a memoir, but it can be better described as a semifictional autobiography. As such it takes its place with two other works written about the same time, Turgenev's *Notes of a Hunter* (1852) and Tolstoy's *Sevastopol Sketches* (1855–56). Dostoevsky could well have been inspired by their example in the sketch-form that he created for the account of his prison-camp years. All three works in fact share the same overriding theme—the encounter of a member of the upper, educated class with the Russian people—and each treats it in his own distinctive way.

Turgenev stresses the spiritual beauty and richness of Russian peasant life, the poetry of its customs and superstitions, and by so doing makes the serf status of the peasants and the casual cruelty of their treatment all the more unforgivable. Tolstoy discovers the Russian peasantry amidst the besieged bastions of Sevastopol and is astonished by the calm tranquility of their unassuming heroism—so different from the vanity occupying the consciousness of their upper-class officers dreaming of decorations and promotions. Only Dostoevsky, however, depicts the Russian people *in revolt* against their enslaved condition, implacably hating the nobles who have oppressed them and ready to use their knives and axes to strike back when mistreatment becomes unendurable.

On the very last page of the book, just before his own fetters were struck off and he was once again a free man, Dostoevsky sets down a statement about the convicts that has led to some misunderstanding. "After all," he wrote, "one must tell the whole truth; these men were exceptional men. Perhaps they were the most gifted, the strongest of our people. But their mighty energies were vainly wasted, wasted abnormally, unjustly, hopelessly" (302). Dostoevsky here is obviously protesting against serfdom and the whole complex of Russian social customs that treated the peasant as an inferior species. Those who refused to accept such injustice and revolted against it could well be seen as the "strongest" of the people, whose "mighty energies" had been perverted.

Among the notes left by Nietzsche and later published in *The Will to Power*, there is a reference to this passage. The philosopher wondered whether one of his own subconscious (*unwillkürlich*) aims was not "to return a good conscience to an evil human being ... and the evil human being precisely insofar as he is the strongest human being. Here one should bring in the judgment of Dostoevsky about the criminals in the prison camp."[18] For Nietzsche, presumably, Dostoevsky's peasant-convicts were

---

[18] Friedrich Nietzsche, *The Will to Power*, book 3, cited in Wolfgang Gesemann, "Nietzsche's Verhältnis zu Dostoevsky auf dem europäischen Hintergrund der 8oer Jahre," *Die Welt der Slaven* 2 (July 1961): 129–56.

"evil human beings," whose "strength" derived from having overcome the inhibitions of customary moral constraints. Nothing, however, could have been farther from Dostoevsky's own point of view. Indeed, perhaps the most important conviction he had acquired as a result of his prison camp ordeal was that, even in their worst excesses, the Russian people had never abandoned the moral law proclaimed by Christ.

TWO

THE IDIOT

DOSTOEVSKY'S great novel *The Idiot*, one of the finest works ever written inspired by the image and the ideal of Christ, was composed during a particularly difficult period of his life. To be sure, some other periods of his existence had been equally tumultuous and agitated. There was his arrest as a political conspirator in 1849; the agonizing mock execution to which he had then been exposed; his four years in the prison camp, and the succeeding six of service in the Russian Army. But while such events were nerve-racking and tormenting, he was not, at the same time, attempting to carry on his literary career. And if we examine the conditions under which he wrote his other great novels, it is clear that none was created in such harassing and distracting circumstances as *The Idiot*.

He was, in the first place, then living in Europe, whose culture he admired but whose social and political institutions he abhorred—and which he came to detest even more virulently the more he remained abroad. Presumably, he had left Russia with a new bride, twenty years younger than himself, only for a vacation visit of a few months; but the absence from his homeland unexpectedly continued for four years. Just before leaving he had been pursued by creditors, who threatened to throw him into debtor's prison; and he feared that if he returned as impoverished as he had left, the threat would be carried out. He and his devoted wife Anna Grigoryevna settled first in Dresden, and then in Baden-Baden; next they went to Switzerland, living in Geneva and Vevey; finally they traveled to Italy, residing first in Milan and then Florence. To finance the trip, Dostoevsky had received an advance from Mikhail Katkov, the powerful editor of *The Russian Messenger* in which *Crime and Punishment* had recently been published; and he continued to live on such advances all through this time. It was necessary for him to get to work as soon as possible, both to cover the funds already obtained and, by the installments of a new novel, to earn what was necessary to meet his current expenses.

Aside from this peripatetic existence, several other factors also interfered with all his efforts to satisfy his literary obligations. During an earlier

---

Introduction to *The Idiot* copyright © 2004 by Joseph Frank, originally published in a slightly different form in 2004 in the Barnes and Noble Classics edition of *The Idiot* by Fyodor Dostoyevsky.

trip to Europe, Dostoevsky had been bitten by a passion for roulette (he never gambled excessively in any other way) and had even written a novella, *The Gambler* (1866), whose depiction of the psychological ravages of a gambling fever remains unsurpassed. Ironically enough, he had met Anna Grigoryevna when she had come to help him as a stenographer to meet a deadline with this text; and he had proposed marriage by depicting himself as someone who had to choose between disastrously surrendering to his gambling mania or being rescued by the stability of a new loving attachment.

Once back in Europe, however, it became clear that he had not really overcome his addiction; and the hypnotic lure of the wheel, besides inevitably increasing the impoverishment of the couple, also drew him away from his writing table. The letters that Dostoevsky wrote to his wife from the various resorts with gambling casinos to which he traveled, often imploring her to send money for his return, are among the most pitiful, pathetic, and self-castigating that he ever penned. In the end, however, he managed to conquer his obsession before returning home in 1871; and from that time on, even when residing in Europe on several occasions, he never gambled again.

It was also while working on *The Idiot* that Dostoevsky first became a father. His daughter Sofya (Sonya) was born on March 5, 1868 (according to the European calendar), and Dostoevsky became so upset during the delivery that the midwife finally excluded him from the room. Anna herself later recalled that "at times I saw him sobbing, and I myself began to fear that I might be on the threshold of death."[1] But nothing untoward occurred, and Dostoevsky wrote a week later to his friend, the poet Apollon Maikov, that "Sonya, my daughter, is a healthy, robust, lovable marvellous child, and I spend practically half the day kissing her and can't tear myself away."[2] According to Anna, Dostoevsky was "the tenderest possible father," who would sit by [the baby's] crib for hours on end, now singing songs to her, now talking to her."[3]

One can well imagine the depth of despair into which the Dostoevskys were plunged when, three months later, Sofya caught a chill, contracted an inflammation of the lungs, and was carried away after a week. In another letter to Maikov, Dostoevsky expresses his grief in heart-rending words. "This tiny, three months old being, so pitiful, so minuscule—for me was already a person, a character. She began to recognize me, to love

---

[1] Anna Dostoevsky, *Reminiscences*, trans. and ed. Beatrice Stillman (New York, 1975), 142.

[2] Fyodor Dostoevsky, *Polnoe Sobraniie Sochinenii*, ed. and ann. G. M. Fridlender et al., 30 vols. (Leningrad, 1972–1990), 28/bk. 2:272–73; March 2/14, 1868. Hereafter cited as PSS.

[3] Anna Dostoevsky, *Reminiscences*, 146.

me, to smile at me when I approached, when I, with my ridiculous voice, sang to her, she liked to listen.... And now they tell me, in consolation, that I will have other children. But where is Sofya? Where is that little individual for whom, I dare to say, I would have accepted crucifixion so that she might live?"[4] If the thematic motif of an all-too-untimely death resounds with such poignancy in the anguished outcries of the adolescent Ippolit in *The Idiot*, racked by an advanced tuberculosis, one can surely trace them to the emotions experienced by the author with the death of his little Sonya.

Another aspect of the book can also be linked with the events of Dostoevsky's life in this period. In their wanderings through Europe, the couple passed through Basel on their way to Geneva and paused for a one-day stopover to take in the sights. The cathedral and the museum were the objects of their interest, and it was the museum—or one of its paintings—that anticipatorily provided inspiration for the future novel. Along with much else, they saw the famous canvas of Holbein the Younger, *The Dead Christ*, which enjoyed a widespread notoriety. Indeed, in a book well-known to Dostoevsky, Nikolay Karamzin's *Letters of a Russian Traveller*, it is mentioned as one of the attractions that no conscientious tourist should miss.

The picture depicts Christ separated from all the traditional iconographic accoutrements that usually accompany his portrayal, and Karamzin records the legend that the painter had used the corpse of a drowned Jew as his model. According to Anna's *Diary*, much closer to the event than her later *Reminiscences*, Dostoevsky was so impressed with the painting that he climbed on a chair to obtain a closer look; and Anna was terrified that the law-abiding Swiss would fine him for such a violation of museum decorum. So overcome was he by the canvas that "he pronounced Holbein the Younger a painter and creator of the first rank."

Anna's description of the work, which may be assumed to contain the impressions of her husband as well, stresses that while the body of Christ usually contains "no marks at all of pain and suffering," in this case the opposite was true. "But here the whole form is emaciated, the ribs and bones plain to see, hands and feet riddled with wounds, all blue and swollen, like a corpse on the point of decomposition.... The whole thing," she remarks, "bears such a strong resemblance to a real dead body that I should not like to be left with it in a room alone."[5]

A copy of Holbein's painting turns up in chapter 4, part 2, of *The Idiot*, where Prince Myshkin, who has seen it abroad in Switzerland, remarks: "Why, that picture might make some people lose their faith." It is referred

---

[4] *PSS*, 28/bk. 2:297; May 18/30, 1868
[5] *Dnevnik A.G. Dostoevskoi, 1867 g.* (Moscow, 1923), 361–66.

to again later by the young Ippolit, well aware of being doomed to an early death, who wrestles with the problem that the picture poses not only for him, but for Prince Myshkin as well, and, we may assume, also for the author of these anguish-filled pages. "Looking at such a picture," Ippolit declares, "one conceives of nature in the shape of an immense, merciless, dumb beast, or, more correctly, much more correctly speaking, though it sounds strange, in the form of a huge machine of the most modern construction, which, dull and insensible, has aimlessly clutched, crushed and swallowed up a great priceless Being, a Being worth all of nature and its laws, worth the whole earth, which was created perhaps solely for the sake of the advent of that Being." Ippolit imagines the people who surrounded this dead man as being gripped by "the most terrible anguish and consternation" at the sight of his corpse, though when they parted, "each one bore within him a mighty thought which could never be wrested from him."[6]

For Dostoevsky, we may speculate, the greatness of Holbein the Younger lay in the boldness with which his art confronted the anomalies of the Christian faith. (Modern scholars, though, tend to doubt whether Holbein the Younger had any genuine concern with the religious quarrels of his time, and Erasmus, once a friend of whom he left a famous portrait, thought him opportunistic.) However that may be, it is a similar boldness that Dostoevsky displays in *The Idiot*, and no one can doubt *his* sincerity.

Two

Just as *The Idiot* was written under more adverse conditions than Dostoevsky's other major novels, so the external history of its composition involved a more far-reaching change than can be observed elsewhere. Dostoevsky often shifted plans as he made initial notes for his works, and he continued to do so even after embarking on what he thought would be the final text. *Crime and Punishment*, for example, began as a first-person novella exploring the psychology of a humanitarian murderer; but then, incorporating much of the original novella, it became a larger, third-person work with many more characters. Dostoevsky rewrote a good part of *The Devils*, of which he already had a considerable draft, when the glamorously lethal Byronic dandy Stavrogin emerged as his main character instead of the pathetically lovable member of an earlier generation, the liberal idealist

---

[6] Fyodor Dostoevsky, *The Idiot*, trans. Constance Garnett, Elina Yuffa (New York: Barnes and Noble Classics, 2004), 375. Subsequent page references to this work are cited in parentheses in the text.

Stepan Trofimovich. A change of creative plan in midcourse was therefore nothing unusual for Dostoevsky; but the case of *The Idiot* was more extreme than all the others. In fact, the work that he initially outlined in his notebooks and began to write has only the loosest relationship to the text that finally emerged.

Three notebooks for *The Idiot* exist in the Dostoevsky corpus. Two contain scenarios written before the first chapters were published; the third shows Dostoevsky struggling to find his way amidst the plethora of possibilities opened by the thematic motifs already adumbrated. The prepublication notes can only be described as a fertile creative chaos, and some notion of their bewildering diversity is conveyed by Edward Wasiolek, who supervised their translation into English. "The relationship between characters fluctuates from plan to plan: sisters are and are not sisters, nephews become sons, fathers become uncles. The idiot is sometimes the son of the Uncle, sometimes the nephew, sometimes the foster son, sometimes illegitimate, and sometimes legitimate; acts are committed and die abortively in the next plan, or even a few lines later; people hang themselves but then perhaps don't hang themselves; the same people die by hanging, poisoning, broken hearts or drowning. It is not always clear who is who, where they come from, and where they are going," etc.[7] What *is* clear, however, is that, all through this time, Dostoevsky was searching for an inspiration that continues to elude his grasp.

A character labeled "the idiot" does appears in these early notes and is also described as subject to epileptic seizures; but his personality is the very opposite of what he will later become. At first, he is characterized as follows: "*The Idiot*'s passions are violent, he has a burning need of love, a boundless pride, and out of pride he means to dominate himself, conquer himself. He takes delight in domination."[8] This first conception of "the idiot" is thus more or less the reverse of the later one; but other figures in these notes are endowed with some of the moral qualities that he will later possess. At this point, "the chief character of the novel" is called the Uncle, who is "a usurer," "a hypochondriac, with a deep-seated vanity, pride."[9] But his son is an ideal figure, called "a socialist" by his father, though Dostoevsky writes: "he is not a socialist: on the contrary; he finds in socialism little besides an unrealizable ideal. Economic redistribution, the problem of bread." The son also "preaches about how there is a great

---

[7] Fyodor Dostoevsky, *The Notebooks for "The Idiot,"* trans. Katherine Strelsky, ed. with intro. by Edward Wasiolek (Chicago, 1967), 7–8. I have utilized this translation for my further quotations from the notebooks.

[8] *PSS*, 9:141.

[9] Ibid., 142.

deal of happiness in life, that each moment is a happiness." The word "Christ" then suddenly appears, and the note: "To an extent the son has already impressed the idiot sometime earlier."[10] It is as if Dostoevsky were on the point here of fusing the two, with the idiot taking on some of the attributes of the son; but the connection will not be made until much later. Nonetheless, it is striking that on the margin of this page Dostoevsky scribbles the following sentence, repeated almost verbatim in the novel: "The one thing in the world is spontaneous compassion. As of justice—that is a secondary matter."[11]

Dostoevsky continued to shuffle and reshuffle his various plot ingredients and characters for several months in the helter-skelter fashion indicated by Wasiolek. But while numerous situations and suggestions can be seen in retrospect as embryonic indicators of what lay ahead, "the idiot" still remains "an anguished, contemptuous, endlessly proud personality," though now "*in the end he is agonized by his own role,* and suddenly perceives a solution in love" (italics in text).[12] Just how to present this last mutation, however, remains unresolved.

In November, with only a month left before the first installment of his novel was due, and in the midst of setting down a tentative outline, Dostoevsky desperately adds in italics: "*Give me an idea!*"[13] One can only speculate about what occurred at this time, but there is some reason to believe that the "idea" at which he finally arrived could well have come from another source than the notes for his novel. Dostoevsky's creative imagination was intensely prolific, and he often jotted down ideas for various works simultaneously. One such jotting, which turns up amidst those for the future novel, may well have helped him to discover what that novel eventually became.

This plan, entitled "*A Thought* (Poem), Theme Called 'The Emperor,'" was inspired by an article in a historical journal about an incident that had occurred in the mid-eighteenth century. A one-year-old child had then inherited the Russian throne, and the new empress kept him imprisoned for the remainder of his life. He died at the age of twenty-four, after a young army officer unsuccessfully tried to free him and reestablish him to his rightful place. Dostoevsky develops the various figures (the prisoner is now twenty years old) and dwells on the innocence and backwardness of the isolated captive (he even has to be taught to speak). The beauty of the world as he comes to discover it fills him with rapture; but he is overcome with dismay on learning of all its injustices. When his presump-

[10] Ibid., 151–52.
[11] Ibid., 152 n2.
[12] Ibid., 171.
[13] Ibid., 196.

tive rescuer explains that they are not social equals, he replies: "If you are not my equal, I do not wish to be emperor."[14] It may well be that the guilelessness of the princely prisoner, himself an "idiot" for so many years, and now exposed to both good and evil for the first time, served as a transition figure between the tyrannical and egoistic idiot-character of Dostoevsky's first conception and the sudden appearance of "the idiot" in another incarnation.

In any case, the notes from early November contain a new idea: "He is a *Prince*. Idiot," and then, in the next sentence, "*Prince* Yurodivi. (He is with the children)?!"[15] (A *yurodivi* is a Russian "holy fool," sometimes considered deranged or demented but also endowed with an unearthly aura of transcendence and often uttering a truth concealed by normal social relations.) Some of Dostoevsky's excitement here can be felt in his punctuation as a new image of "the idiot" begins to crystallize, and the formerly vengeful personality of this figure was shifted elsewhere. Of the son, now called Ganechka, Dostoevsky writes: "This is the character that was formerly the Idiot's: magnanimous, bitterness, pride and envy."[16] Many of the definitive plot details now begin to surface in the notes ("the Idiot with the children ... about Mont Blanc, Switzerland"). What occurred is then described in a letter at the end of December, in which Dostoevsky explains to his literary confidante Valerian Maikov that, although he had begun to write a novel (presumably in November), "I threw it all out" and on December 4 "set about the painful task of inventing *a new novel*."[17] The Prince Yurodivi could not be incorporated into any of the earlier scenarios, and his appearance, moreover, confronted Dostoevsky with a challenge he had long endeavored to avoid.

"For a long time already," he confesses, "there was an idea that had been bothering me, but I was afraid to make a novel out of it because it was a very difficult idea and I was not ready to tackle it.... The idea is—*to portray a perfectly beautiful man*.... The idea used to flash through my mind in a somewhat artistic form but only *somewhat*, not in the full-blown form that was needed. It was only the desperate situation in which I found myself that made me embark upon an idea that had not yet reached full maturity. I took a chance, as at roulette" (italics in text).[18] Starting on December 18, Dostoevsky thus set out to write a novel about "a perfectly beautiful man," and in a burst of inspiration he was able to send seven chapters to the journal by January 11.

[14] Ibid., 114.
[15] Ibid., 200.
[16] Ibid., 204.
[17] *PSS*, 28/bk. 2:240; December 31, 1867/January 12, 1868.
[18] Ibid., 240–41.

A day later, in a letter to his favorite niece to whom the novel was originally dedicated, Dostoevsky elaborated on his conception of "the perfectly beautiful man." There is only one such, he explains, and that is Christ, "so that the phenomenon of that boundlessly, infinitely good figure is already in itself an infinite miracle." Earlier attempts had been made in Christian literature to represent such a figure, and for him the finest of all was Don Quixote; but this character was essentially comic, someone at whom the reader was supposed to laugh—tenderly, to be sure. The same was true of Dickens's Mr. Pickwick, "a conception infinitely weaker but still ... tremendous," who generates sympathy because he is unaware of his own worth. Jean Valjean in Hugo's *Les Misérables* is also a Christ figure but of a different caliber: "he engenders sympathy because of his terrible misfortune and society's injustice toward him.... But there is nothing of this sort in my novel, absolutely nothing, and that's why I am afraid it will be a positive failure."[19] Prince Myshkin, indeed, inherits a fortune just after the action gets under way; and while the other characters are struck by his "strangeness," they find his moral purity to be more impressive and disturbing than a source of merriment.

Three

This first section of the novel plunges the prince into the superficially respectable but inwardly corrupt world of Petersburg high society, with a plot intrigue similar to that of Alexandre Dumas Jr.'s *La Dame aux Camelias*, a work referred to in the text (it also served Giuseppe Verdi for his opera *La Traviata*). In both works, a beautiful woman who has been socially disgraced, but is still capable of nourishing the finest feelings, is asked to sacrifice herself in the name of family honor. In Dumas, it is the *demi-mondaine* Marguerite Gautier who submits to the implacable condemnation of society so that the sister of her aristocratic beloved can enter into a proper marriage. In Dostoevsky, it is the queenly Nastasya Filippovna, once the innocent ward and then the helpless mistress of the elegant high official Totsky (a variant of his name is Trotsky, and one rather regrets that it was not used). Totsky now wishes to marry her off so that he can wed one of the daughters of General Epanchin; but the proudly resentful Nastasya refuses to allow herself to be bought and sold in this disgraceful if socially acceptable fashion.

The prince in part 1 finds himself in the midst of this drama, instantly recognizing Nastasya's fineness of spirit and sympathizing with her rage

---

[19] Ibid., 251.

and resentment, although appalled at the self-destructive form it has assumed. Indeed, in the riotous party scene that terminates this first section, he attempts to thwart her decision to debase herself even further by running off with the immensely wealthy merchant's son Rogozhin, consumed by a mad, all-consuming passion for her that bodes no good. When the prince unexpectedly, and to everyone's astonishment, offers her marriage, she replies: "Thank you, prince. No one has ever talked to me like that before.... They've always been trying to buy me, but no decent man has ever thought of marrying me." But of course she refuses ("did you really think I meant [to] ... ruin a child like that?)" (156), and she departs with Rogozhin and his disreputable group to express her contempt for the outwardly estimable but inwardly depraved society that had corrupted her own life.

These early chapters, written at white heat, also contain other notable features. *The Idiot* is the most autobiographical of Dostoevsky's novels, or at least the one in which autobiography obtrudes most overtly. There is the scene, for example, in which the prince attempts to gain admission to the Epanchin mansion from a recalcitrant footman, inclined to think him an impostor pretending to be a relative because of his far from fashionable clothes and modest manner. The prince succeeds in gaining entry, however, after recounting his impressions of an execution by the guillotine that he had witnessed in Europe. Intuiting the agony undergone by the condemned man as he faced the ineluctable certainty of death, which the prince compares with the "torture and agony ... [of which] Christ spoke too," he then muses: "Perhaps there is some man who has been sentenced to death and then has been told: 'you can go, you are pardoned.' ... Perhaps such a man could tell us" (22).

Dostoevsky himself was of course such a man, having experienced these same torments in 1850 during the mock execution staged by Nicholas I to punish the Petrashevsky circle. All of them had been officially condemned to death and then pardoned. The ordeal of this mock execution is utilized again in Prince Myshkin's scene with the Epanchin sisters, who at first tend to regard the unassuming prince as something of a pious fraud. Not only does Dostoevsky here reproduce the exact details of this lacerating event, but he also expresses sentiments similar to those he employed in a letter to his older brother Mikhail just after returning to prison. "Life is a gift," he wrote then, "life is happiness, every minute can be an eternity of bliss."[20] These are the very emotions that Prince Myshkin attributes to a condemned man who then was pardoned: "What if I could go back to life—what eternity! ... I would turn every minute into an age; I would lose nothing" (56). The mock execution again appears when the prince, asked to suggest a subject for a picture to be painted by Adelaida Epanchin, can

---

[20] *PSS*, 28/bk. 1:163–64; December 22, 1849.

think only of the face of a condemned man and a priest holding up a cross. The prince's sensibility is thus haunted by the shadow of eternity, and the absolute sense of moral obligation that he exhibits can be attributed to this overhanging presence.

In *The Idiot* as well, Dostoevsky also draws on his own ailment of epilepsy more explicitly and directly than anywhere else in his writings. Just before the onset of a fit, during which he loses consciousness and is overcome by spasmodic convulsions, the prince felt an "aura" of ecstatic plenitude, which, as we know from other sources, reproduces the sensations felt by his creator. At such moments, the prince became aware of "the acme of harmony and beauty ... a feeling, unknown and undivined till then, of completeness, of proportion, of reconciliation, and of ecstatic devotional merging in the highest synthesis of life." It was a moment of "infinite happiness," which "might well be worth the whole of life" (208). And it was then that the prince "seem[ed] somehow to understand the extraordinary saying [from the Book of Revelations] that *there shall be no more time*" (209). Moments such as these may well have strengthened Dostoevsky's own belief in the existence of a supersensous realm transcending ordinary earthly existence. If so, however, he did not employ it in *The Idiot* for such a purpose. On the contrary, the loftiness of the vision is depicted as a sublime illusion; and when the prince acts under its inspiration, he provokes Rogozhin into an attempt on his life.

This first section of *The Idiot* contains some unforgettable scenes in which the "angelic" character of the prince is superbly portrayed. One such is the story of Marie, a consumptive little slavey in the Swiss village where the prince is being treated for epilepsy. She has been seduced and abandoned by a traveling salesman and then becomes a despised outcast mistreated by everyone and ridiculed by the village children. Moved by her misery, the prince gives her a few francs and persuades the children that she has been unjustly abused and condemned. The last days of her life are thus irradiated by the warmth of their love, and she dies surrounded by their care and devotion. The children, when they observe the prince kissing her out of compassion, are unable to distinguish between this and the kisses exchanged between their parents; and this leitmotif of "the two loves" will later be developed on a large scale in the rivalry between Nastasya Filippovna and Aglaia Epanchin.

The completion of this first part, however, posed new problems for Dostoevsky because he had written it without any overall plan, and it is clear from his letters and notebooks that he scarcely knew how to continue. "As I go along," he wrote to his niece, "various details crop up that I find fascinating and stimulating. But the whole? But the hero? Somehow the whole thing seems to turn on the figure of *the hero*.... I must establish the character of the hero. Will it develop under my pen?" Even though he seemed to see other characters quite clearly, he confesses that "the main hero is still extremely pale."[21] The notes reveal that he continued to struggle with this problem all through the remainder of the book. On the one hand, as he writes, it was necessary *"to show ... the Prince in a field of action"*[22] (italics in text); but on the other, as Reinhold Niebuhr has written of Christianity, "it is impossible to symbolize the divine goodness in history in any other way than by complete powerlessness."[23] Dostoevsky thus was faced with the dilemma of creating a hero lacking all the usual attributes associated with such a figure, but whose moral-religious purity would somehow shine through and redeem his practical impotence.

Four

The Idiot is the most loosely constructed of Dostoevsky's major novels, no doubt because of its sudden emergence but also because of this inherent difficulty of constructing a determining sequence of action for his main figure. After part 1, the book thus breaks up into three alternating narrative strands. One is the Nastasya–Myshkin relationship, which now, however, sinks into the background for lengthy stretches. What occupies the foreground is the prince's attraction to Aglaia Epanchin, the youngest, most beautiful, most headstrong, and most socially idealistic of the three Epanchin daughters. She has been attracted by Myshkin's defiance of social convention as he springs to the defense of Nastasya, who has been externally dishonored but is the innocent victim of circumstances. Aglaia thus characterizes Myshkin, in a famous scene, as "The Poor Knight" of Pushkin's well-known poem, a work that she recites in his presence after having spoken of the "poor knight" as "Don Quixote, only serious and not comic" (229). The third narrative strand consists of all the ancillary episodes that Dostoevsky introduces in such profusion, and which, allowing him to roam far and wide, add so much vivacity and even grotesquerie to what is otherwise a hauntingly tragic story.

The first of these plot-lines centers on the Nastasya–Myshkin–Rogozhin triangle, and on the prince's efforts to rescue the once-violated but now regal and commanding Nastasya from the self-destructive consequences of her own resentment and rage. She had fallen prey to what Dostoevsky called elsewhere (in his first post-Siberian novel, *The Insulted and Injured*) "the egoism of suffering," that is, an egoism turned back upon itself in

---

[21] *PSS*, 28/bk. 2:241; December 31, 1867/January 12, 1868.
[22] *PSS*, 9:242.
[23] Reinhold Niebuhr, *The Nature and Destiny of Man: A Christian Interpretation* (New York: Scribner's Sons, 1949), 72.

masochistic self-hatred and using its own self-punishment as a means of exhibiting its contempt for others. Nastasya dabbles with the potentially murderous passion of the socially inferior Rogozhin so as to display her scorn for such "respectable" gentlemen as Totsky and General Epanchin, who wish to dispose of her life for their own purely selfish ends. Prince Myshkin provided the only exception to this sordid intrigue that she had ever encountered in "respectable" society.

While the threat of Rogozhin's violence hangs over Nastasya from the earliest pages, the notes reveal that Dostoevsky contemplated the possibility of averting what finally seemed the inevitable ending. At one point, he writes: "He [Myshkin] rehabilitates N. F. and asserts ascendancy over Rogozhin. He induces humility in Aglaia," etc.[24] Other notes, however, sketch the murder that will ultimately occur. "When Rogozhin shows him N. F.'s corpse. She was screaming. He kisses the corpse."[25] No final choice was made until later, when Dostoevsky was writing part 4 of the novel; and he thought that readers would be surprised by such a conclusion. "If there are readers of *The Idiot*," he wrote in a letter, indicating his doubts about the novel's success, "they perhaps will be somewhat stunned by the unexpectedness of the ending, but, on reflection, they will finally agree that it had to end this way."[26] No doubt he imagined that, given the Christian aura surrounding the prince, a more positive or "uplifting" termination might have been expected; but he found it impossible to satisfy such a presumed anticipation.

The second plot-line centers on the prince's involvement with Aglaia, who is also being courted by the polished and sophisticated nobleman Radomsky. The latter serves additionally as a commentator on the action from a highly civilized and worldly point of view, both friendly but distant and quite skeptical. The tentative romance between the prince and Aglaia posed something of a critical problem for Dostoevsky because Myshkin's capacity to maintain a normal love relationship remains ambiguous. Some commentators have believed him to be sexually impotent, and as evidence they can cite his remark to Rogozhin: "Perhaps you don't know that owing to my illness, I know nothing of women" (14). These words can be taken simply as a statement of fact about the prince's life up to that point, or as the indication of a more fundamental disability; but there are reasons to doubt that it refers to a physical infirmity. In the first place, although Dostoevsky himself was an epileptic, he was twice married, the father of four children, and is known to have been passionately involved with at least one mistress. Moreover, to interpret the prince in this way would weaken

[24] *PSS*, 9:252.
[25] Ibid., 229.
[26] *PSS*, 28/bk. 2:327; December 11/23, 1868.

one of the important leitmotifs in the book—the conflict in the prince himself between his pure but carnal love for Aglaia and his compassionate love for Nastasya. These differing kinds of love are carefully distinguished in Dostoevsky's notes, as well as by the early scene with the children, and they ultimately come into conflict. Unless we accept the prince's desire to marry as flowing from a normal masculine urge, we seriously undermine the tragic nature of his dilemma.

The romance between Prince Myshkin and Aglaia provides some of the most charming scenes of the book, filled with a tender playfulness hard to find in Dostoevsky elsewhere. It is she who necessarily takes the lead in what would normally be the masculine prerogative of courtship; and even after she does so, the afflicted prince cannot imagine that it was possible for him to experience anything such as ordinary "love" for a woman. Indeed, as he wanders through the park at night in Pavlovsk waiting for Aglaia (a scene that Dostoevsky rightfully referred to later as one of his best), "if anyone had told him at that moment that he had fallen in love, that he was passionately in love, he would have rejected the idea with surprise and perhaps with indignation" (332). Earlier, when Aglaia had read the "Poor Knight" poem, substituting the initial letters of Nastasya's name for those in Pushkin's text, he took it as "a mockery," though everyone else understood it as an indication of her burgeoning romantic infatuation. The scene in which she tries to prepare him for the reception at which he will officially appear as her fiancé, both fearing his social ineptitude and denouncing those who might ridicule it, also beautifully captures the incongruity of their situation.

Prince Myshkin dramatizes Dostoevsky's image of "a perfectly beautiful man," who comes as close as humanly possible to the Christian ideal; but for Dostoevsky there was only "one positively beautiful figure in the world—Christ,"[27] and the appearance of Christ had been "an infinite miracle." There could only be one God-man; and while He remained an eternal aspiration for humanity, such aspiration could never obviously receive its complete fulfillment in purely secular form. Many years before, holding a nighttime vigil at the bier of his dead first wife in 1864, Dostoevsky had jotted down some notes that provide the only direct firsthand glimpse into his religious convictions; and these can serve as a commentary on the prince. Here he writes that "to love man *like oneself*, according to the commandment of Christ, is impossible. The law of personality on earth binds. The *Ego* stands in the way."[28] And as an example of the nefarious effects of this "law of personality," obstructing the perfect fulfillment of Christ's commandment, Dostoevsky astonishingly cites the institution of

---

[27] Ibid., 251; December 31, 1967/January 12, 1868.
[28] *PSS*, 20:172.

marriage. "Marriage and the giving in marriage of a woman ... [is] the greatest deviation from humanism, the complete isolation of the pair from everyone else ... the family, that is the law of nature, but [it is] all the same abnormal, egotistical."[29] The prince's attraction to Aglaia, which normally would lead to marriage, thus runs athwart of the Christian commandment to love all of mankind like oneself.

The love theme of the book comes to a crisis in the climactic scene where the two women confront each other as rivals and demand that the prince choose between them. It is then that Myshkin must decide between his love-as-compassion for Nastasya and his flesh-and-blood love for Aglaia. Nastasya's suffering, her "frenzied and despairing face," initially stirs his heart; he even appeals to Aglaia on her behalf; but this is enough to end his romance with her once and for all. The purest earthly love cannot be reconciled with the universal compassion embodied in the Christian ideal, and the prince is caught in the racking impasse created by this situation. In the final chapters, while making preparations to marry Nastasya Filippovna, the prince still wishes to continue visiting Aglaia; and the narrator confesses that "we find it difficult in many instances to explain what occurred" (525). The prince is inwardly torn, as the highly intelligent Radomsky recognizes, between "two different sorts of love" (535) completely incompatible one with the other. This is why his behavior can no longer be comprehended by the narrator, who only reflects the bewilderment of the community at Myshkin's unwillingness to surrender one for the other as required by existing social norms. Like Christ with the Pharisees, Myshkin has now gone beyond the realm where such norms have any relevance. In the eerie final scene, after Nastasya has fled back to Rogozhin's embittered love-hatred, the prince consoles the hysterical murderer beside the corpse of his victim; and he finally sinks back into the darkness of the epileptic oblivion from which he had emerged at the beginning of the novel.

Five

The third of Dostoevsky's narrative strands contains a whole host of minor characters who enliven, enrich, and diversify the main thematic action in ways that are sometimes ludicrous and grotesque, and whose effect may be compared to the burlesque interludes often included in medieval mystery plays. All these figures are analogically related to Dostoevsky's central motif—the effort fully to incorporate the Christian ideal—and each exhibits a different level of the conflict between some form of moral behavior

---

[29] Ibid., 173.

and the inherent egoism of the human personality. One of the most important is the dying adolescent Ippolit, who becomes the first of the metaphysical rebels later developed in such characters as Kirillov in *Demons* and Ivan Karamazov.

Ippolit emerges as an ideological rival to Prince Myshkin's meekness and humility, rising in revolt against a God who has condemned mankind to suffering and death. When the prince first sees the copy of Holbein's *Dead Christ* in Rogozhin's home, he tells of four encounters that had convinced him that "the essence of religious feeling does not come under any sort of reasoning or atheism, and has nothing to do with crimes or misdemeanors.... But the chief thing is that you will notice it more clearly in the Russian heart than anywhere else" (203). The prince can thus surmount this iconoclastic image of the dead Christ, whose contemplation can very well cause a loss of faith. But for Ippolit the canvas leads to a semicomic public reading of his "Necessary Explanation," which nobody really wants to listen to, and is terminated by an attempt at suicide that rather pathetically fails. Ippolit's youthful mawkishness and self-preoccupation, combined with the sadness of his fate, anticipates some of the black comedy of Beckett. One of the most poignant moments of the book, however, occurs when Ippolit pleadingly asks the prince how best he might die and receives the compassionate but also rather guilty reply: "Pass by, and forgive us our happiness" (479).

If Prince Myshkin embodies the purest and more exalted expression of Dostoevsky's theme, other characters represent it in a completely opposite register. In their case, we see the almost miraculous survival of a moral sensibility in lives where it might be considered to have been completely extinguished. The rascally civil servant Lebedev, for example, is both a lawyer and a fervent expounder of the Apocalypse; and he narrates a gruesome story about medieval cannibalism in the parodistic style of a lawyer arguing for the defense. It appears that, during times of extreme famine in the Middle Ages, cannibalism was widely resorted to; and one such cannibal, who began by eating monks (usually well nourished) and little children, reduced his diet to laymen because he was tormented by his conscience. But finally he went and confessed to the authorities, despite all the tortures he knew would ensue, though he might simply have desisted without saying a word. From which Lebedev concludes that "there must have been an idea stronger than any misery, famine, torture, plague, leprosy and all that hell, which mankind could not have endured without that idea, which bound men together, guided their hearts ... show me anything like such a force in our age of vices and railways" (348). Despite such a disillusioned conclusion, Lebedev himself and all the other minor characters manifest the workings of the same force that is so sarcastically exalted in this harrowing tale.

Such extreme dissonances of tone fill *The Idiot* to a much greater extent than other Dostoevsky novels. But there are also appealing touches of less grisly humor in the cock-and-bull stories of the discredited General Ivolgin, vainly striving to overcome his social degradation by the mythomaniacal adventures he recounts to dubious, half-amused listeners who do not believe a word that he utters. The anecdote about the lapdog tossed out of the window of the railway carriage, after its well-bred female owner had done the same with the general's cigar, demonstrates his refusal to accept so insulting a reprimand; but it turns out, alas, to have been taken from a recent newspaper article. The marvelous story about his relation to Napoleon as a child during the siege of Moscow, in which his innocent words lead to the disastrous Russian retreat in midwinter, is sheer braggadocio worthy of Falstaff and narrated with irresistible skill. Dostoevsky's talent as a satirical humorist has been generally overlooked because of the tragic nature of his themes; but nowhere is it better displayed than in *The Idiot*.

If we place *The Idiot* in the perspective of Dostoevsky's work as a whole, it may well be considered his most courageous creation. Not, however, because he tackled the almost impossible creative task of presenting "a perfectly beautiful man" within the limits of a novel form whose "realism" he wished to respect. It was courageous because, in doing so, he was putting his own highest Christian values to the same test as those to which he had been most opposed. The inspiration for his best novels, before and after *The Idiot*, had been provided by his polemical relation to the doctrines of Russian Nihilism. In the underground man and Raskolnikov, as later in Stavrogin and Ivan Karamazov, he dramatized the disastrous consequences of such Nihilist ideas if taken to their ultimate limits in human behavior. But this is exactly what he does in *The Idiot* as well—except that the values in this instance are those that he himself cherished with a fervor made all the more ardent by his full awareness of their vulnerability.

With an integrity that cannot be too highly praised, Dostoevsky fearlessly submits his *own* most hallowed convictions to the same scrutiny that he had used for those of the Nihilists. What would they mean for human life if taken seriously and literally, and lived out to their full extent as guides to conduct? The moral extremism of his own eschatological ideal, incarnated by the prince, is portrayed as being equally incompatible with the normal demands of social existence as the egoistic extremism of his tormented and tortured Nihilist figures. Dostoevsky thus remained true to his deepest artistic instincts in narrating the career of Prince Myshkin; but no doubt for this reason the reactions of his closest literary allies, as well as the general public, were far from enthusiastic.

To Maikov, as he was working on the fourth section, he wrote: "Now that I see, as through a magnifying glass, I am bitterly convinced that never in my literary life have I had a better and richer poetic idea than the one now becoming clear to me." But he complains about having to rush "full speed ahead," lacking the time even to reread what he has written, and helplessly feeling that "if I had started writing this novel a year earlier and then could have spent two or three months correcting and re-writing, it would have come out differently."[30] However that may be, the novel soon began to make its way; and nine years after it had been published Dostoevsky wrote to a correspondent who considered it his "masterpiece": "Let me tell you that I have heard such an opinion 50 times if not more. The book keeps selling every year, and more as time passes."

Posterity has justified the verdict of Dostoevsky's correspondent about the novel that Dostoevsky undertook as a gamble, as if he were playing roulette. One may say that it is the one and only time he emerged a winner.

---

[30] *PSS*, 28/bk. 2:320–21; October 26/November 7, 1868.

THREE

DEMONS

DOSTOEVSKY'S *Demons* (*Besi*), sometimes also translated as *The Devils* or *The Possessed*, is probably the greatest novel ever inspired by a revolutionary conspiracy; but it was not the book that its author had intended to write. The story of how it came into being in its present form is rather a complicated one, involving Dostoevsky's own literary ambitions, the fact that he was living abroad, and the appearance in the Russian and German newspapers, which he read assiduously every day, of stories about an atrocious crime committed in his homeland by a small cell of revolutionaries.

At the time this news appeared, Dostoevsky had been dreaming of writing another type of novel entirely, one that would center on the loss of religious faith and its recovery; but he felt that he could not create such a work before returning to Russia from his European exile. The cause of his prolonged, four-year sojourn in Europe was not, as in the case of Turgenev, a preference for the amenities of European culture (and a desire to remain close to his mistress, the diva Pauline Viardot). It was simply a need to escape from creditors who, on his return, might have thrown him into debtors' prison. The debts involved, incidentally, had not accumulated because of his own imprudence, as is too often assumed. In fact, they were those of a failed commercial venture of his deceased older brother Mikhail, whose obligations he had voluntarily taken over. Dostoevsky's first idea for what became *Demons* was thus to knock off rapidly what he called a political "pamphlet," in which he could express all his by now bitter hatred of the Russian radicals and their ideology. It might also, at the same time, bring in sufficient income to enable him to return to Russia, where he would settle down to write the great work that he regarded as the culmination of his literary career. But things did not turn out that way at all.

Dostoevsky was living in Dresden, plagued by financial worries and undecided about what to undertake next. He had recently finished *The Idiot*, in which he had tried to depict "an absolutely beautiful man" (Prince Myshkin), who wished both to live in the real world and, at the same

---

Introduction to *Demons* copyright © 2000 by Joseph Frank, originally published in a slightly different form in 2000 in the Everyman's Library edition of *Demons* by Feodor Dostoevsky.

time, to incorporate the highest Christian virtue of totally selfless love. Unfortunately, this novel had not met with the same success as *Crime and Punishment*; nor was Dostoevsky by any means satisfied with it himself. In a letter to the critic N. N. Strakhov, defending what he called his "fantastic realism" ("what the majority calls almost fantastic and exceptional for me sometimes constitutes the very essence of the real"), he nevertheless admitted that "much in the novel [*The Idiot*] was written hastily, much is dragged out and does not come off, but something still does come off. I do not stand by my novel but by my idea."[1]

This "idea," in its broadest sense, was to create a positive artistic image to counter the influence of the ideology of Russian radicalism in the 1860s. The intellectual leaders of this movement—N. G. Chernyshevsky, N. Dobrolyubov, D. Pisarev—are little known except to students of Russian culture, but they exercised an enormous influence and determined the literary-cultural ambiance in which Dostoevsky was writing. These critics and publicists (though Chernyshevsky also wrote a famous and influential novel, *What Is To Be Done?*) not only were atheists who rejected God and the divinity of Christ; they also attempted to substitute for the Christian morality of love and self-sacrifice one based on a purely home-brewed Russian amalgam of Benthamite utilitarianism and Utopian socialist idealism (labeled "rational egoism"). Dostoevsky's great aim was not only to reveal the disastrous human consequences to which such an ideology might lead (as he had done with both the underground man and, more explicitly, Raskolnikov in *Crime and Punishment*), but also to rehabilitate the Christian ideal against all its gainsayers. It is thus not surprising that, even before completing the fourth and last part of *The Idiot*, he should have thought of another embodiment of the same thematic ambition.

In December 1868, writing to his oldest friend, the poet Apollon Maikov, Dostoevsky confides his plan for "a huge novel whose title would be *Atheism*," asking his friend to keep the idea secret ("for God's sake, let this remain between us").[2] The passage is too lengthy to quote in its entirety, but it involves a main character who loses his religious faith and then embarks on a quest to find a substitute ideal. He goes off in search of this alternate faith among a large variety of competing groups: "the atheists, the Slavs and Europeans [i.e., the Slavophiles and Westernizers], the Russian fanatics, anchorites, the priests"; he even flirts with Polish Jesuits but "slips away from them to the depths of the flagellants [Russian sectarians]—and in the end finds Christ and the Russian God." The importance

---

[1] Fyodor Dostoevsky, *Polnoe Sobranie Sochinenii*, ed. and ann. G. M. Fridlender et al., 30 vols. (Leningrad: 1972–1990), 29/bk. 1:19; February 26/March 10, 1869. Hereafter cited as *PSS*.

[2] *PSS*, 28/bk. 2:329n1.

of this project for Dostoevsky could not be more forcefully expressed: "Let me write this final novel," he declares, "and even if I die—I will have spoken out about everything."[3]

It was to take another year, however, before Dostoevsky could get around even to making notes for this project. Instead, to obtain some much needed funds (his wife had just given birth to a daughter), he wrote *The Eternal Husband* with great reluctance, although his expressed aversion to doing so did not prevent him from turning out a small masterpiece, the most classically perfect of all his shorter works. But it was only in December 1869 that he could think of his *Atheism* novel again, which by this time had turned into a much larger idea for a work in several volumes to be called *The Life of a Great Sinner*. Never written as such, this projected series furnished material for *Demons*, as well as for Dostoevsky's two last novels, *A Raw Youth* and *The Brothers Karamazov*.

His ideas for *The Life of a Great Sinner* were sketched in his notebooks between December 1869 and January 1870, and Dostoevsky told Apollon Maikov in the first week of December that he would be sitting down to begin writing "in three days."[4] But just a month later, he excitedly reported to Maikov that he had been inspired by a new theme. "I have tackled a rich idea," he tells him enthusiastically. "I am not speaking of the execution but of the idea. One of the ideas that has an undoubted resonance among the public. Like *Crime and Punishment* but even closer to reality, more vital, and having direct relevance for the most important contemporary issue." Dostoevsky was certain that he would be able to finish this novel by the fall of 1870, and that, since its topicality might have the same financial success as *Crime and Punishment*, "there is hope of putting all my affairs in order and of returning to Russia.... Never have I worked with such enjoyment and such ease."[5]

This is the first reference to *Demons* in Dostoevsky's correspondence, and we can also see the novel beginning to take shape in his notebooks. At the same time, he continued to add material to his "great sinner" corpus (some notes are dated from as late as March 1870). What was the idea that had so suddenly gripped Dostoevsky, and had "direct relevance to the most important contemporary issue"? It was the murder, committed during November 1869, of a young student at the Petrovsky Agricultural Academy in Moscow by a revolutionary group headed by Sergei Nechaev; and one can see why Dostoevsky thought that his proposed idea was "even closer to reality" than *Crime and Punishment*. In that novel, he had *imagined* a crime inspired by the supposedly humanitarian aims of radical ideol-

---

[3] Ibid.
[4] *PSS*, 29/bk. 1:81; December 7/19, 1869.
[5] Ibid., 107; February 12/24, 1870.

ogy; but now "reality" had caught up with what he had foreseen would be the results of "rational egoism" in practice.

News about the crime began to appear in the Russian and foreign press about a month after it was committed; and while it certainly would have attracted Dostoevsky's notice in any case, the name and activities of Nechaev had come to his attention even earlier. It so happened that Dostoevsky's young brother-in-law, Ivan Snitkin, was a student in this very academy and had been visiting with the Dostoevskys in the fall of 1869. Dostoevsky's wife, Anna Grigoryevna, thus attributed the origin of the novel to Dostoevsky's conversations with her brother; but this exhibition of pardonable family pride is highly exaggerated. At most, Ivan Snitkin may have spoken to Dostoevsky about Nechaev's organizing activities at his school before the murder actually took place; but he could have known nothing else. Nor is there any evidence in Dostoevsky's notes that he thought of a novel involving a political murder before the story broke in the newspapers. Indeed, Dostoevsky himself affirmed, in a letter to his editor Mikhail Katkov a year later, that "I know nothing at all about Nechaev, nor Ivanov [the victim], nor the circumstances of the murder, except from the newspapers."[6]

What Dostoevsky learned from these newspapers confirmed some of his worst fears, particularly exacerbated during his self-imposed European exile, about the disintegrating effect that the Western-imported ideas of the Russian Nihilism of the 1860s was exercising on the moral fiber of Russian society. Sergei Nechaev, whose extraordinary force of personality seemed to exercise a hypnotic effect on all those with whom he came into contact, had carried the utilitarian component of "rational egoism" to its farthest extreme. He advocated a total Machiavellianism— one that included deception and falsity not only against one's enemies but also against friends and allies if this became necessary for the cause. In his own case, Nechaev created a completely false myth about himself as having been arrested, and then accomplishing the unprecedented feat of escaping from the Peter-and-Paul fortress (where Dostoevsky himself had once been imprisoned). When Nechaev contacted the veteran revolutionaries Mikhail Bakunin and Nikolai Ogarev in Geneva, enveloped in the aureole of his supposed exploits, he represented himself as the delegate of a powerful and perfectly fictitious underground organization. Pyotr Verkhovensky in the novel presents himself in the same fashion to the awed members of his revolutionary cell, as well as to all those assembled in the superb scene in which "the progressives" of the town gather for a meeting. Dostoevsky read Nechaev's blood-curdling *Catechism of a Revolutionary* (probably written in collaboration with Bakunin) only

---

[6] Ibid., 141; October 8/20, 1870.

after the first part of *Demons* had already appeared. But he was convinced that he had nonetheless created a character, Pyotr Verkhovensky, who embodied all the unscrupulousness and ruthlessness of its precepts; and the *Catechism* itself, though perhaps adding a few extra details, only helped to confirm his creation. Pyotr Verkhovensky, he told Katkov, does not resemble the real-life Nechaev in any way, but "my aroused mind has created by imagination the person, the type, that really corresponds to the crime."[7] The image of this type, however, did not emerge all at once but underwent a crucial metamorphosis as the writing of the book proceeded.

Pyotr Verkhovensky is a product of the ideology of the 1860s, and the members of this generation, almost from the very start, had defined themselves in opposition to the generation of the 1840s (to which Dostoevsky himself belonged). This conflict of generations had been brilliantly depicted in Turgenev's *Fathers and Sons* (the Russian title has "Children" instead of "Sons"), a novel that Dostoevsky greatly admired. Here the main younger character, a medical student named Bazarov, treated members of the older generation with a pitying and condescending contempt. He had no tolerance at all for their high-minded Romantic and idealistic velleities, even though these had played a part in helping to abolish serfdom and had led to a more humanitarian attitude toward the peasantry. But Bazarov had no patience with exalted sentiment of any kind, including that expressed in art, and proclaimed himself a Nihilist who believed nothing except what could be established through science and materialism (he spends a good part of his time dissecting frogs).

This opposition between the generations, so indelibly portrayed by Turgenev, also gave rise to a whole series of polemical exchanges throughout the mid-1860s to which Dostoevsky paid the closest attention, and on which he drew for his own novel. In 1867 he quarreled personally with Turgenev, at least in part because of an anti-Russian tirade in Turgenev's novel *Smoke*; and in the course of their heated exchange of unpleasantries, he advised his fellow novelist to acquire a telescope so that he could see Russia more clearly from the latter's European residence. In reporting on this incident to Maikov, Dostoevsky already anticipates the clash of generations as he would later present it. "The difference [between the generations]," he wrote, "is that Chernyshevsky's followers simply criticize Russia openly and wish for its collapse," while the older radicals of the 1840s like Turgenev, who are "Belinsky's offspring [Belinsky was the greatest literary critic of the 1840s, a political radical and Westernizer], add that they *love* Russia" (italics in text).[8] The tragi-comic quarrel in the

[7] Ibid., 130; July 2/14, 1870.
[8] *PSS*, 28/bk. 2:210.

novel between Pyotr and his father, the marvelously delineated Stepan Trofimovich, whom Dostoevsky both pillories and glorifies at the same time, is already implicit in these words.

Once having decided to write a topical novel, Dostoevsky started by reworking some of his old notes in which embryonic images of his later characters already appear. There is a Romantic poet who calls himself "a pagan" and "deifies nature" (Stepan Trofimovich); there is a lame girl, whose father is a drunken lieutenant, and "who goes begging in a noble manner"[9] (Captain Lebyadkin and his lame sister Marya); there is also the beginning of a political plot. "Nechaev, Kulishov had denounced Nechaev.... The police enter and capture [presumably Nechaev]."[10] Dostoevsky also sketches a romantic rivalry between a Prince, "a pathetic figure," and a Schoolteacher, obviously a moral exemplar; both are competing for the affections of a young girl called the Ward (Darya Shatov), who has been raised by the Prince's mother (Mme Stavrogin). When the Prince seduces the Ward, the mother wants to marry her off to the Schoolteacher with a dowry; but he refuses the dowry and becomes her friend instead. This plot intrigue, provisionally entitled *Envy*, ends with the Prince marrying the Ward because he wishes to emulate the superior moral qualities of the Schoolteacher.

There are also some other features of these early notes that foreshadow the final text. The locale of the action is set in a populous provincial society ("a large group gathered in the rural countryside"[11]), and this somnolent and lethargic world has become infiltrated and undermined by Nihilist ideas. Nihilist ideas are being spread by "a neighbor ... very wealthy, and with students"; even the morally positive Schoolteacher is "a Nihilist up to a point, does not believe."[12] One may see him as a prototype of the later Shatov, also a figure of sterling moral purity and wrestling with the problem of religious faith. Just how these two themes—the romantic and the political—will be interwoven is by no means clear. But the way forward is indicated by another note: "Proclamations. Fugitive appearance of Nechaev, to kill the Teacher (?)."[13] Dostoevsky's question mark indicates his uncertainty as yet, but he has introduced a political murder that intersects with the sentimental intrigue of *Envy*, and this is the path that he will continue to follow, interweaving the private and the political ever more closely as he goes along. His next task is to integrate this plot structure with the ideological conflict-of-generations theme that will provide his novel with so much of its satirical bite.

[9] *PSS*, 9:122–23.
[10] Ibid., 121.
[11] Ibid., 11:59.
[12] Ibid.
[13] Ibid.

An important aid in this task was a review article that N. N. Strakhov had written the year before about a recent biography of T. N. Granovsky, a liberal historian who had enjoyed a brief moment of fame in the 1840s. Strakhov had defined him as "a pure Westernizer," who had sympathized with everything that was "sublime and beautiful" in European culture, but like all the others of the same stripe he had nonetheless been one of the forefathers of the Russian Nihilism that the surviving members of this generation had since been denouncing. Indeed, the detestation was reciprocal, "and the Nihilist children themselves have now taken to renouncing their fathers." Whether Dostoevsky recalled this article, or had it at hand, it certainly inspired a note labeled "*T. N. Granovsky* ... a pure and idealistic Westernizer," whose "aimlessness and lack of firmness in his views ... which ... used to cause him suffering before ... *have now become his second nature* (his son makes fun of this tendency)" (italics in text).[14] Dostoevsky wrote to Strakhov asking him to dispatch a copy of the book about Granovsky as quickly as possible and in a later letter explains: "I wish to speak out about several matters even though my artistry goes smash. What attracts me is what has piled up in my mind and heart; let it give only a pamphlet, but I shall speak out."[15]

Once Granovsky had become the prototype of the character representing the 1840s, Dostoevsky could imagine him very clearly and concretely. "Places himself unconsciously on a pedestal, in the style of relics to be worshipped by pilgrims, and loves it.... Shuns Nihilism and does not understand it.... 'Leave me God and art, and I will let you have Christ.' ... Christ did not understand women.... Literary recollections, Belinsky, Granovsky, Herzen ... Turgenev and others."[16] Stepan Trofimovich does not merely "recollect" all these figures of his generation but also represents them because they become part of his own character as well. Dostoevsky's artistic practice, even if he started as here with an identifiable prototype, was never simply to delineate an individual; he allowed himself the greatest freedom to create by amalgamation a "type" that would portray his conception. Hence Stepan Trofimovich fuses Granovsky with Alexander Herzen, who had attacked Chernyshevsky himself in his slashing article *The Superfluous and the Bilious*, and who defended the importance and dignity of art—just as Stepan Trofimovich does in the unsurpassed fete scene of the novel—against what Herzen called "the Daniels of the Neva." Dostoevsky could thus immediately grasp the character of Stepan Trofimovich in all the pathetic splendor of his faded glory; but it took him

---

[14] Ibid., 65.
[15] *PSS*, 29/bk. 1:116; March 25/April 6, 1870.
[16] *PSS*, 11:65.

a considerable amount of time to arrive at his definitive portrait of Pyotr Verkhovensky.

At first, he saw him as another, though much more sinister, incarnation of Bazarov. Now called "the Student," he "*appears* with the aim of counterfeit money, proclamations and groups of three.... Troubles his father (*Granovsky*) by his Nihilism, his sarcasms, contradictions. Simple, straightforward.... Rebuild the world ... *Bazarov*" (italics in text). This is very far from being the Pyotr of the novel, who is anything but "simple, straightforward," though his relation to his father will remain unchanged. Even less like the final Pyotr is another note, in capital letters: "THE STUDENT AS A HERO OF OUR TIME."[17] The Student would thus be endowed with some of the Romantic, Byronic traits of Lermontov's Pechorin, the protagonist of his famous novel, *A Hero of Our Time*. The Prince is still in love with the Ward, and a group of three kill a character called Shaposhnikov (the later Shatov) for fear of being denounced. They attempt to throw the blame on the Prince, between whom and Shaposhnikov there is a supposed mutual hatred because the Prince has dishonored Shaposhnikov's sister (the Ward), etc. (there is a plethora of plot variations that Dostoevsky tries out to motivate the accusation against the Prince). What originated as the idea of an innocent person being accused of the murder eventually becomes that of an innocent person, Kirillov, voluntarily assuming the guilt.

Once such an accusation against the Prince is made, however, this hitherto colorless and conventional Romantic prop "immediately unravels everything ... obliges Uspensky [a member of the group of three, whose name is that of one of Nechaev's actual accomplices] to confess and firmly denounces to the Governor."[18] The Prince then marries the Ward, as in *Envy*, and Dostoevsky notes: "The principal idea (that is, the pathos of the novel) is the Prince and the Ward—*new people* who have surmounted temptation and have resolved to begin a new regenerated life" (italics in text).[19] The problem, though, is that Dostoevsky had not given much thought earlier to the Prince and now finds himself called upon to provide some adequate motivation for his heroic behavior. "In general," he writes, "at the end of the novel nobody suspects such a strong and ardent character in the Prince";[20] but this implies that he would be portrayed as a mediocrity in the eyes of society throughout most of the text. To avoid such an unpromising prospect, Dostoevsky then conceives of him as a haughty

[17] Ibid., 66–67.
[18] Ibid., 101.
[19] Ibid., 98.
[20] Ibid., 99.

aristocrat, contemptuous of all those around him, but then also endows him with a passionate religiosity. "Despises the atheists to the point of fury, *believes* furiously. Wishes to be a *muzhik*; Old Believer" (italics in text).[21] With this, the political "pamphlet" begins to move into the realm of the religious thematic to which it had been intended as an alternative.

Dostoevsky had expected that he would be able to write his "pamphlet-novel" very quickly, but almost a year after beginning he wrote to Strakhov: "All year I only tore up and made alterations, I blackened so many mounds of paper that I even lost my system of references for what I had written. I have modified the plan not less than ten times, and completely written the first part each time."[22] What was causing him so much difficulty? Part of the answer is that, once Dostoevsky had begun to provide the Prince with a religious motivation, the character began to deepen in a way that he had not foreseen. Until March 1870 he had clung to his initial plan of the Prince and the Ward as "new people," who would emerge triumphant from the machinations of Nechaev and the ordeal of the murder; but suddenly all this is changed. After the Prince unravels the murder plot as before and declares that "it is necessary to believe ... [that] Russia and Russian thought will save humanity ... he [the Prince] prays before icons.... And then suddenly, he blows his brains out.—(Enigmatic personage, said to be mad)."[23] This note turns the Prince into a genuinely tragic character, beset by a crisis of faith like "the great sinner." Dostoevsky's two projects thus now begin to merge in his imagination.

He then immediately develops this new image of the Prince, who would become Stavrogin by the end of March (*stavros* in Greek means cross). In a transitional note, Dostoevsky writes: "The Prince—a man who has become bored. *Product of Russian century*" (italics added).[24] Previously, the Prince had turned for ideological guidance to Shatov and Golubov (the latter the real name of a writer on religious issues, a former Old Believer who had returned to Orthodoxy, and whose articles had impressed Dostoevsky); but now Golubov is dropped, and it is the Prince "who inflames him [Shatov] with enthusiasm, but does not believe himself."[25] A page later, there is a reference to the Prince as having "violated a child of thirteen years of age, which created some stir"; and he is described as "gentle, modest, quiet, infinitely proud and bestially cruel ... all the pathos of the novel in the Prince; he is the hero."[26] What had begun as a satirical depiction of the clash of generations, with Stepan Trofimovich and his son as

[21] Ibid., 100.
[22] *PSS*, 29/bk. 1:151; December 2/14, 1870.
[23] *PSS*, 11:133.
[24] Ibid., 134.
[25] Ibid., 134–35.
[26] Ibid., 136–37.

the central characters, has now become one revolving around Stavrogin, who inspires others with beliefs that he does not share and is himself "a product of the Russian century."[27]

This last phrase is of considerable importance because it helps to clarify the particular social-historical coloring that Dostoevsky will give to his character. The remark about Stavrogin's "boredom," the famous *mal de siècle*, links him with the Russian Byronic type first created by Pushkin in *Evgeny Onegin*; and like Baudelaire and many others, Dostoevsky attributed this sense of ennui to a loss of religious faith, the faith that had previously provided a meaning to the universe and to human life. In an essay dating from 1861, in which he had defended Pushkin's creation against the charge of being merely an upper-class wastrel, Dostoevsky had seen him as the first artistic expression of a crisis of the Russian spirit—a crisis caused by both the assimilation into the Russian moral-social psyche of all the attainments of European civilization and the realization of the European-educated upper class that this assimilation had deprived them of contact with their own native roots (which for Dostoevsky always meant the religious roots still deeply embedded in the soil of Russian peasant life). "The skepticism of Onegin," he had written, "contained something tragic in its very principle, and sometimes expressed itself with malicious irony."[28]

This type then entered into the bloodstream of Russian culture and produced the already-mentioned Pechorin, who combined "an egoism extending to the limits of self-adoration, and a malicious self-contempt." The latest avatar of this Russian Byronism is Stavrogin, whose moral-psychological attributes fit these words to perfection, but who combines them with something new—a malignancy, as the narrator of the novel puts it, that was "cold, calm, and, if one may put it so, reasonable and therefore the most repulsive and terrible that can be." Moreover, the creation of this Onegin-type by Pushkin, as Dostoevsky saw it, then gave birth to the epoch when "our leading men sharply separated into two camps.... The Slavophiles and the Westernizers were also a historical manifestation and in the highest degree national."[29] The Slavophiles, whose ideas Dostoevsky largely shared, believed that Russian culture should (and would) follow an independent path quite different from that of Europe; the Westernizers believed it was essential for Russia to follow the European model of social-cultural development more and more closely. Stavrogin, as the very latest incorporation of this Onegin-type, is thus flanked by the two disciples whom he had indoctrinated, Shatov and Kirillov, and who unfor-

---

[27] Ibid., 134.
[28] Ibid., 19:11.
[29] Ibid., 10.

gettably embody the essence of these two doctrines as Dostoevsky envisaged them (the effort to return to the religious sources of Russian life, on the one hand, the triumph of a self-destructive rationalism, on the other). The structure of this relationship, which has aroused some perplexity, derives from this view of the whole development of Russian cultural self-consciousness.

Dostoevsky had promised Katkov that he would begin sending chapters of his new novel by June 1870 but found himself unable to meet the deadline even though he had been piling up manuscript and constantly adding new ideas and aperçus to his notes. But he was dissatisfied with what he had written and felt that there was a problem he had not yet solved. "The work went slowly," he told his niece in mid-August. "I felt that there was an important error in the whole thing, but what it was—I could not figure out."[30] By that time he had written fifteen signatures (approximately 240 pages), which unfortunately have not survived in their initial form. During July his epileptic attacks had been so frequent and so severe that he found it impossible to write at all (they usually incapacitated him for several days, sometimes as long as a week); but perhaps this respite from composition was a blessing in disguise. In any event, when he returned to his desk in August, "I suddenly saw all at once what the trouble was, and where I had made a mistake ... a new plan appeared in all its proportions.... I struck out everything I had written ... and I began on page 1."[31] This does not mean, however, that Dostoevsky simply discarded the entire manuscript; he told Katkov a month later that twelve of the fifteen signatures had been integrated into the new version, though obviously entirely rewritten.

Dostoevsky never explained to any of his correspondents what he had discovered his "mistake" to have been, but some plausible inferences may be drawn from the notes and comments. In mid-August, under the heading "Something New," we find the following: "And Nechaev appears on the scene like Khlestakov."[32] No longer Bazarov or Pechorin, Nechaev is now seen as the ingratiating, fast-talking impostor of Gogol's *Revisor*, who adapts himself compliantly to whatever role he is cast in by the incomprehension of those around him. Dostoevsky presumably realized that Stavrogin, in becoming an Onegin-type, now embodied the Romantic, Byronic traits formerly attributed to Nechaev-Pyotr Verkhovensky, and the latter is thus recast in a subordinate and semicomic role. As Dostoevsky told Katkov: "To my surprise, this figure [Pyotr Verkhovensky] half turns

---

[30] *PSS*, 29/bk. 1:136; August 17/29, 1870.
[31] Ibid.
[32] *PSS*, 11:202.

out to be a comic figure"; and the reason is that "the whole incident of the murder ... is nonetheless only accessory and a setting for the actions of another character ... (Nikolai Stavrogin),"[33] who is not only "a sinister character" but also a tragic one. Once having reconceived his image of Pyotr Verkhovensky, Dostoevsky solved the problem that had been troubling him subliminally, and he kept his promise to Katkov that he would furnish enough text to begin publishing by January 1871.

Even though Dostoevsky's writing went smoothly from this time on, his problems with the novel were by no means over. A good part of *Demons* was published in installments during 1871, despite the disturbance caused by the Dostoevskys' return to Russia in July (the manuscripts of *The Idiot*, *The Eternal Husband*, and the early drafts of *Demons* were all burned for fear of running into trouble at the border). But publication stopped after the November issue, when part 1 and eight chapters of part 2 had already appeared, and did not resume until almost a year later. The reason was that, in what was intended as chapter 9 of part 2, Dostoevsky describes a visit by Stavrogin, assailed by hallucinations of various mocking "devils," to a nearby monastery to seek for spiritual aid from the monk Tikhon. This name and character come from an eighteenth-century saint whom Dostoevsky admired, St. Tikhon Zadonsky, who plays an important role in *The Life of a Great Sinner* and has been taken over from there (he later also provided inspiration for Father Zosima in *The Brothers Karamazov*). Stavrogin asks Tikhon to read a confession in which he describes his seduction of a twelve-year-old girl, whose suicide he then does nothing to prevent. Dostoevsky was told that Katkov hesitated to print this chapter, but no final decision was taken on its exclusion until just before the November issue of 1872.

Meanwhile, Dostoevsky made attempts at revision, which left the question of an actual rape uncertain. He hoped that this would be enough to satisfy "the modesty" of his editors; he also read this chapter to his literary friends to obtain their advice (which later led to ugly and totally unfounded rumors, handed down to posterity, that he was actually confessing a misdeed of his own). Continuing to forge ahead with the remainder of the book, he wrote on the assumption that his contested chapter would be accepted in its revised form; but publication continued to be delayed. It was only a year later, just before publication resumed, that he received a definitive refusal; and he then worked frantically on the galleys to give his remaining text whatever coherence he could.

One addition, made at the last moment to the original manuscript of part 3, is of some importance—the scene in which the dying Stepan Tro-

---

[33] *PSS*, 29/bk. 1:141; October 8/20, 1870.

fimovich listens to the reading of a passage from St. Luke (Dostoevsky also uses this passage as epigraph) about the devils entering into a herd of swine and drowning in the sea. It is under the inspiration of this passage from the Gospels that the repentant Westernizer declares himself to be one of the devils, and perhaps their progenitor. It is possible that, if Dostoevsky's initial chapter 9 had been accepted, he would have assigned more responsibility to Stavrogin, whose social-cultural coloration makes him the far more plausible (and historically accurate) source of Dostoevsky's ideological devils. The original plot assignment of Stepan Trofimovich as Stavrogin's tutor, who is thus presumably the cause of all the moral-ideological maladies of his pupil, is obviously a structural hangover from the earlier plan before the Prince had been transformed into Stavrogin and taken over the book.

However that may be, chapter 9 vanished among Dostoevsky's papers and was only unearthed in 1922, although parts of it (the dream of a golden age of innocence, mirrored by a classical Greek landscape inspired by Claude Lorrain's painting *Acis and Galatea*), were used in *A Raw Youth*. There has been a continual dispute over whether it still belongs to the book, but the consensus is that it should certainly be read if we are to grasp the moral-philosophical inspiration underlying Dostoevsky's remarkable character. For here we see, as this variant of the chapter tells us, that Stavrogin was not simply a perverse moral monster; he was, rather, carrying out a sacrilegious moral-philosophical experiment on himself to ascertain whether it were true that "I neither know nor feel good and evil and that I have not only lost any sense of it, but that there is neither good nor evil (which pleased me) and that it is just a prejudice."[34] Dostoevsky wrote in a letter that "I took him [Stavrogin] from my heart,"[35] and in my view he meant a heart that was aching because the glamorous radiance of this "product of the Russian century," the finest flower of the Russian absorption of European culture, should have been doomed to such a tragic destiny.

Demons is thus a totally original amalgam, one part of which contains a brilliantly ironic depiction of the conflict of generations in Russian culture and displays all of Dostoevsky's still insufficiently recognized talents as a satirist and a parodist. The portrait of Stepan Trofimovich is unsurpassed in the Russian novel, and the more one knows about the Russian culture of the period, the more one marvels at Dostoevsky's intellectual sophistication, skill, and sureness of touch. The foibles, the weaknesses, the impotence, the self-pampering pretensions of the personage are all there, and the jibes of Pyotr Verkhovensky against his father hit home time and again. One also laughs at the tempestuous vagaries of his beautifully Platonic

[34] *PSS*, 12:113.
[35] *PSS*, 29/bk.1:149; October 9/20, 1870.

relationship with his strong-willed patroness; but we are also shown the genuine sweetness of spirit, the occasional pangs of conscience, and the sincere devotion to the ideal.

For all his detestation of his own generation, Dostoevsky much preferred it to the cold, utilitarian, Nihilist rationalists of the 1860s; and the final chapter of Stepan Trofimovich's last wanderings is a wonderful mélange of tender mockery and slyly humorous reverence. It is also, incidentally, a totally unintended but prescient foreshadowing of what would actually occur a year later, when a new generation of young radicals decided "to go to the people" and were met by them with the same bewilderment that greeted the itinerant scholar. Dostoevsky is more pitiless with the figure of Karmazinov, a caricature of Turgenev, with whom he had a personal bone to pick; but there were also ample social-cultural reasons in the mid-1870s to motivate Dostoevsky's lampoon. The parody of Turgenev's prose-poems perfectly catches their mannerism and is hilariously funny; so is the entire boisterous helter-skelter of the fete scene, with its wicked takeoff on Karmazinov's world-weary farewell to literature that nobody takes seriously. Such a large-scale assault on a fellow writer has no rival, except perhaps Dickens's attack on Leigh Hunt in the Harold Skimpole of *Bleak House*, with which Dostoevsky, a great reader of Dickens, was certainly familiar.

Dostoevsky combines all these pages of irresistible satirical comedy with what seems to be their very opposite, the tragic theme of an unsuccessful quest for religious faith and personal salvation by "a great sinner." He has often been criticized for attempting to unite what seems, at first sight, to be such disparate material; but this criticism misunderstands the nature of his genius and measures him by standards that are quite irrelevant to his poetics. Dostoevsky was one of the few novelists of the nineteenth century (rivaled in this respect perhaps only by Balzac) who could still feel the universe and human life as directly related to the ultimate questions about human life that are posed and answered only by religion. This is one reason why, in reading him, one is so constantly reminded of works produced in the great eras of poetic tragedy, when the relationship of man to the gods or to God was so much more instinctive and spontaneous. In general, characters in the novel do not usually relate their own mundane problems and dilemmas so immediately to the "accursed questions" that never ceased to haunt Dostoevsky himself both as artist and man.

It is no accident that, in *The Brothers Karamazov*, Ivan speaks nostalgically of the time when "it was customary... to bring down heavenly powers on earth"[36] in literature and mentions Victor Hugo's *Notre Dame de*

---

[36] Fyodor Dostoevsky, *The Brothers Karamazov*, trans. Constance Garnett (New York: Barnes and Noble Classics, 2003), 228.

Paris as a modern novel in which a mystery play of this kind is depicted—one in which the Virgin Mary descends to Earth. Dostoevsky, it might be said, tried to do the same with the world of the Virgin Mary (or, to use a more Russian appellation, the Mother of God) in his own mode of "fantastic realism," which remained within the realistic conventions of the nineteenth-century novel but enormously extended their usual range. He made realism "fantastic" by using the extreme situations of melodrama or the criminal adventure novel, which he then elevated to the level of high tragedy by handling their sordid conflicts in terms of the transcendent values of religious faith.

For him, the Machiavellianism of Pyotr Verkhovensky, purely social-political in nature, issued the same challenge to the moral basis of human life and society as did the personal experiment of Stavrogin to abolish his feeling for the distinction between good and evil. Both, in Dostoevsky's imagination, derived from the Western rationalism that he saw as inevitably leading to the replacement of the God-man Christ, with his morality of love, by the Man-god of egoism and power embodied in Stavrogin, in Pyotr, and most nobly of all in Kirillov. It was because Dostoevsky possessed so acute a sense of this relation between the religious and the social that he was able to create the unparalleled and artistically viable synthesis between his "pamphlet" and what he later called his "poem," which was unfortunately weakened—though by no means destroyed —by the suppression of chapter 9.

One of the questions that inevitably arises about *Demons* is whether it should not be judged as an unpardonable slander on the Russian radicals who were valiantly struggling, against impossible odds, to create a brave new world. That the book is certainly hostile to the radicalism of its time goes without saying; but to call it "slander" is very excessive. This would imply that Dostoevsky deliberately distorted and blackened the historical record so as to depict the radicals in the worst possible light. It is true that Dostoevsky gives the Nechaev affair much more importance than it actually warranted in the context of the time; no such widespread disturbances occurred as are depicted in the novel. But so far as the aims and tactics of Nechaev are concerned, as well as his actions and those of his followers, everything in the novel can be supported by what he and they actually did, or, as their propaganda made clear, would have liked to do if given the chance. Nor, in considering this question, should one overlook—though it is usually hardly noticed—the scathing image equally given of the stupidity of the reaction of the authorities in the person of the pitiful Governor-General von Lembke, whose half-crazed attempt at severity only succeeds in throwing oil on the fire of discontent.

It is also worth noting that, while the publication of *Demons* ruined Dostoevsky's standing with Russian progressives and the radical youth (though his repudiation by the young was only temporary), the new radical groups that began to reorganize in the early 1870s very self-consciously set themselves off from Nechaev and the moral miasma of his methods. Such a reaction indicates that Dostoevsky's portrayal of them was hardly as defamatory as has been charged, and it possibly may even have had some effect. Moreover, it was not only the antiradical Dostoevsky who was revolted by Nechaev and his tactics, with all their murderous consequences. Alexander Herzen also denounced the propaganda of Nechaev as leading to the provocation and unleashing of "the worst passions"; and Marx and Engels used the Nechaev affair to have Bakunin and his followers booted out of the First International. "These all-destroying anarchists," they declared sententiously, "who wish to reduce everything to amorphousness in order to replace morality by anarchy, carry bourgeois immorality to its final extreme."[37]

Dostoevsky liked to recite Pushkin's poem "The Prophet" at benefit readings, and he was often hailed as "a prophet" in his own lifetime. Such an accolade was usually stimulated by the references that he made, much like Shatov in the novel, to the future glories of the all-reconciling Christian world civilization that it was the God-given destiny of Russia to bring into being. If anything in his work is truly prophetic, however, it is his depiction of the radicals and the spread of their ideas in *Demons*. One cannot praise too highly the devastating portrayal of how the "fashionable" progressive ideas brought from the capital permeate the stagnating provincial society, and how the "radical chic" of the wife of Governor-General von Lembke, which arouses the envy of Mme Stavrogin herself, only paves the way for such infiltration. The "birthday party" at the Virginskys', which turns into a meeting of the local progressives, begins as a comic adolescent quarrel between a schoolboy and his female counterpart traveling round the country to raise the consciousness of students; but there is nothing comic about the troubled discovery announced by the radical "theoretician" Shigalyov, who has been tackling the problem of defining the conditions for achieving the earthly paradise. "Starting from unlimited freedom," he has noted to his dismay, "I arrive at unlimited despotism."[38] (This has certainly become the most quoted passage in the book.) It is little wonder that a fairly recent (1990) Russian study of the novel should be entitled: *Roman-Preduprezhdenie*—"A Novel of Warning." And the historian and critic Yury Karyakin, writing of the period just after Khrushchev had lifted the curtain on Stalin's crimes against humanity, cites the remark made to him with "a sorrowful smile" by a friend,

---

[37] Karl Marx and Friedrich Engels, *Werke*, 39 vols. (Berlin, 1959–), 18:426.
[38] Fyodor Dostoevsky, *The Possessed*, trans. Constance Garnett (New York: Barnes and Noble Classics, 2004), 402.

"a typical Stepan Trofimovich," with a doctorate in chemistry and who played the flute: "But you know, all this is in *Demons*. I was almost arrested in '36 because I read the novel. Someone denounced me."[39]

What is most remarkable, however, is that Dostoevsky still manages to make the dupes of Pyotr so pathetically and appealingly human amidst all their follies and delusions; they are very far from being scoundrels or villains whose motives are base or ignoble. One should always remember that Dostoevsky had himself been involved in a genuine revolutionary conspiracy in 1849 (it was a secret he kept concealed all his life), whose aim had been the abolition of serfdom; and he never accepted the official view that those who plotted against the state should simply be viewed as criminals. Indeed, just a year after *Demons* had been completed, he admitted in an article that he himself might have become "a Nechaevist ... in the days of my youth."[40]

What he had tried to show in *Demons*, he explained, was that "even the purest of hearts and the most innocent of people can be drawn into committing such a monstrous offence."[41] The group around Nechaev, as he depicts them, are hardly "the purest and the most innocent," but neither are they vile or fundamentally corrupt. They by no means approve of Pyotr's desire to spread disruption and chaos, nor of his instigation of Shatov's murder; but Dostoevsky understood how mass psychology, as well as fear, could overcome the most recalcitrant. He himself had once called Nikolai Speshnev, the leader of his underground group (very probably a biographical prototype for Stavrogin), his "Mephistopheles," which meant that he knew how it felt to be persuaded to act against one's will in the name of a sacred cause. The scene in which Pyotr brings his rebellious pack to heel is a masterful lesson in the psychodynamics of group persuasion.

One could go on indefinitely exploring all the riches of *Demons* on various levels, and its relation both to its author and to the period with which it deals. So far as the latter is concerned, it is practically an encyclopedia of the Russian culture of its time, filtered through a witheringly derisive and often grotesquely funny perspective. Nothing in the European novel compares with it, except perhaps Balzac's *Les Illusions perdues* or Flaubert's *L'Education sentimentale*—the latter most of all because of its equally disillusioned view of socialism, more disillusioned, in fact, than Dostoevsky's. For Pyotr Verkhovensky, who is nothing if not self-conscious, declares to Stavrogin in the scene where he explains his plan to proclaim him Ivan the Tsarevich: "I'm a crook, not a Socialist, ha ha!" Dostoevsky has hardly

[39] Yury Karyakin, *Dostoevsky i Kanun XXI Veka* (Moscow, 1989), 204–5.
[40] *PSS*, 21:129.
[41] Ibid., 131.

been given enough credit for this disclaimer, which allowed Russian critics in the late Stalinist period to argue that he was not in fact attacking Russian radicalism as a whole but only its anarchist wing.

Once, when evoking his past, Dostoevsky recalled how, even before he had learned to read, "I used to spend the long winter evenings before going to bed listening ... agape with ecstasy and terror as my parents read aloud from the novels of Ann Radcliffe." This queen of Gothic mystery thrillers was Dostoevsky's memorable initiatrix to literature, and he never forgot the lessons he absorbed from her during those long winter evenings. His own novelistic technique, as Leonid Grossman pointed out long ago in a classic study, was modeled on both Ann Radcliffe and her successors, especially French ones, who catered to the popular taste for suspense, mystery, and narrative surprise. Dostoevsky was the only Russian writer of his stature to employ these Gothic devices, and he was severely rapped over the knuckles for the "vulgarity" of doing so (a sniffish and snobbish critical tradition that has been regrettably carried into our own day by Vladimir Nabokov). But Dostoevsky, who unlike his rivals wrote for a living, paid no attention to his detractors, and we should be grateful that he shrugged them off. For *Demons* is not only a novel that deals with some of the profoundest issues of the modern world, and indeed of human life—it is also a riveting page-turner, a great read, a thriller par excellence that is impossible to put down.

FOUR

WAR AND PEACE

IT IS SOMETHING of a surprise to realize that Tolstoy's great novel *War and Peace*, which has now become so much a part of the literary heritage of Western culture, was initially greeted with some bewilderment and perplexity. "Taken as a whole," wrote one critic, "this *1805* (a provisional title) offers something strange and undefined."[1] Such a critical reaction was so widespread that Tolstoy felt compelled to respond to it with an essay, "Some Words about the Book *War and Peace*," written in 1868.

"What is *War and Peace*?" he wrote. "It is not a novel, still less a poem, still less a historical chronicle. *War and Peace* is what the author wished to express and was able to express in that form in which it is expressed. Such a statement of an author's disregard for the conventional forms of an artistic prose work might seem presumptuous if it were not deliberate and if there were no precedents for it. But the history of Russian literature since the time of Pushkin not only affords many examples of such a departure from European form but does not offer so much as one example to the contrary. From Gogol's *Dead Souls* to Dostoevsky's *Dead House*, in the recent period of Russian literature there is not a single work of artistic prose at all rising above mediocrity that quite fits the form of a novel, a poem, or a story."[2]

This statement well illustrates the peremptory self-assurance and dogmatism so characteristic of Tolstoy's opinions, which later led him to denounce Shakespeare and most of modern art and literature in his *What Is Art?*. But there is no reason to be too overwhelmed by the forcefulness of his assertions. What is true, however, is that *War and Peace* "is what the author wished to express and was able to express in that form in which it is

---

Introduction to *War and Peace* copyright © 2006 by Joseph Frank, originally published in a slightly different form in 2006 in the Barnes and Noble Classics edition of *War and Peace* by Leo Tolstoy.

[1] *Knizhnyi Vestnik*, nos. 16–17, 1866 quoted in Gary Saul Morson, *Hidden in Plain View: Narrative and Creative Potentials in "War and Peace"* (Stanford: Stanford University Press, 1987), 39.

[2] Lev Tolstoy, "Neskol'ko slov po povodu knigi 'Voina i Mir'" (Some words about the book "War and Peace"), *Polnoe Sobraniie Sochinenii* (*Complete collected works*), ed. V. G. Chertkov et al., 90 vols. (Moscow 1928–1958), 16:7. Hereafter cited as *PSS*. Quoted in Morson, *Hidden in Plain View*, 75–76.

expressed"; and this form *was* something new in the history of the novel. For what Tolstoy created was a combination of the epic and the novel, a fusion of the ancient epic like the *Iliad* or the *Aeneid*, which re-creates the life and history of a whole people, with the more private, personal, and domestic concerns of the novel.

Not that the effort to fuse these two genres had previously been entirely unknown. The enormous influence of the historical novels of Walter Scott in the early nineteenth century had already introduced the epic theme—the life, customs, and traditions of an entire people—into the purely individual preoccupations of the eighteenth-century novel represented by such works as *Moll Flanders* and *Tom Jones*. But the historical novel still differed from the old epic tradition by placing the lives of relatively insignificant individuals at the center of the work rather than the rulers of society (who entered, but only on the periphery), and using the historical context more as background for the working out of private fates than as motivation for the main action of the story.

In Tolstoy, we find these two narrative traditions united in a hitherto unprecedented way by giving them equal importance and alternating them as part of a larger pattern. The novelty of such a fusion in a single work certainly accounts for some of the bafflement it created. "We cannot place this work categorically in any of the familiar literary genres," one critic confessed. "It is neither a *chronicle* [meaning an account primarily of historical events] nor a *historical novel*."[3] Quite true; it is an original combination of the two, which in fact plays each off against the other.

Also, there is still another aspect of the book that is entirely original and has not been sufficiently recognized. For despite the equilibrium implied by the title, the two are not really held in balance as the work proceeds. Indeed, we find Tolstoy advancing the view—and even arguing directly on its behalf in both his text and the theoretical epilogue—that the novelistic vision of reality, so to speak, the purely private behavior of individuals looking after their own most pressing and domestic needs and concerns, is far more important in grasping historical reality than the plans and projects of those who believe they can shape and master the epic flow of history.

Two

By the time he undertook the enormous task of writing *War and Peace*, Tolstoy was thirty-five years old and had already not only led a quite adventurous life but acquired an established reputation as a writer. Born in

---

[3] N. D. Akhsharumov, "1805-i god, soch. grafa L'va Tolstogo," in *Vsemirnyi Trud*, no. 6, 1867, quoted in Morson, *Hidden in Plain View*, 50.

1828 on the estate of Yasnaya Polyana ("clear glade"), which has since become a national Russian shrine, he moved with his family to Moscow when he was two, but at age thirteen he went to live with relatives in Kazan. Educated at home by private tutors, he sketched their portraits vividly in his first published work, *Childhood* (1852). At the age of sixteen he entered the University of Kazan, whose student roster would later include the name of V. I. Ulyanov, better known today as V. I. Lenin. Intending to become a diplomat, he first registered in the department of Eastern languages but then shifted to the faculty of law. Too independent and self-willed a character to submit easily to a routine of studies imposed by others, he was consumed by an intense intellectual curiosity and read omnivorously not only in literature but in philosophy and history as well. He also began to write a diary at the age of eighteen, and he continued to confide his thoughts and record his actions all through his life. As a result, he is one of the best-documented writers in the history of literature.

Tolstoy's inner world in these early years is nothing if not fluctuating and unstable. He was an intensely ambitious and self-scrutinizing young man, perplexedly searching for his own identity. His diary, for instance, is filled with "Rules of Life" that he sets down and pledges to observe, separating them carefully into duties to oneself, duties to one's neighbors, and duties to God; but then he scrupulously acknowledges his failure to live up to any of their requirements. The unrivaled precision with which he will later examine not only the actions but the innermost reflections of his characters (he is now recognized as one of the inventors of the interior monologue as a literary device) is already present in such early analyses of both his own ideals and his shortcomings. Another harbinger of the future can be seen in remarks about history confided to a friend at the age of eighteen: "History is nothing but a collection of fables and useless trifles," he declared, "cluttered up with a mass of unnecessary figures and proper names. The death of Igor, the snake which bit Oleg—what is all this but old wives' tales?"[4]

During all this time, the young Tolstoy was also acquiring a formidable erudition only loosely connected with his studies. A list of what he was reading during his second year as a law student includes "Gogol, Rousseau, Pushkin, Goethe's *Faust*, Hegel."[5] A slightly later list, with annotations as to whether the effect on him was "great, very great or immense," includes, besides the Gospel of St. Matthew, Sterne's *Sentimental Journey*, Dickens's *David Copperfield*, Schiller, Turgenev, Lermontov, and many others. His intellectual and literary aspirations knew no bounds, and during a summer vacation, when he had returned to the family estate and was

---

[4] Quoted in Ernest J. Simmons, *Leo Tolstoy* (New York: Vintage Books, 1960), 1:58.
[5] Henri Troyat, *Tolstoy* (New York: Grove Press, 2001), 51.

"up to my neck in estate management," he wrote his older brother that he was working away at three books. "One is called *Miscellany*, another *What Is Needed for the Welfare of Russia?* and the third is *Observations on Property Management.*... My *Miscellany* will be filled with poetry, philosophy and in general things that are not pretty but are amusing to write."[6] The vague outlines of the future problematics of *War and Peace* can already be detected in these ambitious projects. They still lack, however, the crucial experience of warfare, which will soon be supplied.

Tolstoy was an extremely restless and febrile personality, whose life was filled with abrupt changes of mood that often led to changes of place. After inheriting Yasnaya Polyana in 1847, he left the University of Kazan and devoted himself entirely to estate management, which included the thorny and distasteful task of solving peasant disputes. A two-year stint of this kind was enough; and he relieved its burdens by interludes in Moscow and Petersburg. Here he indulged in disastrous gambling and frequented gypsy cabarets, whose entertainers supplemented the peasant girls easily at his beck and call on the estate. Tolstoy fervently denounced such dissipations in his diary, but it proved impossible for him to resist their allure. The continuous inner struggle that he records between self-discipline and irresistible temptation provided ample personal experience for the emotional oscillations of the characters that will later fill his great masterpiece.

His older brother Nikolay, whom he greatly admired, was serving as an officer with the Russian Army in the Caucasus, and Tolstoy decided to join him when other possibilities of a career seemed far less appealing. Nikolay returned to his regiment after a leave in 1851, and Leo accompanied him as a volunteer for the Russian Army. For six years he thus became immersed in the romantically exotic Wild East of the Russian imagination already celebrated by Pushkin and Lermontov.

Three

Tolstoy would later utilize the impressions and experiences garnered during these years in his novel *The Cossacks*, and also in a number of short stories ("The Raid," "The Wood Felling"). There was a strong Rousseauistic streak in Tolstoy, who wore a medallion with Rousseau's portrait around his neck; and his contact with a world ruled by more elemental values than the social constraints of aristocratic Russian society exercised an important influence on him. To be sure, his day-to-day dealings as a landowner with the Russian peasants had left him with few illusions about their shortcomings. It is no accident, all the same, that he so often depicts positively those

---

[6] Ibid., 50–51.

of his own class who display some of the simplicity and stoical acceptance of circumstance that he found in peasant life and in the Cossack world. Even while still only a volunteer, Tolstoy himself participated bravely in a skirmish with the troops among whom he lived, and who were engaged in continual combat with the Muslim (particularly Chechen) hill tribes along the Russian border. This was an experience he never forgot; and the very last story he wrote, *Hadji Murad*, provides a prophetic anticipation of what present-day Russians are still struggling with in Chechneya. He finally enlisted in the Russian Army as a cadet—a noncommissioned officer—and was assigned to the same artillery regiment as his brother.

Tolstoy's decision to join the army relieved somewhat his anxiety about his future career, "You will not believe how this pleases me," he wrote his aunt. "It will seem strange to you that I do not desire to be free. I've been free too long in everything; and it seems to me now that this excess of freedom has been the principle of my faults, and that it is even an evil."[7] These army years are of course put to very good use in *War and Peace*, and what he felt about them is partially embodied in the same sentiments that he later ascribes to Nikolay Rostov, returning from a furlough to his regiment. "Feeling himself deprived of liberty and nailed down within one narrow, unchangeable framework, Rostov had the same feeling of peace and moral support and the same sense of being at home here ... as he had once felt under his father's roof. Here was none of all that confusion of the free world, where he did not know his proper place, and made mistakes in exercising free choice."[8]

But Tolstoy was Nikolay Rostov only to a certain degree, as he was of so many of his other characters as well, and he had already embarked on another outlet for his overflowing energies. "You recall the advice you once gave me: to write novels," he reminded his aunt. "Well, I've followed it, and my endeavors, about which I shall speak to you presently, are literary."[9] He had already tried his hand at a sketch, *A History of Yesterday* (published only after his death), narrating in penetrating detail the impressions and observations of a single day, and he now embarked on what became his first published novel, *Childhood*, later continued in *Boyhood* and *Youth*. The fundamentally autobiographical nature of Tolstoy's creations is evident from the very start; and though he reshaped his life experiences to conform to his artistic aims, the background of figures and events from his own life is easily discernible. Scholars have tracked all this down with unremitting zeal, and in the case of *War and Peace* it is

---

[7] Quoted in Simmons, *Leo Tolstoy*, 1:93.

[8] Leo Tolstoy, *War and Peace*, trans. Constance Garnett; intro. by Joseph Frank; notes by Lena Lencek (New York: Barnes and Noble Classics, 2006), 359. References to this work are hereafter cited in parentheses in the text.

[9] Quoted in Simmons, *Leo Tolstoy*, 1:92.

possible to pinpoint the presumed originals of most of the nonhistorical figures.

Childhood was greeted with enthusiastic reviews in 1852, and the quality of Tolstoy's gifts was immediately apparent. Turgenev and others were struck by the precision of his analysis of feelings and emotions. These were conveyed through a careful depiction of bodily movement, gesture, and surrounding environment rather than by more conventional rhetorical devices. Tolstoy's notebooks also reveal that he was very conscious of the effects he was seeking to create. A writer he admired was the poet, historian, and politician Alphonse de Lamartine, but he sharply criticizes Lamartine's use of an image describing drops of water from an oar as "comme des perles tombant dans un bassin d'argent" (like pearls falling into a silver basin).

"If Lamartine," he remarks, "Lamartine who is a genius, would tell me what color those drops were, how they fell and trickled along the wet wood of the oar, what little circles they made falling into the water, my imagination would remain faithful to him."[10] Lamartine's image, Tolstoy wrote, led him to visualize, instead of someone rowing, a maid washing her mistress's jewels in a silver basin; and such embellishment distracted from the exactitude of the scene being evoked. Although Tolstoy never expressed any of the agony of a Flaubert slaving the whole day over a page in order to obtain the exact nuance of every word, his manuscripts indicate the extent to which he revised over and over again to satisfy his own standards.

Moreover, Tolstoy's works are never motivated by the working out of a strongly accentuated narrative plot. The use of such a plot ran against the grain of his minute study of character; and he believed that literature was now moving away from such dependence on external narrative action. His admiration for Pushkin was unbounded, but on rereading the famous novella *The Captain's Daughter*, he found it no longer either to his taste or to the way in which, according to his opinion, Russian literature was developing. "Now, truly, in the new tendency, interest in details of feeling replaces interest in events themselves. Pushkin's tales are somehow too bare."[11] Tolstoy knew that such "details of feeling" were his own strong point, and in one of the several unused prefaces he wrote for *War and Peace*, he remarks: "The denouement in the relations of these characters [he had already been writing for a year] I cannot foresee.... Although I have tried very hard to devise from the beginning a novelistic plot and

---

[10] Lev Tolstoy, "Varianty iz vtoroi i tret'ei redaktsii 'Detstva,", *PSS*, 1:178, quoted in Kathryn B. Feuer, *Tolstoy and the Genesis of "War and Peace"* (Ithaca: Cornell University Press, 1996), 19.

[11] *PSS*, 46:187–88 (November 1, 1853), quoted in Feuer, *Tolstoy*, 19.

denouement, I have become convinced that to do so is not in my power, and I have decided, in the depictions of these characters, to be guided by my own habits and abilities."[12]

Tolstoy soon became dissatisfied with army service in the border regions, despite having been commended three times for bravery in action and awarded decorations he never received because his papers were not in order. He requested and was given a transfer, which, after being promoted to a commissioned officer, brought him eventually to Sevastopol, then being attacked by the French in the Crimean War (1853–1856). He was assigned to a battery of guns in the Fourth Bastion, one of the most exposed of the earthworks that surrounded the city, and served there, continually under fire, for about a month and a half. His sojourn in the besieged city led to his *Sevastopol Sketches*, which anticipate *War and Peace* in several respects.

Tolstoy's *Sevastopol Sketches* brought home to his readers both the unassuming heroism and the patriotism of the Russian soldiers, and it contains some withering portraits of the officer class, concerned largely with promotions and social prestige. Most of all, it nakedly portrays the human senselessness and the horror of war. The narrator visits a military hospital where amputations are being performed and addresses the reader: "You will see the wounded man suddenly regain consciousness, cursing with a terrible, harrowing shriek," and watch "the apothecary assistant fling the severed arm into a corner.... you will see war not as a beautiful, orderly and gleaming formation, with music and beaten drums, streaming banners and generals on prancing horses, but war in its authentic expression—as blood, suffering and death."[13]

Prince Andrey Bolkonsky, wounded himself, confronts the same spectacle in Tolstoy's novel, where the amputee becomes Anatole Kuragin, the man who had ruined his life by almost seducing his fiancée, the vibrantly volatile Natasha. This episode is used to provide one of the book's epiphanic moments. For Andrey now weeps over Kuragin, whom he had previously hated with a cold contempt, and he "wept tears of love and tenderness over his fellow-men, over himself, and over their errors and his own." At last he realized that "sympathy, love for our brothers, for those who love us, love for those who hate us, love for our enemies, yes, the love that God preached upon earth" (745) provides the only meaning for a life that he fears he now has lost.

One of the most famous passages in the superb *Sevastopol Sketches* may well be taken as a statement of Tolstoy's own artistic credo—a credo he

---

[12] "The Second Preface," *PSS*, 13:55 quoted in Feuer, *Tolstoy*, 106.

[13] Leo Tolstoy, *Tales of Army Life*, trans. Louise and Aylmer Maude (London: Oxford University Press, 1935), 96.

could well have formulated under the stress of living amidst the harrowing conditions that he describes with such indelible vividness, sober admiration, and mournful astonishment. After one of his most haunting evocations—a temporary peace between the two sides, called to gather up the corpses of the dead—hostilities are resumed; and he cannot help being overcome by the incomprehensibility of the terrible mutual slaughter. Had those enemies not been chatting together amiably and peacefully just a moment earlier?

Indeed, he now cannot avoid asking himself whether the purpose for which he and the others are fighting makes any sense at all. "What I have said," he writes, "perhaps belong to that class of evil truths that lie unconsciously hidden in the soul of each man and should not be uttered lest they become harmful." Where are the heroes and villains of his pages, who might offer some much needed guidance? None exist, and he cannot provide them. All the same, "the hero of my tale—whom I love with all the powers of my soul, whom I have tried to portray in all its beauty and who has been, is, and always will be beautiful—is truth."[14]

Tolstoy retired from the army in 1856, returned to Yasnaya Polyana, and continued to write and to publish a number of short stories as well as a novella, *Family Happiness* (1859), whose main female character undergoes somewhat the same transition from perfervid youthful love to the obligations and satisfactions of married domesticity as does Natasha in *War and Peace*. But Tolstoy's wartime experiences, as well as the impending social-political changes, turned his attention in other directions. The Russian defeat in the Crimean War had led to the liberation of the serfs, and a relatively liberal tsar, Alexander II, had succeeded to the throne. Literature temporarily lost its attraction for Tolstoy, or took second place to the problem of educating the recently enfranchised Russian people for their new responsibilities.

Four

Whatever he undertook, Tolstoy always began at the beginning; and so he established a free school at Yasnaya Polyana that soon grew to several for the education of peasant children. The operations of the school, at which a journal was also published, absorbed most of his activity for the next several years. *War and Peace* was still far in the offing, but one of Tolstoy's lessons, a recital of the account of the Napoleonic invasions of 1812, inspired the children with patriotic ardor. Along with becoming a schoolmaster, Tolstoy also accepted the function of "arbiter of peace"

---

[14] Quoted in ibid., 152.

in the local commission established in his district to settle the numerous disputes between landowners and peasants over the terms of the liberation settlement. Since he was scrupulously honest, his rulings tended to favor the peasants; and he was cordially abhorred by the local gentry who had initially opposed his appointment. He resigned in April 1862, more convinced than ever that individual moral qualities were of far greater importance than civil institutions for the welfare of society.

During this period he also made several trips to Europe, where he met both P. J. Proudhon and Alexander Herzen. Proudhon's book, *La Guerre et la Paix*, has been thought to have exercised some influence on Tolstoy's novel with the same title; but the resemblances are too imprecise to be very compelling. Herzen's marvelous memoirs, *My Past and Thoughts*, begins with a description of the Moscow fires in which his family was caught, and also his father's employment by Napoleon for a message to be delivered to Alexander II. This incident is used in *War and Peace*, where Herzen's father is mentioned by name; and some of Herzen's firsthand recollections of the chaos caused by the fires may also have influenced Tolstoy's depiction. In addition, Herzen wrote some biting pages on Napoleon; and both he and Tolstoy agreed that it is futile to search for any predetermined aim in history. Although Tolstoy and the radical publicist were miles apart on social-political questions, there is no reason to exclude a possible interaction. Many years later, Tolstoy wrote that Herzen stood head and shoulders above any other political thinker he had met in his lifetime.

For all the usefulness of his pedagogical activities, into which he threw himself with his usual intensity, Tolstoy remained dissatisfied with both his personal life and his retirement from the literary scene. More and more the endless, unsuccessful struggle with his sensuality and other dissipations such as gambling began to weigh Tolstoy down. This problem was solved, after several abortive romances, by his marriage to the eighteen-year-old Sofya Behrs, preceded by much initial vacillation and hesitation because of the difference in age. She became his devoted even if increasingly strong-willed spouse, who provided him with the relatively stable and tranquil years during which he wrote *War and Peace* (1863–1869). In addition, it appears that she copied a good deal of the manuscript seven times over; and anyone examining a page of Tolstoy in its initial state, filled with corrections and marginal insertions, can see that this was far from being a routine task.

On Tolstoy's return from the Caucasus, the literary world had welcomed the author of *Childhood* and *The Sevastopol Sketches* with great enthusiasm, but this initial reception had very quickly turned sour. Diplomacy in human relations was not Tolstoy's strong point, and his bluntness of speech almost led to a duel with Turgenev, with whom an initial friendship dissolved into both mutual artistic admiration and mutual personal antipathy.

Despite the hostility he encountered in literary circles, the man who between bombardments had worked on *Youth* in the trench dugout of the Fourth Bastion was not someone who could easily abandon the literary life. The few stories he had published in the intervening years had met with a cool reception; but this probably only piqued the vanity that he constantly accuses himself of failing to overcome. In any case, to pay off a gambling debt he returned to literature by disinterring and publishing the manuscript of *The Cossacks*. *War and Peace* was to come quite soon, but it was preceded by several stories and a little-known satirical comedy, *The Contaminated Family*, ridiculing the fashionable radical ideas of the generation of the 1860s that he loathed even more deeply than Dostoevsky did because he had never been touched by them at all.

Five

The origins of *War and Peace*, which Tolstoy only began to work on seriously in 1863, nonetheless go back to literary projects that began to accumulate in 1856. This was the moment when Alexander II made his epochal statement that it would be better to plan for the liberation of the serfs "from above," rather than to wait for them to effectuate it "from below." At the same time, the noblemen who had been involved in the 1825 conspiracy of the Decembrists, a group wishing to establish a constitutional monarchy, were allowed to return to Russia from exile in Siberia. The Decembrists were members of the gentry who had been influenced by Western liberal ideas acquired during their service as officers with the Russian Army in Europe after Napoleon's defeat. At the accession of Nicholas I to the throne, they had unsuccessfully tried to provoke an uprising in the army; five were executed and the remainder were sent into exile. Among Tolstoy's papers was found a manuscript called *The Decembrists*, the beginning of a work dealing with the return of one such family.

Tolstoy himself referred to such a theme in a letter to Herzen in 1861. "About four months ago I began a novel, the hero of which is to be a Decembrist returning from exile.... My Decembrist is to be an enthusiast, a mystic, a Christian returning to Russia in 1856 with his wife and his son and daughter, and applying his stern and somewhat idealist views to the new Russia."[15] Presumably, a work of this kind already had been

---

[15] Quoted in R. F. Christian, *Tolstoy's "War and Peace": A Study* (Oxford: Clarendon Press, 1962), 21–22.

begun in 1856 and is referred to as such in one of Tolstoy's unpublished forewords. There he wrote: "In 1856 I began to write a story with a definite tendency, the hero of which was to have been a Decembrist returning with his family to Russia. From the present I involuntarily moved to 1825, the period of the delusions and misfortunes of my hero, and I abandoned what I had begun. But even in 1825 my hero was already a grown-up man with a family. In order to understand him, I had to carry myself back to his youth, and his youth coincided with Russia's glorious period of 1812."[16] Tolstoy then found it necessary to recede even further back and to begin in 1805, with the first clash between Russia and the forces of Napoleon.

This initial Decembrist inspiration of the later novel was eventually abandoned but in fact did not vanish; it was rather transferred from the beginning to the end. For in the first epilogue of *War and Peace*, it is clear that Pierre Bezuhov has just returned from Petersburg, where he has been meeting with other highly placed gentry to organize a society that would counteract the repressions and injustices of a government that, after the victory over Napoleon, had become reactionary and obscurantist. Every Russian reader would know that Pierre had become involved with the Decembrists, and the dispute about their aims, opposed by other male members of the family, is passionately absorbed by the fifteen-year-old Nikolay Bolkonsky, the son of the dead Prince Andrey. In response to his question whether his own father, whom he idolizes, would agree with Pierre, the latter reluctantly answers yes. And so, as the book ends, the consequences in the future of its initial inspiration already begin to loom.

One commentator has remarked that, while *War and Peace* is the lengthiest novel in Russian literature (and perhaps, with the exception of Proust, in Western literature as well), compared with the massive manuscripts and draft versions later found in Tolstoy's files it could well be referred to as a "slim volume." One of the challenges Tolstoy faced was to reproduce the historical and ideological atmosphere of the period he was portraying, a problem he had never been forced to cope with before. At first he did so head-on and wrote four explanatory prefaces and four historical introductions to serve as an elucidating framework for the unfamiliar world he was evoking; but none of these were finally used.

Also, in the early drafts he frequently intervened as narrator with information and commentary about his characters. All such interventions were zealously rewritten to eliminate such direct intrusion into the narrative flow. Instead, as in the definitive opening scene, where conversation at a fashionable party mingles personal matters with considerations about Napoleon and the murder of the duc d'Enghien, Tolstoy masterfully in-

[16] Ibid.

tegrated the historical background with his depiction of the private attributes and lives of his characters. Just how laboriously he worked to obtain such an effect can easily be seen from the manuscripts, which contain fifteen versions of this opening scene.

A close study of his revisions also indicates his determined effort, not only to avoid direct authorial commentary, but to downplay as much as possible even third-person narrative presentation. Tolstoy had long ago written that "it is really impossible to *describe* a man, but it is possible to describe the effect he produces on me";[17] and in *War and Peace* it is these latter effects that he uses for his finely honed portraits. Sometimes this is done through what Kathryn Feuer, in her pathbreaking book *Tolstoy and the Genesis of War and Peace*, called the "technique of externalization," the depiction of impressions through a meticulous account of the character as seen through another's eyes. Often, when restricting himself to the character's own point of view, Tolstoy does so very rigorously, carefully indicating the character's own uncertainty about what he or she is observing or feeling. Tolstoy thus avoids as much as possible imposing any narratorial authority on the reader. Percy Lubbock, who in his *The Craft of Fiction* criticizes Tolstoy for not maintaining a consistent narrative point of view, nonetheless was perceptive enough to understand Tolstoy's aim. It was "to give his tale the look of truth ... to raise ... the narrative ... to a power approaching that of drama, where the intervention of the storyteller is no longer felt."[18]

Six

War and Peace opens with the informative scene over which Tolstoy worked so laboriously, and in which he introduces his two main heroes, Pierre Bezuhov and Prince Andrey Bolkonsky. The picture of Petersburg society, with its jockeying for social influence, position, and fortune, sets the tone for how this world will continue to be depicted in the future. Its inhabitants, like the wily and influential Prince Vasily Kuragin, are concerned with nothing but their personal advantage, and his family glaringly illustrates the point. His lecherous son Anatole will almost bring the delightfully exuberant, innocent, and spontaneously warmhearted Natasha Rostova to ruin. His statuesquely beautiful and equally licentious daughter Ellen (frankly called "a whore" in the notes) traps Pierre into a disastrous marriage by the sensuous appeal of her abundantly displayed charms.

---

[17] Quoted in ibid., 32.
[18] Percy Lubbock, *The Craft of Fiction* (New York, 1931), 126, quoted in Feuer, *Tolstoy*, 124.

All through the book she acquires one lover after another, and there is a certain poetic justice in her death. Its cause is a drug she was taking to avoid childbirth, though her friends spoke of angina pectoris and carefully wrapped her demise in euphemisms.

Pierre and Prince Andrey stand out from this world because both wish to find some higher meaning in their lives. As noted of Pierre in a draft note: "Often speaks of immortality, and tormented by the question"[19]— just as Tolstoy was himself. Pierre also leads the same life of drunkenness and debauchery so often lamented by his creator in the *Diary*. Prince Andrey, bored with his life and a tedious marriage to a social butterfly, has joined the Russian Army to fight against Napoleon in search of honor and glory.

In the early sections of the book, the bumbling, awkward though naturally kindhearted Pierre, educated abroad and hardly at home in Russian society—illegitimate into the bargain—is portrayed as someone easily led and manipulated by the Kuragins and their milieu. Even after he inherits the enormous wealth and noble status of his father, which immediately elevates him to the highest rank of society, he is putty in the hands of Prince Vassily and Ellen; but Ellen's affair with the daredevil Dolohov awakens Pierre from his lethargy. He wounds Dolohov in a duel and, breaking with both Ellen and her father, becomes a Freemason. Tolstoy here accurately utilizes an influential movement in the Russian society of that period, whose doctrines imbue Pierre with a new sense of moral responsibility. Tolstoy treats this phase rather ironically, ridiculing the intricacies of Masonic doctrine but nonetheless portraying it as temporarily satisfying the aspirations of Pierre to fulfill some of his moral yearnings.

Pierre's craving for what may be called moral purification, however, is not satisfied until the final pages of the book. Taken prisoner by the French during the occupation of Moscow, though guilty of nothing more than trying to rescue a child in the burning city, he is spared execution. But he witnesses five others being shot and buried, one possibly still living, and this unbearable spectacle "had annihilated in his soul all faith in the beneficent ordering of the universe, and in the soul of men ... and in God" (881). Such faith is restored by two experiences. One is the extreme deprivation and physical hardships he endures both in captivity and while accompanying the French in their retreat. His ability to survive, and even to overcome such suffering, teaches Pierre "not through his intellect, but through his whole being, through life, that man is created for happiness, that happiness lies in himself." He learns "that all unhappiness

---

[19] R. F. Christian, *Tolstoy: A Critical Introduction* (Cambridge: Cambridge University Press, 1931), 106.

is due, not to lack of what is needful, but to superfluity," and "that there is nothing terrible to be dreaded in the world" when such superfluity vanishes (965).

The second is his encounter with Platon Karataev, a simple illiterate Russian peasant whose uncomplaining and even joyous acceptance of existence under the most appalling conditions furnishes Pierre with a living exemplar of the ideal he had vainly been searching for all his life. "Attachments, friendship, love, as Pierre understood them, Karataev had none; but he loved and lived on affectionate terms with every creature with whom he was thrown in life"—including the French who were holding him captive. He existed entirely in the moment, not even being able to repeat words he had just uttered, and felt his life to have "no meaning as a separate life. It had meaning only as part of a whole, of which he was at all times conscious" (886). Platon's speech consists mainly of proverbs, containing the age-old wisdom of the people, and in telling stories illustrating God's inexplicable goodness and mercy. Whether Tolstoy succeeds in creating a credible character with Platon has aroused a good deal of disagreement; and the presumed ideal he provides has also provoked controversy. What is obvious, however, is that Platon foreshadows Tolstoy's own later personal and ideological evolution when, much to the displeasure of his wife, he too attempted to live as close as he could manage to the life-style of a Russian peasant.

Another family and milieu depicted, which differs entirely from the self-seeking and dissolute Kuragins, is that of Prince Andrey. Prince Andrey's father, Prince Nikolay Bolkonsky, had once been a commander-in-chief in the Russian Army but had been sent into exile; and even when this banishment was lifted by Alexander I, he refused to leave his estate. This had become, in effect, his own small kingdom that he ruled with an iron hand, and he was "known in the fashionable world by the nickname of 'the Prussian king'" (probably an allusion to Frederick the Great) (76). He is, in any case, a martinet formed by eighteenth-century ideas that "human vices all sprang from only two sources, idleness and superstition" (76), and he teaches geometry himself to his terrified daughter Princess Marya, who is deeply religious and constantly suffers from his impositions and exactions. Without intending to be cruel, he nonetheless is so in fact; but Princess Marya, understanding that the rigidity of his character is a result of wounded pride, pardons him inwardly with Christian compassion. Prince Andrey, without inheriting his father's ideas, nonetheless retains some of his inflexibility and stiffness of character and arouses as much antipathy as amiability among those he frequents.

Whereas Pierre is searching for a moral ideal, Prince Andrey joins the Russian Army in Austria hoping to find the opportunity for his own "Toulon," the battle that brought fame to Napoleon. His dreams of glory, however, are shattered when he is wounded at Austerlitz after picking up the fallen standard of a retreating regiment and rallying the troops to return to combat. What he now sees, in one of the most often-cited passages, is "the lofty sky, not clear yet immeasurably lofty," which he contrasts with what he had just felt in battle. "How was it I did not see that lofty sky before? And how happy I am to have found it at last! Yes! All is vanity, all is a cheat, except that infinite sky" (253).

When Napoleon, surveying his victory, stands over Andrey's prostrate body on the battlefield, "how insignificant ... seemed to him [Andrey] all the interests that engrossed Napoleon ... with his paltry vanity and joy in victory... compared to the lofty, equitable and kindly sky" (254). Suddenly he becomes aware of the unimportance of glory and military triumph and feels all earthly ambition to be dwarfed by the contemplation of the mystery of nature and of human life.

Like his father, Andrey now retreats from the world and becomes a model landowner, not out of compassion for his peasants but to save himself from remorse because of the advantages of his superior social status. His life alternates between such periods of action and withdrawal, and he returns to the world again after a crucial scene in which the two friends meet after a long separation. Pierre expresses his newfound ambition to help humanity, while Prince Andrey, having seen the futility of his previous desire for "glory," insists that he is only concerned with the welfare of himself and his family. But he is nonetheless troubled by his former callousness toward his wife who has died in childbirth, and her loss has now persuaded him "of the necessity of a future life." After uttering such words, "with a radiant, tender, childlike look ... for the first time since Austerlitz he saw the lofty, eternal sky, as he had seen it lying on the field at Austerlitz, and something that had long been slumbering, something better that had been in him, suddenly awoke" (354).

Andrey thus rejoins the army, and, parallel to Pierre's Freemasonry, becomes involved with the famous and then influential reformer Speransky; but the plans on which he labors for this zealous bureaucrat are so far removed from Russian reality that he is overcome by their futility. Two encounters with Natasha, among the most charming scenes in the book, replace Speransky as the focus of his life, and Andrey and Natasha become engaged. But the marriage is put off for one year at the insistence of the Andrey's tyrannical father, and in the absence of Andrey Natasha yields to the seduction of Anatole Kuragin—though saved from ruin at the last moment. Natasha is plunged into grief and remorse and becomes ill, but the two meet again after Andrey is fatally wounded at Borodino and she nurses him until the end. The scene in which he forgives Anatole Kuragin, whose leg is being amputated, has already been cited. During his last days, he dreams that "Love is God, and dying means for me, a particle of love, to go back to the universal and eternal source of love." But he finds these to be only thoughts, "and something was wanting in them"; he had still not really accepted death. It was only when he did so that those looking after him "felt they were waiting not on him (he was no more; he had gone far away from them, but on the nearest memory of him—his body)" (895–97). Even before his physical death a few days later, Prince Andrey's soul returns, as it were, to that eternal sky that had always intervened to lift him above the vanity of his earthly cares and ambitions.

The Rostov family in Moscow, with its kindhearted, good-natured, and spendthrift head, also contrasts sharply with the self-seeking and manipulative St. Petersburg Kuragins. The most important figure here is the fifteen-year-old Natasha, whose features Tolstoy grasps from the very first. In his notes, he wrote of her: "*Love:* crying out for a husband, two even, needs children, love, bed."[20] She is shown as capricious and flirtatious, yielding to her impulses but normally checked by an equally spontaneous moral instinct (though she will need help when overcome by Anatole Kuragin). She is one of Tolstoy's most irresistible creations, whose youthful vivaciousness—her joy in life and the joy that radiates from her presence—elicits a proposal not only from Prince Andrey but from the totally inappropriate hardened cavalry officer Denisov. Her marriage to Pierre, after a good deal of suffering on both sides, unites the two most appealing figures in the book, and her transformation from a blossoming belle into a solid matron concerned only about the diapers of her babies seems a suitable fulfillment for the life-stimulating and life-sustaining role that she has played throughout the book.

Tolstoy also uses her as a symbol for something essentially Russian that has not been stifled by the European education of the upper class. When she instinctively performs a Russian dance to the music of a balalaika, Tolstoy asks: "Where, how, had this young countess, educated by a French *emigrée* [governess], sucked in with the Russian air she breathed, the spirit of that dance?" (470). Her brother Nikolay Rostov plays somewhat the same role, and in scene after scene he affirms his devotion to the tsar and his instinctive refusal to question his supreme authority. Nikolay finally marries the Princess Marya, deeply imbued with traditional Russian Christianity, and who once dreamed of becoming an indigent wandering pilgrim like the "God's folk" that, despite the disapproval of her father, she entertained in her home. It is Nikolay who tells the incipient Decembrist Pierre, at the end of the book, that if he were ordered to lead a squadron

---

[20] Quoted in Christian, *Tolstoy's "War and Peace,"* 12.

against his brother-in-law and his friends and to cut them down, he would do so without a moment's hesitation.

Seven

Tolstoy's masterly portrayal of military life, already evident in his earlier work, reaches new heights in *War and Peace* on a much larger scale. Without avoiding the cruel human costs of warfare, no other novel can compete with Tolstoy's in the superb panoply he offers of regimental displays and parades, and of battle scenes seen both from a distance and in close combat. Also, as the Vicomte de Vogüé noted in his pioneering book on the Russian novel that brought writers like Tolstoy and Dostoevsky to the attention of the European public, no one could compete with Tolstoy in his portrayal of the life of the court and the upper reaches of society. Tolstoy here was "in his native element," just as he was, after his years in the Caucasus and in Sevastopol, in the many scenes in which the rank-and-file Russian soldiers banter with each other around their bivouacs or while marching to and from their battles.

Nothing fascinated Tolstoy more, at least in this period of his career, than the mysterious force which, as he put it, moved millions of men to march from West to East and then back again, all the while "perpetrat[ing] against one another so great a mass of crime—fraud, swindling, robbery ... plundering, incendiarism, and murder—that the annals of all the criminal courts in the world could not muster such a sum of wickedness in whole centuries" (553). The problem of war and warfare more and more preoccupies Tolstoy as the book moves on, and this evolves into a theory of history whose ideas, scattered throughout these later chapters, are argued theoretically in the second epilogue and brilliantly explored in Sir Isaiah Berlin's *The Hedgehog and the Fox*. Sir Isaiah views Tolstoy as a fox, unremittingly occupied with the minutiae of particulars, while longing for the unitary vision of the hedgehog "who knows one big thing." But Tolstoy himself, though he may have longed to know "one big thing," was unrelentingly critical of those who believed they had attained such semisupernatural mastery of events.

In one superbly satirical scene after another, Tolstoy drives home that those in command cannot possibly anticipate what will occur in the ebb and flow of battle, and thus the uselessness of all the elaborate plans prepared so carefully in advance. It is not such plans that are important but the behavior of such Russian commanders as Prince Bagration and particularly the elderly and battle-scarred Field-Marshal Kutuzov, who becomes the military hero of the book (against a good bit of historical evidence to the contrary). They both respond as if all the randomness were going according to *their* plan, and in this way they support the morale of their troops. Kutuzov, who falls asleep while the battle of Borodino is being discussed in advance, knew "with the wisdom of old age" that battles were lost or won "by that intangible force called the spirit of the army, and he followed that force and led it as far as it lay within his power" (737).

For Tolstoy, it was morale that ultimately decided the course of combat—the morale of the soldiers, and the behavior of individuals like the unprepossessing Captain Tushin, who pays no attention to orders, responds to the immediate situation, and, as only Prince Andrey realizes, is really responsible for the Russian success at Schongraben. Tolstoy thus rejects the "great man" theory of history, particularly as embodied in Napoleon, which attributes military success to the superior capacities of a leader capable of dominating in advance the uncertainties and vicissitudes of the battlefield. All the historical explanations of what occurred in 1812 as the result of forethought or planned decision are ridiculed with biting sarcasm.

As a result, while the epic-historical aspect of his theme becomes more and more prominent as the book proceeds, Tolstoy deliberately inverts all the age-old rules of epic delineation. In the conventional epic it is the heroes, the rulers of their societies, who embody its highest values and take command to guide the course of the action. But in Tolstoy's pages, just as the morale of the individual soldier determines the course of combat, so the private behavior of individuals—acting in their own interests, and paying attention only to their own needs and desires—proves to be the cause of epoch-making historical events.

The unrivaled pages dealing with the occupation of Moscow by the French, and the accidental, involuntary destruction of the city by fire, illustrate this overturning of literary convention with admirable clarity. "Those who left the city with what they could carry away, abandoning their houses and half their property, did so in consequence of that latent patriotism which finds expression, not in phrases, not in giving one's children to death for the sake of the fatherland, and such unnatural exploits, but expresses itself imperceptibly in the most simple, organic way, and so always produces the most powerful results" (761).

In fact, however, the patriotism of such behavior was more than latent; for the Russians, "to be under the government of the French was out of the question; it was worse than anything" (761). *War and Peace* became a great national Russian epic precisely because, among the natural feelings that the people were expressing in their abandonment of Moscow, Tolstoy did not fail to include the patriotism that had become, as it were, an instinct as powerful as all the others. Such patriotism is always stirred from latency into potency by foreign invasion, even when, as was the case with Napoleon, liberation was promised to the Russian peasant-serfs with little or no effect. (The one scene of incipient serf rebellion is easily put down by

Nikolay Rostov.) Instead, in Tolstoy's portrayal, which rather downplays the genuine historical situation, the spontaneously formed Russian guerilla detachments harass the French mercilessly in their disastrous retreat.

Eight

War and Peace is so vast a work, and Tolstoy raises so many problems through both his depiction of character and his theoretical excurses, that the question has inevitably arisen whether one can say anything in general about the focus of the book as a whole. He remarked himself, many years after it was written, that "the most important thing in a work of art is that it should have a kind of focus, i.e., some place where all the rays meet or from which they issue."[21] But he then added that "this focus should not be capable of being completely explained in words." Nonetheless, let me cite in conclusion an effort by R. F. Christian to provide at least a tentative focus for this extraordinary novel-epic.

> Broadly speaking it is the contrast between two opposite states: on the one hand, selfishness, self-indulgence, self-importance, and the attendant evils of careerism, nepotism, vanity, affectation and the pursuit of purely private pleasures; on the other hand, a turning outwards from the self, a groping towards something bigger, an endeavor to surmount individualism, a recognition that the cult of the self is an unworthy alternative to the service of one's neighbor, one's family, the community and the country at large.[22]

One can accept this as a fairly adequate elucidation of the moral-social values that control the book; and it is on this level that Tolstoy's great novel has usually been interpreted. But what gives its pages their universal appeal is Tolstoy's capacity to immerse himself, as well as the reader, so completely in the experience of the moment —to convey Natasha's ecstasy and despair during her first ball with the same intensity as Prince Andrey's glimpse of the sky after Austerlitz, and to have Nikolay proclaim, when his dog seizes the wolf by the throat during the lovingly depicted hunt scene, that "this was the happiest moment of his life" (**460**). The importance of such immersion in the immediate and particular was something Tolstoy always strove to capture, and the dangers of losing sight of the individual for the general was a temptation that he took special care to avoid.

Indeed, in a letter he wrote—but never sent—to the minor novelist P. D. Boborykin in 1865, in full tide of writing *War and Peace*, he makes his own aim very clear. "If I were to be told," he writes, "that I could

---

[21] Quoted in Christian, *Tolstoy*, 150.
[22] Christian, *Tolstoy's "War and Peace,"* 105.

write a novel whereby I could irrefutably establish what seemed to me the correct point of view on all social problems, I would not even devote two hours to such a novel. But If I were to be told that what I should write would be read in about twenty years time by those who are now children, and that they would laugh and cry over it and love life, I would devote all my own life and all my energies to it."[23] Tolstoy later changed his mind on this issue, as he did on so many others, but posterity is lucky that he completed *War and Peace* before he did so. Much more than twenty years have passed, but people are still laughing, crying, and learning to love life along with the unforgettable characters he created.

[23] Quoted in Troyat, *Tolstoy*, 297.

PART II
THE RUSSIAN TRADITION

FIVE

NATASHA'S DANCE:

A CULTURAL HISTORY OF RUSSIA

TO CALL a work designated as a cultural history of Russia "Natasha's Dance" is unexpected, to say the least. What has such an appellation to do with so weighty a subject—and with a book of over six hundred pages? Why so seemingly frivolous a title for an inquiry which, presumably, will unroll before the reader the rich panoply of Russian cultural creations that have for so long excited the interest and curiosity of Western observers? The answer is that Orlando Figes's impressive book is not at all conceived along the lines usually expected on reading the phrase "cultural history."

For a culture, in his view, is not simply a series of literary and artistic productions, and its history more than the theories attempting to explore and explain their significance. Rather, it is the complex of ideas and attitudes that underlie them both and finds expression in every aspect of life—not only in cultural creation, but also "as impressions of the national consciousness, which mingle with politics and ideology, social customs and beliefs, folklore and religion, habits and conventions and all the other mental bric-à-brac that constitute a culture and a way of life."[1] One might say that Figes approaches Russian culture (actually, only Russian culture from the time of Peter the Great; the subtitle is too inclusive) as an anthropologist approaches that of a primitive tribe whose way of life he wishes to fathom, and who finds it embodied in every artifact and every custom and gesture.

The title of the book refers to a famous scene in *War and Peace* in which Natasha Rostov, the finest product of the European education favored by the Russian aristocracy for more than a century, visits the far from luxurious home of a distant relative. He is a nobleman living with his serf-"wife" in the country, and who has, as it were, abandoned that superior attitude to the uncivilized "people" that characterized his class. He strikes up a Russian folksong on his guitar and challenges Natasha, who has never danced

---

Originally published in a slightly different form as "His proudest moment had been when two peasants bowed to the ground, Russian style, and thanked him for his book," *The London Review of Books*, November 28, 2002. Reprinted by permission

[1] Orlando Figes, Natasha's Dance: A Cultural History of Russia (London: Macmillan, 2002), xxvi. Subsequent references to this work are cited in parentheses in the text.

to such music before, to do so now. Suddenly she finds herself performing the native steps with perfect rhythm and grace. "Where, when, and how," asks the narrator, "had this young countess, educated by an émigré French governess, imbibed from the Russian air she breathed that spirit, and obtained that manner which the *pas de chale* would, one have supposed, long ago effaced?" The serf-"wife," along with all the other peasants present, are deeply moved when they saw from such body language that "this slim, graceful countess reared in silks and velvets ... was able to understand all that was in Anisya ... and in every Russian man and woman" (xxvi).[2] One can easily chalk this up to Tolstoy's artistic aim, which was to compose a great patriotic epic portraying the unity of the Russian people in the face of foreign invasion. But Figes, as with all the other artistic works he uses, interprets such a scene as expressing a fundamental historical truth about Russian culture. It is the rise of such a belief, the feeling that caused Tolstoy to express it, and so many others (Dostoevsky, to name only one) to accept it as more than the author's personal conviction, that Figes has set out to elucidate.

What the dance of Natasha reveals is the split between an aristocratic upper class whose mentality, ideas, and values have been shaped by an education along European lines and a vast mass of peasantry still living in a pious, religious world untouched by the Renaissance and Reformation, not to mention the blasphemous European (particularly French) eighteenth century. The dance, however, also manifests the continued existence within the Russian cultural psyche of instinctive responses that reaffirm the values of its own tradition. It is this continual seesaw between the old and the new, the hereditary and the innovative, the fascination with the foreign and the comfort of the customary, that provides Figes with the structure of his weighty work. In fact, as he acknowledges, his book is not so much a history as "an interpretation of a culture," and it is an interpretation governed by this cultural dialectic.

Figes is careful to point out that he makes no claim to having uncovered some "pure, organic, or essential core" (xxviii) of Russian culture in his depiction of this inevitable reaffirmation of native roots. Indeed, he does precisely the opposite: Tolstoy's scene represents a "historical myth" invented out of the necessity to cope with the dilemma created by Russian history, a dilemma that may be compared (though he does not do so) to that of a third-world colonial country compelled to accept totally alien European ideas and values. "Forced to become Europeans, the educated classes had become so alienated from the old Russia ... that when, in Tolstoy's age, they struggled to define themselves as 'Russians' once again, they were obliged to reinvent their nation through historical and artistic

---

[2] Lev Tolstoy, *War and Peace*, trans. L. and A. Maude (Oxford, 1998), 546.

myths" (xxx). But such myths, shaped by literature and art, then became a driving force in Russian cultural life itself.

Ever since, the great problem for Russians has been the incessant struggle to wrest some sort of unity out of these conflicting alternatives. "In a way that was extraordinary, if not unique to Russia, the country's artistic energy was almost wholly given to the quest to grasp the idea of its nationality." What was Russia, "the Tsar's Empire or the muddy one-street village where Natasha's 'Uncle' lived?" (xxvii). This question became posed in other and more complex terms as time went on, but it continued to form the leitmotif, not only of Russian culture itself, but of all those who have studied its modern history; there is nothing original about Figes's point of view. What is original, however, is the vast range of information from both history and all the arts on which he draws, the vigor and intensity of his writing, his telling eye for the dramatic detail, and most of all the unprecedented use he makes of private lives to illustrate his themes. It is in such private histories, he writes, "that we may find ... the unseen threads of a common Russian sensibility, such as Tolstoy had imagined in his dancing scene" (xxxiii). Since Peter the Great, however, this "common Russian sensibility" always contained a European admixture, and Figes criticizes those—not negligible by any means, Rilke, Thomas Mann, Virginia Woolf—who swallowed whole the cultural myth of a completely indigenous "Russian soul." All the great Russians "were Europeans too, and the two identities were intertwined and mutually dependent in a variety of ways" (xxxii). It is precisely this point that his book sets out to elucidate on a grandiose scale.

It contains eight sections, each of which explores another manifestation of this underlying cultural dialectic. Beginning with the establishment of St. Petersburg by Peter the Great, it ends with the lives of the Russian exiles scattered throughout the world by the Bolshevik Revolution. There is thus a loose overall chronological structure, but within each section the material is handled thematically and moves freely from past to present. No attempt is made to integrate its abundance except in the very loosest manner; the reader is simply confronted with a vivid presentation of events, either historical, cultural, or personal, whose juxtaposition evokes the particular thematic admixture that Figes wishes to convey. The first page, for example, reads like a historical novel: "On a misty spring morning in 1703, a dozen Russian horsemen rode across the bleak and barren marshlands where the Neva river runs into the Baltic sea. They were looking for a site to build a fort against the Swedes, then at war with Russia," etc. (4).

The chapter then goes on with Peter "the Tsar of landlocked Russia" dismounting from his horse, carving a cross on the marshy ground with his sword, and declaring: "Here shall be a town" (5). All of the book is written more or less in this expressively descriptive narrative style, which carries the reader along easily in its energetic flow, even though, here and there, one would have wished for a little more analytic clarification.

Two

The subjects covered in Figes's book are so extensive that it is impossible, in a review, to do more then summarize some of their main outlines. His first chapter describes in overflowing and vivid detail the transformation of what was essentially swampland, uninhabited except in the summer by visiting fishermen, into a huge metropolis built at enormous cost of labor and human life. It was an artificial city in which Russians never really felt at home; and their distress is brilliantly limned in Pushkin's classic poem *The Bronze Horseman* (an allusion to the statue of Peter the Great on a rearing charger created by the French sculptor Falconet). Herzen called St. Petersburg a huge barracks, and such military imagery about it became customary.

Just as he had constructed an artificial city, so Peter endeavored to do the same with the Russian upper class, forcing them to assume a synthetic personality by becoming as European as possible. They no longer spoke their own language, trained from their earliest years to speak a foreign one (usually French, but also others as well), and behaved, dressed, and even ate in imitation of European models (there is a page-and-a-half list of the foods from Europe ordered by the immensely wealthy Sheremetev family (23–24). As a result, the European Russian acquired "a split identity" and always felt as if he/she were acting out a theatrical role. This could be seen even in the palaces built by the aristocracy, usually the work of European architects and containing grand reception halls and galleries filled with the paintings, bought by the yard, from European artists (some quite famous). These dwellings were conceived as "an oasis of European culture in the desert of the Russian peasant soil" (24); but there were other parts of the house, "the bedrooms and boudoirs ... the chapel and the icon room ... the servants quarters, where a more informal 'Russian' way of life was to be found" (45).

The strains of this inner division began to show around the end of the eighteenth century. The Russian nobleman, despising his own country and its people, then became a stock satirical type of a whole group of minor writers (Kniazhnin, Kheraskov, Fonvizin). He was contrasted in one way or another with the simple moral virtues presumably to be found either in the Russian past or in the villages. The best-known work of this kind is Griboedov's *Woe from Wit*, whose main character Chatsky, on returning home from abroad, finds Russian life intolerable and flees it once again.

A whole group of late-eighteenth-century travel writers, however, found little to praise (quite the contrary!) when they ventured abroad; and the final blow to this idealization of European culture was dealt by the French Revolution. The highly readable *Letters of a Russian Traveller* of Nikolay Karamzin, which contains a fascinating interview with Kant, ends on a recoil before the reign of terror. As a result, "the idea that the West was morally corrupt was echoed by virtually every Russian writer from Pushkin to the Slavophiles" (65) and continued later by Herzen and Dostoevsky.

The hegemony of European (and particularly French) culture was further undermined by the Napoleonic invasion and the war that followed. This initiates a new phase of Russian culture, expressed in the title "The Children of 1812," which focuses on the generation that fought the war and emerged from it with new ideas and values. The sense of community fostered by the war between the upper-class, Europeanized officers and their peasant soldiers, as well as the experience of living in Europe and observing (as well as enjoying) the amenities of its relative freedom, led to a desire among these young aristocrats to import some of its benefits for their countrymen. Such sentiments resulted in the abortive Decembrist rebellion of 1825, the attempt of a group of such officers to mount a coup d'état before Nicholas I acceded to the throne. One of the main aims of the leaders was to abolish serfdom and bring the peasants the freedom they so amply deserved; but the illiterate peasant-soldiers refused to follow, and when leaflets were distributed calling for a "constitution," they thought it was a female name. The peasants simply had never heard the word before; and this is only one example of the continual discrepancy between imported European ideas and the attempt to apply them in Russian conditions.

All the same, the democratic attitudes of the Decembrists continued to gain ground, and Figes details a whole series of cultural phenomena that document this development. There was a notable attempt on the part of the aristocracy to return to Russian customs and way of life. The vogue for the dacha, the simple country house, dates from this time, and so does a change in women's dress. Powdered wigs and heavy scents were abandoned, as elsewhere in Europe, but Figes notes that "in Russia the fashion for the natural had an extra, national dimension" (109). He sees Pushkin's Tatiana as the embodiment of this ideal (the poet had friends among the Decembrists) and cites her rejection of the glamour of St. Petersburg society "for just my books, the simple joys / of our old home, its walks and flowers / for all those haunts that I once knew" (110).[3] He also stresses the importance of the reference to her nanny a few lines later (there is a quite extensive and informative discussion of the importance

---

[3] Alexander Pushkin, *Eugene Onegin*, trans. J. Falen (Oxford, 1990), 209.

of such peasant nursemaids in inculcating their aristocratic charges with the moral-social religious values of the peasantry). It is the memory of her beloved nanny, who had been forced into marriage as a child but remained faithful to her vows, that inspires Tatiana's decision to sacrifice herself to the husband she does not love. Dostoevsky, in his famous Pushkin speech, also saw her choice as an affirmation of true Russian values, though Figes fails to make the connection.

Russian life thus began to be rediscovered and reevaluated in many ways. The Slavophiles made their appearance around 1830, arguing that Russia need not follow the path of Western historical development. Slavophile folklorists went out to collect Russian folksongs, and Glinka integrated them into his own style in the intensely patriotic opera *A Life for the Tsar* (1831). Gogol latched on to the vogue for folktales, using Ukrainian ones in his *Evenings on a Farm near Dikanka* (1831–1832), on which Mussorgsky drew for his *Night on Bald Mountain* (1861) and Rimsky-Korsakov for the opera *May Night* (1879). The Crimean War (1853–1856) in which Russia was defeated by the united might of England and France fighting along with, and on behalf of, Turkey (Figes might have mentioned Tolstoy's *Sevastopol Sketches* at this point) brought on a new surge of anti-Europeanism and ultimately resulted in the liberation of the serfs in 1861.

Three

Every reader of Russian literature is familiar with the contrast between Petersburg and Moscow that forms one of the symbolic dichotomies of Russian culture. The next section, "Moscow, Moscow," begins with the burning of the city by the Russians during the Napoleonic invasion—a decision that staggered the French and led to their retreat for lack of supplies. In *War and Peace*, Tolstoy wrote that "every Russian felt Moscow to be a mother"; it was, writes Figes, "a symbol of the old Russia, the place where ancient Russian customs were preserved" (151). Even when it was rebuilt in European style, "classical façades were softened by the use of warm pastel colours, large round bulky forms and Russian ornament" (154), in an architectural style labeled "neo-Byzantine." Both Gogol and Dostoevsky established the image of Petersburg as spectrally "unreal"; and they had been preceded by the relentless hoofbeats of *The Bronze Horseman*, who, in pursuing a rebellious clerk daring to question Peter's choice of venue for his city, fixed it as the seat of oppressive power and military might. Moscow, however, was depicted in the memoirs of the period as an oasis of food and drink (some of the details are quite extraordinary, if not particularly mouthwatering), the site of innumerable balls and parties, where families converged in spring with marriageable daughters.

Moscow was also the birthplace of a movement dedicated to producing an indigenous Russian art no longer slavishly imitative of European models. Six large volumes of *Antiquities of the Russian State* (1864–1853), published by an artist who restored a palace of the Kremlin, "provided artists and designers with a grammar of historic ornament which they could incorporate in their own work" (173). Crafts that had died out in Petersburg (icon painting, cheap popular prints, lacquer work) were still alive in Moscow. These crafts continued to flourish because of the "old-style merchant taste that dominated the art market in Moscow" (173). A neo-Russian style was thus created, and it was a wealthy Moscow merchant, Pavel Tretyakov, who established his famous gallery of Russian art at this time. A group of young musicians (Balakirev, Mussorgsky, Borodin, Rimsky-Korsakov) revolted against the German-dominated tastes of the Petersburg Conservatory and developed a self-conscious Russian style incorporating "what they heard in village songs, in Cossack and Caucasian dances, in church chants and ... in the tolling of church bells" (179). The Moscow Opera grew out of this revolt, and so did a new style of acting, the creation of Stanislavsky, for the Moscow Art Theatre.

By the end of the century, Moscow had become a center of artistic experimentation harboring painters like Kandinsky and Malevich, musicians like Scriabin (to whose museum Stravinsky made a pilgrimage in 1962), and poets like Pasternak and Mayakovsky. After the revolution, "it became the Soviet capital, the cultural centre of the state, a city of modernity and of the new industrial society the Bolsheviks wanted to build" (214). Tatlin designed a monument, never built, to express these ambitions—"a giant striding figure to be made out of steel and iron girders, tiered and rounded like the churches of medieval Muscovy" (215). The ancient city became, in effect, "a Soviet Petersburg" (215), and the symbolic roles were reversed as the narrow, confining streets were rebuilt to allow for the vast parades, familiar from old newsreels, to stream through the widened avenues. But "with their armed march past the Kremlin, the citadel of Holy Russia, these parades were imitations of the old religious processions they had replaced" (215). When Hitler besieged the city in the autumn of 1941, there was no question of repeating the flight before Napoleon; the Germans were fought to a standstill. "It was not the Soviet capital but Mother Moscow which was saved" (216).

Four

Russian culture at midcentury, once the serfs had been liberated, was preoccupied with the problem posed by this great mysterious mass whom the upper class and the intelligentsia now sought to fathom. The next section is devoted to this effort and its ramifications, beginning with the "going to the people" movement in the "mad summer" of 1874. At that time, the flower of Russian youth, inspired by feelings of guilt over the iniquities of the past, abandoned their own secure existences to live in the villages. Their aim was to make themselves useful (many had learned handicraft skills or studied nursing as preparation) and to win the confidence of the people, hoping, after doing so, to inspire them to improve their lot. Russian literature had already paved the way in 1852 with Turgenev's sympathetic images of peasant types in *Sketches from a Hunter's Album* (he said that the proudest moment in his life had been when two peasants he encountered bowed to the ground Russian-style and thanked him for the book). Nekrasov's epic poem *Who Is Happy in Russia?* (1863–1876), which included snatches of peasant speech, "gave a new, authentic voice to 'the vengeance and sorrow' of the peasantry" (223).

Alas, the gap between the mentality of the peasants and their would-be benefactors, as the Decembrists had already learned, was too great to be so easily bridged. In *Demons* (though Figes fails to note this prediction), Dostoevsky had already intuited such an outcome, and the suspicious peasants turned most of these unwelcome intruders over to the police The peasants were not unconscious socialists, as the young people had been led to believe by such guides as Chernyshevsky and Mikhailovsky, nor did they conform to any of the other images about them developed by Herzen and the Slavophiles. Dostoevsky wrote that "the people still stand before us as a riddle" (224),[4] but he then went on to argue that they were immensely superior morally both to the Russian upper class and to Europeans in general.

The "going to the people" movement influenced painters like Ilia Repin (*The Volga Barge Haulers*) and a composer like Mussorgsky (*Khovanschina*), who aimed at transposing the distinctive features of peasant song and speech into his own musical language. The problem of entering into a closer relation to "the people" is then illustrated from the career of midlife Tolstoy, writing *War and Peace* at this time but tormented, as readers of his later novels are well aware, by the injustice inherent in his social position. He strove futilely to become a peasant as far as possible though without relinquishing his privileges, ultimately persuading himself that the simple pieties of peasant life provided a moral norm. But someone like Repin, of humble origin and who came to Yasnaya Polyana to paint Tolstoy's portrait, thought his way of life to be "just hypocrisy" (242).[5]

Once going to the people had proved to be a failure, a general disillusionment set in with the previous veneration of the peasantry's habitual

[4] Feodor Dostoevsky, *Polnoe Sobraniie Sochinenii*, 22:44.
[5] *I. E. Repin i L. N. Tolstoi*, 2 vols. (Moscow-Leningrad, 1949), 2:36.

way of life. The quite delusory image of peasant rectitude fostered by populist ideology and by both Tolstoy and Dostoevsky (more in the journalism of the latter than in his artistic creations) was now replaced by Chekhov's story *The Peasants* (1899), which created a scandal by unblinkingly depicting their lives as sunk in vice and degradation. These were also the years when the growing industrialization of the country created an urban culture drawing the younger generations away from the land; the more educated they became, the less they wished to adhere to the old way of life. The revolution of 1905, which led to the destruction of many estates by the marauding peasantry, eliminated the last illusions of the liberal intelligentsia. And while the revolution led to a kind of constitution, it was quite clear that the socialists wanted not only political changes but social ones as well that threatened the propertied classes. Ivan Bunin's *The Village* (1910) upset any remaining complacency by its hopelessly bleak portrayal of rural existence—to such an extent indeed that for Gorky, who had painfully worked his way out of such an environment, it raised "the question of whether Russia is to be or not to be" (263).[6]

A new myth of the peasantry, however, soon found artistic expression in the Ballets Russes. The workshops of Abramtsevo had already combined a revival of Russian folk arts and crafts with the art nouveau stylizations of the present, and a group of young men (Sergei Diaghilev, Alexander Benois, Leon Bakst) now began to view peasant art in terms coinciding with the new European taste for the exotic and the primitive. For them, such art "was impersonal, symbolic and austere, strictly regulated by the folk-traditions of representation, a mystical expression of the spiritual world yet intimately linked with the collective rituals and practices of village life" (270). The Ballets Russes thus arose from this attempt to create a purely fictive Russian past, using artistic techniques that would appeal to the most sophisticated contemporary taste; and when they first appeared in Paris, they took Europe by storm.

Stravinsky used "the heterophonic harmonies of Russian folk-music" (276) without attempting to adapt them to a European format, and Fokine's choreography for *The Rite of Spring* (1913), instead of being the usual romantic story, was "a succession of ritual acts" (279), whose movements broke completely with the classical conventions of ballet. A Russian painter, also an archeologist, believed he had unearthed some evidence of human sacrifice among the ancient Scythians, and this had been used as the basis of the ballet—for which he designed the costumes based on Russian peasant clothes. After the 1917 revolution, Stravinsky labored long and hard in exile on a ballet called *The Peasant Wedding* (given in Paris in 1923 as *Les Noces*). He saw this work as an attempt to express "the

---

[6] Maxim Gorky, *Letters* (Moscow, 1964), 54.

ur-Russia, the ancient peasant Russia that had been concealed by the thin veneer of European civilization since the eighteenth century" (284). This was the only Russia to which, during the years of his exile, Stravinsky could manage to feel any allegiance.

Five

No study of Russian culture can afford to underestimate its Christian heritage, and Figes does it ample justice as he goes "In Search of the Russian Soul." Attention is centered on the monastery of Optina Pustyn, which Dostoevsky used as a basis for his portraiture of monastic life in *The Brothers Karamazov*. Like Gogol, Tolstoy, and the Slavophile critic-philosopher Ivan Kireevsky, he had visited this remote and isolated sanctuary while working on the early chapters of his novel. Optina Pustyn, in addition to publishing translations of the Greek Fathers, was the center of a nineteenth-century revival of a mystical doctrine called Hesychasm, which emphasized the divine mystery of the Christian faith because "God cannot be grasped by the human mind (for anything we know is inferior to Him)." The official Church, whose relatively uneducated parish priests were not much respected by the population, looked with disfavor on such ideas, especially since they were also combined with a social mission of relieving poverty and injustice.

Russian Christianity was taken over from Byzantium and thus lacked any central dogmatic authority like Roman Catholicism. When Byzantium fell, the idea arose that Russia had now become the Third Rome—"the last remaining seat of the Orthodox religion, with a messianic role to save the Christian world" (300). Russian Christianity was not a religion of doctrine but of ritual, and when an attempt was made in the seventeenth century to bring Russian ritual into conformity with the Greek, a split (*raskol*) developed between the official Church and the Old Believers, who regarded such reforms as the handiwork of the Antichrist. A large proportion of the Russian population thus abandoned the official Church (it is impossible to estimate how many, but Figes cites at least twenty million by the beginning of the twentieth century) and then fractured even further into various sects. These all elaborated different beliefs, some of them quite fantastic, but at their heart "was the ancient Russian quest for a truly spiritual kingdom on this earth" (307), which might be found in "Holy Rus." Myths developed of the existence of such a kingdom somewhere at the far edges of the Russian land, or even, like the city of Kitezh, sunk under a lake and "only visible to the true believers in the Russian faith" (308).

Gogol, like the Slavophiles, cherished the idea of "the Russian soul"—a people united in "their willingness to sacrifice their individual egos for a higher moral goal" (313), as could be seen in their communal way of life, their peaceful nature, and their humility, which made them far superior to the selfish individualism rampant in the bourgeois West. Gogol's work, particularly the first part of *Dead Souls*, revealed with biting satire the ravages of the quest for filthy lucre evident even in Russia; but the second and third parts would display "the 'Russian principle' of Christian love" (315) in action. Alas, Gogol could not manage to create such a world and instead published his *Selected Passages from Correspondence with Friends*, whose unctuous kowtowing to the existing conditions of serfdom was condemned even by his closest friends. In the end, filled with despair despite several visits to Optina Pustyn during these last years, he starved himself to death.

Dostoevsky too sought to find solace in the monastery in 1878 (his three-year-old son Aleksei had just died suddenly of an epileptic fit, inherited from his father); Figes speaks of "several trips" (325), but only one was made. The scene in *The Brothers Karamazov* in which Father Zosima attempts to comfort the grieving peasant women is taken from a similar event in the monastery; and the figure of Zosima as well as Father Ferapont were probably influenced by Dostoevsky's perusal of *The Life of the Elder Leonid* (1876), though perhaps less exclusively than Figes suggests. No mention is made of the eighteenth-century cleric St. Tikhon Zadonsky, probably because he could not be linked to the monastery, even though Dostoevsky had much earlier expressed admiration for his writings and intended to include him in a novel.

Succinctly outlining Dostoevsky's literary career, Figes points out that "the type of socialism to which he subscribed [in the 1840s] had a close affinity with Christ's ideals" (328). His experiences in the prison camp (described in his 1862 autobiographical memoir, *House of the Dead*) destroyed whatever illusions he may have cherished about the ingrained virtues of the Russian peasant. But the memory of a boyhood incident, when one of his father's serfs had comforted him as a frightened child, persuaded him that the criminals and murderers among whom he lived were not cynical and unredeemable evildoers. "From the distant memory of a single peasant's kindness, he made a leap of faith that all Russian peasants harbored Christ's example somewhere in their souls" (331). The same leap of faith is made in relation to the larger, perennial issue of theodicy, the existence of evil in a world presumably created by a God of love.

Ivan Karamazov refuses to accept a world in which the suffering of the innocent (children) is necessary for the eternal harmony of the ultimate reconciliation; and Dostoevsky struggled with this tormenting problem all through his post-Siberian career. But whatever resolution he managed to envisage is intimately intertwined with "the redemptive quality of the Russian peasant soul" (334), which could be perceived only by faith and not reason. It was such a faith that allowed Dostoevsky to discern that "the capacity for suffering"[7]—not in a material but a moral sense, the self-sacrifice for another—was "the truly Christian essence of the Russian peasantry" (336). He also suggested that it might become a significant force for social betterment if, as Father Zosima proclaims would someday come to pass, the Russian Church substituted its "moral sanction" for the impersonal laws of the state and Russia became a theocracy. In one of his last articles, picking up a well-known term from the radical Herzen, Dostoevsky labeled this as "Russian Socialism"; and Figes aptly comments on the irony of the ferociously antiradical Dostoevsky proclaiming a "vision of a democratic church [that] remained close to the socialist ideals which he espoused in his youth" (339).

Tolstoy lived quite close to Optina Pustyn (he had sometimes walked there in earlier years), but in 1910, ten days before he died, he left home stealthily and bought a railroad ticket to the nearest station. By this time he had rejected all the doctrines of the official church and preached "a practical religion based on Christ's example as a living human being" (342). He had become a Christian anarchist who, refusing to accept all church and state authority, had been excommunicated in 1901. But this only increased his enormous influence, which, as one conservative publicist wrote, was shaking the throne of Nicholas II, whereas Tolstoy's throne was beyond the grasp of the tsar. Even though few people read Tolstoy's religious writings of the 1880s, his novel *Resurrection* (1899), which attacked all the institutions of the tsarist state, had been a sensational best seller. Tolstoy was not a revolutionary, however, but a Christian pacifist who refused to countenance violence, though he vehemently denounced all the social evils—"poverty and inequality, cruelty and oppression" (342)—so rampant and not only in Russia alone.

Very much obsessed with death, he depicted the moment of dying unforgettably in his great novels; but unlike Chekhov, whom he went to visit in the last stages of the latter's tuberculosis, he could not accept it with equanimity. Chekhov, though not a believer, was by no means areligious and very often depicts with great sympathy characters who are searching after faith. Indeed, he saw the need for a faith of some kind to be an essential aspect of the Russian character. But he brushed aside Tolstoy's "mystical conception of death as a spiritual release, the dissolution of personality into a 'universal soul'" (349). In Tolstoy's memorable *The Death of Ivan Ilich* (1886), the sole "spiritual release" for the dying man is the presence of a young peasant lad Gerasim, who sits with him at night and tries to ease his physical discomfort simply as an act of human solidarity with someone in his last moments. Others of Ivan Ilich's Europeanized upper-

---

[7] Feodor Dostoevsky, *A Writer's Diary*, trans. K. Lantz, 2 vols. (London, 1994), 1:135.

class milieu tried to reduce death "to the level of a fortuitous, disagreeable and rather indecent incident" (349)[8] from which they turned away with distaste; but Gerasim accepted it as a normal part of life and felt a human duty to ease the misery of this inevitable moment as best he could.

Such a serene acceptance of death among the peasantry had earlier been portrayed by Turgenev, among others, and became a cultural myth that continues up to Solzhenitsyn's *Cancer Ward* (1968). The peasants, in any case, believed in a spirit world in which the souls of the dead continued to exist and influence those still living, whether for good or evil. Allusions to such a belief can be found in *The Brothers Karamazov* when Father Zosima consoles the grieving mother, and little Ilyusha asks his father to scatter bread on his grave "so that the sparrows may fly down, and I shall hear and it will cheer me up not to be lying alone" (353).[9] As for Tolstoy, he breathed his last, after leaving the monastery, in the house of a stationmaster on the railroad line, sheltered by his family from an Optina monk sent to reconcile him with the church. He was buried at Yasnaya Polyana, without the benefit of official rites, but even the police knelt when the assembled crowd began to intone an ancient Russian chant.

Six

While most of the book dwells on the relation of Russian culture to Europe, Figes also devotes a rather speculative section, "The Descendants of Genghiz Khan," to the Eastern and Asiatic cultures that intersect with Russian cultural development. The modern painter Vladimir Kandinsky as a young man traveled to the northern Komi region of the country to study the shamanistic beliefs of its Finno-Ugrian people; and it is quite possible that he had some Komi blood in his veins. It is astonishing, at least for this reader, to learn how many eminent names in Russian culture of the past and present derive from Tatar origins, including Boris Godunov himself—the descendant of a Tatar khan named Chet.

Russia had been conquered by the Mongols in the thirteenth century, and, after the breakup of their power 250 years later, a large Mongol population settled in Russia, intermarrying with the Slavs and entering into the service of the Russian state. Many common words in Russian are taken from the Tatar, and "There is also reason to suppose that the shamanistic cults of the Mongol tribes were incorporated in the Russian peasant faith"

---

[8] Lev Tolstoy, *The Death of Ivan Ilich and Other Stories*, trans. R. Edmonds (Harmondsworth, 1960), 140.

[9] Feodor Dostoevsky, *The Brothers Karamazov*, trans. D. Magarshack (Harmondsworth, 1988), 906.

(371). Figes goes so far as to suggest that the Russian "holy fool," so familiar from Russian literature as a Christian exemplar, may also have had shamanistic origins. There is great resistance to such a notion in present-day scholarship—Dimitry Likhachev, "the leading twentieth-century cultural historian of Russia" (367) is cited—and the period of the Mongol conquest is generally seen as detrimental because it cut off Russia from European cultural developments. Nonetheless, there has always been a certain ambiguity in the Russian relation to Asia. Russia's geography placed it on a borderline between West and East, and the adjective "Asiatic" was used by European observers like the Marquis de Custine to characterize the peculiarities of Russian life. Although the Russians desired to be considered Europeans, when they were rejected and felt misunderstood even someone like Pushkin would refer threateningly to the Asiatic expanse of his native land.

Even while engaging in imperial conquest in the Caucasus and Central Asia, the Russian attitude was not, according to Figes, that of the Western cultural superiority exhibited by the Europeans (making them the great exception to Edward Said's castigation of Western *Orientalism*). Indeed, the Russians were not at all averse to admiring and assimilating the cultures they were subduing. The Cossacks were an instance of such assimilation, and their portrayal in Tolstoy's *The Cossacks* (1863) illustrates the point. Lermontov at first fought bravely against the Chechens but then wrote poems denouncing the Russian atrocities in the course of their conquest. In his great novel, *A Hero of Our Time*, the main character Pechorin falls in love with the daughter of a Circassian chief and learns her language. The Oriental influence on Russian music has already been mentioned and continues to blossom in *Prince Igor* and *Scheherezade*. A little-known critic, Vladimir Stasov, who exercised a wide-ranging influence, developed theories linking Russian ornament with Persian art and considered the Russian *byliny*—the epic oral folk poetry of the people—as "Russified derivatives of Hindu, Buddhist and Sanskrit myths" (393). Stasov wrote the original scenario for Rimsky-Korsakov's *Sadko*, full of the wonders of shamanistic magic, but the composer refused to go along and turned the work into a celebration of "the demise of paganism and the triumph of the Christian spirit in Russia" (399). Nonetheless, such theories were also used to justify the Russian invasion of Central Asia, and "the idea that Russia had a cultural and historical claim in Asia became a founding myth of the empire" (414).

This notion of a Russian claim to Central Asia was bolstered by the theory that a pre-Christian "Scythian" civilization also formed part of Russia's cultural heritage. Support for such a view was furnished by the discovery of a rich treasure of Scythian artifacts by the same ethnographer-artist, Nicholas Roerich, who had inspired *The Rite of Spring*. It was then taken up by a group of "Scythian" poets, the most famous of whom was Alexander Blok. Blok saw the Russian Revolution as an expression of this primordial Scythian drive, which Europe either had to join or be destroyed. Andrei Bely's remarkable Symbolist novel *Petersburg* is also built on this East–West dichotomy, and one of the characters envisages a vast carnage as "thousands of Tamerlane's horsemen ... poured down on Rus'" (423).[10] Among the emigrés, a group of scholars known as the Eurasians—the best-known being the linguist N. S. Trubetskoy—attempted to give a theoretical foundation to the notion that Russia had developed a unique "Eurasian" culture combining the merits of both East and West. Such notions had some influence especially among the émigrés, but they quickly vanished as being too speculative to taken seriously. Just as with the Ballets Russes, it was among the artists that these ideas had the greatest resonance and most fruitful impact. While Western artists traveled to foreign climes in search of primitive cultures or adapted exotic styles, Russians like Malevich, Kandinsky, or Chagall "took their inspiration from the art of the Russian peasants and the tribal cultures of the Asiatic steppe" (426). Even the abstract art of Kandinsky contains shapes and hieroglyphs that can be identified as Finno-Ugrian shamanistic symbols.

Seven

The final two sections of Figes's sweeping inquiry deal with the Soviet period and Russian culture in exile. The old intelligentsia that remained in the country, like the great poetess Anna Akhmatova, suffered years of material hardship and cultural ostracism. They represented the Russia that the Bolsheviks wished to transform, not only materially but spiritually as well— in some sense, though Figes does not make this point himself, taking up the task begun by Peter and wishing to carry it even further. "Trotsky waxed lyrical on the 'real scientific possibility' of reconstructing man" (447). Architects made plans to build communal houses that would eliminate egoistic individualism, though few were ever constructed, and the palatial dwellings of the past, like the Fountain House of the Sheremetev family (whose construction was portrayed at the beginning of the book), were split into small apartments, one of them being occupied by Akhmatova. Such accidental historical intersections are unobtrusively used throughout the book as symbolic illustrations of both the ruptures and continuities of Russian culture.

[10] Andrey Bely, *Petersburg*, trans. R. Maguire and J. Malmstad (Harmondsworth, 1983), 167.

Lenin was reported to have said that "for us the most important of all the arts is the cinema" (451),[11] no doubt because it could impart a message directly by images to a semiliterate public. The montage technique, in which a quick succession of images communicates a specific meaning, was the invention of Lev Kuleshov, who established a workshop that trained Pudovkin and Eisenstein. This type of film also required a special technique of acting based on mime and gesture, in which, as with Buster Keaton and Charlie Chaplin, the actor's body became "a biomechanical device for the physical expression of emotions and ideas" (462). Meyerhold, who had made two movies before 1917, trained his actors so that a story could be told purely through physical gesture. Like Lenin, he was also an admirer of the "time and motion" studies of the American engineer F. W. Taylor, which he wished to apply in his own domain. One of his friends was the ardent Taylorite Alexei Gastev, who envisaged the complete mechanization of human life and personality as the task of the future (it was against such views that Zamyatin created his unsurpassed dystopia *We*). Another friend was the flamboyant Vladimir Mayakovsky, whose *Mystery-Bouffe* (1918) he staged with the poet playing a leading role. The suicide of Mayakovsky in 1930 marked the end of the era when the artistic avant-garde was able to employ its talents with relative freedom on behalf of the revolution.

With the rise of Stalin, all artistic endeavor was regimented into the service of the state. "The one and only task of Soviet literature," declared one influential journal, "is the depiction of the Five-Year plan and the class-war" (471).[12] Conformist mediocrity became the key to success, and the same was true for the other arts as well. Writers like Zoschenko, Bulgakov, Zamyatin, and Pilnyak were hounded, and when Eisenstein undertook to base a film on a greatly altered version of Turgenev's story *Bezhin Meadow*, his view of collectivization was deemed unsatisfactory and the film was burned. Shostakovitch's opera *Lady Macbeth from Mstensk* was also violently denounced, and when Meyerhold courageously spoke out in its defense he lost his theater. Three years later he was arrested, tortured to obtain a "confession," and finally shot. Mandelstam too, a close friend of Akhmatova, was arrested, released, imprisoned again, and finally died in a camp of a heart attack. "Poetry is respected only in this country," he remarked with bitter irony. "There is no place where more people are killed for it" (482).[13]

On the invasion of Russia, Stalin was forced to appeal to the people in the name of the patriotic and religious values of the Russian tradition,

---

[11] *Samoe vazhnoe iz vsekh isskustv. Lenin o kino* (Moscow, 1963), 124.

[12] Cited in H. Borland, *Soviet Literary Theory and Practice during the First Five-year Plan, 1928–1932* (New York, 1950), 24.

[13] Nadezhda Mandelshtam, *Hope Against Hope*, trans. M. Hayward (London, 1981), 159.

and a sense of relief was felt by the intelligentsia despite all the enormous suffering that came in its wake. As a character comments in *Dr. Zhivago*, the "menace of death [was] a blessing compared with the inhuman power of the lie" (488).[14] Art was no longer required to conform to the crippling party-line materialism of the recent past, and an area of relative freedom thus opened allowing artists fallen into disfavor to participate in the war effort. Akhmatova's poem "Courage" (1942) presented the war as a defense of "the mighty Russian word" and, in a broadcast speech from besieged Leningrad, "appealed to the city's entire legacy, not just to Lenin but to Peter the Great, Pushkin, Dostoevsky, and Blok, too" (491). Shostakovich's Seventh Symphony, dedicated to "the city of Leningrad," was performed in the bombed-out Great Hall of the Philharmonia and broadcast on loudspeakers throughout the city. Eisenstein collaborated with Prokofiev to produce *Ivan the Terrible*, with whom Stalin had come to identify himself, and whose first part won the Stalin Prize in 1945. But Eisenstein was given a personal dressing-down by Stalin over the second part, not released until 1985, which depicts Ivan, like Boris Godunov, suffering agonies of conscience over his misdeeds.

The victory over Hitler, contrary to all expectations, led to even severer strictures on intellectual and cultural life under the ferule of Andrei Zhdanov. Soviet triumphalism was glorified everywhere, in the sciences as well as the arts, arousing ridicule in some quarters and incredible acceptance elsewhere from even highly qualified fellow-travelers. Akhmatova and Zoschenko were publicly denounced, and the works of Shostakovitch, Katchaturian, and Prokofiev censured as alien to the tastes of the Russian people. As the Cold War heated up, a campaign against "cosmopolitanism" (a code word for anti-Semitism) placed everyone of Jewish origin in jeopardy, including even the most eminent figures. Vasily Grossman, who had gained fame as a war correspondent, depicted the Soviet and Nazi regimes as parallel in his great novel, *Life and Fate* (1980), first published in Switzerland more than twenty years after his death. In Pasternak's *Dr. Zhivago* (1957), smuggled out of Russia, "the novel's central theme is the importance of preserving the old intelligentsia" (510). Pasternak also came under attack for having visited Akhmatova and helping her financially, and Shostakovitch managed to keep afloat only by writing music for films. In his later chamber music, beginning in 1944, he began to employ Jewish themes and continued to do so up until the very end.

Russian readers, accustomed to look for hidden, allegorical meanings in what they read, were offered ample fare in the copious production of science fiction, given new life by the space program of the 1950s. The authors of these extremely popular works are hardly known in the West, but their

---

[14] Boris Pasternak, *Doctor Zhivago*, trans. M. Hayward and M. Hari (London, 1988), 453.

visions of a far-distant world stressed "the eternal need of human beings for ethical relationships, freedom, beauty and creativity" (514). Much to the dismay of communist hardliners, spiritual values were once again being affirmed. The same was true in science fiction movies such as *Solaris* by Andrei Tarkovsky, whose theme was the preservation of "human values in which every Christian culture, even Soviet Russia's, sees its redemption" (516). In Tarkovsky's *Stalker* (1979), the central character is the contemporary equivalent of a "holy fool," who revives the "national myth" that a search for faith is typical of the "Russian soul." His remarkable film *Andrei Rublev* (1966) was a celebration of the tradition of icon painting, of which Rublev was one of the greatest practitioners, and brought to life all the national-religious associations that accompanied such works of art. Evidences of the same tendency also began to appear in literature, and Akhmatova could write that even though "from beneath the ruins I speak / ... they will recognize my voice /... and ... they will believe in it once more" (520).[15] When she died in March 1966, thousands turned out to pay her a last homage.

The Russian Revolution scattered three million people over the face of the Earth, among them some of the most highly gifted of a nation whose cultural achievements in the previous century had astonished the world. At first Berlin was the largest colony, where the main shopping street was renamed "Nepski Prospekt." There was a movement to return home, and the noted novelist Alexei Tolstoy was among the first to go. Others, like the gifted poetess Marina Tsvetaeva, were filled with the same nostalgia later expressed in Nabokov's wistful evocation of his early years in the memoir, *Speak, Memory!* Many moved to Paris when Berlin became too expensive, and the French capital then became the center of the Russian emigration. The older émigrés felt that their mission was to keep alive the Russian culture being destroyed, as Bunin put it, "by the modernist corruptions of left-wing and Soviet art" (540). In a series of novels and stories, he created an idyllic image of a happy rural Russia, quite the opposite of that depicted in *The Village*, but which he acknowledged to be "an Elysium of the past" (541).[16]

Some, like Rachmaninov, remained unchanged in exile; his work had always been strongly influenced by Russian religious music and expressed a sense of loss and alienation. Vladimir Nabokov performed the unusual feat, after publishing nine novels in Russian abroad, of shifting to English, which as a child he had learned to read even before his native tongue. But he too was consumed by nostalgia, and in his brilliant *Pale Fire* (1962)

---

[15] Anna Akhmatova, "Leningrad, 1959," in *The Complete Poems of Anna Akhmatova*, trans. J. Hemschemeyer (Edinburgh, 1992), 716.

[16] J. Woodward, *Ivan Bunin: A Study of His Fiction* (Chapel Hill, 1980), 164.

created an imaginary land, *Zembla* (*zemlya* in Russian means earth), which may be, as he put it himself, a "pure invention or a kind of lyrical simile of Russia" (551).[17] In his delightfully humorous *Pnin*, he depicts the misadventures of an exiled professor unable to adapt to life elsewhere than in his ex-homeland. Exile also led to a revival of neoclassicism in the Ballets Russes under the aegis of Stravinsky and the young George Balanchine, but a neoclassicism that was felt as returning to an eighteenth-century Russian tradition. There was, at least on the surface, no nostalgia in Stravinsky, who abandoned his previous nationalist style and even used Latin for the text of his oratorio *Oedipus Rex* (1927).

Those like Tsvetaeva, who could not endure exile and followed the example of Alexei Tolstoy, led a difficult and precarious existence. Even Prokofiev, lured back to relative luxury and given unusual freedom, could not escape being attacked for "formalism" by Zhdanov and, though producing numerous scores, lived in relative seclusion. Like Shostakovich, he turned to chamber music in these last years to express his distress. The biggest catch of all was Maxim Gorky, a revolutionary icon, who, before leaving for exile, had taken up arms against the abuses of the Leninist regime between 1917 and 1921 without entirely abandoning his faith in revolution. The worsening political situation in Europe and the blandishments of Stalinism led to his return in 1931. He was heaped with honors and privileges, but the man who had opposed Lenin became "a thorn in Stalin's side as well" (572). Some are likely to find that Figes glides too lightly over the Soviet exploitation of his prestige, to which he hardly opposed any resistance, but he raised his voice against the hounding of other writers and did the best he could to protect many who were threatened.

Eight

The book ends with a symbolic episode embodying its main theme, but with a reversal of its beginning. No one had appeared to repudiate his Russian heritage more vehemently than Stravinsky, who even tried to deny the Russian roots of such a work as *Rite of Spring*. "I borrowed nothing from folk pieces" (563),[18] he asserted, without convincing anyone, but his later music is very ostentatiously non-Russian in character. He became a French citizen, lived in the United States, and even the casual mention of the Soviet Union was enough to throw him into a rage. But when he finally returned to Russia for a visit in 1962, accompanied by his close

---

[17] Cited in B. Boyd, *Nabokov: The American Years* (London, 1992), 464.
[18] Igor Stravinsky, *Chronique de ma vie* (1935), quoted from the English translation: *An Autobiography* (New York, 1962), 53.

friend the American conductor Robert Craft, the latter was astonished at the transformation he observed. Suddenly the man he knew, or thought he knew, became someone else, and "I see that half a century of expatriation can be forgotten in a night" (581).[19] Stravinsky was anxious to meet Shostakovitch, and though the two men hardly spoke at all (except to acknowledge a common dislike of Puccini), their encounter "was a symbol of a cultural unity which in the end would triumph over politics" (585). They were reunited at a banquet that evening, where, as Craft remarks, the increasingly tipsy speakers all abased themselves "before the mystery of Russianness, and so, I realize with a shock, does I. S., whose replies are soon overtaking the toasts" (586).[20]

It is this "mystery of Russianness" that Figes has been so lavishly exploring all through the preceding hundreds of pages, which become occasionally repetitious when he traverses the same ground in different contexts but remarkably succeed in never being dull. The present review hardly can do justice to the overflowing richness of the work, which has no parallel in English or, so far as my knowledge goes, in any other language including Russian. No doubt specialists will find many bones to pick, as is only inevitable in a work so ambitious; a few have already turned up here in passing. But the effort to create a synthesis of this kind, covering two centuries and so many fields, should not be judged by the same standards as a scholarly monograph. And whatever criticisms can be made, one can only be grateful to Orlando Figes for the extraordinary task he has undertaken and accomplished with such indefatigable scholarly zeal and linguistic brio. Anyone with even the slightest interest in Russian culture, or indeed with modern European culture in general, should eagerly accept his invitation to join in Natasha's dance.

---

[19] R. Craft, *Stravinsky: Chronicle of a Friendship* (New York, 1994), 317.
[20] Ibid., 328.

SIX

A LIFE OF PUSHKIN

IN HIS NEW LIFE of Pushkin, T. J. Binyon leaves the reader in no doubt as to the chief aim of his massive work. He begins with a brief preface, detailing the meteoric rise of the poet's reputation from the very first public knowledge of his youthful compositions, its temporary decline during the mid-nineteenth century, and its restoration culminating in the dedication of a monument to him in Moscow in June 1880. This occasion was marked by a celebration lasting for several days and by numerous speeches from attending literary celebrities, the most famous being that of Dostoevsky. Boldly asserting that Pushkin was, as Gogol had said, "an extraordinary, and perhaps unique manifestation of the Russian spirit,"[1] Dostoevsky claimed that his "universal responsiveness" (xxvii) his ability to embody himself in characters of other nationalities, remains unrivaled elsewhere in world literature; and he thus foreshadowed the great historical task of the Russian spirit, which was to unite all nations into "a final brotherly agreement in accordance with the law of Christ's Gospel" (xxvii).

This speech created a sensation; and though very little in Pushkin's work corresponds to such a reading, it was from this time on that he became more than a poet. He assumed the stature of "a symbol, a myth, an icon" (xxviii), whose work was utilized for the most diverse purposes. Both the tsarist empire and the Soviets used him for their ends: the post-Soviet Bank of Russia issued a coin with a picture of Pushkin holding a goose-quill and with portraits of his personages in the background; even Coca-Cola "ran an advertisement featuring lines from his most famous love lyric" (xxix). The aim of Binyon's book is to break with these various exploitations of the poet's image, and to synthesize the vast amount of Russian scholarship that has exhaustively explored every aspect of Pushkin's life; he wishes "to free the complex and interesting figure of Pushkin the man from the heroic simplicity of Pushkin the myth" (xxix). This estimable purpose is carried out with impeccable scholarship, extending far beyond Pushkin's personal life and including not only his friends and acquaintances, but also the epoch in which he lived.

Originally published in a slightly different form in *The New Republic*, January 19, 2004. Reprinted by permission.

[1] T. J. Binyon, Pushkin: A Life (New York: Alfred A. Knopf, 2003), xxvii. Subsequent references to this work are cited in parentheses in the text.

Those interested in Pushkin's work, however, will have to look elsewhere. "Literary analysis has been eschewed," Binyon writes, "as being the province of the critic, rather than the biographer" (xxix). Pushkin's works are of course mentioned, briefly summarized, and often cited to illustrate one or another biographical point. Every chapter begins with an epigraph taken from his poetry—but very little more. Such a sharp separation between the life and work, however, may very well be disputed.

The best works of literary biography combine the two, and presumably our interest in the life of an important literary figure is prompted by the desire better to understand his work. Why concern oneself with the life of a writer if not as a means of obtaining additional insight into his/her creations? To limit one's perspective, as Binyon does, is to impose restrictions that hardly enable a non-Russian reader, unfamiliar with Pushkin's work, to understand the reason why he has become a "myth" at all. One also misses any attempt to evoke the timbre of Pushkin's poetry, as was done many years ago in D. S. Mirsky's little book—and so well, that it inspired Edmund Wilson to learn Russian. The translations that Binyon offers are his own, and literally accurate. But in two instances I have used others, more ambitious in attempting to transmit some of the irresistible elegance and vibrancy of Pushkin's language.

Two

Pushkin was born into a family that, to say the least, provided him with a mixed heritage. On his father's side he could trace his ancestry back to the *boyar* class, the feudal aristocracy that had ruled Russia until Peter the Great created a new service nobility in the eighteenth century. On his mother's side he was the descendent of a far more exotic strain, a Negro child brought back from Constantinople by a Russian ambassador there, given as a present to Peter, and then adopted by the monarch. The boy was baptized with Peter as his godfather, educated as an army officer, and spent a number of years in France at a military school; eventually, he took the name of Gannibal (Hannibal). He had a distinguished military career, produced seven children by a second wife, and Pushkin's mother was the daughter of one of his sons. The poet was proud of both lineages, alluding to one boyar ancestor in his play *Boris Godunov* and leaving an unfinished story, *The Blackamoor of Peter the Great,* based on the rather remarkable life of his African forbear.

From his very earliest years Pushkin was surrounded by an extremely cultivated and literary atmosphere. Although his father was a ne'er-do-well, not looking after his estates at all, he had a taste for French literature, was an inveterate theatergoer, and read Molière to his children. Pushkin's uncle Vasily had a reputation as a minor poet, and some of the leading literary lights of the day—Nikolay Karamzin, Vasily Zhukovsky, Konstantin Batyushkov—were visitors to the Pushkin residence. There is a tradition that the six-year-old Alexander left his toys to listen with rapt attention to a conversation between his father and Karamzin; but Binyon refuses to take it too literally. All the same, there is no doubt that at the age of seven the childish Pushkin stayed awake at night writing poems, and he created comedies in French at the age of ten (French was the language spoken in the home). After reading Voltaire's *La Henriade* a bit later, he produced a parody of it in six cantos.

Pushkin was at first educated by foreign tutors, who found him a recalcitrant pupil, and his family thus decided to send him to school. A new Imperial Lycée was about to open at Tsarksoe Selo to train young men for government service, and through influential friends they obtained his admission after he passed a cursory examination. The friendships made during Pushkin's years at the Lycée (1811–1817) proved to be very important for the burgeoning young poet, who had had very little family affection. Pushkin was not a particularly good student but became known for being able to produce poetic epigrams (some of them quite obscene) for any and every occasion, and he was nicknamed "the Frenchman" because of his encyclopedic knowledge of that country's literature. Two other poets among his classmates also took their place in the annals of Russian literature: Anton Delvig, who became Pushkin's closest friend all through his life, and Wilhelm Kuchelbecker, who was exiled to Siberia for taking part in the Decembrist uprising. Although Binyon does not mention such matters, Kuchelbecker may well have furnished some traits for the figure of Lensky, the young poet just home from Gottingen and full of German Romantic *Schwarmerei* in *Eugene Onegin*, who is killed in a duel with the title figure.

Pushkin became known not only for his ability to turn out verses but also for the impetuosity of his character and his sexual arousability (as a fellow student wrote, "merely touching the hand of the person he was dancing with ... caused his eyes to blaze, and he snorted and puffed, like an ardent stallion in a young herd" [36]). The Emperor Alexander I complained to the school authorities when Pushkin, in a dark corridor, mistook a lady-in-waiting of the empress for her maid and overwhelmed her with "indiscreet caresses" (38). He was also rebuked for sending verses to a lady whose husband had recently died, and who was two months pregnant, imagining himself to be in bed with her. Other types of poems as well came from his pen, and he began to publish in 1814 at the age of fifteen. Twenty-four poems were printed while he was still in the Lycée, all but one under pseudonyms.

The poem to which he signed his name, "Recollections in Tsarskoe Selo," was written on assignment for recital at the examination for his junior year. Among those present was the greatest poet of the preceding age, Gavrila Derzhavin, and Pushkin later described the excitement created by this attendance. He read his own poem "standing two paces away from Derzhavin ... and when I reached the line where I mention Derzhavin's name, my adolescent voice broke, and my heart beat with intoxicating rapture" (33). The older poet expressed his enthusiasm for the poem and said "that a second Derzhavin will appear in the world ... he is Pushkin" (34); and Zhukovsky, after reading the poem, called Pushkin "the hope of our literature" (34). From this time on his fame spread beyond the Lycée walls, and he was accepted as the uncontested rising star of the new generation of writers.

Three

Pushkin graduated at the age of eighteen and was assigned to a post in the Foreign Ministry. There is not a single reference in his letters to this nominal position, which he treated more or less as a sinecure; in answer to an inquiry about him, the head of the Lycée remarked "that he does nothing at the Ministry" (44). He joined a society of writers who called themselves *Arzamas* (a small town noted for nothing except its geese), whose aim was to make fun of another, more solemn assemblage founded by the Admiral Shishkov "to defend 'classical' forms of Russian against foreign infection" (48).

At the same time, Pushkin was also associating with others—officers in the army and civil servants—who had been classmates or acquaintances and were deeply concerned with politics. Many had been with the Russian Army occupying Paris after the victory over Napoleon, and, impressed by the greater freedoms enjoyed by their European counterparts, they had begun to organize for what became the abortive Decembrist revolt in December 1825. As Binyon writes, "a number of the future Decembrists were his [Pushkin's] close friends.... He frequented houses in which they held meetings; he shared many of the political views of their programs" (57). His diary for example, contains an entry reporting a morning spent in conversation with the twenty-three-year-old Pavel Pestel—an officer in the Chevalier Guards and later one of the leaders of the uprising—whom he calls "one of the most original minds I know" (57). Pushkin did not conceal his sympathies with those who refused to accept any longer the absolute despotism of the tsarist regime, and he ostentatiously paraded in the stalls of a theater with a picture of the murderer of the duc de Berry that bore the inscription: "A Lesson for Tsars?" (59). It was such bravado, however, that led his more cautious friends to conclude that he was untrustworthy, and he was not invited to join any of the secret societies they were forming to take action.

His poetry of this period reveals what Binyon calls his "conservative liberalism," which was not antimonarchical at all but requires the monarch to respect his own laws. The poem "Liberty: An Ode," in which such sentiments were expressed, was not published in its entirety in Russia until 1906. Another poem, "The Country," denounces serfdom and contains the famous quatrain:

> Will I see, o friends! A people unoppressed
> And Servitude banished by the will of the tsar,
> And over the fatherland will there finally arise
> The sublime Dawn of enlightened Freedom? (54)

Another poem was addressed to Peter Chaadaev, later an important philosopher but then an elegant officer with the reputation of a dandy, whom Pushkin had met while at Tsarskoe Selo and whose friendship he valued very highly. Chaadaev, a Freemason, had been initiated into the plans of the Decembrists but took no part in the actual events. The poem concludes: "Russia will start from her sleep, / And on the ruins of autocracy / Our names will be inscribed" (61). None of these poems, as well as others mocking the police and censorship, were published; but *samizdat* is an old Russian tradition and, as one observer wrote, "there was scarcely a more or less literate ensign in the army who did not know them by heart" (61).

As a framework for the depiction of Pushkin's life in St. Petersburg, Binyon uses the sparkling first chapter of *Eugene Onegin*. The stylish protagonist of Pushkin's great novel in verse, after carefully choosing the appropriate garb—the poet apologizes for being forced to use so many French words—indefatigably dashes from the French restaurant to the ballet, and then on to a fashionable ball. Much of Pushkin's time was spent in exactly the same manner, combined with the (more often than not) successful pursuit of youngish wives who had been married off to elderly dignitaries. He also frequented bordellos and contracted infections, which, requiring him to remain at home in bed, apparently provided his only leisure time. He was then working on his first long poem, "Ruslan and Lyudmila," and one of his friends, reporting on its progress, remarks in a letter: "If he were to have three or more doses of clap, it would be in the bag" (90).

Pushkin was also an ardent gambler, staking and losing large sums that he could not afford and then borrowing to pay such debts of honor. He once lost the manuscript of his first volume of poems in this way, and publication was delayed until he could buy it back. Poor Dostoevsky never went that far! Pushkin was also quick to take umbrage at what he thought was any insult to his dignity, and he acquired a reputation as a duellist.

"Mr. Pushkin has duels every day," wrote the wife of Karamzin; "thank God, not fatal, since the opponents always remain unharmed" (67). Alas, this was not always to be the case; and one can only wonder at the poet capable of writing so feelingly about the death of Lensky, killed in a senseless duel over nothing, who nonetheless himself flared up at the slightest provocation and acquired a reputation for hairtrigger susceptibility.

An extreme obscurantism reigned in the last years of the rule of Alexander I, who had come under the influence of mystical and irrational currents of thought. The relative liberalism of a Pushkin poem like "Liberty," not to mention the scurrilous and often semipornographic denigration of authority in his numerous epigrams, was called to the tsar's attention by a disgruntled patriot, the founder of the new University of Kharkov. Alexander was outraged, and Pushkin barely escaped being sent to Siberia or the Solovetsky islands on the White Sea, infamous for the harshness of its climate. Karamzin exacted from him a pledge that he would write nothing against the government for two years; and it was only through the influence of such powerful friends at court that the tsar relented. Pushkin did not escape being sent into exile, but it was to the Southern Territory of Russia, where he was assigned to the chancellery of the general in charge of Russian interests in that region.

Four

Pushkin spent four years in the south of Russia, traveling in the Caucasus and the Crimea, gathering impressions for such poems as "The Prisoner of the Caucasus" and "The Fountain of Bakhchisaray," and setting down the first stanzas of *Eugene Onegin*. It was at this time that he began to read Byron in a French prose translation, and the Byronic influence on his work became apparent. One work in particular written during these years later caused him as much trouble as his political poetry had done previously. Professing to be "a militant atheist" (137) at this time, he mocked the general's orders that his staff attend church services ("If only Christ's blood were, let's say, Lafite ... or Clos de Vougeot" [138]); and in "The Gabrieliad," he turned out "a blasphemous parody of the Annunciation" (138). The beautiful Mary is impregnated not only by God but by Satan in the guise of a handsome young man, and then by the angel Gabriel. "One, two, three—" the weary Mary exclaims, "how can they keep it up?" (139).

Pushkin himself, resentfully vegetating in this obscure outpost of the Russian Empire, amused himself as best he could with amorous adventures (including a Greek courtesan reputed to have been a mistress of Byron), gambling, and occasional duels. He had several passionate affairs, however, with more respectable mistresses. One, particularly fervent, was with the Jewish wife of a shipping merchant in Odessa and led to an outburst of remarkable poems. Although Pushkin's service superior General Vorontsov, aware of his fame and his supporters in high places, was extremely lenient with his lapses, the general's patience ran out for several reasons. Pushkin—along with others to be sure—was one of the lovers of his wife, and the poet had taken it into his head that the general had insulted him by a request that he investigate a plague of locusts in the region. The general complained about him to St. Petersburg, and his friends could do nothing because a letter in which he boasted of his atheism had come to the attention of the authorities. It was thus decided to assign him to forced residence in the family estate of Mikhailovskoe, which the Empress Elizabeth had given to Abram Gannibal in 1742.

Alexander I has perhaps never received sufficient credit for his service to Russian literature in forcing Pushkin to lead a relatively isolated and tranquil country life between 1824 and 1826. "In just over two years," Binyon writes, "Pushkin completed *The Gypsies*, composed a mass of lyrics, wrote a historical drama in blank verse [*Boris Godunov*], and added nearly a hundred stanzas to *Eugene Onegin*" (236). For company there was a cultivated family on a neighboring estate, close enough to be reached on foot; and in *Eugene Onegin* he pays tribute to the narrow waist of one of the two daughters (with whom he had an affair two years later). Evenings were often spent in the company of Pushkin's peasant nurse, Arina Rodionovna, who regaled and amused him with folk songs and fairy tales. "How charming these tales are," he wrote in a letter. "Each is a poem" (201). Although critics concerned to stress Pushkin's immersion in the culture of the Russian people have emphasized the importance of such an influence, Binyon simply mentions it in passing. However, he cites the lines from the poem "Winter Landscape," in which Pushkin depicts how he passed the long evenings in her company:

> Sing me a song of how the bluebird
> Peacefully lived beyond the sea;
> Sing me a song of how the maiden
> Went down for water in the morning. (201)

This innocent and poetically productive occupation was not his only distraction, however, and a visitor to Mikhailovskoe noticed among the serf girls one who was unmistakably pregnant. A poem of Pushkin's had excoriated the widespread propensity of landowners to take sexual advantage of their helpless female serfs; but no more than Tolstoy could Pushkin resist the temptation. The girl went to Moscow with her family, and Pushkin asked friends there to look after her and the future infant, a boy who died a month and a half after being born. He later arranged for her freedom, and she married a nobleman whose service rank was higher than the poet's.

A good deal of Pushkin's time was also taken up with attempts to escape from his rustic incarceration, and he invented an imaginary illness that required treatment in Riga or Dorpat, border cities that would allow him to flee abroad. This plan became so complicated and so far-fetched that Binyon can only compare it "to the exploits of the Scarlet Pimpernel" (214), and the authorities who received Pushkin's petition, accompanied by a lachrymose letter from his mother, were only puzzled by the request. But Alexander I died suddenly in November 1825, and Pushkin saw in his decease a new hope of being freed by the successor to the throne.

Five

The Decembrist revolt occurred at this time, led by officers who were either close personal friends or acquaintances of Pushkin. Indeed, when asked by the new tsar, Nicholas I, where he would have been on the day of the revolt if he had been in Petersburg, he replied courageously: "I would have been in the ranks of the rebels" (242). Moreover, many of the officers arrested and questioned referred to the influence of his work, and the effect of what one called "Mr. Pushkin's freedom poems" (223). Perhaps this was one reason that Nicholas wished to see him in person and ordered him brought back to the capital. The interview went very well, and when Pushkin complained about the censorship, Nicholas declared that he alone would now take over the task. This new arrangement, which pleased Pushkin at first, turned out to be even more stifling than the old. The tsar could not be approached directly, his word was final, and even the reading of new works to Pushkin's friends was forbidden before they were officially approved. The publication of *Boris Godunov* was delayed for a number of years because the tsar, who actually read it (those were the days!), thought it would be more suitable as "an historical tale or novel in the manner of Walter Scott" (254).

Pushkin had thus now been placed under the personal supervision of the tsar; and though he had been assured that he was free, the secret police kept a sharp eye on all his comings and goings. Even though the tsar's interest provided some protection, and in fact the poet had now become a staunch supporter of the throne, Pushkin's reputation as a subversive continued to cause him trouble. A poem written years before had denounced the guillotining of one of his favorite French poets, André Chenier, during the French Revolution; and this was now brought to the attention of the secret police with the added title "December 14" (the date of the Decembrist uprising). His protest about Chenier was thus mistakenly thought to apply to recent events, which had led to the execution of five of the Decembrists; but he extricated himself easily from the charge, only being reprimanded for allowing the circulation of a manuscript not approved by the censorship. Another early work caused trouble when two serfs complained to the metropolitan of St. Petersburg that they had been corrupted because their master read to them from "The Gabrieliad." Pushkin at first rashly denied having written the sacrilegious lampoon; but when pressed in the name of the emperor, he wrote a letter to Nicholas acknowledging his guilt and asking for (and receiving) pardon for a transgression of his youth.

Pushkin now once again led the same debauched and ruinously expensive life already familiar from his past, much to the disapprobation of his friends. His patriotic ardor, though, led him to try and enlist in the Russian Army, then engaged in hostilities against both Persia and Turkey. Having been turned down, he decided to go south independently to observe the war in which his brother and numerous classmates from Tsarksoe Selo were now taking part. Six years later he used the trip to write his prose *Journey to Ezerum*, a work that contains, as Binyon remarks in one of his few literary observations, battle scenes comparable to both Stendhal and Tolstoy. Pushkin also strongly supported the Russian cause in the war against its Polish provinces that broke out in 1830, and he was worried that Europe might interfere. What Binyon rightly calls his "chauvinist, imperialist" (377) side appears in such a poem as "To the Slanderers of Russia," an answer to the chorus of Europeans reviling his homeland. It is worth noting that his friend Vyazemsky, along with a group of younger writers, was highly critical of this poetic defense of a bloody suppression. Less controversial were the satirical literary polemics he engaged in over criticisms of the recently published chapter 7 of *Eugene Onegin*.

Most of all, however, he was now concerned to find himself a wife. He had decided to marry, for reasons he could never explain to himself, and perhaps only because, as he wrote in chapter 8 of *Eugene Onegin*, "Blessed is he, who was youthful in his youth / ... Who at twenty was a fop and a rake / And at thirty advantageously married" (241). At age twenty-nine he was turned down several times because the extremely affluent families of the women to whom he proposed did not think it was "advantageous" for their daughters to marry *him*. Aside from his shady reputation, great poet or not, he had no family fortune on which such a union could be based. At last he found a notably beautiful eighteen-year-old, Natalya Goncharova, whose once-wealthy family was willing to accept him. Binyon comments on the peculiarity of his letter to her mother asking for her hand—a letter that eloquently outlines all the reasons why he would *not* make an acceptable husband. Could he, perhaps subconsciously, have been trying to provoke a refusal, and thus "tell himself that fate did not wish him to become a married man?" (327).

He did become one all the same, but not before a three-month burst of creativity in the solitude of a country estate recently inherited from his uncle. There he wrote all of the *Tales of Belkin*, thirty lyrics, his four *Little Tragedies* (which include *Mozart and Salieri*), and two more chapters of *Eugene Onegin*. An additional chapter, placing Eugene among the Decembrists, was burned (though Binyon fails to mention that fragments, written in a sort of code that scrambles the lines, exist in a notebook and contain what Roman Jakobson called "an openly incendiary and antitsarist reflection"[2]). Three years later, retiring to the same estate from the whirligig of social life, in six weeks he wrote his marvelous *The Bronze Horseman* (in which the antinomies that continue to dominate Russian culture, *pace* Binyon, are expressed with incomparable mythical power), and also the superb story *The Queen of Spades*, not to mention poems and verse tales.

Six

Married life involved considerable extra expense, which plunged him even more heavily into debt; and his wife, whose charms attracted the attention of the emperor (though there is no evidence of any further intimacy) adored the endless social merry-go-round. There was hardly an evening when the couple could not be found at a dinner or a ball, and this became more than a personal preference when he received a court appointment as gentleman of the chamber. Such gentlemen, usually much younger men, were required to attend all court functions, and Pushkin took the supposed honor as a kind of insult. In one poem he speaks of himself as "a tired slave" (427), and he struggled laboriously to reconcile his literary preoccupations with his obligations as a father (he and Natalya had four children) and husband. He nonetheless managed to turn out a history of the Pugachev uprising, the peasant revolt of the eighteenth century that shook the reign of Catherine the Great, even traveling to the locality to interview survivors. His brief but impressive novel, *The Captain's Daughter*, treats the rebel with a surprising impartiality and creates character types that set the pattern for many Russian novelists of the future. In addition, he also published a good deal of critical journalism as well as continuing to express his inmost feelings through lyric poetry.

As well as enjoying the heady excitement of fashionable festivities, Natalya was also an irrepressible flirt, and many letters from her husband, sometimes lightheartedly, sometimes seriously, warn her of the dangers of this proclivity. Had not Pushkin himself portrayed in *Eugene Onegin* the terrible consequences to which it might lead? Nothing untoward occurred

---

[2] Roman Jakobson, "Marginal Notes on Eugene Onegin," in *Selected Writings* (New York: Walter de Gruyter, 1971), 293.

for several years while Natalya continued to bask in masculine admiration; and there is no evidence that she ever overstepped permissible bounds. But finally she attracted the attentions of a handsome young French officer, a Royalist in exile serving with the fashionable Chevalier Guards, George d'Anthès, who was also the adopted son of the Dutch ambassador to Russia, the Baron van Heeckeren. The relations between father and nominal son aroused a good deal of comment because, to cite one memoirist, "at that time buggery was widespread in high society" (518). However that may be, d'Anthès conceived a violent passion for Natalya Pushkina that he displayed quite openly, and which soon also became the subject of Petersburg tittle-tattle. Although repulsing his advances, she was flattered all the same, and he refused to cease his pursuit.

One day Pushkin received an insulting letter designating him as a member of the society of cuckolds (who sent this document has never been established), and he challenged d'Anthès to a duel. His friends, however, as well as the baron made desperate efforts to circumvent such an encounter, and it kept being put off. Indeed, d'Anthès even married Natalya's sister, who had always been infatuated with him, and Pushkin then withdrew his challenge. But d'Anthès still continued to pay court to Natalya in public, and even the emperor intervened to reassure the poet that he knew Natalya to be spotless (which only proved to what extent the couple had become the talk of the town). Pushkin thus found his social position more and more exasperating and untenable, and he challenged d'Anthès again. Two days later he died from his wound. His opponent left Russia, fathered four children with Ekaterina Goncharova, and ended as a senator under Louis Napoleon.

In his Pushkin speech, Dostoevsky concluded by declaring that Pushkin, in dying young, had taken "some great secret to the grave. And so we must puzzle out this secret without him."[3] Voices in the audience shouted that Dostoevsky himself had solved the secret, but a mountain of Russian scholarship ever since has belied this precipitous conclusion. No more than with any other great writer is there a single "secret" to be found in Pushkin's brilliantly multifarious work; but English readers interested in his complex character and incandescent life can find no more reliable place to start than Binyon's book.

---

[3] Fyodor Dostoevsky, *A Writer's Diary: 1877–1881*, trans. K. A. Lantz, ed. Gary Saul Morson (Evanston: Northwestern University Press, 1993), 2:1295.

SEVEN

OBLOMOV AND GONCHAROV

ANYONE with a claim to literacy is familiar with the names of Tolstoy, Turgenev, and Dostoevsky, and at least can cite some of the titles of their most famous works. But Goncharov and his novel *Oblomov*, of which a new and very snappily colloquial and readable translation has just been published—who has ever heard of them? Well, Samuel Beckett for one, who was told to read *Oblomov* by his mistress Peggy Guggenheim and soon signed some of his letters to her with this cognomen. I recall my teacher at the University of Chicago long ago, the renowned classicist David Grene, who had been a fellow student of Beckett at Trinity College, Dublin, once telling me that the future famous writer was well-known for his penchant as a very late riser and missed classes for this reason. Since the main character of *Oblomov* also finds it very difficult to leave his couch, and whether he succeeds in doing so or not (literally as well as symbolically) constitutes the main thread of the extremely tenuous action of the novel, Beckett's instant attraction to this character is easily comprehensible. There is also good reason to believe that the figure in *Waiting for Godot* bearing the Russian name of Vladimir is a tribute to this unexpectedly Slavic aspect of Beckett.

Nor can any of the titles of the more famous Russian writers, aside from their familiarity, rival Goncharov's in having provided a new word to the Russian language. Open any Russian dictionary and you will find the word *oblomovschina* there, defined, in the first that comes to hand, as "carelessness, want of energy, laziness, negligence," and specifying its origin in Goncharov's novel (where the word itself is used). Scarcely any other novelist Russian or otherwise (except perhaps Cervantes) can boast of having created a character whose attributes have left such an indelible impression both on the vocabulary, and hence as well on the national psyche, of his country.

So who was Ivan Goncharov, and why has the character he created taken on such ineradicably symbolic proportions? He was born in 1812 in a town on the Volga named Simbirsk, which struck all who came to visit it, such as the poet Lermontov, as the epitome of "sleep and laziness.... Even

---

Originally published in a slightly different form in *The New Republic*, January 29, 2007. Reprinted by permission.

the Volga," he wrote, "rolled here slower and smoother."[1] Goncharov himself later agreed that "the whole appearance of my home town was a perfect picture of sleepiness and stagnation."[2] He came from a very prosperous merchant family and was one of the few Russian writers of this period descended from such a background. When he wished to study at the University of Moscow, it was necessary for him to obtain freedom from the guild of merchants in order not to be forced to follow in his father's footsteps. Despite climbing the ladder, as he did, to the highest ranks of the civil service, and even being appointed tutor to a presumed inheritor to the throne who died prematurely, it would appear that Goncharov could never shake off a certain sense of discomfort deriving from this relatively lowly origin. He was known for his shy and retiring personality, and such reticence may well be attributed to a lingering uneasiness over his status in the carefully delineated Russian caste society. The merchant class in Russia had very little, if any, contact with the Western European values that had shaped the aristocracy and was generally regarded as backward and obscurantist. Goncharov was perhaps inwardly unable to overcome the psychological results of this inauspicious heritage despite his outward success.

Goncharov's father died when he was seven, and a tenant of the family, an ex-naval officer of noble birth who was also a Freemason, moved into the main house on the family estate, thus becoming a substitute father (whether literally or not is unclear). His presence and influence clearly opened Goncharov to a wider cultural horizon and a more elegant and sophisticated way of life than was customary among the merchant class. It may also have provided Goncharov with a tenant–landlord pattern later used in *Oblomov* in reverse. There, the upper-class antihero ultimately marries the lower-class landlady who has unstintingly taken care of all his material needs, and whose devotion allows him to sink into a restful if self-defeating torpor. Curiously enough, in his later years Goncharov also assumed responsibility for the family of his manservant, whose widow and her three children were taken into his home and, since he never married, constituted an otherwise absent family. Here he was following a pattern already portrayed by Oblomov, who derives some satisfaction from tutoring the children of his landlady by a former marriage.

Goncharov very early learned French and German, as well as the less widespread English, and read widely in the Romantic literature of the period. Initially sent to a School of Commerce at the urging of his mother, he later spoke of this establishment with loathing and was then allowed to

---

[1] Galya Diment, *Goncharov's Oblomov: A Critical Companion* (Chicago: Northwestern University Press, 1998), 8.
[2] Ibid.

enroll in the department of philology at the University of Moscow. Here he came into contact with some of the leading minds of that period, when Romantic Idealism, imported from Germany, was all the rage in Russian culture. In contrast with literary rivals like Turgenev and Tolstoy who inherited fortunes, and more like Dostoevsky, dependent on his writings for his income, Goncharov also was forced to earn his living. On graduation he entered into the civil service bureaucracy; and some notion of how he regarded his post can be gathered from the pages in which he describes Oblomov's reaction to the brief period in which he too served in a similar situation.

Reared in the lap of comfort and indolence, Oblomov had instinctively assumed that his life would continue to be much the same in the bureaucracy. "Imagine his dismay when he saw packages flashing by marked 'urgent' and 'extremely urgent,' when he was made to write out and copy all kinds of papers and documents, rummage in files, fill writing pages as thick as your arm whimsically referred to as 'notes.'" Worst of all was that "a couple of times they even got him out of bed in the middle of the night to make him write some 'notes.'... Everything had to be done fast, everyone was always rushing somewhere non-stop.... The dreariness of it filled him with dread: 'it doesn't seem to leave a moment for living!' he complained." It is not surprising that, when Oblomov carelessly sends a document off to Archangel instead of Astrakhan, he decides to retire rather than "to face the music."[3]

Unlike that of his fictional creation, Goncharov's civil service career was eminently successful; but perhaps he felt something similar. In any event, he astonished all those who knew him by accepting an appointment that required him to travel around the world on a mission assigned to an admiral of the Russian Navy. In 1852 he became the secretary to Admiral Putyatin, entrusted with the task of inspecting Russian possessions in North America (they were never reached) and more importantly with seeking a commercial treaty with Japan (that was never concluded). Goncharov kept a notebook throughout his travels and later published sketches of his impressions and observations in a work entitled *The Frigate Pallas* that met with some success. It was written in the ironically subdued, semihumoristic style also cultivated in *Oblomov* (which he had already begun but found difficult to complete).

On his return, Goncharov accepted a position in the censorship that supervised Russian publications and retained it until his retirement in 1867. This of course exposed him to fierce criticism from the radicals, and even some of his more moderate friends found it difficult to accept the notion

---

[3] Ivan Goncharov, *Oblomov*, trans. Stephen Pearl (New York: Buni and Banigan, 2006), 44–46. Subsequent references to this work are cited in parentheses in the text.

of a writer turning into a censor. "If I wrote the devil knows what," he complained in a letter to a friend, "even then there would be no compassion for me, if only because of my title and position."[4] Nonetheless, Goncharov's record, based on his censorship reports, indicates that Russian literature may well have benefited from his supervision. No one studying Russian nineteenth-century culture can fail to be struck by the extent to which, contrary to what occurred after the Soviet takeover of power, radical criticism of the prevailing regime managed to appear in print. Of course Russian writers used what came to be known as Aesopian language, which expressed their subversive ideas indirectly; but everyone knew how to read what was implied in the figurative imagery. Goncharov was criticized by other censors for his "liberalism," and he approved some extremely radical articles on the assumption that, as he wrote in one report, "extreme views show themselves to be flimsy before strict science and die away from the contact of critical analysis."[5]

Despite the rigid self-control that allowed him to pursue a successful career, Goncharov was nonetheless assailed by inner obsessions that led to an episode whose equal it would be hard to find elsewhere in literary history. He began to work on *Oblomov* simultaneously with another book, which eventually became his third novel, *Obryv* (*The Precipice*); and he often spoke of his plans for this latter work with Turgenev. In 1859, while *Oblomov* was appearing in installments, he accused Turgenev, with whom he had been on the best of terms, of having stolen some of the ideas for *The Precipice*. Turgenev, he claimed, had initially used these ideas in his own novel *A Nest of Gentlefolk* (1859), and then a year later in *On the Eve*. The offended Turgenev asked that other members of their literary circle pass judgment on Goncharov's accusations, and several agreed to read Goncharov's plans and the novels in question.

Their decision was that the relations between the plans and the novels were too indistinct to justify Goncharov's charge; whatever similarities existed arose from the fact that both had been created "on the same Russian soil."[6] Even a member of this impromptu jury, known as being close to Goncharov, wrote that "my friend Ivan Alexandrovich played a very unenviable role in this event"; and he praised Turgenev for behaving with "that particular grace which is the property of decent people of highly educated society."[7] Turgenev broke off all relations with Goncharov, but the two were presumably reconciled, at least in public, at the funeral of a member of the jury in 1864. As such an incident demonstrates, Goncharov was

---

[4] Milton Ehre, *Oblomov and His Creator: The Life and Art of Ivan Goncharov* (Princeton: Princeton University Press, 1974), 45.
[5] Ibid., 49.
[6] Ibid., 56.
[7] Ibid.

very far from being an engaging or ingratiating personality and had very few intimate friends. Dostoevsky, who admired *Oblomov*, once wrote of its author that he embodied "the soul of a petty official, not an idea in his head, and the eyes of a steamed fish, whom God, as if for a joke, has endowed with a brilliant talent."[8]

Despite the decision of the literary jury, Goncharov continued to believe that Turgenev had pilfered his conceptions; and his delusion reached such a pitch that he claimed Turgenev was not only using them himself but passing them along to French friends such as Flaubert and a whole host of other writers (the Goncourts, George Sand, Alphonse Daudet, etc.). Indeed, he even went so far as to write that Flaubert's *L'Education Sentimentale* is "simply an abbreviated *Precipice*." When his own novel was harshly criticized as "reactionary" and proved to be a failure with the public, Goncharov consoled himself with the illusion that its lack of success was because his own thematic inspirations had already been used by others. "What an effect this novel could and should have made," he wrote, "if only they [Turgenev and his accomplices] had not run ahead with their copies."[9] It is little wonder that he spent the last years of his life in relative solitude.

Goncharov was by no means a prolific writer, and he published only three novels. His first, *A Common Story* (1847), which aroused the enthusiasm of the important critic Belinsky and also earned the praise of a Tolstoy just beginning his literary career, had been written without much difficulty. A chapter of *Oblomov*, the famous dream of his childhood, appeared in a collection of new writing published in 1849; but the novel itself was only completed ten years later, in a burst of inspiration that surprised Goncharov himself. As for *The Precipice*, his letters contain endless complaints about the lack of a similar inspiration, though it was finally finished at the urging of the editor of an important journal. To be sure, Goncharov's obligations as bureaucrat and censor gave him less time than others to devote to literary composition; but his notion of "realism" also proved a hindrance to the seemingly effortless productivity he so obviously envied in his presumed imitator, the perfidious Turgenev.

Goncharov's understanding of "realism" is expressed in an exchange of letters with Dostoevsky, one of the contributors to an anthology of well-known writers he was editing in 1874. A famine had raged a year earlier in the province of Samaria, and the proceeds from this volume were to be used for famine relief. Dostoevsky sent in a series of *Little Sketches*, one of

---

[8] Fyodor Dostoevsky, *Polnoe Sobranie Sochinenii* (Leningrad, 1972–1990), 28/bk. 1:244; November 9, 1856.

[9] Ehre, *Oblomov and His Creator*, 59.

which contained the depiction of a priest whose behavior indicated a certain influence of the fashionable Nihilism of the radicals. Goncharov found this portrait unconvincing and expressed this opinion to Dostoevsky, who replied that priests of this kind were nonetheless beginning to exist. His sketch, he insisted, had been taken from life; such a type was coming to birth. Goncharov riposted that a type is formed only "when it has been repeated many times, or been noticed many times, has become customary and is well known to all."[10]

Dostoevsky's sketch of this burgeoning type did not appear, but it is easy to see how the creator of Raskolnikov would be especially alert to social-cultural phenomena of this kind while Goncharov's own literary horizon was limited by his preconception of "the typical." Its advantage, however, is that it allowed him to endow a character like Oblomov with an almost mythical stature. For in a resounding article entitled "What Is Oblomovschina," the radical critic Nikolay Dobrolyubov hailed the central figure of his novel as the epitome of all those "superfluous men," beginning with Pushkin's Evgeny Onegin and continuing in works by Alexander Herzen and Turgenev (the term comes from Turgenev's story, *The Diary of a Superfluous Man*) that formed a subgenre of the Russian novel up through the 1860s and beyond. Dostoevsky's Nikolay Stavrogin in *Demons* may be considered an effort to provide this type with a religious-metaphysical foundation beyond Goncharov's range.

The reader first meets Oblomov in part 1 of the novel at the age of "thirty-two or three," past his first youth but hardly decrepit. The description of his face already indicates the vagaries of his character, which will be developed at great length and in endless variations. "A thought would flit, bird-like, randomly across his face, glint briefly in his eyes, light on his gently parted lips, hide in the furrows of his brow and suddenly vanish; then his whole face would radiate an even glow of unconcern. This unconcern would pass from his face into the lineaments of his body, into the very fold of his dressing gown" (1). This depiction already indicates the pattern of Oblomov's life—a capacity to be roused momentarily by "a thought," which invariably arises as a response to some aspect of external social existence, and then his relapse into "an even glow of unconcern."

A few paragraphs later, the dressing gown is referred to again as being "of Persian cloth, a real Oriental robe without the slightest European touch.... The sleeves, in true Asiatic fashion, were much wider at the shoulder than at the wrist" (2). Like many other details, which at first appear only casual, this robe takes on symbolic proportions as the book advances. Some critics have interpreted it as a reference to an "Asiatic"

---

[10] Ivan Goncharov, *Sobranie Sochinenii*, 8 vols. (Moscow, 1955), 8:459

tendency of the Russian national character; and Oblomov's efficient and successful friend Stoltz, whose father is German, certainly forms a "Western" contrast to Oblomov's indolence and practical helplessness.

Oblomov occupies only one room of an apartment containing four, spends most of his time lying on a couch, and very rarely stirs from his outwardly opulent but, so far as care is concerned, totally neglected dwelling. He is looked after by a faithful manservant named Zakhar, who both scorns and adores him, and much prefers to have a drink with other lackeys and flunkeys to performing household chores. Goncharov obtains a classic comic effect (Don Quixote–Sancho Panza) by the amusing and sometimes heated exchanges between the two that continually contrast bleak reality with decayed grandeur and exalted daydreams.

A number of people come to visit the recumbent Oblomov on the first day of spring, treated as a holiday in Russia, and several unsuccessfully invite him for a drive to one of the outlying suburbs of Petersburg. Goncharov was a master of satirical parody, and he takes potshots here at various targets. Most relevant is a writer named Penkin, an advocate of "the realistic tendency" in literature, who advises Oblomov to read a sensational work about to be published called "The Love of the Bribetaker for the Fallen Woman." It depicts, he enthuses, "all the workings of society . . . the weak but corrupt dignitary and his whole retinue of duplicitous officials"; but when Penkin compares it to Dante and Shakespeare, Oblomov objects "and almost rose to his feet in amazement" (19). Sounding as if he had just read the *Poor Folk* of Dostoevsky, he vehemently reacts: "Show us your thief, your prostitute, your pompous idiot! But where's the human being, where's the humanity in all this?" (20). Oblomov's weaknesses and failures are most often comic, but Goncharov raises him above the level of caricature by these occasional outbursts of genuine identification with the feelings of others—a capacity most valued by those closest to him in the novel, his friend Stoltz and the woman he almost marries, Olga Ilyinskaya.

A famous setpiece of this first section is the chapter on "Oblomov's Dream," which overcomes him as he falls asleep after pondering his continual failures to behave like others in meeting the obligations of real life. "Futile regrets about the past and the bitter recriminations of his own conscience pricked him like sharp needles. He strove desperately to find some guilty party on whom he could shift the burden of these recriminations" and decides, relievedly, that "it's all Zakhar's fault" (81). This obviously self-evasive answer on the personal level, this refusal to assume the burden of responsibility himself, is yet essentially true if extended to include the world that had given birth both to Zakhar and himself, the world that he recalls in his dream.

What Goncharov evokes here has been accurately called a pastoral idyll, and it is difficult briefly to do justice to its intermixture of lyric celebration with gentle satire. It is a world in which nature and man live in a state of eternal harmony; nature contains nothing menacing or threatening; even death comes naturally and without suffering to those who pass quietly away in old age. People contentedly exist in a self-enclosed universe with little or no knowledge of others, and when peasants took their grain "to the nearest river port on the Volga," it was "the equivalent to them of Colchis and the Pillars of Hercules of classical Greek mythology" (86).

Image after image from both nature and literature is used by Goncharov to emphasize the placidity and tranquility of this way of life, so different from the Romantic pageantry of Sir Walter Scott, with "its ancient bard, a wild goat for ... supper and a ballad sung by a young damsel to the accompaniment of a lute" (85). Instead, life for the young Ilya Ilyich, as well as his parents and all the others of similar rank who shared the life of Oblomovka, went undisturbedly and unquestionably on its unending rounds of "christenings, namedays, family celebrations, fast and feast days, noisy dinners, gathering of relatives, welcomes, congratulations, formal occasions of tears and smiles" (102). All work was done by the army of peasant-serfs who appear in the background from time to time to be rebuked, as Oblomov always does with Zakhar, for one infraction or another of their appointed tasks.

The young Ilya Ilyich was guarded by peasant nannies who stirred his imagination with horrific tales taken from Russian folklore as well as others recounting the "derring-do of Ilya Mouromets" (97) (his namesake); and they both left "an indelible impression on the young Oblomov's mind and imagination" (98). Carefully protected from doing anything that might involve the slightest possibility of injury, he is unable to play with the other children. Sent to a school run with German rigor by Stoltz's father, it was there that the two boys became lifelong friends; but Ilya's own family sought any excuse (and even invented some) to keep him at home and spare him the presumed hardships of the Stoltz schooling. To satisfy its requirements he was aided by his friend Andrei, who plays the same role in Oblomov's later years, and whose character, partly shaped by his Russian mother, is softened by his contact with Russian tenderness and emotivity. If there is any social-cultural moral to be derived from *Oblomov*, it would be that Russia needs a fusion of the two.

One of the problems in the interpretation of *Oblomov* is to what extent Goncharov, while unsparing in his portrayal of Oblomov's defects, nonetheless retains a certain affection for what seems, at first sight, as an indictment of the world that gave him birth. The radical Dobrolyubov was entirely right in viewing Oblomov's character as an implied attack on the social milieu from which he came; and a whole line of criticism simply expands and develops this view of the book. But this milieu is portrayed with such loving detail, and the satire is so muted and even affectionate, that it has raised questions about the "ambiguity" of Goncharov's own point of view. It is perfectly clear in any case that, while grateful for Dobrolyubov's enthusiasm for his novel, he did not share the latter's radical principles. Vladimir Korolenko, a noted turn-of-the century writer, acutely remarked: "Goncharov, of course, mentally rejected 'Oblomovism,' but deep inside he loved it with profound love beyond his control."[11]

Part 1 ends with the arrival of Stoltz, previously only evoked in Oblomov's dreams and musings or mentioned by the narrator. Parts 2 and 3 are occupied by Oblomov's involvement with Olga, a young girl that Stoltz has known since childhood and introduces to his friend. Stoltz initially saw her "merely as a delightful child full of promise," who possessed a "sunny temperament" and was free of any "spurious sophistication" (165). Intrigued by Oblomov, about whose peculiarities she had been informed by Stoltz, she decides to rescue him from his inertia and, as it were, to bring him back to life.

Oblomov had avoided romantic entanglements during his early years in Petersburg, even though there had been numerous opportunities, "because of the trouble involved in establishing such close relations" (47). He particularly avoided "the pale 'damsel in distress' type, usually with dark eyes hinting glisteningly at 'tormented days and harrowing nights'" (47). (This is a good instance of how Goncharov uses his seemingly objective third-person narrative voice to carry on his polemic with Romantic stereotypes, and occasionally with stock reactions of the reader that he anticipates and ridicules.) Nonetheless since Olga, reversing the usual relation of the sexes, takes the initiative in this instance, Oblomov is caught up in emotions he had never experienced before.

The course of their relationship is narrated with a great deal of wry humor as Olga carries out her intention of transforming Oblomov's life —partly, it is suggested, to satisfy her own vanity. "And it would be she who would work this miracle, the shy, silent Olga whom no one had ever listened to before and who had barely experienced life herself—yes, she would bring about this transformation!" (179). The intricacies of their romance are marked by a skillful use of symbolic detail—the aria *casta diva* (sacred goddess) from Bellini's *Norma*; a sprig of lilac that she hands to Oblomov but then throws down in a moment of pique; the reports she requires him to write of the books he claims to have read; and when he carelessly utters an opinion about art, even a visit to the Hermitage—the equivalent for Oblomov to a trip to the ends of the Earth. Oblomov continually doubts that so attractive a young woman could become seriously involved with a hopeless idler like himself, and his own oscillations are noted by the narrator with both penetration and amusement. Oblomov

---

[11] Diment, *Goncharov's Oblomov*, 13.

even writes her a lengthy letter claiming to renounce her for her own good; but eventually they become secretly engaged.

Olga insists, however, that their engagement remain undisclosed until Oblomov takes up the burden of actually traveling to his estate where they will presumably live, accomplish its necessary repairs, and investigate the continual diminution of the income from his three hundred peasant-serfs. Incapable of occupying himself with such financial details, he is being systematically swindled by the bailiff left in charge. Although tormented by the mysterious status of his connection with Olga, which led to social embarrassments only adding to his inner dismay, and continually assuring her of his imminent departure, he proves unable to keep his word. Meanwhile, forced out his apartment, he moves to one in an isolated "street with no houses, just fences and grass, with ruts in the dried mud" (259).

On his first visit, he notices the bosom of the landlady high and solid like "a pillow on a couch" (262). After moving in, the face of the landlady, though she was dressed shabbily and incongruously, "projected an impression of simple good nature," and "her bust, even though covered as it was ... could have served as a model for a painting and sculpture of a firm, healthy and substantial bosom without even a suggestion of immodesty" (261). Never inactive for a moment, always occupied with accomplishing some necessary household task, Agafya Matveyevna's bare elbows were always in movement, and when she bent her back, Oblomov "could see underneath a clean skirt, clean stockings and round, plump legs" (267). Most important of all, Oblomov would suddenly be confronted with a hand mysteriously appearing and offering him something tasty and delicious to eat or drink.

Goncharov thus discreetly suggests both the erotic attraction of the landlady, divorced from any of the tasks imposed by a union with Olga, and the return, as it were, to the childhood delights of Oblomovka. Ultimately, this leads to the replacement of the increasingly disillusioned Olga by the devoted Agafya, dedicated entirely to Oblomov's happiness as she understood it. Olga eventually marries the much more suitable Stoltz, and both intervene to rescue Oblomov and Agafya, whom he too finally marries, from the clutches of her brother and his rascally cohort who have concocted a scheme for bleeding them dry. All these twists and turns of the action are given a larger significance by a passage in which Stoltz, contemplating his own marriage, reveals the literary ancestry of Goncharov's creation.

> With a smile and with blushes alternating with frowns, he watches the endless procession of love's heroes and heroines file past: he saw Don Quixotes in steel gauntlets and ladies of their imaginations remaining true to each other through fifty years of separation; he saw ruddy-cheeked shepherd boys with their bulging innocent eyes and their Chloes, minding their lambs. Powdered marquises with their knowing glances and lewd smirks paraded past him in

their frills and furbelows; behind them came the Werthers who had shot, hanged and strangled themselves; there were the faded spinsters in their convents shedding the endless tears of the lovelorn; there were the mustachioed latter day heroes with their flashing eyes, the witting and unwitting Don Juans, the sophisticates who tremble at the very suspicion of love but secretly adore their housekeepers—the procession went on and on. (397)

Oblomov is thus placed in this literary line as merely the latest incarnation of a perennial theme.

Oblomov is not only located in such an expanded literary-historical context, but his tirades from time to time also raise ultimate questions about the meaning of human activity and human life itself. Accused of *oblomovschina* by Stoltz, Oblomov answers back "with a strange, searching look," but "mildly and without heat": "Isn't everybody looking for the same thing as me? ... Surely the purpose of all this hustle and bustle of yours, all these passions, wars, trade and politics is to achieve precisely this very peace and quiet, to strive for this ideal of paradise lost?" Stoltz can only reply that "Russia needs hands and heads to develop and restore its inexhaustible resources" (157), but this is no real answer to the scope of Oblomov's query. The same theme arises much later when Olga, living a married life of perfect happiness, is overcome by an inexplicable sadness for which she can find no evident cause. Stoltz can only console her by replying that "yes, that's the price we pay for Prometheus's fire, but don't think of it as a burden or a curse" (407). One feels Goncharov here reaching out for Dostoevskian themes that he felt incapable of exploring, but which, if only in passing, give Oblomov's character much more than a social-cultural purport.

All the same, it is the social-cultural implications first analyzed by Dobrolyubov that continue to provide Goncharov's novel with its ever-renewed topicality. It is no surprise that Lenin (incidentally, also born in Simbirsk) time and again refers to Oblomov as a figure embodying all the forces opposing the transformation of Russian society that he wished to bring about. Nor could Gorbachev resist invoking Oblomov to characterize those opposing his policy of perestroika. Still another facet of the book's appeal, however, also ought not to be overlooked. For as the excellent British Slavist Richard Peace has written, *Oblomov* "has significance beyond that of its continuing relevance to Russian society and Russian culture. Happy, indeed, would be the reader who behind laughter at Oblomov's subterfuges ... would not be aware, too, of an uneasy feeling of self-recognition."[12]

---

[12] Richard Peace, *Oblomov: A Critical Examination of Goncharov's Novel* (Birmingham: University of Birmingham, 1991), 3.

EIGHT

LYDIA GINZBURG, *ON PSYCHOLOGICAL PROSE*

LYDIA IAKOVLEVNA GINZBURG is not a name widely known outside Russia except to Slavists, but this excellent translation by Judson Rosengrant of perhaps her most important book, *On Psychological Prose*, should help to introduce her to a larger public. Until a few years before her death in 1990, when she was eighty, one could hardly say that her reputation was widespread even in Russia, except in scholarly circles. There she was highly respected as the author of a series of impressive studies of Russian writers, including Lermontov (1940) and Alexander Herzen (1957), as well as on such broader literary subjects as the Russian poetic tradition (*On the Lyric*, 1964).

The present book, however, brought her increased attention when it was first published in 1971 because it deals with both Russian and Western European writers in a manner running completely counter to the Marxist-Stalinist insistence on the inherent virtues of the Russians and the inherent shortcomings of the Europeans. *On Psychological Prose* treats Vissarion Belinsky, Nikolai Stankevich, Turgenev, and Herzen on equal terms with the duc de Saint-Simon (not the Utopian socialist of the 1800s, but his great-uncle, the memoirist of the court of Louis XIV whom Proust so much admired) and the Rousseau of the *Confessions*. Tolstoy, who dominates the last three chapters, is discussed along with Benjamin Constant (*Adolphe*), Stendhal, Balzac, Flaubert, and Proust.

Soviet Russian readers were not accustomed to such impartial and judicious handling of foreign writers, who were most often denounced rather than studied, even in the work of specialists. Moreover, the book ends with a chapter on the question of individual moral responsibility as raised by Tolstoy—a question that was not supposed to trouble good Soviet citizens since it had been answered once and for all by the Bolshevik Revolution. So Ginzburg's subtly subversive emphasis gave her presumably innocent work of scholarship a distinct ideological edge.

The young Lydia Ginzburg's circle of friends included both her Russian Formalist teachers at the Institute of the History of Arts in Leningrad (Boris Eikhenbaum and Yuri Tynianov among others) and many of the

---

Originally published in a slightly different form as "Subversive Activities," *New York Review of Books* 41 (20). Copyright © 1994 *The New York Review of Books*. All rights reserved. Reprinted by permission.

leading Russian writers of the 1920s and 1930s such as Mayakovsky, Blok, and Mandelstam; she was especially close to Anna Akhmatova. Teaching at the institute herself until it was closed by Stalin in 1930, Ginzburg then found work giving adult education courses in factories and wrote a detective novel, *The Pinkerton Agency*, for adolescents. Between 1947 and 1950 she obtained a post at Petrozavodsk University north of Leningrad, one of the provincial schools considered safer for Jewish intellectuals in those years than institutions in the larger cities. The publication of her memoirs, based on the journal she kept all her life, brought her additional fame in the 1960s, and she continued to produce books and articles throughout the 1970s.[1]

Her considerable personal influence is evoked in an essay by Irina Paperno (now teaching at UC Berkeley): "For us," she writes, "the generation that began to study literature in the 1960s and 1970s, conversations with Lydia Ginzburg became one of the most important parts of our education.... Informal as they were, these conversations were always experienced as events, for in this way Lydia Iakovlevna included the younger generation in the oral tradition of cultural inheritance, into the 'domesticity' of Russian cultural life."[2]

Ginzburg thus became a link with the past for the younger people who were devoted to her; and for many years she also held open house for the foreign Slavists and students who sought to penetrate beneath the frozen Soviet surface. In 1988, two years before her death, she was awarded the Lenin Prize, at a time when, as one writer acidly remarked, it was no longer a disgrace to receive this honor.

On Psychological Prose may prove somewhat disconcerting to Western readers because the word "psychology" is usually taken here to mean a study of inner, private lives. One might expect yet another book about what Erich Kahler called "the inward turn of narrative," the movement of prose literature from epic heroics and picaresque travels to the exploration of states of feeling and, ultimately, the stream-of-consciousness. Ginzburg, however, uses the term in the sense of "social psychology," the ways in which character and personality are formed from myriad impressions, sensations, and feelings, under the influence of both internal needs and external models. These models are usually derived from the social norms

---

[1] Her last book was *On the Literary Hero* (1971). After that, she published volumes of essays and reminiscences: *On the Old and the New* (1981), *Literature in Search of Reality* (1987), and *A Person at a Writing Table* (1989).

[2] See Irina Paperno, "Beyond Literary Criticism," *Canadian-American Slavic Studies* 19 (Summer 1985): 184. This issue of the journal is entirely devoted to Ginzburg, and its contributors are mainly younger North American Slavists. Many of them made her acquaintance during their study and research jaunts to the then Soviet Union.

of a particular period and, very often, from the type of personality-ideal expressed in the literature of that period. Ginzburg thus sees a very fluid boundary between literature and life and speaks of an "aesthetic potentiality" present everywhere in social life itself. (She uses the word "aesthetic" in a very broad and rather vague sense, to mean the organization of experience according to one or another dominating idea or ideal, which then becomes self-conscious in art.)

For Ginzburg all of human existence is filled with principles of organization that give it form and structure, and "social man" comes into being by absorbing "shared norms and ideals, images that not only have a social function but that also possess aesthetic coloration."[3] To show how the rituals of social life embody part of this inbuilt "aesthetic potentiality," Ginzburg points to parades, uniforms, and the ceremonial dress obligatory for certain official duties. She also stresses the "mutual interpenetration in life and in literature of images of personality" (10)—so that a work such as *Werther* could cause a wave of suicides. Ginzburg's attempts to correlate art and social life in this way have produced a new approach to Russian culture called "the semiotics of behavior"—a study of the ways in which literary models and historical reality interact. And she has been hailed as a pioneer by numerous scholars who have applied and developed her suggestions.[4]

Since art and social life mutually affect each other in forming images of personality, Ginzburg takes a special interest in types of writing that arise directly, without any artistic intention, from social experience. The first section of her book is devoted to the stormy and painfully revealing correspondence between the literary critic Vissarion Belinsky and the young Mikhail Bakunin (not yet the anarchist and all-destroying revolutionary); the second, to writers of memoirs and autobiographies such as Saint-Simon, Rousseau, and Herzen; the third, to novelists who are able to write without the responsibility to fact that constrains the others. This progression obviously represents an increasing degree of self-consciousness and autonomy in transforming social experience into aesthetic images; but Ginzburg is very far from considering such freedom as unconditional as might at first seem the case.

---

[3] Lydia Ginzburg, On *Psychological Prose*, trans. and ed. Judson Rosengrant (Princeton: Princeton University Press, 1994), 11. Page references to this work are hereafter cited in parentheses in the text.

[4] See a collection of such writings, *The Semiotics of Russian Cultural History*, ed. Alexander Nakhimovsky and Alice Stone Nakhimovsky (Ithaca: Cornell University Press, 1985). Ginzburg is credited in the introduction with giving "the first explicit formulation of [this] new approach" to Russian cultural history (8).

On the contrary, she values semidocumentary genres precisely because they have a freedom of their own—a freedom from prevailing aesthetic standards and conventions. Artists tend to conform to the dominant social, cultural, and aesthetic standards of their time, and they seldom break free of the conventions governing contemporary novels, poems, and stories. But "literature located outside traditional canons," Ginzburg remarks, "is sometimes able to furnish unusual, even startling insights into spiritual life, thereby anticipating the future discoveries of artists" (6).

The correspondence between Belinsky and Bakunin from the 1840s, in her view, thus prepared the way for the Russian social-psychological novel of the 1860s and 1870s; memoirs and autobiographies made possible a new understanding of individual personality quite outside the literary practice of their time, and, in the case of Alexander Herzen's memoirs, to a sense of individual character as defined by, and expressive of, a historical or ideological situation. For Ginzburg, such tendencies then converge in the social-psychological realism of the classic Russian novel and particularly in Tolstoy. Her book thus has an external structure deriving from the distinction between artistic and documentary prose, as well as an internal one that traces her own distinctive view of this historical and literary evolution, culminating with the works of Tolstoy. The internal account is by far the more interesting, and it is regrettable that Ginzburg does not give it greater emphasis.

At first sight, the correspondence between Belinsky and Bakunin (as well as between other members of what was known as the Stankevich circle) may seem to have little interest except to students of Russian literature. In fact, Ginzburg uses it to illuminate one of the most widely noted and distinctive features of the nineteenth-century Russian novel as compared with those produced in the West. It is soon evident to any of its readers that virtually all the great characters of Russian literature are portrayed, not only as individuals with particular traits and temperaments, but also as the self-conscious bearers of certain ideas and social-cultural attitudes that give them a particular historical significance.

Turgenev's Rudin, modeled on the young Bakunin, is not only an unhappy nobleman too weak to elope with the young woman he loves but also a Romantic Idealist "superfluous man" of the 1840s, whose weakness is typical of the social impotence of his class and generation. Pierre Bezuhov in *War and Peace* is not only the bumbling, good-hearted scion of Russian high society betrayed by his naïveté into a disastrous marriage but someone whose Masonic affiliations and devotion to his fellow prisoner, the peasant Platon Karataev, reflect important tendencies in Russian culture. Raskolnikov not only is a desperate young man who commits murder to break out of an oppressive personal situation, but he does so under the influence of the radical ideas that were, as Dostoevsky said, "in the air" of his time.

Critics have often explained that in tsarist Russia arguments about such political and philosophical matters could be carried on only in novels, which, as a source of amusement and recreation, enjoyed a certain freedom from political constraint, and in which dangerous thoughts could be implied or suggested rather than stated, or imputed to fictional characters. There is a good deal to be said for this explanation; but it will now have to be supplemented by the more sophisticated perspective that Ginzburg provides.

Tracing the "conception of man" worked out by the Russian intelligentsia of the first third of the nineteenth century, in its movement from German idealism to one or another form of materialism and supposedly scientific determinism, she writes: "First came the romantic idealization of personality, then the meticulous investigation of that personality in terms of philosophical categories, and finally the transition, especially clear-cut in Belinsky, to realistic determinism—the analysis of the individual human being in relation to his social conditionality [i.e., to the most minute, prosaic, and down-to-earth details of his daily existence]" (28).

The second and third stages of this process were the most important, and it is very easy to be amused and astonished at some of the examples that Ginzburg produces of how the most abstract philosophical concepts became intermingled with the most elemental experiences of human existence. One of Bakunin's sisters, for example, who had become engaged to the poet and philosopher Nikolai Stankevich just five weeks before his death, sat beside his corpse and consoled herself by writing (in German) that "in and of itself the material world is nothing but only through its internal union with the spirit has my being, my I, received its reality" (45), continuing with several more pages on the relation of the finite and the infinite.

Herzen, in a famous passage of *My Past and Thoughts*, later described the 1840s as a time when "everything in fact spontaneous, every simple feeling, was raised to an abstract category and brought back without a drop of living blood, as a pale algebraic shadow." Herzen's mockery was justified, as Ginzburg sees it, but it tells only part of the story. For "this habit of detailed and at the same time generalized examination of psychic life laid the groundwork" for what became the Russian novel, whose outstanding feature is "that in it ideology permeates the material of ordinary social life, and that the facts of private life are raised to the level of philosophical generalization" (64–65).

During the 1840s, to be sure, "ordinary social life" had hardly been touched at all by such reflections. It was Belinsky who finally brought it into view, and whose letters Ginzburg analyzes with great detail and acuity to show how he gradually broke free from the metaphysical dualism produced by Idealist thought. Instead of relegating the practical and the empirical to a status inferior to that of the Spirit, the plebeian Belinsky, forced to earn his living as a critic by turning out monthly articles, found it impossible to forget about such trivial matters as money (as his gentry friend Bakunin did all too easily). Bakunin paid no attention to "finite" personal debts, which shrank to insignificance beside his "infinite" mission to spread the gospel of the Spirit. When Belinsky reproached him for his negligence, he replied that he had seen "evidence of eternal degradation in [Belinsky's] letter about scrupulousness and kopecks.... 'You do not even want to hear about kopecks,'" Belinsky retorted, "'but you want to have them—it makes no sense. You speak only of the inner life, but you pay a significant tribute to the external one; it is not logical'" (90).

For Belinsky, individual moral responsibility extended to every aspect of life, even that of "the despised kopecks." By insisting that idealist notions must be anchored in ordinary reality, as Ginzburg writes, he "extended the responsibility of creative endeavor to the whole of life's content" (92). Ginzburg thus maintains that "the intellectual life of the Russian intelligentsia of the 1830s and 1840s was the medium in which were first crystallized those ideas that later found expression in the spiritual experience and writings of Tolstoy and Dostoevsky" (99).

In fact, many similarities exist between the moral and spiritual crises discussed in the letters of Belinsky and his friends and those appearing later in both the life and work of the two great Russians. The famous passage in which Belinsky passionately protests against the sacrifice of the individual to the Hegelian Universal undoubtedly influenced Ivan Karamazov's refusal to accept the injustices of God's world in his conversation with his brother Alyosha about the suffering of innocent children. The resemblances are striking, and Ginzburg is by no means the first to point them out; but she gives Dostoevsky's use of Belinsky fresh importance as part of a more general thesis.

Sometimes, however, Ginzburg is carried away by her doctrine that documentary literature anticipates the novel. It is simply not true that Belinsky's emphasis on ordinary social circumstances, and what she calls their "cause-and-effect" relation to personality, "were still beyond the reach of the novel of the first third of the nineteenth century" (83). Belinsky's letters, to be sure, were published (and even then partially) only in 1875; but the impact of his critical articles had been felt long before then. In Dostoevsky's *Poor Folk* (1845), which Herzen praised as the first Russian social (and socialist) novel, the lives of the characters are deeply affected by their humiliating poverty and inferior social position. No wonder that Belinsky rapturously hailed the book, for reasons that Ginzburg helps us to appreciate more fully. But her eye is too much on Belinsky's letters and too much on Tolstoy to give Dostoevsky the credit he deserves for this early achievement.

Two

Beginning with the early nineteenth century, Ginzburg's book then goes back to the seventeenth and eighteenth centuries to deal with Saint-Simon and Rousseau and then returns to her starting point with Herzen. Saint-Simon, whose memoirs describe life in the court of Louis XIV and the first eight years of Louis XV, was undoubtedly the greatest portraitist of individual character up to his own time: his unprecedented images break all the rules of the reigning literary genres and the conventions of a polite society governed by the most rigid etiquette. At the climax of his portrait of a highly placed court charmer, he notes her heavy jowls and rotting teeth; the brother of the king, the duc d'Orleans, was "a small, pot-bellied man mounted on stilts, so high were his heels, who always dressed like a woman, all in rings, bracelets, and jewels of every kind" (136). One easily understands why the manuscript he left lay buried in the files of the French Ministry of Foreign Affairs for seventy years after his death, and even then was published only in fragments.[5]

Saint-Simon thus was one of the first writers to react against the prevailing literary codes, and to loosen social and cultural constraints by direct empirical observation. In this respect he may be seen as a distant precursor of the nineteenth-century novel. But he was still a man of his time, who continued, as Ginzburg writes, to see personality as a mechanistic assortment of "qualities governed by passions" (122); one succeeded the other, and there was no connection between them. He had no awareness of what she calls the "fluidity of consciousness" (129), the manner in which contrary tendencies could exist in a single personality and form a unity, even if a contradictory one. By contrast, Rousseau's great accomplishment in

---

[5] Erich Auerbach, with his unrivaled knowledge of the Western literary tradition, has written that "the best and most famous portraits from earlier memoirs pale before his, and in all European literature there have probably been only a very few writers capable of giving their readers such an abundance of human characters, each so patently specific and homogeneous, and each so fully revealing the very basis of the individual's life." Erich Auerbach, *Mimesis* (Princeton: Princeton University Press, 1953), 416. Ginzburg refers to Auerbach's book, though not to this passage, and knows it very well. Indeed, there is a good deal of similarity in their critical interests—both were concerned with the history of how moral-social conventions codified in literary norms gradually were overcome by "reality."

his *Confessions* was to show how personality is modified by all the circumstances and impressions that impinge on a person's life.

For Ginzburg, Rousseau's grasp of the complexity of these pressures is what makes him so important a forerunner of the nineteenth-century novel. In turning down, despite his poverty, an offer to meet the king and accept a royal pension, Rousseau gives a variety of reasons that Ginzburg summarizes as follows: "Thus his bladder affliction, his awkwardness and confusion in society, his love of liberty, and his dread of taking trouble all stand, simultaneously, as reasons for his decision. Rousseau revealed the presence of a multiplicity of coexisting impulses deriving simultaneously from different sources—the physiological, the psychological, and the social—in as much as the individual is subject to the influence of all these spheres at once" (188).

Rousseau brought the same type of what we now call "overdetermined causality" to bear on the less edifying aspects of his life, for which, as Ginzburg notes, he judged himself very harshly, while implicitly excusing himself through the very profuseness of the enumeration of his weaknesses.

Ginzburg then turns to Herzen's *My Past and Thoughts*, to which she had devoted her much appreciated book in 1957, and concentrates on the "conscious historicism" that pervades this magnificent autobiographical panorama of Russian culture between the 1820s and the 1860s. No such conscious grasp of their own historical situation can be found in either Saint-Simon or Rousseau, while for Herzen, steeped in Hegel, the historical moment was the very air he breathed. His awareness of history, as Ginzburg illuminatingly shows, penetrates to the most intimate details of private life (his own as well as others'), so that social and historical considerations cannot be separated from psychological ones.

Herzen's friend Nikolai Ketscher, for example, a member of the intelligentsia, married a poor, uneducated orphan girl brought up by Old Believers, and who thus "possessed all the prejudices of esoteric religion and all the fantastic notions of old Russian society" (209). The marriage was a disaster; and Herzen typically turns this private mishap into "the clash of two different cultural stages, of two different 'ages of man' " (209). The infidelity of his own wife, who betrayed him with the radical German poet Herwegh, caused Herzen agonies of grief; but for him it was more than a personal tragedy, it was a clash between "two different historical formations"—a naively idealistic and trusting Young Russia and a treacherously corrupt bourgeois West.

Herzen's work was thus an indispensable step toward the historical self-awareness that marked the grasp of character of the Russian novel; and Ginzburg also sees an even closer link between Herzen and Tolstoy in the similarity of their narrative manner. Both use an explanatory commentator

(Herzen as himself, Tolstoy as third-person observer) who "theoretically explains the general patterns that governed the acts, gestures and words" (208) of a particular character before illustrating these patterns through the scenes and dialogue that follow. This is a well-known trait of the Tolstoyan narrator and clearly distinguishes him as quite different from Turgenev's unobtrusive narrators or Dostoevsky's unreliable ones.

For Ginzburg, the great period of the Russian novel peaks with those of Tolstoy, which are "the high point of nineteenth-century analytical, explanatory psychologism" (221). All the developments she has been tracing thus far culminate in Tolstoy, and she argues that he gave them "a fundamental change in ... direction" (232). Just what this change involves is not very clear, though it seems to mean the final eradication of the boundaries between documentary and artistic literature, and with this the attainment of a hitherto unexampled freedom and range (at least in the novel) in depicting personality. "The documentary nature of Tolstoy's psychological inquiries," she writes, "freed his heroes from the strict laws governing artistic modeling of the individual human being" (246). This does not mean that Tolstoy was writing autobiography instead of novels; but she insists that the close relations between his personal diaries and his novel are more than merely an incidental fact of his creative life. For Tolstoy's heroes "not only address the same problems of existence that he addressed, but ... they address them in the same psychological form and in relation to virtually the same everyday circumstances that he himself was faced with" (245).

Ginzburg realized, of course, that realism in the novel already had a history, but she tries to show that a true, "explanatory" realism in relation to personality had not been achieved in the past. The novelists she discusses are all French (Mme de Lafayette, Constant, Stendhal, Balzac, Flaubert); she seems to know little of English literature, where the realist novel (Defoe) arose directly out of journalism and has a different history (from documentary literature to the novel) from the one she traces. Her suggestive point about the French novel is that, beginning with *La Princesse de Clèves* and even including Stendhal and Balzac—who began to see personality as shaped by historical and social circumstances—the characters' central conflicts are invariably conceived as a "clash" between "the opposing principles" of passion and duty, ambition and love, patriarchal moral values and social success. It is only in Flaubert's *L'Education Sentimentale* that a novel's psychological analysis begins to approach the minute dissection of opposing velleities, impulses, and rationalizations that were initiated much earlier by Rousseau and perfected by Tolstoy.

To illustrate her argument, Ginzburg provides a telling analysis of the great final scene, in which Frédéric Moreau rejects the temptation to make love at last to the now white-haired Mme Arnoux, the ideal woman of his lifelong desire: "Frédéric suspected that Madame Arnoux had come to offer herself to him, and once again he was seized by a furious, ravening lust, stronger than any he had known before. But he felt something inexpressible, a repulsion, and something like the dread of incest. Another fear held him back, that of feeling disgust later. Besides, what a problem it would be! And impelled simultaneously by prudence and by the desire not to degrade his ideal, he turned on his heel and started to roll a cigarette" (238).

It is the very multiplicity and contradictoriness of this tangle of motives—the effect of growing older, the sudden eruption of lust, dread of incest, bourgeois prudence, a last shred of Romantic idealization—that determine Frédéric's response, which Mme Arnoux takes for "chivalry." What Flaubert still lacks, however, is the sociohistorical dimension; and though the revolution of 1848 is part of the novel's background, Ginzburg says quite accurately that "the historical atmosphere surrounding the hero of *L'Education Sentimentale* does not penetrate very deeply into his spiritual experience" (239). History was not an essential element in the construction of personality for Flaubert as it would be for the Russians.

Having celebrated Tolstoy for the unprecedented density and complexity of his social and psychological analysis—so unprecedented, indeed, that contemporary critics, joined by Turgenev, often upbraided him for the "superfluity" of his details—Ginzburg goes on to speak of a "pre-Tolstoyan" period in the history of the novel. Tolstoy thus, in her view, created a new era in the novel, and her claim recalls the very similar one made for Dostoevsky by Mikhail Bakhtin, against whom, one suspects, she is carrying on a concealed polemic.

Ginzburg wrote with great respect of Bakhtin elsewhere, without concealing her resistance to his idea (in fact highly exaggerated) that Dostoevsky's "polyphony," the presumed liberty with which he allows his characters to express their own points of view, precludes the author's dominance over his novel.[6] And in a classic gambit of Russian criticism, she contrasts the two writers in order to justify her view of Tolstoy as the superior artist. "If psychologism means the investigation of spiritual life in all its contradictions and depth," she admits, "then it would be odd, to say the very least, to exclude Dostoevsky" (259). But he went his own way and "departed from classical nineteenth-century psychologism, the basic principle of which was explanation, whether explicit or concealed" (259). Dostoevsky's main characters all act according to motives that come from a dominating idea, and they are more or less removed from the ordinary

---

[6] "By no means everybody (very far from it)," she says, "will agree that there is no definitive authorial word in Dostoevsky." See the interview in *Voprosy Literaturi* 4 (1978): 188.

routine of life that Tolstoy explores so minutely. Nor, as Ginzburg put it elsewhere, did Dostoevsky believe it possible (or desirable) to account for human behavior, as Tolstoy does, by tracing its many interrelated and determining causes.[7]

For Ginzburg, then, Tolstoy was the founding father of the modern novel, and she insists that "one may find in him the seed of everything that twentieth-century literature would later elaborate to the full extent." Among such features, she lists the "stream of consciousness" (as in Anna Karenina's inner monologue on the way to the station where she throws herself under a train), "the unconscious, the subterranean currents of conversation, and the use of extended, vividly marked details." Ginzburg refers disparagingly to the view (first proposed by Dostoevsky himself) that Tolstoy "is a classic who belongs irrevocably to the past"; but she sometimes seems to acknowledge that her own view may not be persuasive today. With a distinct sense of pique, she writes that contemporary man "finds it more interesting to conceive of himself in Dostoevskian terms, since doing so allows him to focus his attention on himself" (243).

In a chapter on "direct discourse," Ginzburg examines at great length Tolstoy's method of explanatory narration and increases one's suspicion that Ginzburg is implicitly debating with Bakhtin; for this is precisely what Bakhtin saw as retrograde and outmoded in Tolstoy. Ginzburg is arguing the same case, on the level of technique, that was made thirty years ago by Wayne Booth, in his *Rhetoric of Fiction*, against the then-reigning critical prejudice in favor of an invisible narrator. Booth too refused to accept the notion that an assertive narrator was necessarily an artistic defect. But Ginzburg is less interested in technique as such and more in Tolstoy's use of direct discourse to unmask in advance the egoism and vanity that often lie concealed in the most innocuous and banal conversations, as well as to describe the ebb and flow of feelings that can "determine" the most casual remark. Printing a long passage from the epilogue to *War and Peace* with the passages in direct discourse marked by italics, Ginzburg concludes that

---

[7] "Dostoevsky," she writes cogently, "occupied a peculiar position among his contemporaries because he made the metaphysical understanding of the freedom of the will a constructive moment of his novels, the driving force of the behavior of his characters." See *On the Literary Hero*, 83. Dostoevsky had a very acute understanding of the moral consequences of Tolstoy's pursuit of causality and wrote a clever and amusing parody of it that should be better known. In it Dostoevsky is discussing *Anna Karenina*, and why he believes that Levin's newfound faith will soon disappear. The reason is that Kitty will have stumbled over the root of a tree. "If she stumbled, it was because she could not have not stumbled; it is perfectly obvious that she has stumbled for this reason or for another reason. It is clear that everything had depended on laws that could be rigorously determined. And if this is so, then science is omnipresent. Where then is Providence? Where is human responsibility? And if there is no Providence, how can one believe in God? And so on and so forth. Take a straight line and extend it into infinity." F. M. Dostoevsky, *Diary of a Writer* (July–August, 1877), chap. 2, part 4.

"Tolstoyan dialogue collapses without this system of analytical connections that establish why and to what end a person says what he says, and that consequently confirm the determined nature of what is being said (in the same way that they confirm the determined nature of every other phenomenon)" (294).

Tolstoy's sense of an inescapable determinism controlling all human behavior leads to Ginzburg's final, and extremely rich, chapter on literature and ethical values. Since literature is concerned with human behavior, she insists, "there is therefore an indissoluble bond bestween literature and ethics" (319). Literature and ethical norms have been related in a bewildering variety of ways over the centuries, but for Ginzburg the mid-nineteenth century posed a new problem. Before then, however acute the tensions between the two may have been, "the commandments of God and the absolute transcended the individual and were therefore beyond dispute" (321). But the combination of atheism and individualism in the mid-nineteenth century, along with the ascendancy of realism as the literary voice of a scientific determinism, brought with it the question of how people could justify a commitment to values other than those of their own egoism. "How can that general significance be established without resorting to transcendental premises?" (324), she asks, in what was certainly a daring question in the Soviet Union of 1971.

Ginzburg discusses this issue with regard to Tolstoy's own moral and religious crisis in his *Confession*, in which he describes how he was tempted to commit suicide. She also attributes the widespread influence of Schopenhauerian pessimism, which affected Turgenev as well as Tolstoy, to the same unresolved dilemma over the source of values. Even those dedicated to revolutionary action, like Herzen, she writes, could find no way "to substantiate the necessity for the humanistic goals of that action" (327). This quandary confronted all of Russian literature and culture in the mid-nineteenth century, and of course not Russian culture alone. What became central was "the sociopsychological issue of how to reconcile determinism with the fact of guilt and individual responsibility" (332). For without the "working hypothesis" that a person is free and morally responsible, no portrayal of spiritual life—or for that matter, action of any kind—is possible (as Dostoevsky had shown with caustic irony in the first part of *Notes from Underground*, though Ginzburg does not mention the work in this connection).[8]

In fact, Tolstoy's work and life reveal the continuous struggle between these two aspects of his world view—on the one hand, the determined nature of all human behavior; on the other, his view of the individual as

---

[8] For a discussion of *Notes from Underground* that highlights this very question, see my *Dostoevsky: The Stir of Liberation* (Princeton: Princeton University Press, 1986), chap. 21.

unmistakably free and morally responsible. The "philosophical duality" of Tolstoy's beliefs has been magisterially laid bare by Isaiah Berlin with regard to the understanding of history, and Ginzburg's fine explorations of the concrete moral choices of Tolstoy's characters provide a valuable supplement to Berlin's "The Hedgehog and the Fox." Tolstoy's characters, she writes, are never good or evil in themselves, but they respond to particular situations according to a hierarchy of values whose highest stage is "higher than intuitive compassion or intuitive closeness to the earth (Nikolai Rostov), or than immanent creative energy." This highest stage is a "condition of faith that was accessible to all, but especially to simple, uneducated people, a condition of faith in the absolute validity of the experience of shared bonds that is given to Tolstoy's unbelieving intellectuals only as a possibility" (351).

As should be amply clear by now, much of the value of Ginzburg's book is found in its details rather than in any overriding thesis, and what is most impressive are her continual flashes of insight about particular issues, especially about the way social and literary stereotypes are formed and broken. She is unlikely, though, to have anywhere near the same impact as Bakhtin, for one thing because she sadly lacks a talent for exposition, for another because she cannot match him in historical range or theoretical boldness. Her strong point is close, careful, and patient elucidation rather than sweeping and often highly dubious speculations. Nor is she likely to persuade many readers that the true father of modernism is Tolstoy, though she makes a good case for giving him more credit as a technical innovator than he has previously had. Technique is not everything, however, and Dostoevsky was right in assigning Tolstoy's still relatively stable and well-ordered world to a landowning gentry past that had irrevocably vanished.

All the same, Ginzburg's book is well worth the attention of anyone seriously interested in literature, and not only that of the nineteenth century. Her perceptive observations on the relation between literary and documentary genres are quite relevant to present-day arguments about the relativity of the literary canon, and she has illuminating things to say on every page about the interaction between varying historical conceptions of human personality and literary creation. One hopes, indeed, that the moment may be as propitious for her as it was for Bakhtin, whose reception in the West was strongly conditioned by the overheated revolutionary atmosphere of the 1960s. His account of fiction as liberated from the author (as presumably in the novels of Dostoevsky) and from moral and social norms (as with Rabelais) strongly suited the apocalyptic temper of the period. The recent attempts to reconsider the relations between ethics and literature (in the work of Wayne Booth and Martha Nussbaum, among others) may provide a climate for a more sympathetic reception of Ginzburg than might have been anticipated a few years back.[9] And perhaps the time has also come for a new, sobering appreciation of what Ginzburg describes as Tolstoy's fundamental task, the slow, stubborn, and relentless search (so congenial to her own critical temperament) for the "foundations of the good" that could withstand even the withering effects of Tolstoy's own disillusioning scrutiny.

Postscript

Long before I knew anything about Lydia Ginzburg except her fame, I accidentally discovered that she was familiar with my own work. One of the foreign students she welcomed happened to have studied with me at Princeton; and on returning, he told me that he had noticed a copy of my volume of essays, *The Widening Gyre* (1963) on her bookshelves. These essays had nothing to do with Russian literature and long preceded my own later work on Dostoevsky.

Her possession of this volume indicates the wide range of her own interests, and I later found a reference to my essay on spatial form in her book, *On the Literary Hero*. In this essay, widely recognized in Anglo-American criticism as well, I characterize the avant-garde literature of the early 20th century (Eliot, Pound, Joyce, Proust) as ahistorical both in technique and thematic significance. In a reduced version, this essay was later (1987) translated into Russian in a volume devoted to outstanding articles of non-Russian literary criticism (*Zarubezhnaya Estetika I Teoriya Literaturi XIX–XX vv*). It is quite possible that Ginzburg's referral may well have called this essay to the attention of other Russian scholars.

---

[9] See Wayne Booth, *The Company We Keep* (Berkeley: University of California Press, 1988), and Martha *Nussbaum's Love's Knowledge* (Oxford: Oxford University Press, 1990). Also see Nussbaum's comment: "It is striking that in the last few years literary theorists allied with deconstruction have taken a marked turn toward the ethical." After citing examples from Jacques Derrida and Barbara Johnson, she adds: "No doubt a part of this change can be traced to the scandal over the political career of Paul de Man, which has made theorists anxious to demonstrate that Deconstruction does not imply a neglect of ethical and social consideration" (29, n52).

NINE

RICHARD PIPES, *RUSSIAN CONSERVATISM AND ITS CRITICS*

RICHARD PIPES has had an extremely distinguished career both as an historian specializing in Russian history and culture and as a member for two years of the National Security Council serving under President Reagan. The two books under review here, *Russian Conservatism and Its Critics* and *Vixi: Memoirs of a Non-Belonger*, deal with both these aspects of his life, and one helps to illuminate the other. His views on Russian history, particularly as they related to the ex-Soviet Union, attracted the attention of politicians like Senator Henry Jackson, and he was invited to testify before Senate commissions and finally to accept a temporary position on the National Security Council. His memoirs offer an extremely interesting, if highly partisan, glimpse into the people and personalities that affected American policy toward Russia during the Reagan era; but it is not with this aspect of his activity that we shall be mainly concerned. It is primarily with his views on Russian history, which for a long period placed him in opposition to the ideas then prevailing among students of the subject. These views are again amply illustrated in his most recent book on Russian conservatism; and his memoirs help to clarify the manner in which his particular interpretation of Russian history evolved and took its final shape.

Pipes provides a vivid picture of his childhood and personal life as a member of an assimilated Polish-Jewish family before and after arriving in the United States at the age of sixteen. As an adolescent, he had led a very active, if independent, intellectual life; and in a notebook entry, written just before his family quit Poland, he depicts himself during the bombing of Warsaw by the German Luftwaffe. "We slept fully dressed ... I slept alone on the 6th floor reading Nietzsche's *Will to Power* ... or writing notes for my essay on Giotto."[1] He was interested in art, music, and philosophy rather than history, and while "in the late 1930s I heard muffled sounds of appalling events taking place in the Soviet Union ... I had no idea what these were and I was not terribly interested in finding

---

Originally published in a slightly different form in *The New Republic*, May 15, 2006. Reprinted by permission.

[1] Richard Pipes, Vixi: *Memoirs of a Non-Belonger* (New Haven: Yale University Press, 2003), 5.

out."[2] Examining his later views, however, he now concedes that "coming from Poland, a country which had bordered Russia for a thousand years and lived under its occupation for over a century, I unconsciously shared Polish attitudes toward Russia"[3] —attitudes that could only have been highly critical.

Such a background was quite different from the innocence he encountered at a small college in Ohio, which he entered quite haphazardly after arriving in the United States. Word had gotten around that he read Nietzsche, and the vice president of the school told him to put Nietzsche aside because "I should not lose faith in mankind, people were basically good and life fair."[4] It was no wonder that he found it impossible to persuade his American interlocutors, who were staunchly Republican and isolationist (how times have changed!) of the monstrosities of Nazism. But Pipes's own experience, which included the endemic anti-Semitism of Polish culture (although relatively mild compared to what occurred under German occupation), had acquainted him with other aspects of people and human life. What he says about the attitude of Polish Jewry toward the German occupation, from which he and his family were luckily able to flee, also helps to illuminate some of his later views.

The Orthodox Polish Jews, living in communities isolated from the modern world, were scarcely aware of what to expect (or so he continues to believe). But even the assimilated, though more apprehensive, still incredibly assumed they could survive, as Jews had always done in the past, by making themselves useful to the conquerors in carrying out the tasks of ordinary life (fortunately his father was more prescient). Most refused to recognize that "the people they had to deal with now were motivated not by economic self-interest but by insane racial hatred—a hatred that could not be appeased."[5] To assume that the motivation of one's enemy is essentially similar to one's own can be a fatal error; and according to Pipes, the majority of scholars who studied the Soviet Union after the end of the Second World War were guilty of precisely such a misjudgment.

He learned Russian while serving in the U.S. Army during the war, picking it up very easily because of its similarity to his native Polish. As a graduate student at Harvard after being demobilized, he initially intended to study philosophy and law; but he shifted his attention to Russian history. His first book, which focused on the problem of nationalism and communism in the formation of the Soviet Union, already brought him into opposition to the reigning ideas on the subject. Even George Kennan,

[2] Ibid., 47.
[3] Ibid., 81.
[4] Ibid., 43.
[5] Ibid., 9.

"a well-informed and clear-headed expert,"[6] assumed that the numerous nationalities of which Soviet Russia was composed bore the same relation to each other as the various states in the United States. Pipes's studies convinced him of the erroneousness of such an analogy, and that Russia was "a multinational empire." "I was left in no doubt," he writes, "that should central authority in Russia weaken again, as had happened in 1917, the empire would fall apart. This prediction was vigorously contested by nearly all Russian specialists,"[7] but events have proven him to have been correct.

Pipe's hard-nosed views of Russian communism inevitably tended to bring him into conflict with what he calls "the Sovietological community,"[8] and he offers a polemical but quite persuasive analysis of its deficiencies. Large-scale concern for the Soviet Union began at the end of the Second World War and took off after the launching of Sputnik. It was thus shadowed by the prospect of a nuclear conflict that was to be avoided at all costs, and emphasis was placed on the similarities rather than the divergences between the two countries. Moreover, the instinctive American assumption that all people are much the same as themselves led to an implicit misinterpretation of Soviet Russian behavior. Whatever misunderstandings existed, it was taken for granted, could be ironed out by greater contacts and exchanges of ideas. "The net result of this methodology was to depict communist societies as not fundamentally different from democratic ones, a conclusion that reinforced the policy recommendations that we could and should come to terms with them."[9] Pipes cites one well-known scholar who wrote that probably one could find no "significant difference between the way New Haven was administered and any city of similar size in the Soviet Union."[10] Those who disagreed, like Pipes, were more or less ostracized by colleagues in the academy, who avoided inviting them to symposia and colloquia. An occasional ironic remark in the memoirs reveals the pique that he still continues to feel at such mistreatment in the past.

One result, however, was to lead him toward the study of those aspects of Russian culture and society that offered the most glaring contrasts with those of the West. After completing his work on nationalism, his attention thus focused on the study of Russian conservatism. As he rightly says, this subject has hardly received much attention from Russian scholarship either at home or abroad. The leading histories of Russian culture, even those written before the revolution, focused on opponents of the tsarist regime

---

[6] Ibid., 72.
[7] Ibid., 74.
[8] Ibid., 135.
[9] Ibid.
[10] Ibid.

who were advocating changes and reforms. But one reason for studying conservatism, he explains, was his attempt to answer the question of why "a government that had seized power in the name of the most radical ideals ever conceived [turned] so quickly into a bastion of reaction, exploiting radical slogans exclusively for purposes of external expansion."[11] Another was that, as he jotted down in a notebook (1956–57), "the conservative movement in Russia is much more indigenous, national, than either liberalism or socialism, [whose] intellectual content was largely imported from the West, whereas conservatism was local both in inception and development."[12]

The first product of this ambition was the rescue from relative oblivion of an important memoir written by the little-known (outside of Russia) but quite important author and historian Nikolay Karamzin, who occupies a significant place in Russian literature as well as Russian thought. Karamzin wrote the first widely read *History of the Russian State*, as well as stories that influenced Dostoevsky among others; and his account of his travels in Europe in the early days of the French Revolution includes a fascinating visit with Kant, who graciously explained to his foreign guest what he meant in the *Critique of Practical Reason*. Pipes, however, concentrates on a memoir that Karamzin wrote for Alexander I just before the Napoleonic invasion of Russia. Alexander was rumored to have been contemplating some measures limiting the powers of autocracy, and "Karamzin argued on the basis of historical evidence that absolutism was Russia's 'Palladium' or protective shield."[13] This "memoir" had never been translated, or even published in Russian in the scholarly edition that Pipes provided; and he thus performed a valuable service in making it more available.

Pipes has been a very prolific author, with thirty-eight books to his credit, but although frequently lecturing on the topic and being constantly preoccupied with the problems posed by the peculiar nature of Russian society, none until *Russian Conservatism and Its Critics* has been specifically devoted to Russian conservatism. In his view, Russia differed from all other European countries because, even after the monumental attempt of Peter the Great to transform it in conformity with the Western model, its rulers clung stubbornly and immutably to their own autocratic privileges instead of evolving along representative-democratic lines. In an influential book, *Russia under the Old Regime* (1974), Pipes expounded a wide-ranging theory that appeared to explain this anomaly.

[11] Ibid., 76.
[12] Ibid.
[13] Ibid., 77.

Briefly stated, it was a view of Russian society as being "patrimonial," a term initially used by Hobbes and then taken over and amplified by Max Weber. What it means is that when "the prince organizes his political power ... in the same essential manner as he does his authority over his household, there we speak of a *patrimonal state* structure."[14] The tsar thus "owned" everything within the state, which is simply considered his own property. No one individual or group has any right to counteract his power, nor is any distinction made between society and the state. Such a regime is different from despotism because "a despot violates his subjects' property rights; a patrimonial ruler does not even acknowledge their existence."[15] In his new book Pipes cites Machiavelli, who in the sixteenth century contrasted the sultan of Turkey with the king of France by pointing out that the former was "a ruler who treated his subjects like slaves"[16]; and Russia was much closer to Turkey in this respect than to any European country. This "patrimonial" mind-set, as it were, continued to dominate Russian politics up through the collapse of the Soviet Union and even, perhaps, beyond.

Russian Conservatism contains a useful summary of these ideas and of a later, more wide-ranging historical inquiry, *Property and Freedom* (1999), which buttresses Pipes's ideas with sections on England as well as material from anthropology and natural history. He begins by citing his old favorite, Nikolay Karamzin, who wrote that "autocracy has founded and resuscitated Russia," and that "any change in her political constitution has led in the past and must lead in the future to her perdition" (1). Why should this notion have had such a long Russian life? The chief answer, according to Pipes, is that "throughout European history, the existence of private property constituted the single most effective barrier to unlimited royal authority inasmuch as it compelled the kings to turn to their subjects for financial support and, in the process, to concede to them a share of political power" (3).

Other factors also enter, such as the submissive habits inculcated by the Mongol conquest of Russia for two centuries, and, by contrast, the influence of Roman law on European monarchies. Even feudalism in the West played a part because it involved a contract between lord and vassal, with mutual obligations on both sides that theoretically placed restraints on the power of the lord—something totally unknown in Russia. The control of the purse strings, however, is certainly the most crucial difference. Pipes

---

[14] Max Weber, *Wirtschaft und Gesellschaft* (Tübingen, 1947), 2:684; in Richard Pipes, *Russia under the Old Regime* (New York: Charles Scribner's Sons, 1974), 22.

[15] Pipes, *Russia under the Old Regime*, 23.

[16] Richard Pipes, *Russian Conservatism and Its Critics* (New Haven: Yale University Press, 2005), 22. Hereafter references to this work are cited in parentheses in the text.

cites a whole host of authorities, beginning in the thirteenth century, to illustrate that "the sanctity of private property was an axiom of European political thought and practice" (3).

Political controversy in Russia began about 1500, but the documentary evidence concerning it is very scarce and unreliable. Moreover, it had nothing to do with politics as such but rather with questions regarding church property and how it should be administered and controlled, as well as with ideas considered heretical. One group known as the Judaizers, some of whom were eventually burned at the stake, "translated into Slavonic the Pentateuch, Maimonides ... as well as Western secular works" (31). The opposing sides represented what would become a standard pattern of Russian culture—the conflict between ingrained native customs and reformist ideas from abroad. "The reformers were men like Maxim the Greek and Nil Sorsky, who had come from foreign countries or who had traveled there and mastered other languages;" against them stood Joseph of Volokolmansk and his followers, "who neither knew nor wanted to know about foreign ways.... Joseph and his adherents considered Russia 'Holy' and God's land ... they were frightened of 'corrupting' Russia under foreign influence even of Greek origin."

In Joseph's own writings, which are nothing but citations from one authority or another, he raised the tsar to hitherto unknown heights by declaring that while the monarch "in his being is like other men, in his authority he resembles God Almighty." To obey the sovereign "is tantamount to obeying God" (35). This deification of the Russian ruler continued in the sixteenth century. Ivan IV (the Terrible) was crowned with the title of tsar (Caesar) by the metropolitan of the Russian Church, a title later endorsed by the patriarch of Constantinople. After the fall of the Byzantine Empire, this led to the influential doctrine of Russia as the Third Rome, the head of the entire Christian community, summarized by the monk Filofei: "Two Romes have fallen, the third stands, and a fourth will not be" (39). This claim was buttressed with all sorts of pseudo-historical myths linking Russian history "with that of the Biblical Jews and ancient Romans.... In his dialogue with the Papal envoy ... Ivan IV claimed that he was descended from a brother of Augustus Caesar and that Russia had received her Christianity directly from the apostle Andrew" (41). Religion thus was used to reinforce the power of the state and offered no "alternatives to the status quo" (42).

The issue of autocracy was raised for the first time in a purely secular context by a Lithuanian, Ivan Peresvetov, who advised the tsar to disregard the inherited aristocratic boyar class and follow the example of Mahomet II, the conqueror of the Byzantine Empire. Mahomet collected all taxes himself, placed the nobles on a salary, and promoted by merit instead of rank; he also abolished slavery. The aim of this advice was to make the tsar even more powerful and independent, but on the basis of purely historical and nonreligious considerations. Contrary counsel was given in an exchange of letters between Ivan IV and a Muscovite noble, Prince Andrei Kurbsky, who had lost an important battle and fled to Catholic Lithuania fearing the wrath of the tsar. Living abroad, Kurbsky had read Aristotle and Cicero and refers to "laws of nature" that presumably rule over tsars as well; he thus advises Ivan to welcome "the counsel of eminent men of the realm." But Ivan replied: "How can a man be called an autocrat if he does not govern by himself," and he compared '"the rule of many" to be like "the folly of women" (44).

It was only under Peter the Great that "political theory in the true sense of the term, not as a mere compilation of opinions ... first emerged in Russia" (52). Peter's determination to Westernize his country led to the importation of ideas derived from such authors as Bodin, Hobbes, Locke, and others as well. Hence he adopted the novel (for Russia) notion "that the ruler and his subjects had joint responsibility for promoting the "common good." As a result, instead of merely issuing decrees, in some instances he even condescended to explain their purpose. In practice, however, he "carried on the patrimonial tradition [and] denied Russians any aspirations of their own" (53), since "the common good" included state service not only for the nobility but for all Russians. Peter's execution of his own son Alexis also led to a spate of writings by erudite scholars arguing that the absolute authority of the tsar gave him the right to bequeath his patrimony to anyone he wished and to exclude his eldest son.

The inconsistency that one observes in Peter, who desired both to adopt Western ideas and to stifle their consequences, continued to haunt all attempts to reform Russian institutions. Nowhere is this more apparent than with Catherine the Great, the friend of Voltaire and Diderot, who even drew up a *Nakaz*, "a kind of philosophical treatise defining the principles of good government" (70), four-fifths of which was cribbed from Montesquieu's *Spirit of the Laws*. But Catherine, as Pipes notes, "borrowed from him in a highly selective manner, ignoring his doctrine of freedom and the separation of powers as freedom's precondition" (69). Montesquieu distinguished between monarchy and despotism by viewing the first as ruled by "fixed and established laws," whereas in the second, "one alone directs everything by his own will and caprice" (69). Montesquieu himself considered Catherine to be a despot, despite her efforts to appear otherwise.

Especially after the French Revolution broke out, she brooked no opposition to her own authority, even persecuting and finally imprisoning a harmless publicist named Nicholas Novikov, who had established a printing press that, among its usual philanthropic and mildly satirical publications, also issued the first overt attack on serfdom. Novikov had joined a Masonic lodge in Moscow to which Karamzin also belonged, and he was active as well in organizing famine relief—though Catherine herself had written to Voltaire that "in Russia there is no peasant who does not eat a chicken whenever he feels like it" (65). To explain such a delusory statement, Pipes offers a choice between hypocrisy and "intellectual schizophrenia"—deciding for the latter, in which wishes are detached from realities.

The same situation occurred with Catherine's grandson Alexander I, who told his Swiss tutor La Harpe that "once crowned he would convene a representative assembly to draft a constitution that would divest him of all authority" (79). All sorts of reforms were discussed by Alexander and a group of intimates who had lived abroad, and a document guaranteeing freedom of speech and religion was drawn up and supposedly to be announced at Alexander's coronation. "But for some reason this was not done, and it remained a dead letter" (80). One of Pipes's heroes, Michael Speransky, helped to write this document, and his name may be more familiar to nonspecialists in Russian history than most of the others.

Readers of *War and Peace*, which Pipes regrettably does not mention, will recall that Prince Andrey Bolkonsky at one point serves in Speransky's cabinet. At first, much impressed with Speransky's ideas about reform, he undertakes the task assigned him of revising the Civil Code; "and with the aid of the *Code Napoleon* and the Institutes of Justinian he worked at formulating the section on Personal Rights."[17] A bit later in the book, he thinks of the impressions gathered during recent trip home to his estate, and of his experiences with the peasants. "Mentally applying to them the Personal Rights he had divided into paragraphs, he felt astonished that he could have spent so much time on such useless work."[18]

Tolstoy's image of Speransky is thus quite deprecatory, and Pipes believes that the merits of this statesman have been neglected in accounts of Russian thought because officials of the tsarist establishment are not usually considered part of the country's intellectual life. Also, the full extent of his "reform projects" were not entirely known until the twentieth century. Still, he gained the admiration of Napoleon, who jokingly offered to trade a kingdom for him, and he was the first Russian political thinker to stress the importance for a government of obtaining the support of public opinion. He saw the governments of his own day as evolving inevitably from autocracy to republicanism, with Russia being at a stage where it was gradually moving from the former to the latter. He also prophetically defined the problem that, as Pipes sees it, would continue "to plague Russia for the next one hundred years." "What a contradiction" Speransky wrote:

---

[17] Lev Tolstoy, *War and Peace*, trans. Louise Maude and Aylmer Maude (Hertfordshire: Wordsworth Editions, 1993), 340.
[18] Ibid., 367

"to desire sciences, commerce and industry and to thwart their most natural consequences; to wish the mind to be free and the will to be in shackles" (84). Speransky's downfall was caused at least in part by the criticism of his ideas by the Karamzin who Pipes had studied long before, and to whom he now returns for another run-through. In Karamzin's view, unlimited autocracy was the only possible form of government for Russia.

The last years of the reign of Alexander I, despite the victory over Napoleon, were marked by an obscurantism that appeared to eliminate any possibility of liberalization; but this eventually led to the Decembrist uprising of 1825. The Russian armies had occupied France and Germany for three years, and such a prolonged contact with European life made the Russian nobility aware, as one of them put it, that "it was possible to have civic order and flourishing kingdoms without slavery" (91). Various secret societies were thus formed, which developed plans to replace uncontrolled autocracy. One group preferred constitutional monarchy; another, more radical, opted for a republic. On the death of Alexander, they attempted to seize power in a coup more public than the palace revolutions of the past; but it was ludicrously unsuccessful and easily overcome by the new tsar, Nicholas I. Five Decembrists were hanged, and more than one hundred sent into exile to Siberia. The effect of the Decembrist revolt was thus only to strengthen the conservative, pro-autocratic forces already ruling Russian affairs.

Pipes then goes on to discuss writers like Pushkin and Gogol, both of whom supported the regime of Nicholas I in their own way though their opinions are only remotely related to actual politics. Pushkin flaunted some liberal tendencies as a young man and was a friend of a number of Decembrists; but he ultimately concluded that "in Russia it was the government that has always led in education and enlightenment" (97). Gogol's pietistic *Selected Correspondence with Friends*, whose religious message contained an implicit defense "of serfdom and class privilege," aroused the fury of the radical critic Belinsky, who labeled him an "advocate of the knout, apostle of ignorance, champion of obscurantism, eulogist of Tatar ways" (111).

Much less familiar, though quite important, is Pyotr Chaadaev, who was influenced by French Roman Catholic opponents of their own revolution such as Bonald and Joseph de Maistre (the latter had lived in Russia for a number of years and wrote a book entitled *Soirees de St. Petersbourg*). A former dandy and elegant Guards officer, Chaadaev shocked his contemporaries by declaring that Russia had no future because it had adopted Christianity from miserable Byzantium, "the object of profound contempt of the Northern nations" (105). Declared insane by order of the tsar, he later changed his mind and wrote an *Apology of a Madman*, in which he argued that the barrenness of Russia's past augured well for its future since the way was clear for innovation. The Slavophile movement was partly a response to Chaadaev and glorified a mythical version of the Russian past as based on peaceful acceptance of autocratic rule rather than the violence of the West. The Slavophiles also developed "a political theory which in some ways was innovative" (109). State and society were sharply separated; and while unlimited autocracy had its legitimate sphere in the first, the state had no right to "encroach on the private lives of its citizens" (110). Of course nothing came of this second idea in practice.

Russia's defeat in the Crimean War led to a series of reforms under Alexander II, the tsar-liberator, that initiated a new era in Russian history. The serfs were freed in 1861, "city councils and rural *zemstva*" (councils) were created that included peasant deputies, "and Russia for the first time got an independent judiciary and trial by jury" (117). As a result, "Russian conservatism now was broadened to include the nation at large"; but while in the past it had been cosmopolitan, "it now acquired nationalistic and in more extreme cases, chauvinistic, xenophobic and anti-Semitic forms" (117). Pipes then turns to a figure like Mikhail Katkov, the influential magazine editor who published Turgenev, Tolstoy, and Dostoevsky. Beginning as an admirer of English constitutionalism, he ended by asking for the abolition of trial by jury and the deprivation of the autonomy of the universities. Less prominent is Iury Samarin, a conservative of a distinguished noble family who helped to write the legislation freeing the serfs. But he opposed any weakening of the autocracy, even though he was in favor of freedom of speech and press and other reforms, because the Russian people were not yet capable of dealing with the issues of government. The Slavophiles also became more viciously reactionary as time went on, and Pipes speaks of their most influential spokesman Ivan Aksakov as "anticipating the notorious *Protocols of the Elders of Zion*" (135) in his fulminations against the Jews.

Dostoevsky also makes his appearance in this section, although Pipes rightly says that "his greatness ... lay not in political analysis ... but in the grasp he had of the underlying psychological implications of radicalism, which he understood better than any of his contemporaries" (137). Indeed, he not only understood it but portrayed it with such power and insight that one wonders whether, in opposing radicalism, Dostoevsky did not also inadvertently arouse sympathy for it at the same time. It is hardly accurate, however, to speak of him as having had "a brief youthful flirtation with radical ideas" (136). His so-called flirtation, as Pipes fails to mention, included membership in a secret underground organization in which he played an active role and that hoped to stir up a revolution against serfdom. Dostoevsky's affiliation with such a group became public knowledge only long after his death, and he lived with this secret all his life. This helps to explain both his devotion to Alexander II, who had accomplished Dostoevsky's revolutionary aim, and his ability to portray his major radical characters as locked in irresolvable moral-psychological conflicts. The solution could be found only in a genuine Christianity that Dostoevsky tended to identify with Russian Orthodoxy, and thus with a return to the beliefs of the traditionally Christian Russian people—which included unfailing devotion to their autocratic tsar, whose family, as Pipes might have informed his readers, included admirers of Dostoevsky's novels.

One of Dostoevsky's intimates in the later years of his life was Konstantin Pobedonostsev, the procurator of the Holy Synod, the highest nonclerical official of the Russian Church. Initially a professor of civil law at the University of Moscow, he had also been the tutor of Alexander III, who succeeded to the throne after the assassination of his father by the radical Nihilists. These latter had turned to terrorism after having been unable to make any headway among the people. Pobedonostsev was influential in persuading his ex-pupil against carrying out the extremely modest reform that, as a means of combating Nihilist influence, was being considered at the time of his father's death. This reform would have consisted of allowing committees elected by city councils and *zemstvas* to consult with the government, and whose function would be purely advisory. But such a proposal reminded its opponents too much of the Estates-General convened for advice by Louis XVI at the beginning of the French Revolution, and it was put aside. Instead, the tsar issued a manifesto declaring that he would maintain an unalloyed autocracy, and Katkov welcomed it "like manna from heaven" (142). In a book translated as *Reflections of a Russian Statesman* (1896), Pobedonostsev denounced all the institutions of Western democracy as leading to disaster.

Pipes also includes in this section the fascinating and original figure of Konstantin Leontiev, sometimes called the Russian Nietszche, who does not fit into any of the usual categories. His contempt for modernity was based partly on aesthetic grounds—an admiration of the diversity of life that he found in the Orient (he served as Russian consul for ten years in various parts of the Turkish Empire). He developed an anti-Hegelian theory of history as consisting of diverse cultural-historical types that anticipated Spengler, and he advocated the "freezing" of Russian development by the autocratic monarchy to prevent Russia from evolving along Western European lines. With little or no influence during his lifetime, one of his perorations has since achieved some notoriety. In it he asked whether Moses ascended Mt. Sinai, the Greeks built their "graceful Acropolises," the Romans waged the Punic Wars, Alexander the Great invaded the Orient, "apostles prophesied, martyrs suffered, poets sung, painters painted and knights shone at tourneys only so that a French, German and Russian bourgeois in his ugly and comical attire would enjoy life" (148–49). Pipes might have also mentioned that Leontiev criticized *The Brothers Karamazov* for being too strongly affected by the hope of a Christian transformation of earthly life. The critic finds no warrant for this in the New Testament and traces it—correctly, in my opinion—to a residual Utopian socialist influence.

The last two chapters of the book deal with what Pipes calls "conservative liberals," that is, a group of publicists and one or two politicians who were strong supporters of the monarchy but believed that, without weakening its powers, the autocratic rule could nonetheless profit from more consultation with *zemstva* organizations closer to local concerns. Nothing of the sort occurred, however, and Pipes considers "the most fatal mistake committed by Tsarism in the late 19th century" to be the rejection by Nicholas II, shortly after his coronation, of the numerous requests addressed to the crown that he move in this direction. "By repelling the moderates, it pushed them into the hands of the radicals" (167).

Nonetheless, in October 1905 a general strike that paralyzed the country led to the promise to grant the country a constitution and an elected legislature. This was done, but the provisions of the constitution were constantly violated. Pipes's hero at this point is Peter Stolypin, hailed as "Imperial Russia's last great statesman" (174), who became prime minister in 1906 and was assassinated in 1911. One of his major aims was to abolish the peasant commune, which had been seen both on the right and left as the bulwark against the formation of a European proletariat. But it had not prevented the formation of a rural Russian proletariat, and it served as a brake on the economic initiative of the peasantry.

What Stolypin desired was the formation of a class of small peasant landowners, who would provide a bulwark against revolutionary upheaval because of their ownership of property. He also proposed, unsuccessfully, a sweeping series of reforms that would have reversed "the tradition of Russian governments of treating society as a body without legitimate interests of its own, whose sole function was to serve the state" (177). A few years later the Russian Revolution broke out, and "a new form of autocracy came into being, far more despotic and lawless than the previous one" (173). Lenin defined the "dictatorship of the proletariat" as "power that is limited by nothing" (173–74), and the Russian patrimonial tradition thus continued to reign adorned with new, Marxist-Leninist trappings.

There is a passage in *Vixi* in which Pipes describes an idea that occurred to him after comparing his impressions of visits to both Soviet Russia and China. "Ideas accommodate themselves," he concluded, "to the cultural soil on which they fall. Thus Marxism in Scandinavia, where traditions of property and law were relatively strong, evolved first into social democracy and then into the democratic welfare state. In Russia, where both traditions were weakly developed, it reinforced the autocratic, patrimonial heritage."[19] The persistence of this heritage came to my mind when, in the *New York Times* on February 4, 2006, I read an interview with Andrei Ilarionov, who had been an economic adviser to Vladimir Putin before resigning in protest in December.

What caused his resignation was the efforts being made by Putin to reappropriate the private-sector companies that had been acquired by individuals, and to establish what Ilarionov calls state-corporatism over which Russian citizens have little or no control. Are we not seeing here the reappearance of the patrimonial tradition, now in a refurbished pseudo-capitalist guise? Pipes's book, besides being a sweeping and valuably informative historical survey, thus may help us better to understand some of the anomalies of post-Gorbachevian Russia.

---

[19] Pipes, *Vixi*, 118.

PART III
THE DOSTOEVSKIAN ORBIT

TEN

DOSTOEVSKY AND ANTI-SEMITISM

LET ME BEGIN with something of a confession. My own work on Dostoevsky originally began by my interest in his relation to the radical ideology of his time. It seemed to me to have been neglected, particularly in Western interpretations of his work, perhaps largely through ignorance. The Russian scholarship, though factually of great value, was hampered by ideological limitations. My focus was therefore on his relation to radical ideology, and the question of his anti-Semitism seemed to me a relatively unimportant issue that did not enter significantly into those aspects of his work in which I had the most interest.

The best book on his anti-Semitism is still the late David Goldstein's *Dostoevsky and the Jews*, published first in French in 1976 and in English in 1981.[1] It so happened that David Goldstein was a close personal friend, with whom I collaborated on editing a translation of selected letters of Dostoevsky still in print. He asked me to write an introduction to the English version of his book, and it was then that I was confronted head-on for the first time with the problem of Dostoevsky's anti-Semitism.

Previously I had thought that such a topic was rather similar to the old story about a mythical Academy of Sciences, which announced a competition for papers about the elephant. One of the entries it received was entitled "The Elephant and the Jewish Question." But after reading the book, I changed my mind. It was perfectly true that, in the corpus of Dostoevsky's work as a whole, the Jewish Question played a very minor role. Indeed, except for one character in his semifictional prison memoirs, one scene in *The Brothers Karamazov*, and one article on the subject, it never appears as such except in side remarks. But there is no question that, for every admirer of his novels and stories, it poses a very serious challenge.

This challenge may be formulated in the following way. What we find in Dostoevsky's work, among a good deal else that shall have to be neglected here, is an intense humanity, an intense concern and empathy for those who have been oppressed and humiliated. Dostoevsky is the unsurpassed portrayer of the tortures and torments of the downtrodden sensibility, of those, as he wrote himself, who have been insulted and injured. The

---

This is the text of a lecture given at Harvard University in the fall of 2002.
[1] David Goldstein, *Dostoevsky and the Jews* (Austin, 1981).

crimes that are committed in his books are invariably inspired by a desire to rectify in some way a world in which such injustices exist.

The murders committed by Raskolnikov, for example, misguided though he may have been, were still nominally perpetrated for the benefit of mankind. Pyotr Verkhovensky in *Demons* is the leader of a group that commits a murder for political reasons. He is someone who has rejected morality of any kind for political expediency; but even he expresses a twinge of pity for the miseries of mankind that may be improved in the future. *The Idiot* is the novel in which Dostoevsky tried to portray his positive Christian ideal, one that is too sublime to be fully realized in this world except by Christ himself. But there is one sentence that sums up the moral goal toward which he thought all of mankind should strive. "Compassion was the chief and perhaps the only law of all human existence," thinks Prince Myshkin.[2] And while this thought comes to him in the euphoric period just before an epileptic fit, it still expresses Dostoevsky's highest positive ideal.

One can well understand why the Russian Jewish readers of Dostoevsky's own time would have been greatly moved by this appeal for compassion as the supreme moral virtue. They would certainly have felt, or would have liked to feel, that the universal compassion he advocated applied to them as well; and this is why they became so troubled by the anti-Semitic aspects of his writings. But it was not only a century and a half ago that this problem troubled readers and admirers of Dostoevsky.

In 1980 a Russian Jewish scientist named Leonid Tsypkin published a novel called *A Summer in Baden-Baden* that first appeared, incidentally, in a Russian-language journal in New York though Tsypkin was living in Russia. This book again illustrates, with great poignancy, how contemporary this issue is for Russians of Jewish origins who admire Dostoevsky.[3] One of its narrative strands is focused on Dostoevsky himself, whose life is dramatized with great expressive power. But this is not what concerns me here. Another strand is my main concern—the one that attempts to cope with the author's self-questioning about his own fascination with, and admiration for, Dostoevsky.

Such admiration is greatly troubled by Dostoevsky's anti-Semitism, which the author finds it so difficult to comprehend. How could it be that a man so sensitive to the suffering of others should not have uttered even a single word in defense or justification of a people persecuted over several thousands of years? Tsypkin also remarks on the peculiar fact that the Russian scholars who have gained a practical monopoly on the study of Dostoevsky are mainly of Jewish origin. Why this Jewish preoccupation

---

[2] F. M. Dostoevsky, *Polnoe Sobranie Sochinenii*, 30 vols. (Leningrad, 1972–1990), 8:192. Hereafter cited as *PSS*.

[3] See chapter 11, "In Search of Dostoevsky."

with Dostoevsky? In my own opinion, the answer lies in the persistent attempt to fathom, or at least to comprehend, the mysterious anomaly that lies in his work. On the one hand, there is the intense sensitivity to human suffering; on the other, the adamant refusal, at least after a certain point in his career, to extend such sensitivity to the Jews. This is an issue that bothers not only his Russian Jewish readers but all those who read and admire his works and are not anti-Semitic themselves.

Let us now take a look at the evidence of the work itself. The first item related to this question is one that, if it was ever written, has been lost. All we know is its title: *The Jew Yankel.* Dostoevsky mentions this in a letter of 1844, at the very beginning of his literary career, and refers to it as a play that he has finished.[4] At this time he was also translating Balzac's novel *Eugénie Grandet* and working over his own first novel, *Poor Folk*. It was also the moment when he was shifting from the writing of Romantic tragedies to the new realism championed by the influential critic Vissarion Belinsky. The idea of writing a play about a figure whose name indicates his lowly origins thus fits in with this trend.

The Jew Yankel is a minor character in Gogol's novel *Taras Bulba*, which glorified the military exploits of the Cossacks then fighting the Poles. Yankel is depicted there as a wretched, cowardly, and miserable figure, interested only in saving his own skin and accumulating money. The avariciousness of the Jews, of course, is a stock trait of their depiction in European literature as a whole. Taras Bulba, though, had once saved Yankel's life, and Yankel thus undertakes the dangerous task of smuggling his erstwhile benefactor into Warsaw. This involves a certain inner struggle in Yankel because he knows that a price has been placed on the head of Taras. "He was ashamed of his avarice," Gogol writes, "and tried to stifle the eternal thought of gold, which twines like a snake about the soul of a Jew."[5] He did stifle it in this instance, though Taras rewards him richly in any case. The Jew Yankel then became a prototype for the portrayal of the Jewish character in Russian literature. How Dostoevsky would have handled his own version of it remains unknown.

In Dostoevsky's novels and stories of the 1840s, there are numerous demeaning and uncomplimentary references to Jews that were part of Russian common speech and Russian attitudes. But no Jewish character is portrayed. It was only in his prison memoirs, published in 1861, that such a figure appears. Named Isai Fomich Bumstein, and based on one of the author's fellow convicts, Bumstein (not the convict's real name) may well have been the first Jewish person with whom Dostoevsky had had any prolonged contact. He is also one of the very few Jewish literary characters

---

[4] *PSS*, 28/bk. 1:86.
[5] N. V. Gogol, *Polnoe Sobranie Sochinenii*, 14 vols. (Moscow, 1940–1952), 2:130.

of the time given more than a type-name like Yankel and portrayed as an individual. Jews were not allowed to live except in the outlying provinces of the Russian Empire, and it was not until the 1860s that certain exceptions were made. In any case, Dostoevsky provides a detailed portrait of this prison-mate, treated as a comic figure and caricature said to resemble Gogol's Yankel.

The other convicts taunted Isai for their own amusement, "simply for fun," as Dostoevsky writes, "just as one teases dogs, parrots, or any sort of trained animal."[6] In these conversational exchanges, though, we see Isai giving back as good as he got. Dostoevsky assures us that everybody was fond of him, and nobody was ever offensive to him. He was a skilled jeweler who also worked for people in the town (Solzhenitsyn comments with amazement in the *Gulag Archipelago* that the convicts Dostoevsky describes had enough energy to work after-hours). This was certainly not the case in Soviet camps, where the inmates were worked to the limits of exhaustion—and even beyond. Bumstein was also, as was to be expected, a moneylender, and almost everyone was in his debt.

The portrait of Bumstein that Dostoevsky offers certainly contains extremely unattractive features; but it is hardly viciously hostile. Various commentators have interpreted it in diverse ways, and Goldstein divides them into three groups. Some see the image as definitely anti-Semitic; others think the opposite; and those in the middle believe that the attitude of Dostoevsky cannot be summed up in any sort of categorical formula. I would place myself among this middle group. As a matter of fact, one of the most baffling and even infuriating aspects of this whole question is that, even when Dostoevsky is at his most explicitly and overtly anti-Semitic, he will then advocate a practical position that appears to be the exact opposite. How seriously should this latter be taken? It is really impossible to say with any assurance, and we shall come back to this issue.

But let me turn to Bumstein again, and to Dostoevsky's portrayal. However caricatural it is, there is no indication of any hostility. Bumstein is simply one of the curiosities of the Russian world that the author happens to encounter in his prison surroundings. It is this absence of overt hostility that inclines me to conclude that the treatment of Bumstein is not *malignantly* anti-Semitic as this term has come to be understood. He and the author simply live in different worlds that do not intersect, and to evidence hostility, instead of amused contempt, would be to imply a degree of preoccupation that does not exist. Goldstein is an extremely harsh critic of Dostoevsky's anti-Semitism; but even he notes that in the famous bathhouse scene of the book, which Turgenev compared to Dante, "it is

---

[6] Fyodor Dostoevsky, *The House of the Dead and Poor Folk*, trans. Constance Garnett (New York: Barnes and Noble Classics, 2004), 119.

with sympathy, if not affection, that he [Dostoevsky] evokes 'the blissful countenance of my prison comrade and barracks mate, the unforgettable Isai Fomich."[7]

One of the pioneering works in English on the problem of Russian literature and anti-Semitism is that of Joshua Kunitz, published in 1929 and now quite out of date.[8] But it is still useful for certain basic distinctions. At first, Jews were depicted in stereotypes taken from European writers like Shakespeare, Marlowe, or Walter Scott by writers who had little or no acquaintance with them at all. This is the case with Pushkin or the now-forgotten dramatist Nestor Kukolnik, who Dostoevsky cites in his essay on "The Jewish Question." A bit later, with someone like the Ukrainian Gogol to whom Jews were more familiar, there was the contempt already noted, not always as good-natured as we see in Dostoevsky. But the early 1860s saw the liberation of the serfs and brought about another change, quite temporary and short-lived though of relevance to our topic.

In this era of relative liberalism, several of the most onerous laws regarding Jews were abolished. They were now free to live in certain areas from which they had been excluded, and a general feeling prevailed, especially among the intelligentsia, that efforts should be made to integrate them into Russian society. When a journal in 1858 printed an article against Jewish emancipation, claiming they were unworthy of such benevolence, three other journals printed a protest signed by everyone of prominence in cultural life at that moment. Dostoevsky, it should be noted, had not yet returned from Siberia. In November 1861, as a follow-up to these efforts, it was decreed that Jews with doctorates from a university should be allowed to serve in all government offices and settle anywhere in the country.

The Jewish question was thus a matter of great relevance at this time. Dostoevsky and his brother Mikhail had founded a journal called *Time* in January 1861, and their magazine naturally took a stand on this issue. In each of the four items they printed touching on Jews, they strongly supported the cause of greater tolerance. The most important of these interventions concerned the Jews (obviously a very small number) with doctorates. The Slavophile journal *Day*, even though its editors had signed the earlier petition, now protested that a Jew could thus become the procurator of the Holy Synod, the nonclerical body administering the affairs of the Orthodox Church. They argued that Jews do not accept Christian ideals and ethics, and while they should have full freedom to develop in their own way (even to live anywhere in Russia), they should not be allowed to have administrative or legislative rights.

---

[7] Goldstein, *Dostoevsky and the Jews*, 21.
[8] Joshua Kunitz, *Russian Literature and the Jews* (New York, 1929).

Time took up the cudgels to defend the Jews against this attack. It printed an unsigned article whose author may have been Dostoevsky (he was managing editor) or one of the other contributors to the journal. In any case, Dostoevsky as editor would have sponsored its publication. It should also be noted that, as editor, he often added notes to articles about one or another point that he disagreed with or wished to be qualified; but no such note appeared here. The tone of the article is more one of sorrow than of anger.

"Pitiful friends," it said, "who do more harm to Christianity than do its enemies." As for a Jew becoming procurator of the Holy Synod, the article finds the raising of this possibility "superfluous, unnecessary, and uninteresting." "If there is something in Judaism threatening to Christianity," the writer argued, Christianity can only find protection in its own faith, not by passing laws against the Jews. In the end, this could lead to burning or hanging them, on the ground that after all they had crucified Christ. The article concludes: "It is not this spirit ... that inspired the teachings of Him in whose name *Day* is apparently speaking. The teachings of peace, love, and concord should have prompted other thoughts and other words." The Slavophile journal replied to this attack by printing an article about the Talmud with distorted references aimed at showing that Jews could not be entrusted with government service. *Time* then replied with an eighteen-page article by a Jewish journalist disproving these allegations.[9]

It would be difficult to find a more pro-Jewish position in the context of the period, and one should perhaps keep this in mind when Dostoevsky protests later that he is not an anti-Semite. There is a tendency in the literature—it is found in Goldstein—to dismiss this pro-Jewish stance as a tactical maneuver in the heated literary polemics of the period. Dostoevsky wished his journal to preserve a reputation as "progressive" while in fact entering into polemics with radicals like Nikolay Chernyshevsky and his journal *The Contemporary*. The implication is that this article cannot (or should not) be taken as representing Dostoevsky's own genuine and sincere views.

There is of course no way of establishing this point one way or the other. Was this objection to *Day* only a polemical ploy, or does such an idea represent something more fundamental for Dostoevsky that continued to exercise its influence? It is worth noting that, in a jotting he set down in the very last month of his life, he uses much the same terms. This note does not concern the Jews, and in writing it he probably had in mind his

---

[9] See Goldstein, *Dostoevsky and the Jews*, 39–40; also V. S. Nechaeva, *Zhurnal M. M. i. F.M Dostoevskikh, "Vremya," 1861–1863* (Moscow, 1972), 29.

own depiction of an auto-da-fé in the Legend of the Grand Inquisitor. But the issue is the same—the use of force to suppress religious views that one rejects or even abhors. "For me," he wrote, "there is only one moral model and ideal, Christ. I ask: Would He have burned heretics—no. So that means the burning of heretics is an immoral act."[10] With this note in mind, one can accept the earlier article as perhaps a journalistic maneuver without discrediting it entirely as expressing something that Dostoevsky felt (and continued to feel) very deeply. The self-contradictions already mentioned in his attitude toward the Jews may thus well be taken as the reflection of an inner conflict between his inbred anti-Semitism and his Christian ideals.

The 1860s is the period of Dostoevsky's marvelous burst of three great novels, to be followed by the fourth, *The Brothers Karamazov*. In one of my volumes, I labeled it "the marvelous decade." There is very little here that concerns anti-Semitism directly, but Jews do enter the novels in several ways. One is the sentence in *Crime and Punishment* depicting the intellectually sophisticated villain Svidrigailov before he shoots himself. He does so in the presence of a Jewish fireman wearing an Achilles helmet and speaking garbled Russian. "His face [the fireman's] wore that look of eternal peevish affliction that is so sourly imprinted on all the faces of the Jewish tribe without exception."[11] The combination of this remark and the Achilles helmet, with its evocation of a heroic classical past, has led to a rash of interpretation that there is no need to go into here.

Goldstein notes that the late émigré critic Wladimir Weidlé, whose penetrating insights into Russian culture I admire, saw nothing symbolic in this scene, and I am glad to have his support for my own point of view. If there is any symbolism here, it is perhaps that of Svidrigailov's own hopelessness and despair. The world for him has been transformed into a nightmare of evil and corruption. He has just awakened from a dream in which he had given shelter from the rain to a little five-year-old girl, and she had turned into a shameless prostitute. The narrator here, though nominally objective, is conveying Svidrigailov's desolate vision of the world in these last moments, and the remark about the Jews constitutes part of this vision. To give it a marked anti-Semitic significance seems to me, in this instance, greatly exaggerated.

There is no Jewish character in Dostoevsky's next novel, *The Idiot*, but it contains the first appearance of "the Rothschild idea." Dostoevsky could well have come across such a notion in his socialist days in the 1840s. Some of these early Utopian socialists were quite anti-Semitic (Fourier in

[10] *PSS*, 27:56.
[11] *PSS*, 6:394.

particular), and Dostoevsky belonged to the Petrashevsky circle, whose leader wrote that "some clever banker like Rothschild"[12] always took advantage of the banking system and the stock market.

In his wonderful memoirs, *My Past and Thoughts*, Herzen describes how James Rothschild forced the tsar of all the Russias, Nicholas I, to release the money of an estate left to him though he was a political exile. Rothschild is here called "King of the Jews," whose power equals that of the greatest monarch, and there are numerous references to this appellation in the notes for *The Idiot*. Dostoevsky also was familiar with Heine's *On the History of Religion and Philosophy in Germany*, with its ironically amused account of the regular visits of the papal envoy in Paris to the office of James Rothschild to pay interest on the papal debt. One of the Christian characters in *The Idiot* expresses the ambition to squeeze money out of people and become like the "king of the Jews" (which would indicate that such ambition is hardly only a Jewish trait), and there is a side remark of the same kind but nothing else. However, this equation of the Jews with the ability to exercise power on the world scene because of their wealth was to remain with Dostoevsky and reappear several years later in the *Diary of a Writer*.

The Jewish issue also arises in *Demons*, Dostoevsky's next novel, but in a different form. Here it appears indirectly in the character of Lyamshin, one of the members of the radical group of Pyotr Verkhovensky. Lyamshin is of Jewish origin, as the narrator remarks, but he is completely assimilated and there is nothing Jewish about his appearance or behavior, except perhaps that he serves as a kind of entertainer. He plays the piano very well, improvises on it, and in the novel invents a musical contest between the "Marseilaise" and "Mein Lieber Augustin" to illustrate the Franco-Prussian War.

He has all the demeaning personal traits of the Jew Yankel, and it should be noted that he could mimic various Jewish types as well as a woman giving birth. This latter feat parodies one of the most moving scenes of the book, the birth of a child to the wife of Shatov, who is murdered by the revolutionary group. Lyamshin is not present at the killing of Shatov, and when he shows up he breaks down completely and begins to scream in some sort of inhuman voice. There is also a rumor that he had desecrated an icon, but if so, this offense was committed with the collaboration of a genuinely Orthodox Russian peasant. When he confesses to knowledge of the murder, he behaves abjectly, unlike the others who retain a modicum of dignity, and he even offers to act as a spy.

The image of Lyamshin here fits in with the transformation in the status of Russian Jewry that occurred during the 1860s. The Jews had been of-

---

[12] Goldstein, *Dostoevsky and the Jews*, 59.

fered the possibility of assimilation, and Lyamshin is an example of this new type. Kunitz notes its appearance, and Dostoevsky, whether deliberately or not, was following a trend evident in other writers as well. The earlier contempt turned to hatred in this period, to use Kunitz's terms, and thus the older patronizing anti-Semitism took on a new and much more virulent form. But should the portrait of Lyamshin, considered in the context of the novel as a whole, be taken only as displaying anti-Semitism? Certainly he presents a quite repellent image; but one should note also the savage satire of other elements of Russian society. To take only one example, the dim-witted numbskull of a governor-general totally unaware of what is going on, who allows chaos to break loose and amuses himself with manipulating a toy theater. Even though Lyamshin's character fits the anti-Semitic stereotype (he is also terribly tight-fisted about money), he hardly stands out sufficiently from the others, in any negative way, to justify a charge of arrant bigotry.

It is during the 1870s that Dostoevsky's concern with the Jewish question takes on a new intensity and a new animosity. By this time some assimilated Jews, many of whom were converted to Orthodoxy, had begun to assume an important place in Russian society and were no longer living on its fringes. Much of the railroad construction of the period, for example, was financed by Jewish capital, whether of Russian origin or coming from abroad. And there was also Dostoevsky's growing uneasiness over the mounting influence of the radicals on the young generation, as well as the vehemently patriotic passions excited by the Russo-Turkish War of 1877–78. England was the chief supporter of Turkey at this time, and Dostoevsky never forgot that its prime minister, Disraeli, was what he called a Spanish Yid.

I have been criticized by the English Slavist Aileen Kelly, whose work I value very highly, for having linked the increasingly anti-Semitic utterances of Dostoevsky in these years to such extraneous socioeconomic and political matters. Kelly sees Dostoevsky's anti-Semitism as rooted in the millenarianism that begins to appear in his journalistic writings of the 1860s, and then occupies an increasingly prominent place in his *Diary of a Writer* beginning in 1873. But there is no trace of anti-Semitism in the articles of the 1860s (quite the contrary, as we have seen). There are all sorts of uncomplimentary references to Jews there, as well as to other nationalities like the Poles and the Germans (Dostoevsky was very xenophobic), but nothing like the blatant anti-Semitism that came later.

Kelly views Dostoevsky as fixed and immutable from the 1860s on in a millenarian frame of mind rooted in the belief that Russia was destined by God to save the Christian world. In the past, as Norman Cohen has shown in his classic *Pursuit of the Millennium*, such millenarian expectations inevitably led to anti-Semitic pogroms. My own view is that a more or less normal anti-Semitism (if I am allowed such a phrase) was always there, as it was in Russian culture as a whole, but that its intensification in the 1870s was consistent with the changes taking place in Russian life. Dostoevsky was always responding to these changes and did so quite specifically, for example, to the evolution of radical ideology. The same occurred with his anti-Semitism. This was sharply exacerbated in the 1870s because of the conditions already mentioned, and by the general disillusionment, which Dostoevsky shared to a great degree, with the initial hopes stirred ten years earlier by the reforms of Alexander II.

In 1873 Dostoevsky began to print the articles of his *Diary of a Writer* in the extremely conservative journal *The Citizen*, of which he became the editor for about a year. Three years later he began to publish his *Diary* as an independent monthly, and it became the most widely read publication of its kind ever to have appeared in Russia. It is in the *Diary* that Dostoevsky's anti-Semitism shows up in its most naked and belligerent form. Here, in article after article, we find him belaboring the Jews in the most insulting language. He never missed a chance to berate "the crowd of triumphant Jews and kikes that has thrown itself on Russia ... kikes ... both of the Hebraic and Orthodox persuasion."[13] He depicts them as sucking the lifeblood of the liberated but hopelessly indebted peasantry, and as ruthless batteners on the misery of others. Like James Rothschild, they are also concealed masters and manipulators of world politics as well.

The Jewish readers and admirers of Dostoevsky (and even of the *Diary*, which contains two of his most beautiful short stories) wrote in to protest. Dostoevsky carefully filed these letters but answered only two of them, one from a young girl named Sofya Lurie he had met earlier in Petersburg. The other was from a convict in a Moscow prison named Arkady Kovner (a Russianized form of his name), whose letter was so impressive that Dostoevsky said "he had rarely read anything more intelligent."[14] Dostoevsky knew nothing of Kovner's background, but the latter had written two books in Hebrew attacking the narrowness and obscurantism of the traditional Hebrew education he had received and the literature it had produced. He then became a journalist in Russian and wrote a regular column for the moderately conservative journal, *The Voice*. Later he worked for a bank and was jailed for embezzling enough funds (and no more than that amount) to allow him to flee to the United States with his fiancée. An extremely interesting book about him was written by the pioneer Dostoevsky scholar Leonid Grossman in 1924 and is available in English.

Dostoevsky replied to him with great respect in their exchange of letters and even agreed if possible to help him place his manuscripts (he had writ-

[13] *PSS*, 22:81.
[14] *PSS*, 29/bk 2:139.

ten a novel and a play). Whether he kept this promise has not been established. But Kovner's cogent and hard-hitting objections to Dostoevsky's anti-Semitism provoked Dostoevsky's article "The Jewish Question." It was written as an answer to Kovner, sections of whose letter are cited in the text. Dostoevsky protests that he is not anti-Semitic but tries to pile up evidence proving that the "merciless" economic exploitation of the peasant population by the Jews justifies what he has written against them.

There is also another aspect of the article that must be mentioned, and which fits in with Dostoevsky's previous interest in "the Rothschild idea." By this time he had come under the influence of an influential book written by Yakob Brafman, a Jewish convert to Orthodoxy who taught Hebrew in a seminary. Brafman's book published the records of a *kahal*, that is, the official body recognized by the tsarist government to administer Jewish communities until 1844, when they were abolished. But Brafman insisted in his commentary that they still existed underground, as it were (which was true) but then charged quite falsely that they formed, as Simon Dubnow wrote, "a secret, uncanny sort of organization which wielded despotic power over the communities and incited the Jewish masses against the state, the government and the Christian religion." The Jews thus possessed a "state within the state" that allowed them to take advantage of whatever difficulties occurred to the Christian country in which they were living.[15]

Dostoevsky attributes the astonishing longevity of Jewish survival to the power of their "national idea." This he defines as "alienation and estrangement from others," and "the belief that Jehovah will one day gather them together in Jerusalem ... and will use his sword to bring down all the other peoples to sit at their feet."[16] What the Jews also represent is the triumph of materialism, the triumph of the flesh-god Baal that Dostoevsky had denounced when he visited the World's Fair in London in 1862–1863. He thus begins to speak in other articles of all of European culture as being "Yiddish" because the accumulation of wealth, as he sees it, has become the only aim of European life. He thus sees the Jews not only as controlling European life because of their financial power, but also as somehow undermining from within its previous Christian ideals of brotherly love and self-sacrifice.

Nonetheless, at the end of this diatribe, there is a sudden about-face in the section called "A Universal Man." Here Dostoevsky uses material from the letter sent to him by his other Jewish correspondent, Sofya Lurie. This contained a description of the funeral of a Protestant German

---

[15] Simon Dubnow, *History of the Jews in Russia and Poland*, 3 vols. (Philadelphia, 1918), 3:88.

[16] *PSS*, 25:313–15.

obstetrician who had looked after families of all religions, but she narrated instances of his special kindness to the Jews. The entire community turned out for the funeral, Jews included, who asked for special permission to allow a synagogue chorus to sing though this was never done otherwise for a non-Jew. Dostoevsky also imagines a picture being painted of the good doctor taking off his shirt and tearing it so that a Jewish baby he has just delivered to a desperately poor family could be swaddled. "The solution of the Jewish problem, gentlemen!" he writes.[17]

It is in this context of charity and benevolence that Dostoevsky announces, in spite of everything said before, that he is in favor of granting full civic rights to Jews—"because this is Christ's law, because this is a Christian principle." But he immediately qualifies this by making it dependent on the absence of anything that may lie "buried among some far deeper mysteries of their law and makeup."[18] What these could be remains unknown. Perhaps their "state within the state" or their inability or unwillingness to overcome their alienation and estrangement. The sincerity of this about-face, after the blistering indictment that has gone before, has often been questioned. And again there is no way of deciding one way or the other. But it is possible to see it as the most glaring example of Dostoevsky's inner wrestling with himself over the Jewish question. He was, after all, a master in depicting the wrenching struggle of characters *against* the innate moral convictions of their conscience, and perhaps we have here another instance of such a moral-psychological conflict taking place within himself.

Dostoevsky wrote two novels during the 1870s. One, *A Raw Youth*, is not among his greatest and has no Jewish characters. However, the main figure, Arkady Dolgoruky, is a young man possessed by "the Rothschild idea," though in a form that is not exclusively self-centered. Searching for another ideal, he asks his father Versilov about the fate of society as a whole. The latter predicts a general bankruptcy, and then "the reign of the Yids," when the paupers will annihilate the shareholders and take their place. Versilov is a character who adopts the most extreme and self-contradictory opinions, and everything he says is thus subject to doubt in the novel, where he finally collapses and tries to shoot himself. But the effect of such a prediction, standing alone, reinforces the anti-Semitic animus of Dostoevsky's articles. In these, he was himself overtly envisaging such a fate for the European world.

The worst example of anti-Semitism, however, occurs in Dostoevsky's last and greatest work, *The Brothers Karamazov*. It occurs in the scene between Liza Kokhlakova and Alyosha Karamazov, who represents Dos-

---

[17] Ibid., 90–92.
[18] Ibid., 87–88.

toevsky's image of a new generation inspired by a Christian social idealism that he hoped was coming to birth. Liza is a hysterical adolescent, partially crippled by illness, with a sadomasochistic character. She has read a book about the torture of a Christian child by a Jew and asks Alyosha if it is true that Jews kidnap Christian children at Passover and slaughter them. Why they would do this is not explained but was well understood (the blood was supposedly used in the preparation of matzoh). This is the ancient blood-libel charge, first leveled against the early Christians (all Jews, of course) by pagans, and then taken over by later Christians for the Jews. The blood is supposed to be necessary for ritual reasons. This charge is still going strong, as anyone can see by looking up "blood libel" on the Internet.

Liza is portrayed as so mentally ill that she claims to enjoy the image of a crucified Christian child suffering for four hours and would like to have eaten pineapple compote, a great delicacy at that time in Russia, while watching the suffering. Her obvious pathology thus would seem to undermine the validity of the blood libel accusation. But when she asks Alyosha whether what she had read is true, he can only answer: "I don't know." This leaves open the possibility that such a charge *could* be true, and since Alyosha is Dostoevsky's ideal spokesman, his evasiveness in this instance has the effect of a confirmation.

A trial of this kind, though the blood libel was never openly mentioned, had been going on in Russia while Dostoevsky was working on these chapters. He often inserted such material, taken from accounts of the very latest crimes reported in the newspapers, into his texts. In this instance, the reformed Russian law courts acquitted the defendants, against whom there was no evidence whatsoever. In a letter Dostoevsky objected to this decision, declaring that the Jews were "beyond doubt guilty,"[19] though on what basis he had come to this conclusion we do not know. The defense lawyer in this case was one that he intensely disliked, and who had won an acquittal in the famous Vera Zasulich case with Dostoevsky in the courtroom. Since Vera Zasulich had shot and wounded a high official, there was no question about her guilt; but she was acquitted because of the brutality of the official, and this may have influenced Dostoevsky's judgment. Perhaps we should be grateful that he was cautious enough to have Alyosha express ignorance.

There is still another instance that should be mentioned of Dostoevsky's increasing anti-Semitic obsession in these very last years. In his famous Pushkin speech, he declared the Messianic mission of Russia to be that of bringing about "the universal brotherhood of peoples." But for the first time he spoke of this mission as being "the general unification of all people

[19] *PSS*, 30/bk. 1:59; March 28, 1879.

of all the tribes of the great Aryan race."[20] This was the one and only time that he used the word "Aryan," which thus limits the universality of this ambition and certainly excludes the Jews. He died shortly afterward, and we do not know whether this noxious notion would have been developed. Someone who was very close to him at this time, the great philosopher Vladimir Solovyev, later criticized his ideas very harshly for the obvious contradiction between their so-called Christian universalism and his xenophobia and anti-Semitism.

Much more could be said of Dostoevsky's Messianism, which often (Aileen Kelly is only one example) has been linked to his anti-Semitism. It has been argued that he saw Russia as taking up the role of the "God-bearing" people, which the Jews had proclaimed for themselves, and he thus regarded them as rivals who had to be denigrated and disgraced. But this is a speculative topic that I do not wish to enter into here. I have simply tried to discuss the historical and literary record so far as it can be established. Doing so has been a painful task because Dostoevsky is a writer in whom I find so much else to admire. But this has been the experience, I believe, of the majority of those numerous Jewish scholars who have occupied themselves with his work.

[20] *PSS*, 26:526.

ELEVEN

IN SEARCH OF DOSTOEVSKY

During his all-too-brief life (he died at the age of fifty-six), Dr. Leonid Tsypkin was indistinguishable from many other middle-class professionals in the Soviet Union. He was born in Minsk of Jewish parents, both of them doctors; part of the family was wiped out in the Stalin terror, part after Minsk fell to the Germans in 1941. His immediate family escaped because a grateful ex-patient made room for them in a truck. The young Leonid himself went on to become a research doctor, a pathologist, a member of the Institute for Poliomyelitis and Viral Encephalitis, the author of a hundred medical articles on his specialty. But his scientific career suffered as a result of Stalin's anti-Semitic campaign and the emigration of his son and daughter-in-law to the United States in 1977. His own efforts to emigrate proved in vain.

A picture of him shows a round-faced man with rather fleshy features sitting before a microscope, from which, one imagines, he has just lifted his head. The expression on the face is pensive, contemplative, the penetrating eyes turned away from the camera and looking beyond it, as if broodingly pondering over what he has just seen. There is no trace of "the eternal expression of resentful affliction which is so sharply etched on every Jewish face" (as Dostoevsky wrote in *Crime and Punishment* of the Jewish fireman with his incongruous "Achilles helmet" who watches the despairing Svidrigailov take his own life).[1]

We are concerned with Dr. Tsypkin here because, as well as pursuing his honorable if unfortunately hampered medical researches, he also nourished a passion for literature, particularly for Dostoevsky, and devoted whatever time he could to literary composition. Only one work of his, the volume written between 1977 and 1980, was published in his lifetime (he died on the very day it began to appear in a Russian-language journal in the United States). Although he wrote several others, they were only printed, along with the republication of *Summer in Baden-Baden*, in a very small Russian edition financed by his son. So far as is known, the volume attracted hardly any attention in the Russian press. Luckily, however,

---

Originally published in a slightly different form in *New York Review of Books* 49, 9. Copyright © 2002 *The New York Review of Books*. All rights reserved. Reprinted by permission.

[1] Feodor Dostoevsky, *Crime and Punishment*, trans. Jesse Coulson, ed. George Gibian (New York: Norton, 1989), 432.

the foreign newspaper version of the brief novel led to its translation by a small English publisher, and Susan Sontag accidentally found this English edition while browsing among the bookstalls in London. On perusal, the short novel turned out to be so striking and unusual that she got in touch with the author's American family, learned the facts about the doctor's life, and arranged for its publication here—for which we can all only be grateful.

The title refers to the five weeks spent in Baden-Baden by Dostoevsky and his recently married wife Anna Grigoryevna, twenty years younger, during July–August 1867. These were the years during which, whenever he went abroad and was within reach or easy traveling distance of a roulette table, he was overcome by an irresistible gambling fever (though after 1871 he never gambled again, despite several trips to Europe). While in Baden-Baden he also had a rancorous encounter with Turgenev—one that has left its traces in Russian cultural history—who had taken up residence in that city. His relations with Turgenev until that time, though strained and touchy, had still been tolerably friendly. Just before the quarrel, Dostoevsky had even been mulling over whether to ask him for a loan (although an earlier one had not yet been repaid). However, the novel is by no means confined only to this period of Dostoevsky's life, and the author does himself a slight injustice by this choice of title. Far from being restricted only to this relatively brief visit to the famous spa, it roams over the entire extent of Dostoevsky's career, ranging from the debut of his literary career in the 1840s to the very last days of his life in 1881. Indeed, if one wished to characterize the book more accurately, it might be called, perhaps, a "Rhapsody on Dostoevskian Themes," or a series of "Variations on Dostoevskian Motifs."

The musical analogy suggests itself spontaneously because the book consists in large part of the uninterrupted flow of the author's strikingly imaginative transformations of Dostoevsky's life, based on a thorough knowledge of the original biographical sources as well as of Dostoevsky's works. There is no division in chapters or other segments, and the unusual style proceeds with an impetus that rarely relinquishes its grip on the reader. The author hardly stops to complete sentences, which roll on with one clause succeeding another, connected only by an "and" or separated with a dash. The unit of closure is the paragraph, which pauses for a moment but then starts up again with the same precipitous movement, as if the writer had just stopped to catch his breath.

The fadings in and out now so customary in the cinema also come to mind because the transition from one subject to another, often involving a change of time and place, is usually made through associative memory-links. This is not unlike what occurs in the stream-of-consciousness novel (Joyce, Woolf, etc.), but this stream-of-consciousness is not focused on the purely private sensations and feelings of the narrator. Most often it is entirely dominated both by imaginative transcriptions of incidents from Dostoevsky's biography, which become fused with that of the characters in his novels, and to a lesser extent by the evocation of other Russian writers and their works (Pushkin, Turgenev, Ivan Bunin, Tsvetaeva, Solzhenitsyn). The largest part of the book is thus cast in this technique of psycho-narration,[2] in which a third-person narrator enters freely into and out of the consciousness of the characters being created. In this case it is Dostoevsky, his wife, and the various people, particularly Turgenev, who play an important role in Dostoevsky's life, while the narrator himself tends to merge with the figures about whom he is writing.

There is also another narrative level, first-person and autobiographical, that interweaves with the episodes devoted to portraying Dostoevsky. Here Dr. Tsypkin himself speaks, and the book begins with a description of his departure for Moscow on a journey to Leningrad specifically to visit the Dostoevsky Museum in that city and take photographs of the surrounding neighborhood. From time to time the author thus emerges from Dostoevsky's world and brings his own (twentieth-century Russia) into relation with it, sometimes with a bitterly ironic thrust at the total indifference of the vast majority of its inhabitants to the moral-cultural issues that so preoccupied the past and continue to maintain their relevance. As for himself, he is engrossed, as we see, with Dostoevsky; and this consuming interest not only provides an external motivation for his musings and reshapings of the Dostoevskian world, but also an internal dynamic of self-probing that imparts a particular poignancy to this voyage.

As the narrator sits in a lurching and swaying railroad carriage at the start of his journey—superficially only from one city to another, but more deeply into the world of Dostoevsky as well as into himself—a few sentences will convey the striking vividness of his sensory evocations and the headlong quality of his style. "Moscow stations flashing into view and vanishing again behind me like the scattering of some invisible hand—each snow-veiled suburban platform with its fleeting row of lamps melting into one fiery ribbon—the dull drone of a station rushing past, as if the train were roaring over a bridge—the sound muffled by the double-glazed windows with frames not quite hermetically sealed into fogged-up half-frozen panes of glass," etc.[3] Here the style communicates the movement and the sights and sounds of the train as impressions flash by; but the impressions of Dostoevsky's life appear and vanish with a similar kaleidoscopic rapidity.

---

[2] I take the term from the excellent book of Dorrit Cohen, *Transparent Minds* (Princeton: Princeton University Press, 1978), chap. 1.

[3] Leonid Tsypkin, *Summer in Baden-Baden*, trans. Roger Keys and Angela Keys (New York: New Directions, 2003), 1. Subsequent references to this work are cited in parentheses in the text.

The narrator is trying to read a book while being tossed to and fro in the railroad car, one filched from the library of an aunt, and he has had it rebound to prevent its falling apart. It is "the *Diary* of Anna Grigoryevna Dostoevskaya produced by some liberal publishing-house still possible at that time ...—with dates given in Old Style and words and whole phrases in German and French and without translation ... a transliteration of the shorthand notes she had taken abroad during the summer following her marriage" (2). Susan Sontag in her introduction seems to confuse this book with Anna Dostoevsky's *Reminiscences* ("aboard a train bound for Leningrad the narrator ... opens a book ... the *Reminiscences* of Dostoevsky's wife" [xii]), but these two works are not the same.

The *Diary*, containing the unaltered shorthand notes made by Anna Dostoevsky in compliance with her mother's request that she keep some account of her journey, was first published in 1923. The *Reminiscences*, partly written on the basis of her diary at the very end of Anna Dostoevsky's life, were put together and published from her manuscripts in 1925, seven years after her death, by the pioneer Jewish Dostoevskian Leonid Grossman. This latter volume covers Dostoevsky's entire life and draws very selectively on the *Diary*, whose on-the-spot entries, often revealing Dostoevsky in a far from favorable light, were later revised and bowdlerized. It is this first book, with its picture of an unadorned Dostoevsky, that the narrator is treasuring so carefully (it was only republished in 1993). "Why was I now on my way to Petersburg—yes, not to Leningrad but precisely to Petersburg?" he asks as he emotionally prepares to plunge into the world of Dostoevsky's own life and time. "Why was I reading this book *now*, in a railway-carriage, beneath a wavering, flickering, electric-light bulb, glaring brightly at one moment, almost extinguished the next?" (3). The entire book provides, if not an unequivocal answer to this question, at least an understanding of why it gnaws at his conscience and confronts him with a moral dilemma.

Reading about the journey of the Dostoevskys while engaged on his own, the narrator describes their departure for Dresden, passing through Vilna, "where they are constantly pestered by loathsome little Jews thrusting their services on them" (2). (The contrast between the *Reminiscences* and the *Diary* is brought out by Dr. Tsypkin's own remark that "perhaps after she [Anna Grigoryevna] got to know Grossman, there is no mention at all of the loathsome little Jews on the stairs" [3] who show up in the *Diary*.) In Dresden the couple go to the art gallery every day "as people in Kislovodsk drop in at the kursaal to take the waters" (5), and this triggers the recollection of a long queue thronging to a show at the Pushkin Museum in Moscow where "the Sistine Madonna" was once displayed—the same Madonna whose photograph "in a wooden frame, hangs in the Dostoyevsky Museum in Leningrad above the leather couch on which the writer died" (4).

Shifting back to Dresden again, and following the *Diary*, the narrator conveys the opinion of the couple that the Germans are "a dim-witted bunch" (2) who cheat all the time, and barely treat them with minimal courtesy. Dostoevsky becomes infuriated when "some Saxon official with fleshly red nose and yellowish eyes, his whole appearance that of a drinker," is carefully served in a hotel restaurant while they are insultingly neglected. In a rage, Dostoevsky pounds the table with his fist, "and he even began to shout at [his wife] as if it were her fault that the two of them had gone there together" (6). The *Diary* itself contains ample evidence of this unjust shifting of guilt, with Dostoevsky turning on the totally innocent and inexperienced Anna again and again to vent his frustration. The narrator accurately expresses the resentment that she feels and expresses in the *Diary* (whose shorthand Dostoevsky was unable to read), but whose external manifestations she kept under careful control for the sake of her marriage.

Another recollection occurs at this point, however, as the narrator's focus shifts from the *Diary* to *House of the Dead*: "had he himself [Dostoevsky] not stared sycophantically into the yellow-lynx eyes of that drunk, red-nosed swine of a commandant—yes! that was the one brought to mind by the Saxon officer just now" (6). The narrator then evokes one day in the prison camp, when Dostoevsky was feeling ill and lying on the bunk during working time, and this officer shouted at him "with all the strength of his bullish throat" (6) to get back to work. And another image from those prison-camp years intervenes at this point, that of witnessing a punishment: "the victim lying motionless as he was beaten with birch-rods, leaving bloody weals on his back and buttocks" (6), and then getting to his feet with dignity and leaving without so much as a glance at Major Krivtsov, the sadistic prison-camp commandant.

"Would *he* have managed to keep so silent and leave the guard-room with such dignity" (6) if condemned to endure the same punishment? (So far as is known, Dostoevsky was never flogged, though rumors to that effect circulated throughout his lifetime; but the narrator evidently refuses to give them any credence.) He imagines Dostoevsky, rather, as having "walked with head lowered—no, not walked, but almost ran—humiliating in itself—and when he reached the officer he stared at him, not a firm, hard look, but with pleading eyes" (7). The memory of those "yellow, lynx-like eyes," with all their humiliating associations, crops up again and again to form one of the image-clusters that structure the narrator's depiction of a continually insulted and injured Dostoevsky.

Another such image-cluster is nautical, appearing whenever reference is made to the account in the *Diary* of Dostoevsky's courtship and marriage. The abrupt change in Anna's hitherto peaceful and uneventful life becomes that of the experience of a storm at sea. Once the two had met, "her world had begun to sway and swirl—on a ship in the middle of a storm, a gigantic wave had swept all the rigging and even the handrails away, leaving only the mast" (14), to which she felt only she alone was able to cling. Such clinging to the mast reappears whenever Anna feels her marriage to be threatened; and their sexual relations are transformed into the imagery of swimming—"swimming with large strokes, thrusting their arms in unison from the water to take great gulps of air into their lungs" (9). But a countercurrent prevents him from moving in unison with her, "and strangely this current, bearing him away ... seemed to turn into the yellow eyes of the commandant with dilated predator pupils" (9), which then brings back the terrible details of the flogging, described as if inflicted on Dostoevsky himself. He hated all these imaginary "invisible witnesses" peering through the grilled windows because they had seen his humiliation, and they then blend with the faces of the waiter and the Saxon officer.

Just as this fictional Dostoevsky is haunted by such debilitating memories of his prison-camp years, so another image-cluster emerges from recollections of his literary debut. His first novel, *Poor Folk*, had been hailed as a masterpiece by the leading critic of the time, Vissarion Belinsky [there is an error in the translation here that speaks of *White Nights*, a later short story, while the original Russian text cites the proper work], but then his swollen vanity alienated the group of young writers gathered around the critic (Goncharov, Nekrasov, Turgenev, et al.). These distressful events also continue to bedevil Dostoevsky, and they come to the fore in the pages devoted to his gambling during the stay in Baden-Baden.

The couple often took walks in the mountains surrounding the city, and these are then used symbolically, with Dr. Tsypkin's fertilely inventive extrapolations, to express Dostoevsky's sense of success or failure, of exhilaration or despondency, depending on his luck at the gambling tables. When winning, he was conquering the mountain heights unhinderedly, the summit "covered with virgin snow, gleaming silver in the rays of the sun or even reflecting gold—and as for the others—Turgenev, Goncharov, Panayev, Nekrasov—they all remained below at the foot of the mountain, hand in hand in some round-dance, enveloped in the fetid mists of the lowlands" (59). This "round-dance" keeps recurring, appearing either above or below Dostoevsky depending on whether he is winning or losing. And when "he tumbled downhill," these round-dance figures become amalgamated with others—"a purple face with lynx eyes," and "women's faces, too—and were they not the ones which had peered through the barred window to the guardroom?" (62).

These examples should be enough to illustrate the remarkable texture of the present book, and the expressively creative manner in which Dostoevsky's life and work are conveyed. In a bravura passage, inspired by the hallucinatory intensity of Dostoevsky's gambling obsession, the narrator brilliantly portrays him rushing back and forth between home and casino, pawning everything the pair possesses to make up his losses. "He would seem to be performing the most extraordinary movements, one moment turning into a juggler with black tights, white kid gloves and a black top-hat, skillfully throwing engagement rings up into space along with dresses and Anna Grigoryevna's fur hat and just as skillfully catching them in mid-air." He then becomes a ballet-dancer, "twisting on his own axis in pirouettes," and she emerges "swathed like Carmen in a shawl," clicking castanets and tossing him her jewelry and her dress after disrobing. And he "would fling necklaces, rings, dresses and shawls into the air, juggling them skillfully ... but the objects he was throwing into the air did not return" (80–81). No one who has read this depiction of Dostoevsky, "executing the complex steps of a divertissement against the background of Baden-Baden's red-brick houses" (80), is ever likely to forget it.

Turgenev appears not only in the "round-dance," but also in the account given of their famous meeting. The author here is drawing on two sources, Anna's *Diary* and a much more detailed version a month later contained in Dostoevsky's letter to an old friend, the poet Apollon Maikov. Dr. Tsypkin recasts them in his own terms, which reproduces the atmosphere of their encounter without being literally accurate. Dostoevsky had always been put off by Turgenev's condescendingly aristocratic simulacra of friendliness, and he had hated, along with a good many others, Turgenev's most recent novel, *Smoke*, considered as anti-Russian. Dr. Tsypkin catches the atmosphere beautifully ("Ah! It's you, said Turgenev in his woman's falsetto, greeting his guest with that ingenuous smile, full of joy and amazement" [52]), while Dostoevsky sat there "feeling like some wretched dropper-in, or, to be more accurate, beggar, although he wasn't begging for anything" (53). It is then, stung by an invented reference (purely fictional) to his penal servitude, and enraged by *Smoke*, that Dostoevsky asks: "So why don't you to go Paris and buy a telescope so you can examine Russia from there" (54). Again, when Dostoevsky (fictionally) demeaningly remarks "that your novel is German through and through" (54), Turgenev replies: "I take your words to be praise.... A literature that has given us Goethe and Schiller" (54). The basis for all this, as Dostoevsky explains in his letter to Maikov, is that in the course of their conversation he accused Turgenev of having declared himself to feel more German than Russian.

One could go on endlessly exploring the fascinating but by no means uncritical or hagiographic portrait of Dostoevsky offered here, or rather, of the Dostoevskys, since Anna Grigoryevna is given her rightful place. Dr. Tsypkin sympathetically describes her during the turbulence of these early months of their marriage, when Dostoevsky, as we have said, abusively turned on her again and again, only to return and lament the unfairness and injustice of his intolerable mistreatment and ask for forgiveness on his knees. And at this point, in the midst of a gambling scene in which he is "flying downhill," the narrator strikes off an analysis of his character that provides it with much more than a purely individual relevance.

> We think up convenient theories designed to soften the blows continually rained on us by fate or to justify our own failures and weaknesses?—and is this not the explanation of the so-called crisis which Dostoevsky went through during his penal servitude?—could his morbid pride ever become reconciled with the humiliations to which he was subjected there?—no, he had only one way out: to consider these humiliations as his just deserts—"I bear a cross, and I have deserved it,' he wrote in one of his letters—but in order to bring this about he had to represent all those earlier views of his, for which he had suffered, as erroneous and even criminal—and this he did, unconsciously of course—the human psyche's need for self-preservation. (88)

Since this is a novel, there is no need either to accept or reject such an interpretation as claiming any definitive biographical truth; we are dealing with the Dostoevsky created by Dr. Tsypkin, and brought to indelible life in his pages.

This passage, however, provides one of the climaxes of the book—the narrator's quest, as it were, for an understanding of Dostoevsky. But there is also another quest embodied in the frame-narrative, the search for an understanding of the narrator's own predilection for the novelist. This question is directly posed when, on arriving in Leningrad, he stays at the apartment of an elderly friend whose deceased husband had been a medical colleague, a urologist also of Jewish origin. His hostess asks the narrator if he is "still keen on Dostoevsky," adding, "Only don't talk about it at the Brodskys." The father of this family was "an academician," and the sons "engaged in some kind of secret work," but they "ate nothing that was not kosher" (114) and observed all the Jewish holidays. For them, the name of Dostoevsky was evidently anathema, and the narrator understands why perfectly well.

Leafing through a prerevolutionary copy of the *Diary of a Writer* that he finds on the bookshelf, he stumbles on the article "The Jewish Question" in which Dostoevsky attempted to justify his anti-Semitism. And this leads into a vividly evoked parade of characters and allusions from Dostoevsky's novels (Lyamshin in *Demons*, the cunning moneylender Isai Fomich among the convicts in *House of the Dead*, the fireman already mentioned in *Crime and Punishment*, the Christian child supposedly crucified by a Jew in *The Brothers Karamazov* (a crime that Alyosha Karamazov refuses either to affirm or deny), as well as the entire panoply of vicious anti-Semitic charges unrolled in the article. And the good doctor read all this with "a pounding heart," trying to understand why "a man so sensitive in his novels to the suffering of others, this zealous defender of the insulted and injured ... that this man should not have come up with even a single word in the defense or justification of a people persecuted over several thousands of years—could he have been so blind? Or was he perhaps blinded by hatred?" (116). Dostoevsky denied harboring any such hatred on religious grounds, but the article in question and his letters indicate that he considered the Jews to be ruthless exploiters of the misery of others, if not even worse.

Dr. Tsypkin belonged to this "tribe," as Dostoevsky calls the Jews, and so did "the many friends and acquaintances of mine with whom I had discussed the subtlest problems of Russian literature" (116). So did the whole array of Russian scholars and critics (seventeen names are listed) "who have gained," as he notes with melancholy irony, "almost what amounts to a monopoly in the study of Dostoevsky's literary heritage." Susan Sontag comments on this preoccupation, remarking that "Tsypkin has no better explanation than the fervor of Jews for the greatness of Russian literature—which may remind us that the German adulation of Goethe and Schiller was in large part a Jewish affair.... Loving Dostoevsky means loving literature" (xix). Well, yes, but it also means something else less easy to acknowledge and less self-congratulatory.

For how does Dr. Tsypkin answer his own question? At first he compares this Jewish adoration with "a cannibalistic act performed on the leader of an enemy tribe" (116), presumably to acquire his powers; but then it becomes "using him as a safe conduct—something like adopting Christianity or daubing a cross on your door during a pogrom—although one cannot exclude the simple fervor of Jews here which has always been particularly strong in questions of Russian culture ... and which, in any case, completely accords with the preceding supposition" (116). The love of literature is thus noted but absorbed in what might be called the symbiosis syndrome, both perfectly genuine but also a means of self-protection that has been a perennial feature of Jewish cultural history and identity. Sontag's German comparison is another excellent example of the same phenomenon.

This question and its problematic then acquires a special pathos in these concluding pages, where, after reading Dostoevsky's article, Dr. Tsypkin falls asleep and dreams. In a jumble of images, he again sees a supplicating Dostoevsky capering, prancing, and dancing before those from whom he seeks favors or approval, walking on a tight-rope, his face covered by "the mask of Harlequin from which tufts of his gray beard protruded" (117) and being thrown into one humiliating situation after another. When he crawls to a mirror, "to straighten his appearance ... instead of himself in the mirror he saw the puny figure of Isai Fomich, without any clothes on and with the breast of a chicken" (119). Dostoevsky himself has now become transformed into the most manifestly Jewish figure he had ever depicted; and as Dr. Tsypkin well knew, but avoids including, the very idea of such an amalgamation would have filled Dostoevsky with horror. Once, having been wiped out at the tables in Wiesbaden and searching for a Russian priest at night to ask both for solace and a loan, he had almost entered a Jewish synagogue by mistake, thinking it a Russian church. He wrote Anna that he felt "as though I had had cold water poured over me,"[4] and it may have been more than coincidental that from this moment on he never gambled again, though he had promised to stop and failed many times before. Could he have interpreted his mistake as a warning from on high—he believed in such omens—that his gambling fever was bringing him close to becoming a Jew?

However that may be, nothing more is made of the dream at this point; the narrative shifts to the autobiographical mode, and we are back in the Leningrad flat with the narrator and his old family friends. They chat about personal matters, and then of the Leningrad Blockade, when his aged hostess, who worked in some scientific institute, tells of "how the people actually ate the dogs and cats, and one "would see frozen corpses ... and how people would collapse before her very eyes, freezing to death on the same spot" (120). The conversation then turns to the arrests of the head of her institute, "a famous chemist" (120), released through the intervention of Romain Rolland, and the disappearance of her husband taken into custody, who suddenly turned up again one day to everyone's surprise. Such anecdotes seem to have little to do with Dostoevsky but in fact serve a thematic function. They bring out the interconnection between the intimate Jewish world of Dr. Tsypkin and the common Russian fate, thus reflecting back indirectly on Dostoevsky's harshly condemnatory pages.

As the narrator gropes his way through the darkening Leningrad streets, walking toward various locations associated with the novels ("Raskolnikov's House or the Old Moneylender's House" [122]), he appreciatively comments on some of the imposing architecture and finally finds his way to the Dostoevsky Museum. Intermingled with his impressionistic glimpses are events in Dostoevsky's life that took place in one or another of the venues that he traverses (the place where the strolling novelist was knocked down by an irate beggar, against whom he refused to testify). The visit to the museum, filled with Dostoevskian memorabilia, brings on an account of the final three days of his life, but now less frenetically agitated and (suitably) more reverential. Past and present blend as the narrator imagines "the flames of two candles standing on the desk and the

---

[4] Feodor Dostoevsky, *Polnoe Sobranie Sochinenii*, 30 vols. (Leningrad, 1972–1990), 29/bk. 1:198; letter of April 16/28, 1871.

photograph of the 'Sistine Madonna' floating in the clouds with the Child, which was hanging above the couch on which the dying man lay, and outside the windows was a wintry Petersburg night—just as it looked now at this moment most probably" (139–140). Just before death Dostoevsky was again climbing a mountain, viewing "not only the earth with all the vanity of its inhabitants ... but all the terrible secrets of those distant planets"; then the sun vanished and "he sank down into terrible, fathomless darkness" (143).

For all his identification with Dostoevsky, the narrator is nonetheless assailed, as he emerges to search for the trolley car that will take him home, not only by the question that had plagued him from the start, but by a sense of alienation he has not been able to shake off. "Why had I come here under cover of darkness, walking along these empty and godforsaken streets like a thief?" (145). And why, in the museum, "or other places connected with him [Dostoevsky]" (145), had he trailed behind, or stood aside, as if all this were no concern of his? What was the meaning of the dream, "in which, in the end, [Dostoevsky] turned into Isai Fomich? Was this not "only the pathetic attempt of my subconscious to 'legitimize' my passion" (145)? Earlier, "the human psyche's need for self-preservation" had impelled Dostoevsky to overcome debasement by renouncing his past. The same need, expressed in Dr. Tsypkin's dream, has now transformed Dostoevsky into a Jew so as to overcome the debasing awareness of his anti-Semitism. The narrator has thus himself become a typical Dostoevskian character, torn between what his mind tells him is distressingly true and what his heart (his "passion") refuses to accept. Could this resemblance be the underlying reason for the strange power that his favorite writer exercised on Dr. Tsypkin's psyche? It certainly helps us to comprehend, in any case, the particular features of Dostoevsky that he places in the foreground of his compelling portrait.

So ends this little poetic masterpiece, which opens up vistas not only in relation to Dostoevsky but also to Russian literature past and present. There is no room here to comment on the sparkling page or two devoted to Pushkin; or the sudden appearance, after the Dostoevsky–Turgenev spat, of the unnamed but unmistakable figures of Solzhenitsyn and Sakharov (along with Elena Bonner) suddenly emerging with imagistic monumentality to renew the Westernizer–Slavophile fray one hundred years later, though it had supposedly been made obsolete "by the coming to power of the workers and the peasants" (54). Similarly, Dr. Tsypkin's reliving of the Russian-Jewish ambiguity in relation to Dostoevsky brings to mind that of the journalist Arkady Kovner, whom Dostoevsky was in fact answering in the article on "The Jewish Question" that the doctor peruses.

The enigma of Dostoevsky's anti-Semitism has thus bewildered his Jewish readers for more than a hundred years, and no doubt it will continue to be endlessly debated. But Dr. Tsypkin has done much more than offer another run-through of the well-worn arguments. Like Dostoevsky in *his* novels, he has embodied his quarrel with himself over the novelist into a touchingly impressive artistic achievement.

TWELVE

ARKADY KOVNER

ADMIRERS of Dostoevsky both in his time and ours have been disturbed and puzzled by the anti-Semitism that became so virulent in his writings in the 1870s. One of his contemporaries took the trouble to make his objections known in a letter to the famous author and provoked a reply from him in several letters and a notorious essay in the *Diary of a Writer*. The name of this correspondent is Avraam Uri Kovner, and he is the subject of Harriet Murav's *Identity Theft, The Jew in Imperial Russia and the Case of Avraam Uri Kovner*.[1] If not for his exchange of letters with Dostoevsky, it is unlikely that he would be known at all today—or only to a very small group of specialists concerned with the obscure literature written in Hebrew, Yiddish, and Russian by Russian-Jewish writers in the middle and late nineteenth century

Kovner's correspondence with Dostoevsky, however, gave his name a certain prominence once he became known as the source of Dostoevsky's essay on "The Jewish Question." And since Dostoevsky's relation to this issue is one of the most intractable that his commentators have to grapple with, the career of Arkady Kovner (he also called himself Albert) has attracted some attention in its own right. Who was this figure, whose letters so impressed Dostoevsky that he singled them out for an answer? Other letters addressed to him, whose Jewish provenance he carefully noted, received no such reward.

Although Arkady Kovner would scarcely have aroused the curiosity of posterity except for this relation with Dostoevsky, he became notorious in his own time for quite a different reason. In 1875, while working as a Russian correspondent for the St. Petersburg Discount Lending Bank, owned by a Jewish financier and philanthropist, Kovner swindled the bank of 168,000 rubles and was caught while trying to escape to the United States with his fiancée. His trial excited a great deal of interest, was assiduously covered by the press, and was probably known to Dostoevsky. Although engaged at the time in writing *A Raw Youth*, the novelist con-

---

Originally published in a slightly different form as "Without a Label," *The New Republic*, May 24, 2004. Reprinted by permission

[1] Harriet Murav, Identity Theft, *The Jew in Imperial Russia and the Case of Avraam Uri Kovner* (Stanford: Stanford University Press, 2003). Subsequent references to this work are cited in parentheses in the text.

stantly scoured the newspapers and journals and was particularly interested in the abundant crime reporting of his day. Kovner's first letter to Dostoevsky was sent from Butyrki prison in Petersburg; and it may well have aroused his interest, not only for the acuity and penetration with which his work and ideas were discussed, but also because Kovner was behind bars. One should remember that Dostoevsky himself had lived in solitary confinement in the Peter-and-Paul prison for approximately a year after his own arrest in 1850.

However that may be, Kovner's correspondence with Dostoevsky is only one incident in a life whose details offer a pathetically illuminating glimpse into the world of the Russian Jewish Pale (the western provinces of the Russian Empire), and the lives of the small group of young men struggling to break out of its cultural as well as geographic confines. Arkady Kovner was born in 1842 in what is now Vilnius (Vilna), a haven of Jewish learning for generations. At the beginning of the nineteenth century, it also became the center for an attack on the reigning ecstatic and mystical Jewish religious movement known as Hasidism. The Hasidists were assailed by those advocating an opposing current of thought known as Haskalah, which aimed both to free Jewish life from its devotion to a past conditioned by exclusion and oppression, and to bring it into relation with the modern world. Moses Mendelssohn had been the chief inspirer of this movement in Germany, and his example soon spread to Eastern Europe.

Two years before his death in 1909, Kovner published some autobiographical essays, *From the Notes of a Jew* (the title is worth noting, since by this time he had become, at least legally, a Christian convert), from which the details of his early life have become known. He was the third of eleven children, who grew up in destitution so extreme that he recalls his father weeping over the accidental loss of four rubles in the street. His father gave lessons and his mother sold grain products, but they lived more or less off the meager bounty of his father's brother, a well-known scholar who had published a book of commentaries on the Talmud. A maternal uncle, who once visited the family, was the first person Arkady ever saw wearing European clothes.

At the age of four he studied the Hebrew Bible, at six the Talmud, and at seven he wrote a play in Hebrew verse about Esther, the Jewess who became queen of Persia and rescued her people from genocide. At nine he was placed in a rabbinical seminary run by the Russian government and staffed with Haskalah teachers. A star student was his older brother Savelii, who later entered the University of Kiev, became a doctor, and wrote in Russian a book on Spinoza as well as others on the history of medicine. But Arkady became ill after a year and was placed by his parents in a yeshiva, a more traditional Hebrew school. He found the rote learning of the Talmud that he encountered there more stultifying than enlightening, and he bitterly criticized it later. "I knew from the 'forbidden books,'" he writes, "that somewhere there breathed and lived a whole world for which such questions as: was it permissible to use an egg laid by a chicken on a holiday... were irrelevant. But this enchanting, alien world was inaccessible to me" (23).[2] The conditions of life that yeshiva students endured were literally appalling. They slept in the room in which they studied, in abominable hygienic conditions, and were fed by various families in the village willing to nourish them out of charity.

Kovner was married off at the age of eighteen against his will, without having become acquainted with his bride before the ceremony, and no truly intimate relation of any depth existed between them, though she gave birth to a daughter and later to a son. He continued his Talmudic studies, supported as was customary by his wife's family, but his brother Savelii urged him to break away and come to Kiev. Arkady finally did so, pocketing a pearl from his mother-in-law to pay for the trip. Following the author of a life of Kovner in Yiddish (1955), Murav calls this his first "theft," implicitly accusing him of falsehood in telling Dostoevsky that the bank swindle was his only crime. That the two are comparable hardly seems persuasive, and it is worth noting that, so far as can be judged, this petty infraction was not held against him when he returned to his family again for a brief period before leaving once more. Some agreement was reached on this occasion so that his wife had the right to remarry, and as a matter of fact she did so twice.

It was in Kiev, where he supported himself as a tutor in a Jewish family and remained for four years, that Kovner began to publish in the Hebrew-language press. As he later wrote to Dostoevsky, "this was in the sixties, when Russian literature and young people were celebrating the honeymoon of progress" (32). The serfs had just been liberated by Alexander II, other reforms were being advocated and introduced in many aspects of Russian society, and for a few years—very few—Russian life seemed to be following the path leading to enlightenment and progress. A new group of radical Russian publicists held the center of the stage and inspired the young Jewish intellectuals of the time.

The most intransigent of these writers was Dimitry Pisarev, "who ... is best-known for his nihilism, his refusal of all authorities, and his rejection of high culture and aesthetics in favor of science and utilitarianism" (32). Murav cites a Russian-Jewish novella by S. R. Ansky, *Pioneers*, to illustrate Pisarev's popularity among Jewish students who considered themselves "free-thinkers." Kovner became a devoted disciple, and it was through Kovner that Pisarev's ideas entered into the Jewish press. Some years later Dostoevsky dramatized Pisarev's point of view in his novel *Demons*, where

---

[2] A. G. Kovner, "Iz zapisok evreia," *Istoricheskii vestnik* XCI (March–April 1903): 1001–2.

in the satirically tumultuous fete scene a character asks whether the works of Pushkin or a pair of boots are more useful to Russian society.

Kovner posed a similar question about "usefulness" in the articles he began to publish in Hebrew beginning in 1864 and in a book entitled *The Inquiry* (*Heker davar*). These works produced a storm because they assailed the preference of Hebrew authors for poetry over prose, for stylistic embellishment rather than contemporary concerns, for the cultivation of, and preoccupation with, the Hebrew language to the point at which "there was no Hebrew literature in the European sense of the word" (42). Without wishing to abandon the study of Hebrew, Kovner spoke of it as being "transitional"—as it were, a way station toward the adoption of European languages. One can well imagine the indignation this aroused in the small circle of readers to whom it was addressed.

By this time Kovner had moved from Kiev to Odessa and become a staff member of a Hebrew newspaper called *The Mediator* (*HaMelitz*), which had published his first articles. His notoriety attracted readers, but he soon quarreled with the editor and even secretly wrote a letter to the governor-general accusing the newspaper of being "an obstacle to the education of the Jews and their rapprochement with the Russian population" (50). The governor wisely ignored it, but Kovner's reason for having taken such a step remains unexplained; Murav cites a pamphlet by a Hebrew poet with whom Kovner corresponded that refers to the "crookedness" of the editor.

Kovner's second book in Hebrew, *A Bouquet of Flowers*, was aimed directly at the newspaper. It consists of passages quoted from its pages followed by Kovner's "sarcastic commentary" (51), which sometimes cites other works to reinforce his ridicule. He also included an alphabetized list of curse words in Hebrew to ease the task of all those he knew would lash out at him with fury. Murav rather belabors this polemical creation with an elaborate commentary, viewing it as raising "the problem of identity and subjectivity that is a core question of acculturation," and concluding that Kovner here displays the lack of "an inner core of selfhood" (52). Why this carefully composed and ironic attack reveals a lack of "selfhood" simply escapes me; nor is it particularly illuminating to learn that "his parody resonates with a postmodern view of subjectivity as a nodal point for various messages and discourses, constituted in and by language" (52). The argument is of course about language since it involves the use of Hebrew; but the issues it raises are scarcely "constituted in and by language." Her book is occasionally marred by this sort of theoretical overkill, which dissolves historical reality into a blur of fashionable notions about acculturation and postmodernism. Fortunately, Murav is also a serious and solid historical scholar, who informatively fills in the background of this little-known world with diligent particularity.

Kovner followed his own advice to abandon Hebrew and began to write for Russian-language Jewish newspapers; but life became impossible for him in Odessa after the publication of his second book. A stint as a tutor in the Ural Mountains was followed by a transplantation to St. Petersburg in 1871. There he obtained a post on the influential newspaper *The Voice* and published a novel whose title, *Without a Label*, indicates his own ambition. The book deals with the lives of university students, none of whom is specifically Jewish, but Murav convincingly demonstrates that the important ones contain character traits ordinarily attributed to Jews in Russian society. One, named Renkov (an acronym for Kovner), is a thoroughgoing Nihilist who insists "there is no purpose whatsoever in the life of any human being" (78). Murav cites a similar passage from one of Kovner's letters but rightly remarks that in his journalism "his ethical vision embraces the universal values he had once described himself as abandoning" (82).

The Voice was in favor of the assimilation and Russification of the Jews that was encouraged during the early years of Alexander II's reign but was regarded with considerable disfavor and trepidation by the conservative elements of the Jewish community. Kovner wrote a feuilleton called "Literary and Social Curiosities" that appeared regularly in 1872–1873, and Murav's chapter is the only serious discussion of it easily available in English. A feuilletonist could comment freely on whatever topic struck his fancy, and "political events, theatrical performances, art exhibits and current court cases all appear together in the space of a single feuilleton" (84). Dostoevsky's *Diary of a Writer*, which began to appear in 1873 and later blossomed into a monthly periodical, may be considered a feuilleton writ large. Many of the topics that Dostoevsky touched on are also broached by Kovner—"corporal punishment in the schools ... ongoing trials in the new jury courts, suicide, domestic violence and the difficult position of women in Russian society generally" (92). Like Dostoevsky, Kovner also attacks the growth in Russia of a modern industrial economy—"stock market[s], banks, railroads, insurance companies, and especially speculation" (95).

One of Kovner's favorite targets was *The Citizen*, the weekly founded by Prince Meshchersky and which Dostoevsky edited in 1873–1874. Kovner wondered at the anomaly of the social-humanitarian author of *Poor Folk* and *House of the Dead* taking over the helm of such a committedly conservative publication, and he also criticized Dostoevsky's latest and most ferociously antiradical novel, *Demons*. The plot is based on the assassination of one of the members of a small revolutionary faction by his comrades out of fear of betrayal. Kovner accused Dostoevsky of not being "a true artist" because, after the public trial of this group for murder, he reproduced in his novel "whole sections of stenographic accounts of ready-made characters and ready made speeches" (98)³ (a charge not at all true), and his characters, in any case, were all "raving maniacs." He ridiculed Dostoevsky's insistence on "the need for suffering" (98) and asked whether the Russian people had welcomed the Tatar invasion or regretted the end of serfdom. One article in the *Diary of a Writer* refers indirectly to such barbs, though it is primarily devoted to an exchange of insults between two other Russian journalists of the time. In his letter to Dostoevsky, Kovner confesses that he had done his utmost "to enter into a personal polemic with you, to challenge you to battle"; but "you silently ignored all my outbursts and did not gratify my egotism."⁴

Kovner lived in the home of an impoverished Jewish widow with four children and fell in love with her oldest, tubercular daughter, Sofia. By this time he was supporting his family in Vilna, his ex-wife and two children, and helping, as much as he could, the indigent family of his beloved, whom he taught to read and write. Because of some disagreement with the influential editor of *The Voice*, he resigned and obtained a lowly position at the bank, where he was badly paid and badly treated. He wished to marry Sofia but lacked the means; he lived in fear of being deprived of his post; and he finally decided on the theft, which was carried out through a forgery of the signature of the bank's Jewish director.

The trial, as already remarked, was a notable public event, and the prosecutor, N. M. Muraviev, later became minister of justice. Sofia's testimony and that of one of her sisters, who spoke of Kovner as behaving "as if our papa had risen from his grave" (119), obviously impressed the jury, who gave Kovner a relatively light sentence—guilty, but deserving of mercy. He was sentenced to four years in a penal battalion but took advantage of a legal technicality to avoid this penalty and was simply sent into exile in Siberia. While waiting in prison Kovner wrote to Dostoevsky, and Murav devotes a chapter to their exchange of letters.

By this time, she has decided, on the basis of one article in *The Psychoanalytic Quarterly*, that Kovner is "an imposturous personality" (125), whose whole life consists in assuming various roles; he is an impostor through and through, guilty of "identity theft." In relation to Dostoevsky, he assumes the role of a Raskolnikov in *Crime and Punishment*, the motive for whose crime (or so Dostoevsky's character thought initially, and quite sincerely) was "humanitarian." To quote the novel: "For one life taken, thousands saved from corruption and decay!"⁵ Kovner himself wrote to

---

³ A. U. Kovner, "Literaturnye i obschestvennye kur'ezy," *Golos* (St. Petersburg, January 18, 1873): 1–2.

⁴ Leonid Grossman, *Confession of a Jew*, trans. Roanne Moab (New York, 1975), 76.

⁵ Feodor Dostoevsky, *Crime and Punishment*, trans. Jessie Coulson, ed. George Gibian (New York: Norton, 1989), 56.

Dostoevsky that, after carefully "decid[ing] that all banks are based on principles of delusion and swindle,"[6] he resolved to commit his crime in order to come to the aid of all those dependent on him as well as others of "the insulted and injured" (this phrase being the title of one of the lesser-known Dostoevsky novels).

Murav, however, concludes that "the real motivation of Kovner's crime is difficult to pin down" (135). She even suggests that Kovner's explanation of his crime in Dostoevskian terms may have sprung from some remarks made by the prosecuting attorney. Less merciful to Kovner than the jury—though one assumes that, like most Russians, they were hardly too favorably disposed to Jews—she refuses to be taken in by Kovner's assumed Raskolnikov identity. The outstanding Russian scholar and Dostoevskyist Leonid Grossman, who wrote a small book on Kovner in 1924, was the first to explicate the comparison with *Crime and Punishment*; but Murav substitutes for the tormenting personal situation in which Kovner was caught a cloud of references invoking Bakhtin, Lydia Ginzburg, Peter Brooks (on confession as accusation), etc. According to her, "Kovner's dialogic address to Dostoevsky was overdetermined, marked both by the drama of acculturation and by the kind of literary confession typical of Dostoevsky's heroes" (136).

One can agree with Murav that Kovner's letters to Dostoevsky, especially the first two, were carefully composed and written to obtain specific ends; but it is difficult to see them, as she tends to imply, only as calculated fakeries based on imitating the literary manner of their recipient. Dostoevsky himself, who hardly can be suspected of naïveté in such matters, took them very seriously and wrote Kovner: "I have rarely read anything more intelligent than your first letter to me (your second is a special case)."[7] Kovner appeals to Dostoevsky for help in publishing a play that had been singled out for praise in a competition, as well as a story that had been approved by the censorship. Dostoevsky agreed to help, but neither was published and both have been lost.

More important, he told Kovner that he accepted his explanation for his crime; in other words, that it was not committed solely for sordid reasons of material gain but for worthier aims. He thus exonerated Kovner from the onus of being considered a common criminal. When Kovner added, however, that he felt no remorse whatever for the crime, Dostoevsky remonstrated, though with considerable tact ("I myself am not better than you or anyone," he wrote) that here Kovner had gone too far. "There is

---

[6] Grossman, *Confession of a Jew*, 76.
[7] Feodor Dostoevsky, *Polnoe Sobranie Sochinenii*, 30 vols. (Leningrad, 1972–1990), 29/bk. 2:139; February 14, 1877.

something higher than the conclusions of reason and all kinds of attendant circumstances to which everyone must submit ... it's much better if I forgive you than if you forgive yourself."[8]

One would expect that, in view of Kovner's situation, he would be, if not obsequious, then at least as deferential as possible. To be sure, he praises Dostoevsky as a writer in terms that the novelist obviously found insightful. Dostoevsky even comments, after Kovner chose *The Idiot* as his favorite novel, that "all those who have spoken of it as my best work have something in their mental formation that has always struck and pleased me"[9] (thus including Kovner in this select group). But while, according to Murav, Kovner supposedly assumes the identity of a Dostoevskian character, even she has to concede that "he took on a role that no Dostoevskian character ever played. *He defended the Jews*" (143, italics added). Indeed, Kovner's letter contains a blistering attack on Dostoevsky's failure to recognize the rights of Jews to full civic equality in Russia. "Are you *really* incapable," he writes bluntly, "of attaining to the fundamental law of any social life that all citizens of a country, if they bear all the duties necessary for the existence of the country, must enjoy all the rights and advantages of its existence.... Why must all Jews be limited in rights, and why must there be special punitive laws for them?" (144).[10] Moreover, he cannot understand Dostoevsky's "hatred of the *zhid* [an insulting word] which appears in almost every issue of your *Diary*."[11] As he remarks, "I have suffered more than a little because [of the prejudices of my people].... But I will never concede that unscrupulous exploitation is in the bloodstream of the Jewish people."[12]

Murav sees all this as part of a complicated interplay between the two in which they "seek to implicate each other in their disingenuous confessions—Kovner with respect to his crime, Dostoevsky with respect to his attitude toward the Jews" (147). Kovner in some sense involves the author Dostoevsky in his crime, while Dostoevsky, parrying Kovner's charge that he is anti-Semitic, cites a remark in Kovner's letter as evidence that *he* hates the Russian people. Dostoevsky's chapter on "The Jewish Question" in the *Diary of a Writer*, written as a direct answer to Kovner's letter, cites passages from it without mentioning the author's name. In reply to Kovner's accusations, Dostoevsky accuses the Jews of sucking the lifeblood of the Russian peasantry, assails Judaism as containing a Messianic claim to world domination, and attacks the Jews for maintaining a state of their own inside the state in which they live, thus giving them more power

[8] Ibid.
[9] Ibid.
[10] A. U. Kovner, Letter to F.M. Dostoevsky, 3 June 1877.
[11] Grossman, *Confession of a Jew*, 82.
[12] Ibid.

than the helpless Russian peasant. Nonetheless, he ends with a call for granting Jews full civic equality—unless, to be sure, their religion contains "deeper mysteries"[13] that make this impossible (just what this means is left unspecified).

Murav's discussion of these letters places the two correspondents on an equal footing, but this hardly does justice to the facts. She refuses to give Kovner any credit for what, from a nontheoretical point of view, can only be considered an act of courage and dignity. He could not restrain himself from challenging, on behalf of the Jews, the very person—a famous and influential author into the bargain—from whom he was hoping to obtain some alleviation of his extremely difficult situation. Indeed, while continuing to ask for help in placing his manuscripts, and willing to accept Dostoevsky's assurance that he is not an anti-Semite, Kovner nonetheless objects sharply to a passage in the article. Dostoevsky had written that, if the Jews had the power, they would turn the Russians into slaves, skin them alive, and slaughter them to the last man. Although Kovner calls this an "unintentional paradox" (151),[14] since Dostoevsky had also written feelingly about the Jews in another section and advocated according them civic equality, Kovner nonetheless retorts: "How can the Russian people not hate the Jews, when its best representatives publicly express their opinion of the latter as wild beasts?" (147).

Kovner's later life in Siberia was not an unhappy one. He found private employment almost immediately, and with the help of his former prosecutor, Muraviev, he ultimately obtained a post in a government agency auditing state finances. (!) Why Muraviev, a notorious anti-Semite, came to Kovner's aid remains a mystery. As the situation of the Jews in Russia worsened considerably in the latter half of the century, Kovner sent a lengthy memorandum to Muraviev, later published as a book (*The Language of Facts: About the Isolation of the Jews*), once again advocating that they be granted civic equality. He married a much younger Gentile woman, nominally becoming a Christian (Jews were not allowed to intermarry), and spoke of his so-called conversion only as a legal formality. Murav agrees that "the conversion is meaningless from the perspective of religion," but she nonetheless views it as "a way of negotiating a new reconciliation between Jewish and Russian identity" (175). How this could be "a reconciliation" once again escapes me; it is, if anything, a renunciation of Jewish identity for practical purposes.

Kovner wrote privately not only to Muraviev but to Tolstoy as well (Murav seems to have missed this epistle, to which Tolstoy never replied). He also wrote another novel, *Around the Golden Calf*, which is discussed

---

[13] Feodor Dostoevsky, *PSS*, 25: 87–88.
[14] A. U. Kovner, Letter to F. M. Dostoevsky, June 3, 1877.

too briefly to form any adequate idea of its contents. A valuable chapter, however, is devoted to Kovner's correspondence with V. V. Rozanov, much more copious than his letters to Dostoevsky. Although little known outside Russia, Rozanov is now considered one of the most original prose stylists of his time and was an extremely idiosyncratic if somewhat disreputable figure. As a young man he had married Dostoevsky's headstrong and intransigent ex-mistress, Apollinaria Suslova, considerably older than himself. She refused later to give him a divorce, though he lived with another woman and fathered several children. He also wrote a still-valuable book, *Dostoevsky and the Legend of the Grand Inquisitor*, which is one of the first serious attempts to cope with the religious-philosophical implications of Dostoevsky's novels.

As a philosophical essayist, Rozanov published in both reactionary and progressive newspapers at the same time, writing in each from a completely opposite social-political point of view. But he ranged far more widely, and one of his favorite topics was sex. He was a fervent opponent of the ascetic aspects of Christianity (he has sometimes been called the Russian Nietzsche) and praised the Biblical Hebrews for integrating their religion with a concern for the body and its functions; he was particularly impressed with circumcision as a link between man and God. But his approval of the ancient Hebrews did not extend to their modern descendants, and he was a regular contributor to the most Judeophobic newspaper of the day, *New Times*.

His correspondence with Kovner has never been published in its entirety and remains in the Manuscript Division of the Moscow Library. It is regrettable that Murav, who consulted the original documents, did not provide a more detailed and balanced account of their contents. Kovner's first letter took issue with the accuracy of some aspects of Rozanov's articles on Jewish rituals and Judaism; and much of it deals with such questions. Kovner apparently wrote quite freely about his sexual life, in response to Rozanov's promptings, and even prepared "a diary of his exploits, written in the style of Casanova" (168). But one letter of Kovner's also contains an indignant outburst about the Kishiniev pogrom in 1903, urging, though without success, that Rozanov denounce it publicly. "How disgusting," Kovner wrote, "that *New Time* is completely silent about the Kishiniev pogrom" (174).[15] He also criticized an article of Rozanov's very bluntly several years later because of its anti-Semitic description of the presumed innate characteristics of the Jewish people.

In a brochure published in 1906, "What I Believe," Kovner repeats some of the arguments he made against religion in his letter to Dostoevsky, but also holds up for admiration a first-century Jewish rabbi, Hillel, who

---

[15] A. U. Kovner, Letter to V. V. Rozanov, April 17, 1903.

founded an extremely influential school of Talmudic interpretation. Hillel was also famous for his response to the challenge of defining the essence of Judaism in a few words. "What you do not wish to happen to you," he replied, "do not do to your neighbor; that is the essence of the entire Torah; all the rest is commentary."[16] Rozanov refers approvingly to this book, and presumably to Hillel as well, in his sympathetic obituary of Kovner, ironically enough printed in the *New Times*. Labeling the deceased "a Jewish Pisarev," Rozanov also identified him as "the very same [person] who in February of 1877 wrote Dostoevsky a letter in defense of the Jews" (196).[17]

In her introduction, Harriet Murav explains that she chose to study her subject because "in his many efforts at transculturation, Kovner assumed different names, languages and ideologies and modified his autobiography depending on his listener" (2) This is perfectly true, and the value of her study lies in her depiction of the various cultural worlds in which he moved and the interaction of his fate with other Russian-Jewish intellectuals faced by the same extremely tormenting problems of transculturation. But she tries too hard to adapt his personality to the dialectic of her general categories, and this causes her to pay insufficient attention to his deep burning sense of indignation at social injustice—especially when it concerned the Jews. He always refused to remain silent on this subject, no matter to whom he was writing and whom he might offend. As a footnote, let me cite from her bibliography the information that the first book Kovner wrote in Hebrew was republished in Tel Aviv in 1947.

---

[16] *The Babylonian Talmud*, Shabbat 31a.
[17] V. V. Rozanov, *Okolo tserkovnykh sten* (St. Petersburg, 1906), 409.

THIRTEEN

J. M. COETZEE, *THE MASTER OF PETERSBURG*

J. M. COETZEE is a subtle and complex writer whose works invariably contain more than appears on their seemingly pellucid surfaces. He made his reputation with novels that focused on the psychological tension created in the white South African psyche by the social and human anomalies of apartheid. But his special gift is to raise this particular conflict, through a certain starkness of treatment and careful choice of detail, into a parable of the master/slave relationship in all colonial circumstances, in all unjust structures of power. In addition to such works, Coetzee also produced a strange little book called *Foe*, which was essentially a rewriting of Robinson Crusoe by a female narrator washed ashore on the island of the original Crusoe, who sees many things not contained in the first version, and who unsuccessfully struggles to persuade Defoe to convey her version of events after she returns to England accompanied by the silent Friday, whose thoughts and feelings she tries to fathom.

Such a work reminds us that Coetzee, who taught at the University of Capetown in his homeland, South Africa, but now teaches in Australia and has become a citizen of that country, is a professional linguist and literary scholar as well as a novelist. He sometimes prefers to express his ideas by means of literary pastiche as well as through his highly stylized treatment of contemporary South African life; and his new book is another contribution to this genre of pastiche. *The Master of Petersburg* draws not on the beginnings of the English novel but on the mid-nineteenth-century Russian novel, in particular on a number of Dostoevsky's creations, great and small. The central figure of the novel is Dostoevsky himself. Another important protagonist is the revolutionary Sergey Nechaev, whom Dostoevsky portrayed, though with no attempt at literal exactitude, in *Demons*, and so it might be thought that *Demons* is Coetzee's most important source; but he has culled from many places for his own purposes.

Coetzee's story begins in 1869, when Dostoevsky began the writing of *Demons* and was living in Dresden with his second wife, afraid to return

---

Originally published as "*The Master of Petersburg* by J. M. Coetzee," *The New Republic*, October, 16, 1995), 53–57. Reprinted by permission.

to Russia because he might be thrown into debtors' prison. In the novel, though, he returns to St. Petersburg with a false passport because he is notified that his stepson, Pavel Isaev, has died. Dostoevsky did have a stepson, the child of his first wife, whom he brought up as his son, and who was a rather feckless though by no means delinquent young man. Pavel, or Pasha, held a number of clerical jobs until his death in 1900. Coetzee thus plays fast and loose with the historical record by killing off Pavel Isaev in 1869; and this raises a more general problem about the book.

Other events that are simply recorded in Coetzee's novel, such as Dostoevsky's adulterous affair in St. Petersburg, or his supposedly catching a glimpse of Nechaev and Bakunin together at a meeting of the League for Peace and Freedom in Geneva, have no basis in fact. Coetzee is a novelist, of course, and he has the novelist's right to play with history. Still, it is regrettable that he did not include a warning to his readers, many of whom will be unfamiliar with the details of Dostoevsky's biography, not to take his fiction as fact. Many will no doubt do so, for the same reason that, as Dostoevsky complained, people thought he had murdered his wife because this was the crime imputed to the narrator of *House of the Dead*.

The fictional Dostoevsky thus arrived in St. Petersburg to gather up Pasha's effects and to look into the causes of his death. Coetzee's opening pages, rather than reminiscent of *Demons*, recall the atmosphere of Dostoevsky's little-known early story "The Landlady," which is somewhat atypical of his work and written in a garishly Romantic style in imitation of Gogol's Ukrainian tales. Coetzee's Dostoevsky moves into the rooming house in which Pasha lived and soon enters into a passionate love affair with the enigmatic landlady, much like the young intellectual Ordynov in Dostoevsky's story. And though Coetzee's tonality is a good bit more subdued, his fictional Dostoevsky drifts through the action in much the same semihypnotic fashion as Ordynov drifts through "The Landlady," which some critics have taken to be (mistakenly, in my view) a dreamlike hallucination of the main character. *The Master of Petersburg* is written in a very similar register, and Coetzee makes no attempt to provide any realistic psychological motivation for his figures and their actions. Rather than a novel, one might use a musical analogy and call Coetzee's book a poetic fantasia on Dostoevskian themes; it should be read as such a work, and not approached with more conventional expectations as a work of fiction.

The fictional Dostoevsky is portrayed as obsessed by Pasha's death (like so many other Coetzee characters in the grip of different obsessions), and in some obscure way refusing to surrender him to the oblivion of the grave. Motifs from Dostoevsky's work are interwoven with the character's attempt to cope with the sensation of loss produced by Pasha's death, which he feels as really his own. "I am the one who is dead, he thinks; or rather, I died but my death failed to arrive."[1] Just as Prince Myshkin is haunted by the thought of what a condemned man feels in the few moments before the fall of the guillotine, so Dostoevsky here "cannot bear ... the thought that, for the last fraction of the last instant of his fall [Pavel jumped, or was pushed, from a height], Pavel knew that nothing could save him, that he was dead. He wants to believe Pavel was protected from that certainty ... [but] he wants to believe in order to etherize himself against the knowledge that Pavel, falling, knew everything." By thinking such a thought, Dostoevsky imagines that he is identifying himself completely with Pavel, who is "thinking in him, he thinking ... in Pavel. The thought keeps Pavel alive suspended in this fall" (20).

When he goes to pick up Pavel's confiscated papers at the police station, Dostoevsky is informed of Pavel's connection with the Nechaev conspiracy, an underground revolutionary group that murdered one of their members for suspected treason. Readers will think of Raskolnikov's visits to a similar police station, and Coetzee teases them (and amuses himself) by allowing his fictitious Dostoevsky to clarify an obscure sense of having once been in an exactly similar situation. "Somewhere to the side falls the nagging shadow of a memory: surely he has been here before, in this very ante-room or one like it, and had an attack or a fainting fit!" (31). Yes, indeed! He had been here before as Raskolnikov, summoned to pay an IOU and fainting when he hears talk of the murder he has just committed.

Pasha's papers contain a list of people condemned to execution by Nechaev's revolutionary group, The People's Vengeance; and the councillor Maximov, who physically resembles the magistrate in *Crime and Punishment* ("a bald man with the tubby figure of a peasant woman" [31]), suggests that perhaps Pavel's death, rather than an accident or suicide, was a murder by the Nechaev group. Dostoevsky expresses horror and then revulsion at Pasha's links with Nechaev but at the same time sees the revolutionary as the embodiment of a much larger force. What moves Nechaev and accounts for his uncanny influence is not "ideas" (the historical Dostoevsky would have contested this formulation), but "a spirit, and Nechaev himself is not its embodiment but its host; or rather, he is under possession by it" (44). For all his historically accurate hatred of Nechaev, Dostoevsky is finally stirred to protest by Maximov's scornfully detached reading of an awkwardly romantic story written by Pasha, which contains a note of social protest by including the murder of a lecherous landowner about to rape a young peasant girl.

Dostoevsky instinctively springs to Pasha's defense against Maximov's amused contempt, and his tirade broaches what will soon become an im-

---

[1] J. M. Coetzee, *The Master of Petersburg* (London: Secker and Warburg, 1994), 19. Subsequent references to this work are cited in parentheses in the text.

portant thematic motif. For Dostoevsky accuses Maximov of suppressing his enjoyment of everything that, as an upholder of the law, he presumably wishes to combat and destroy. Of the murdered landowner, Dostoevsky says: "[D]o you suffer with him, or do you secretly exult behind the arm that swings the axe? You don't answer? Let me tell you then: reading is being the arm and being the axe and being the skull; reading is giving yourself up, not holding yourself at a distance and jeering" (47). As for Maximov's pretense of merely enforcing the law: "Do you not truly want to chop off his [Nechaev's] head and stamp your feet in his blood?" (47).

Literature here, for Coetzee's Dostoevsky, involves a total imaginative participation with all the figures of the story, not only with the victim but also with the murderer revenging an injustice; and Maximov has no right to feel morally superior to the ruthless revolutionary he is pursuing. The fictional Dostoevsky in this way reveals both his view of literature as a surrender to every facet of good and evil projected in a text, and his own capacity to transcend his hatred of Nechaev by viewing Maximov as equally guilty of reveling in bloodshed. One suspects here the influence of Mikhail Bakhtin's suggestive (but somewhat exaggerated) view that the source of Dostoevsky's greatness as a writer is precisely this ability to identify with all his characters to an equal degree, and to allow them unlimited freedom to express their own point of view.

The theme that dominates Coetzee's early chapters—Dostoevsky's desire somehow to keep Pavel alive in memory and his guilty despair at his failure as a father—becomes quite tedious after a while, and less and less artistically persuasive. Luckily, it is taken up and fused with the Nechaev theme, which is far more interesting. Nechaev's group finally contacts Dostoevsky, first through a roly-poly female emissary and then through a transvestite Nechaev, incongruously clad and carefully powdered but with hairs sprouting on his chin. Nechaev insists that the police killed Pavel and appeals to Dostoevsky, as an ex-revolutionary, to take up the struggle again on the side of his murdered son. Nechaev's passionate plea makes Dostoevsky think of "Christ in his wrath.... The Christ of the Old Testament, the Christ who scourged the usurers out of the temple." But he replies to Nechaev's accusation that "all you can do is mumble and shake your head and cry" with a telling retort. "Is it the voice of the people you obey, or just your own voice, a little disguised so that you need not recognize it?" (104).

The fictional Dostoevsky becomes more and more involved with Nechaev, whom he describes in terms used by the historical Dostoevsky for Stavrogin. "He is a sensualist. He is an extremist of the senses. He wants to live in a body at the limits of sensation, at the limits of bodily knowledge" (114). Nechaev takes him to the decrepit tower in Petersburg from which Pavel fell (or was thrown), and they climb it on a storm-tossed night with "the roofs of St. Petersburg glinting in the rain, the row of tiny lamps along the quayside" (118). Nechaev accuses Dostoevsky of having neglected Pasha, unerringly touching the sorest spot of his conscience ("We were his family when he had no family" [119]); and as the two men shriek in the howling wind while they clamber above the city, Coetzee craftily anticipates the reader's reaction to the staginess of this effects. "In fact the whole scene—two men on a moonlit platform high above the streets struggling against the elements, shouting over the wind, denouncing each other—is false, melodramatic" (120): these words are supposed to transcribe Dostoevsky's reaction to what he is experiencing.

The final chapters in which Nechaev and Dostoevsky verbally cross swords constitute the ideological climax of the book and set "the spirit of justice" against what might be called the spirit of freedom. What will happen, Dostoevsky asks, "once the tempest of the people's vengeance has done its work and everyone has been levelled? Will you still be free to be whom you wish? Will each of us be free to be whom we wish, at last?" (184). Dostoevsky invokes Shigalyov's theory of equality praised by Pyotr Verkhovensky in *Demons* ("if another Copernicus were to arise he should have his eyes gouged out" [185]); but Nechaev replies with an apocalyptic image of total destruction, as a prelude to a perpetual regeneration, which radicalizes even the historical Nechaev and his mentor Bakunin.

The future, for Nechaev, is a revolution "when everything is reinvented, everything erased and reborn: law, morality, the family, everything." The "old way of thinking" will be abolished and (anticipating Mao) "the peasants will be the teachers and the professors will be the students.... Everyone will be reborn with a new heart" (189). When Dostoevsky mentions God, Nechaev rapturously replies that "God will be envious ... [and] the angels will stand around us in circles singing their hosannas" (190). Even more, the souls of the dead, the soul of Pavel Isaev, will arise and walk the Earth again. Imitating the Christ of the Legend of the Grand Inquisitor, Dostoevsky embraces Nechaev, "breathing the sour smell of his carbuncular flesh, sobbing, laughing, he kisses him on the left cheek and on the right" (190). Still, in a last feeble effort to resist being swept away, he threatens Nechaev with eternal damnation. But Nechaev charges him with ignorance of theology and invokes the apocryphal legend of the Mother of God who, making "a pilgrimage to hell to plead for the damned" (201), refuses to desist until all have been forgiven (the historical Dostoevsky uses this legend in *The Brothers Karamazov*).

Finally, at the end of Coetzee's book, street fighting between the students and police has broken out, fires are burning, and "a cloud of smoke hangs over the city" (234). (Coetzee may have been thinking of, and magnifying, what occurred in St. Petersburg in 1862.) Dostoevsky feels that he has been defeated by Nechaev, that he "has lost because, in this debate, he does not believe himself" (201–2) He leafs through Pavel's papers, and we are met for the first time by Dostoevsky's self-awareness as a writer. For what Pavel (or his master Nechaev, as well as the landlady) did not understand is that "I pay too ... I pay and I sell: that is my life. Sell my life, sell the lives of those around me.... Sell you, sell your daughter [Matryona], sell all those I love.... A life without honour; treachery without limit; confession without end" (222). All this has led to a terrifying awareness of his own uncertainty, which requires him, if he is to continue to create, "to put aside all that he himself is, all he has become, down to his very features, and become as a babe again" (240).

By the end of the book, in the chapter significantly called "Stavrogin," Coetzee seems to equate Dostoevsky as a writer—or writing in general—with the efforts of this Byronic dandy transformed into metaphysical rebel to wipe out the boundaries of good and evil. Dostoevsky does not appear as a writer at all until this last chapter, but finally he sits down to compose in Pavel's room, determined to "refuse the chloroform of terror or unconsciousness," and instead, "to live in Russia and hear the voices of Russia murmuring within him. To hold it all within him: Russia, Pavel, death." No longer merely the victim of epilepsy or madness, he willfully becomes their vehicle: "not to emerge from the fall unscathed ... to wrestle with the whistling darkness, to absorb it, to make it his medium; to turn the falling into a flying, even if a flying as slow and old and clumsy as a turtle" (234–35). But he also feels, as he unpacks his writing case, that he is engaging in an act of betrayal.

What Dostoevsky writes, in the empty pages in Pavel's notebook, is a reconstitution of Pavel's life in the landlady's apartment, garnished with details taken from Stavrogin's confession, the suppressed chapter of *Demons* published only after Dostoevsky's death, which recounts his seduction and violation of a young girl. What he has written is "an assault upon the innocence of a child. It is an act for which he can expect no forgiveness" and is in effect a temptation of God. "Now God must speak, now God dare no longer remain silent." He imagines himself standing outside his own soul, "somewhere he stands and watches while he and God circle each other." Writing thus involves the loss of one's soul, it is a challenge to God, and he feels again that "he has betrayed everyone; nor does he see that his betrayal could go deeper" (249–50). The book ends with the action unresolved; we do not know how or why Pavel died, or whether the fictional Dostoevsky returns to Dresden. And Dostoevsky is left only with a sense of complete emptiness and dispossession, his mouth filled with the bitter taste of gall. "They pay him lots of money for writing books, said the child [Matryona], repeating the dead child [Pavel]. What they failed to say was that he had to give up his soul in return" (250).

This is an enigmatic and rather puzzling book whose aim is difficult to unravel. Clearly Coetzee is not attempting, like a historical novelist, to convey any sort of historically correct image of Dostoevsky's life in 1869; he prefers to make use of his writer's liberties and to invent his own details. He makes only a very perfunctory stab at filling in the St. Petersburg background, and the effect that he creates is more somnambulistic than realistic. What, then, is he trying to do?

Coetzee, one must remember, is a South African writer, and it may be that he felt himself to be living (until very recently) in a society even more repressive than that of Russia in the nineteenth century, and poised like Russia on the edge of a revolutionary upheaval. Dostoevsky is the greatest novelist of modern revolutionary crisis, of the clash of values that such a crisis involves. It is not difficult to understand why Coetzee, who has used the pastiche of *Foe* to dramatize the issues of feminism and multiculturalism, should use Dostoevsky in the same way to express the dilemmas racking his own society. Coetzee may well have lived the clash between the spirit of justice and the spirit of freedom with all the intensity of Dostoevsky.

But there is also, as we have seen, the problem of writing and the writer, which Coetzee presents so poignantly; and here perhaps he is obliquely taking into account his own personal situation in South African literature. There has never been any ambiguity about his unswerving hostility to the abominations of apartheid, now happily a thing of the past; but he has been harshly criticized in his homeland because his novels did not attack these evils in any overt, socially propagandistic manner. A typical charge, made in 1982, accused him of giving "privileged attention to the predicament of a liberal petty bourgeois intelligentsia."[2] Even the publication, a year later, of his intensely moving *Life and Times of Michael K*, whose central character is black or a person of color vainly seeking to lead a normal, peaceful life, did not put an end to such brickbats. In 1986 another critic attributed Coetzee's increasing international fame "to the muddled pathos of the position of the white South Africans,"[3] which gives such fiction as his its worldwide appeal. Coetzee himself has commented somewhat sadly on the difference in his status at home and abroad.

The Master of Petersburg, then, may be an implicit act of self-defense, a defense of the writer's obligation in an explosive revolutionary period to

---

[2] Michael Vaughan, "Literature and Politics: Currents in South African Writing in the Seventies," *Journal of Southern African Studies* 9, 1 (October 1982): 137.

[3] Lars Engle, "Outrageous Meaning: The Fiction of J.M. Coetzee," *Threepenny Review* 24 (Winter 1986): 5.

participate creatively in all sides of the human bedlam, even at the cost of personal self-abandonment. Such an obligation seems to stir Dostoevsky when he rewards Nechaev with the kiss of Christian forgiveness, while being left himself only with a tragic sense of loss and self-betrayal. Is this novel more a self-revelation than may appear at first sight? We can only speculate. One thing, though, can be stated unequivocally: Coetzee is a fascinating and mysteriously compelling writer.

FOURTEEN

DOSTOEVSKY AND EVIL

IN THE SPRING OF 2002, a colloquium on the problem of evil, sponsored by the Nexus Foundation, was held at the University of Tilburg in Holland. I was a member of a panel assigned to discuss Dostoevsky, certainly the modern writer who has given the thematic of evil one of its most powerful expressions. Our keynote speaker was the South African novelist J. M. Coetzee, who, however, sprung a surprise on his fellow panelists and the audience by not speaking about Dostoevsky at all. Instead, he read a sketch supposedly written by a fictional personage already familiar from his work, a writer like himself named Elizabeth Costello, presumably invited to speak at precisely such a conference on precisely such a topic; and she finds herself rebelling at the task she had assumed.

Her own experience with evil, as she now horrifiedly recalls, was of having been badly beaten by a would-be lover, whom she had carelessly picked up as a young student out of self-indulgence and a youthful search for adventure. After accompanying him to a rooming house, she finally refused her favors; and his frustration then turning to sadism, he beat her so brutally and relentlessly that, among other injuries, he broke her jaw. This had been her own personal experience with evil, the release of demonic forces in a human personality—-forces, she had concluded, that craved satisfaction in her thwarted lover even more strongly than his initial demand for sexual surrender. The encounter left her with a psychic-emotional scar that had never healed; and although she had since become a successful novelist and essayist, she had never utilized this traumatic episode in her works. It had been too painful for her to resuscitate even in some altered artistic form. Now she was wondering why she had accepted the invitation to speak as a writer at a conference on evil. For she had begun to doubt whether *anyone* should be encouraged to depict its all too widespread ravages in the modern world, and whether those who did should be approved and applauded.

This question had become acute for her because she had recently read a novel describing the trial and execution of the German Army officers who had attempted to assassinate Hitler. Ironically entitled *The Very Rich*

Originally published in a slightly different form in *The Partisan Review*, March 2003. Reprinted by permission.

Hours of Count von Stauffenberg—thus evoking late-medieval and Renaissance celebrations of the peaceful pursuits and glories of royalty—the book had finally revolted her to the core. "All was going well enough until she came to the chapters describing the execution of the plotters."[1] The horrifying and repugnant details employed here showed these more or less aged notables being stripped physically of any shred of human dignity, and being mocked and taunted by their executioner with the most revolting particularities ("how the shit would run down their spindly old-man's legs"). This was more than she could endure; reading such pages made her "sick with the spectacle, sick with a world in which such things took place, until at last she pushed the book away and sat with her head in her hands" (158).

The word that came to her mind at this point was "obscene," and she had determined to object to the generally accepted opinion that the use of such material was necessarily desirable. Was she then in favor of censorship? Not at all in the usual sense—that is, of some external authority setting limits to what could or could not be portrayed. But inwardly, she had now come to question the belief, indigenous to Western culture as a whole, that "unlimited and illimitable endeavor" was unquestionably beneficial, and the accompanying conviction "that people are always improved by what they read." Furthermore, she is not at all sure that "writers who venture into the darker territories of the human psyche always return unscathed" (160). What troubles her above all is that, while appalled and repelled by the book, she had not been able to push it away entirely. It had resisted her feelings of revulsion and disgust, and she feared that some of the "absolute evil" it depicted had, as it were, also infected her; "she felt, she could have sworn, the brush of Satan's hot, leathery wing" (178).

Coetzee depicts the inner debate of his feminine alter ego with all the insinuating subtlety of his talent; but he does not allow her conclusion to remain unchallenged. Indeed, after she had expressed such ideas in her paper, a member of the audience arises to contest her point of view. Moreover, Coetzee undermines her even further when she recalls that, in her own work, she had no more spared the feelings of the reader than the author she is now reproving. For she had "shown no qualms about rubbing people's faces in, for instance, what went on in abattoirs. If Satan is not rampant in the abattoir, casting the shadow of its wings over the beast ... where is he?" (179). Those familiar with Coetzee's writings will recognize to what extent the preoccupations of Elizabeth Costello intersect with some of his own. But this is not my topic, and I shall not pursue any

---

[1] J. M. Coetzee, *Elizabeth Costello* (New York: Viking, 2003), 158. Subsequent references to this work are cited in parentheses in the text.

further the question of whether the self-doubt of his female novelist can be attributed to the author himself. In any case, the issue he (she) raises, the issue of how far an author should go in defaming the human race, so to speak, remains totally unresolved; the narrator of the sketch proposes no solution to her dilemma

The crucial question raised by Coetzee, however—one that has been debated endlessly ever since Plato exiled those poets from his republic who did not portray the gods with sufficient reverence—was taken up somewhat later by another outstanding novelist, the Peruvian Mario Vargas Llosa. His own works are immensely varied, but some, for example, *The Feast of the Goat* (2000), portray naked evil in images perhaps less physically degrading than those of Coetzee's imagined novel but equally ruthless. Vargas Llosa clearly felt provoked by the views of his fellow novelist and responded brilliantly in his own terms, but in fact elaborating on the argument of the questioner from the audience who had risen to challenge Ms. Costello's talk. "Perhaps we would be able to read what Mr. West [the author of the Stauffenberg book] wrote," this person had said, "and learn from it, and therefore come out stronger rather than weaker" (175).

Vargas Llosa picks up this point by remarking that the act of reading a book does not in itself make anyone better or worse. "The manner in which a poem, a novel, a play works on the sensibility or on a character varies to infinity, and much more as a result of the reader rather than of the work. To read Dostoevsky may, in some cases, lead to traumatic and criminal consequences, while on the other hand it is not impossible that the spermatic iniquities of the Marquis de Sade have increased the percentage of virtuous readers, vaccinating them against carnal vice." Similarly, some readers of the novel that so appalled Ms. Costello might have been strengthened in their hatred of sadistic cruelty.

All this being true, the question still remains of whether an author should be relieved of *all* responsibility for the effect created by his work. Coetzee's spokesperson perhaps goes too far by implying that certain aspects of human evil should be off-limits for literary depiction; but Vargas Llosa perhaps also goes too far in freeing writers of *any* responsibility for the possible consequences of their works. Might not Ms. Costello's outcry of "obscenity" have been caused by the *manner* in which the author reimagined the scene of execution—not so much the event itself, which could well have held the victims up for admiration, but the author's choice to stress unrelievedly an effort to humiliate and degrade them as much as possible? Indeed, there seems to be such a suggestion in the Coetzee text when Ms. Costello asks: "Where could West have got his information? Could there really have been witnesses who went home that night ... [and] wrote down, in words that must have scorched the paper, an account of what they had seen?" (158). Manifestly not, so far as we know: West was writing a novel. The details chosen to evoke the scene are his own creation, and her horrified response cannot simply be fobbed off as a private reader reaction.

This whole discussion arose in connection with Dostoevsky; and though Coetzee never mentions his name, it may not be overly speculative to assume that the reflections of Ms. Costello also contain an implicit reference to his novels. Indeed, in his own day the same sort of charge was often made against Dostoevsky that Coetzee/Costello makes against Paul West. The so-called heroes of his major novels are criminals who either commit murder themselves or motivate others (in the case of *The Idiot* unwittingly) to carry out their evil intentions. In *Demons*, the "hero" Stavrogin is not only guilty of incitement to murder but also of pedophilia, leading to the despairing suicide of a hapless twelve-year-old girl that he does nothing to prevent. (To be sure, the chapters containing the pedophilia episode were not published in Dostoevsky's lifetime, but rumors about their scabrous content were widespread; and they are now published as an appendix to every edition of the text.) In any case, there is no question that Dostoevsky was constantly skirting the moral bounds that most serious writers in the nineteenth century imposed on themselves, or the bounds imposed by the various censorships of the time.

If reading Dostoevsky's novels can possibly lead to criminal consequences, it is thus not simply, as Vargas Llosa might lead us to believe, because readers have the option of using them any way they please. The works do, after all, grippingly portray criminal impulses and criminal deeds, and nobody depicted the horror of the murder of an innocent more unsparingly than Dostoevsky in *Crime and Punishment*. He takes us into much the same region as Paul West; yet the effect of Dostoevsky's unflinching explorations of evil turn out, for most readers, to be quite the opposite of those that Ms. Costello finds unbearable. They may have been brushed by Satan's wing, but only for a moment and not indelibly. How does Dostoevsky achieve this result, which neither the views of Coetzee nor those of Vargas Llosa help us to account for? The question is worth examining here at a little more length.

Dostoevsky's early work from 1840 to 1849, when he was arrested because of his association with the supposedly revolutionary Petrashevsky circle, reveals no traces of the preoccupation with violent crime that would later play so important a role in his works. Rather, he was concerned to depict the minuscule torments and travails of the educated lower class of St. Petersburg, members of the huge government bureaucracy that labored to administer the vast reaches of the Russian Empire. All these were the "poor folk" that he portrayed in his first novel and early stories, victims rather than evildoers. Their greatest fear was that they might, in some way, infringe the constricting social-cultural taboos that marked their place in society; that they might be considered to be "free-thinkers" by their superiors and thus ground down even more relentlessly. All are obsessed with a pathological sense of guilt as a result of such fears; and in the most extensive portrayal of such a schizophrenic consciousness in *The Double*, the character ends in a madhouse. In only one story, *The Landlady*, do we come across someone possibly guilty of a serious crime—the elderly merchant Murin, who may once have been a robber chieftain of Volga bandits. But this story, an imitation of Gogol's Ukrainian folktales, is too full of Romantic trappings to be taken seriously on this level.

There is one work in this period, however, hardly more than a slight sketch, in which something that might be considered a crime is committed; but it is really only a pitiful misdeed. The story is called *An Honest Thief*, and the oxymoronic title tells it all. A hopelessly destitute and incurable drunkard, in order to buy more vodka, steals a pair of breeches from a benefactor who has taken him in out of charity; and the thief becomes so filled with remorse that he dies of grief. It is a textbook example of the "sentimental Naturalism" for which Dostoevsky became known at this time, and in itself of minor importance. But there is one passage in the original text—Dostoevsky suppressed it in revision for some reason, and it is thus very little known—that is important for my purposes. The thief's benefactor is trying to explain what occurred to a third party and asks his listener not to "despise a man who has fallen; that's what Christ, who loved all of us more than himself, told us not to do." And since "he died from grief and a bad conscience ... he showed the world ... he was a human being all the same." Men can struggle against vice; "it's not born with you—here today, it can be gone for good to-morrow; otherwise, if we were destined to stay depraved all through the ages because of original sin, Christ would never have come to us."[2]

This is of course the utterance of a character in a story, and I am well aware that it is a flagrant critical error to assume that it speaks for the author himself. Moreover, it is quite in keeping with the character, a simple-minded pensioner (a retired soldier, a man of the people) who would naturally use Christian references in his speech. All the same, I will risk attributing it to the author because I believe it tells us something fundamental about Dostoevsky's view of human nature and its relation to evil. The Augustinian condemnation of humanity because of original sin has had much less influence in the Eastern Orthodox Church than in Roman Catholicism. There was thus very little obstacle to Dostoevsky's acceptance of the French Utopian Socialist Christianity that began to make headway at this time among "progressive" Russian intellectuals. This Christianity saw nothing in human nature to prevent translating the love-ethic of Christ into worldly, secular, and particularly social-political terms; and it was this love-ethic that dominated all of Dostoevsky's writings in this early period.

---

[2] *PSS*, 2:426.

Dostoevsky's arrest in 1849, and the four-year sentence he spent in a hard-labor prison camp in Siberia, marked a crucial turning point in his life—as he later wrote himself, it marked what he called "the regeneration of his convictions,"[3] a phrase that has been interpreted in a bewildering variety of ways. But one thing is certain: whatever the effect of these prison-camp years, it was linked to an encounter with evil for which he was totally unprepared. Nothing had provided him with any inkling of the moral anarchy that reigned, without any check, in the midst of the prison-camp world into which he was thrown. "I was surprised and confused," he wrote in *House of the Dead*, "as though I had heard nothing of all this and had not suspected its existence. Yet I had heard of it and knew of it. But the reality makes quite a different impression from what one hears and knows."[4] Most of the convicts had committed at least one murder, if not several; they also stole from each other incessantly, lied, cheated, and drank themselves into stupefaction. Describing life among them, Dostoevsky speaks of "everything being defiled and degraded."[5]

In some sense, these four years can be seen as a test of the view of human nature set down in *An Honest Thief*—the view that, even among those having surrendered to the temptation of evil, repentance and regeneration was always possible. And in the little-read but indispensable masterpiece *House of the Dead* (Tolstoy's favorite among Dostoevsky's works), he portrays, along with much else about prison-camp life that must be neglected here,[6] the gradual passage of this test, and the reassurance that human nature—even among thieves and murderers—was not incurably corrupt. Mainly this is done indirectly—by indicating time and again, for example, without stating it explicitly, that many of the murders were peasant responses to the intolerable mistreatment and injustices this class customarily suffered at the hands of their superiors. More important, perhaps, was that the atrocities of these peasant-criminals had not obliterated their moral sense. For Dostoevsky describes their behavior at the Easter services when each "brought his poor farthing," feeling that "in God's eyes we are all equal." And "when with the chalice in his hands the priest read the words ' ... accept me, O Lord, even as the thief,' almost all of them bowed down to the ground with the clanking of chains, apparently applying the words literally to themselves."[7]

---

[3] Fyodor Dostoevsky, *The Diary of a Writer*, trans. Boris Brasol ((Salt Lake City: Peregrine Smith Books, 1979), 152.

[4] Fyodor Dostoevsky, *The House of the Dead and Poor Folk*, trans. Constance Garnett (New York: Barnes and Noble Classics, 2004), 82.

[5] Ibid., 14.

[6] For more details, see my *Dostoevsky: The Years of Ordeal, 1850–1859* (Princeton: Princeton University Press, 1983), chaps 6–11.

[7] Ibid., 230.

A transformation thus took place in Dostoevsky's relation to the peasant-convicts, one that provides the underlying thematic structure of *House of the Dead*. His feelings gradually evolved from the first shock of horror to that of a more sympathetic comprehension and even, at last, admiration. In a passage that misled Nietzsche, who thought Dostoevsky was providing confirmation for his own effort to go beyond conventional ideas of good and evil, Dostoevsky even wrote: "Perhaps, indeed, they [the peasant-convicts] were the most gifted, the strongest of all our people."[8] But he never describes this evolution from within, never, for reasons that may be both external (censorship) and artistic (his aim of reporting on prison-camp life), depicts his own feelings directly. It is only seventeen years later, in a famous article included in his *Diary of a Writer* (1876), "The Peasant Marey," that he provided a psychological supplement to his prison memoirs.

Here he begins with a sharp and swift evocation of an Easter week celebration in the camp, when the convicts could drink, carouse, and quarrel to their heart's content; and he looked on with a feeling of deep loathing at the raucous turbulence and brutality unrolling before his eyes. To escape, he walks outside the barracks and meets a cultivated Polish prisoner, who tells him in French: "I hate these bandits."[9] Returning then to lie down on the plank bed where all the convicts slept, he recalls a childhood incident when, frightened by the cry that a wolf was in the forest where he was strolling, he ran for succor to a peasant plowing in the fields, a serf owned by his father, named Marey.

The kindly peasant calmed the frightened child with what Dostoevsky describes as almost motherly tenderness, reassured him that there was no wolf, and sent him home after blessing him with the sign of the cross. As this recollection came flooding back, it also brought about a complete reversal in Dostoevsky's earlier revulsion against the spectacle of peasant-convict barbarity. "I remember, when I got off the plank bed and gazed around, that I suddenly felt I could look on these unfortunates with quite different eyes.... That despised peasant with shaven head and brand marks on his face, reeling with drink, bawling out his hoarse, drunken song—why, he may have been that very Marey; after all, I am not able to look into his heart."[10]

This is no longer the "sentimental Naturalism" of Dostoevsky's early period, the appeal not to judge the pathetic "crime" of the hopeless drunkard too harshly because he died of grief. The crimes of those in *House of the Dead* are instances of evil far surpassing anything Dostoevsky could

---

[8] Ibid., 302.
[9] Dostoevsky, *Diary of a Writer*, 206.
[10] Ibid., 210.

personally have met with earlier; but he still refuses to believe that such evil is immitigable and irreparable. Concealed in the human heart is also the kindness and compassion of Marey; and this contains the possibility of remorse and redemption. It is these responses that Dostoevsky now searches for (and finds) beneath the repellent exterior and even the horrendous crimes.

Although Dostoevsky's novel and stories are filled with Christian sentiments, imagery, and allusions, explicit firsthand statements about his religious convictions are quite rare. One of the very few is contained in a notebook entry from April 1864, written during an all-night vigil at the bier of his first wife. "To love man like *oneself*, according to the commandment of Christ "he scribbled then, "is impossible. The law of personality on earth binds. The Ego stands in the way." Evil is thus an inherent attribute of the human condition; only "Christ alone could love man as himself, but Christ is a perpetual eternal ideal to which man strives and, according to the law of nature, should strive."[11] It is thus a law of (human) nature to strive to realize the ideal of Christ; and since human nature also contains another law, that of personality, it is thus locked into an eternal battle with itself. These words condense and express what Dostoevsky had learned in the prison camp, which had immeasurably broadened and deepened what may be called the honest-thief paradigm of his early years.

In his *Diary of a Writer* (1873), Dostoevsky vividly exemplifies the same vision by citing a poem of Nekrasov entitled "Vlas." He is a religious pilgrim who in the past had been a godless reprobate, flogging his wife to death and consorting with thieves and highwaymen. But after falling sick and experiencing a vision of the tortures of Hell, he takes an oath and becomes a pilgrim wandering through the land and collecting "offerings for God's church":

> Filled with grief past consolation,
> Dark of face, erect, and tall,
> He passes on with gait unhurried,
> Through the village, through the town
>
> But never word passed e'en his lips,
> A book, an icon at his side,
> Strong chains of iron round his hips,
> To overcome his sinful pride.[12]

This poem uses Russian peasant imagery to express the conversion of the sinner, and there is no doubt that Dostoevsky believed the Russian folk character in particular to be more amenable to such transformations

---

[11] *PSS*, 20:72.
[12] *PSS*, 21:32

than the people of other nations; but we may disregard the nationalistic slant of his ideas, which play little or no role in his artistic creations. Indeed, the intellectually sophisticated and highly cultivated characters of his novels undergo the same moral mutations as the untutored Vlas. What is common to both is the struggle of moral conscience to live up to the "perpetual eternal ideal" of the love-ethic of Christ, despite the impossibility of ever truly accomplishing this endless task here on Earth. All of Dostoevsky's best works depict this struggle without flinching at portraying evil; but its manifestations are, if not balanced, then certainly mitigated, by the torments of conscience unleashed in the psyche of his main characters.

Let us open *Crime and Punishment* and look at the commission of the murder by Raskolnikov—a murder motivated, or so at least he believed, by "humanitarian" motives. "Because she was so short the axe struck her full on the crown of the head.... Then he struck her again and yet again with all his strength, always with the blunt side of the axe and always on the crown of the head. Blood poured out as if from an overturned glass.... Her wide-open eyes looked ready to start out of their sockets, her forehead was wrinkled, and her whole face convulsively distorted."[13] Or let us look at the murder of the simple-minded Lizaveta, who comes into the room by accident. "When she saw him run in, she trembled like a leaf and her face twitched spasmodically; she raised her hands to cover her mouth, but no scream came.... He flung himself forward with the axe; her lips writhed pitifully, like those of a young child when it is just beginning to be frightened and stands ready to scream, with its eyes fixed on the object of its fear....The blow fell on her skull, splitting it open from the top of the forehead almost to the crown of the head and felling her instantly."[14]

One would be hard put to match such grisly details in either the European or the Russian novel of the same period, but their effect is ultimately offset by the intensity of Raskolnikov's inner suffering and his final inability to endure his total estrangement from the rest of humanity. Besides the murders, there is perhaps the even more shocking metamorphosis, in Svidrigailov's dream, of the pitiful little five-year-old girl he stumbles on, shivering and crying, who a bit later smiles at him seductively "with the face of a courtesan, the brazen face of a mercenary French harlot."[15] This anticipates Stavrogin's pedophilia but is immediately countered by Svidrigailov's appalled reaction and his own suicide that follows shortly thereafter. Even Dostoevsky's deepest-dyed villain, himself guilty of despi-

---

[13] Feodor Dostoevsky, *Crime and Punishment*, trans. Jessie Coulson, ed. George Gibian (New York: Norton, 1989), 66.

[14] Ibid., 68.

[15] Ibid., 431.

cable crimes, cannot endure this vision of childish innocence transformed into shameless vice.

One can find example after example in Dostoevsky's works of the same boldness in depicting evil at work and the same effort to overcome its effects. But there is no point in continuing to pile up passages; we can go directly to his last and greatest work, *The Brothers Karamazov*, in which this issue is raised explicitly with a towering power and brilliance that makes it one of the few rivals to the Old Testament Book of Job. Nowhere else in Dostoevsky—nowhere, perhaps, since Dante and Milton—can we find a panoply of horrors displayed in such profusion. The Turks who cut children from their mother's womb, or throw others who have been born into the air to catch on their bayonets while mothers look on; the "feeble little nag" mercilessly beaten "on its weeping, on its 'meek eyes'[16] (a detail already used in *Crime and Punishment*); the poor little five-year-old girl brutally beaten, thrashed, and kicked by "cultured parents," then locked in an outhouse and forced to eat her excrement; the serf-boy torn to death by hunting dogs before his mother's eyes for having thrown a stone that lamed a favorite dog—all this leads Ivan Karamazov to denounce God and the world of "diabolical good and evil" that He created.

Shortly after sending off this section of the novel, which also contains the Legend of the Grand Inquisitor, Dostoevsky wrote in a letter that Ivan's devastating accusation would be answered by the preachments of Father Zosima. But many readers, myself included, have found these worthy sentiments, no matter how impressively and movingly expressed, to be rather weak in the face of Ivan's accumulation of moral monstrosities. Later, when the novel had been completed, Dostoevsky wrote in his notebook—more accurately, in my view—that the *entire* work was really the answer to these chapters. And this answer is given by the triumph of moral conscience in the three main characters, as well as in the murderer Smerdyakov. For while refusing to overlook that God permits all the evils denounced by Ivan, Dostoevsky also remained firm in his assurance that the God-man Jesus had been sent to stir the conscience of mankind in its eternal struggle against iniquity.

This is hardly the place to explore in any detail the multiple ways in which Dostoevsky's great novel embodies this theme. The most obvious is Dimitry's last-minute inability, despite his seething rage and resentment, to strike the fatal blow against his justifiably hated father. But the most direct answer to Ivan's horror at the world God had created, and which leads to his bitterly disillusioned declaration that "everything is permit-

---

[16] Fyodor Dostoevsky, *The Brothers Karamazov*, trans. Constance Garnett (New York: Barnes and Noble Classics, 2003), 223.

ted," is given by the pages in which his own responsibility for the murder begins to pierce through his consciousness. The gradual inner awareness of his own culpability and his efforts to suppress it; the three almost somnambulistic visits to Smerdyakov to seek reassurance; the marvelous black comedy of the Devil's hallucinatory visit (a product of Ivan's own schizophrenic psyche); his final collapse and mental breakdown—all this remains unsurpassed as an image of moral conscience at work, a conscience for whose injunctions, as the Devil rightly mocks, Ivan's reason offers no justification whatever.

It is thus not the views of Father Zosima that give Dostoevsky's novel its enduring sublimity (quite the contrary!) but the masterly portrayal of the influence of moral conscience, an influence in each case convincingly adapted to the personality and situation of the character portrayed. Such influence can be felt and understood quite independently of Dostoevsky's own convictions (his view, for example, that conscience cannot exist without a belief in immortality), or indeed, of that of the readers themselves. So that while Dostoevsky does not spare his readers the evil that he so vividly represents, he invariably counterbalances its effects by insisting on the ineradicability of a moral conscience that even the most hardened evildoer will not be able to escape.

It is time now, however, to return to Elizabeth Costello and examine her plight a little more carefully. Why has the book of Paul West brought on the crisis that had led her to the advocacy—reluctant, to be sure—of an inner censorship? Describing what the author must have intended, she speaks of it as a "wager with himself: to take as his subject a handful of bumbling German career officers unfitted by the very code of their upbringing to plotting and carrying out an assassination, to tell the story of their ineptitude and its consequences from beginning to end, and to leave one feeling, to one's surprise, authentic pity, authentic terror" (162–63). Nor had she felt any objection to the book until the scene of the hanging, with its deliberate degradation of the prisoners, and particularly the portrait of the hangman, the butcher, to whom West gives "a voice, allowing him his coarse, his worse than coarse, his unspeakable gibes at the shivering old men he is about to kill, gibes about how their bodies are going to betray them as they buck and dance at the end of the rope" (168).

This, as we know, is Paul West's conception; as author he is responsible for the manner in which he depicts this episode; and there is no evidence here of pity, only terror and even horror. It is such horror that leads Costello to level against him the charge of "obscenity," and to arrive at her extreme conclusion. "To save our humanity, certain things that we may want to see (*may want to see because we are human!*) must for ever remain off-stage. Paul West ... has shown what ought not to be shown" (168–69). But has West shown what really ought not to be shown, or has he rather shown it in such a way that its impact leads to Costello's charge? Has she gone too far in wishing to outlaw such a scene entirely, and assuming that the only other possibility is to accept it unobjectionably as it stands (leaving its effect, as Vargas Llosa had insisted, to the vagaries of the reader)?

Coetzee's sketch ends without any resolution, but nonetheless its final paragraph expresses an unfulfilled longing. Costello yearns for "some confrontation leading to some final word"; perhaps, if she met Paul West in the corridor by accident, "something should pass between them, sudden as lightning, that will illuminate the landscape for her, even if afterwards it returns to its native darkness" (182). Nothing of the sort occurs; but one cannot help thinking that the person Costello really wishes to meet, rather than Paul West, is an incarnation of Dostoevsky. Is not such a wished-for sudden illumination typical of *his* poetics, and would it not have flared up again in the scene that so afflicted the distraught Costello? Would he not have found a spark of humanity *somewhere* in the sadistic ghastliness that West portrays? And is it not possible that Coetzee, with his perfect command of the Dostoevsky corpus— as we know from his *Master of St. Petersburg*—and who likes to play literary games, might have read his story to lead off a Dostoevsky panel precisely for this reason? If so, he would only have been following in the footsteps of Dostoevsky, who so often preferred to present his positive values *a contrario*—by dramatizing the unhappy fates of those who disregarded or distorted them with disastrous consequences.

PART IV

TWENTIETH-CENTURY ISSUES

FIFTEEN

ANTON CHEKHOV

CHEKHOV BIOGRAPHERS are a very lucky breed. They do not have to face the problem of spending a good deal of time studying the life of someone whom they may end up by disliking intensely. One famous example is the perhaps now-forgotten book by Lawrence Thompson, who was selected by Robert Frost himself to be his official biographer. After literally living with his subject, the critic found the poet to be very far from admirable; and the work he produced bore clear evidence of this shift of sentiment.

In my own case, after spending more years than I like to recall with Dostoevsky, there was also a somewhat related inner struggle. On the one hand, I admired his literary genius and his capacity to portray guilt-ridden figures unable to stifle their moral conscience—a conscience that one assumed was his own. On the other, there was my hostile reaction to many of the social-political ideas he accepted and propagated in the later phase of his life. Moreover, although Dostoevsky was not the monster portrayed by some biographers, who was at least implicitly guilty of all the crimes depicted in his novels (there were rumors to this effect during his lifetime), he was a notoriously difficult and prickly personality. Indeed, his attitude toward foreigners who questioned him about his work, as we know from the account left by the Vicomte de Vogüé (whose book on the Russian novel brought Dostoevsky to the attention of the European literary world) was anything but friendly. No such problems bother students of Chekhov, whether Russian or otherwise. On the contrary, it is difficult to think of a writer of equal fame and importance who, on close inspection, proves to be such an admirable and sympathetic human being.

Rosamund Bartlett's work *Chekhov: Scenes from A Life* is not a conventional biography, which unrolls the often-depicted facts of Chekhov's life once again, but rather a study of Chekhov's environment—of the Russian world in which he lived and had his being. Her book is inspired by the idea that, since "it is difficult for us to penetrate Chekhov's character through his relationships with people because of his inscrutability and reserve, perhaps our emphasis should be shifted to his relationship with the places in which he lived."[1] Her reader thus receives a plethora of lively,

---

Originally published in a slightly different form as "Why Sakhalin?," *The London Review of Books*, February 17, 2005. Reprinted by permission.

[1] Rosamund Bartlett, *Chekhov: Scenes from A Life* (London: Free Press, 2004), xvii. Subsequent references to this work are cited in parentheses in the text.

brightly written, and quite interesting information about all sorts of adjacent and ancillary aspects of Chekhov's life, ranging from the ancient Greek past of his birthplace Taganrog to the Chekhov Museum opened in Sri Lanka in 1999. Her chapters proceed geographically, as it were, according to the succession of places in which Chekhov lived or to which he traveled; the events of his career, so far as they relate to such locations, are filled in regardless of when they occurred. Luckily, the book also contains a vivid account of Chekhov's human and cultural environment, though this is not placed in the foreground. The selection of letters edited and translated by Bartlett, in collaboration with Anthony Phillips, provides a valuable supplement (and are quite marvelous in their own right!) to what she herself calls "an impressionistic approach." Such an approach is not for Chekhovian neophytes, who would do better with the biographies by Ronald Hingley or Donald Rayfield among others; but for devotees it provides a very lively read.

The history of Taganrog, a southern Russian city on the Sea of Azov, goes back to the Scythians and the ancient Greeks, not to mention the Mongol and Ottoman empires, and is explored at length in a first chapter ranging from Herodotus to the Crimean War. The city was heavily bombarded in this latter conflict by the British fleet, and Chekhov's father and mother (he was not yet born) moved inland to escape the siege. Tolstoy was then writing his *Sevastopol Sketches*, and Bartlett suggests (no reference is given) that many years later, when Tolstoy had become "something of a paternal figure" for the much younger writer, "the war would be a favorite topic of conversation for Chekhov and Tolstoy when they were both living in the Crimea for health reasons" (20). It was also the war that impelled Chekhov's mother to press his father, whose own father was a freed serf, to raise the funds necessary to join the merchant class exempted from military service.

Pavel Egorovich Chekhov thus became a *meshchanin*, a member of the merchant class and the proprietor of a small grocery that "sold everything from rhubarb to castor oil and was open at all hours" (28). The merchants as a group were looked down upon in educated Russian society and had been satirized as ruthlessly grasping and immovably obsolescent in outlook in the plays of A. N. Ostrovsky. One of this playwright's important themes was the pitiless domestic tyranny that reigned in such households. Chekhov experienced such remorseless tyranny in his own childhood, and Bartlett devotes a subchapter to this "merchant background," later depicted in several important stories. She follows other biographers in assuming that, despite Chekhov's specific denial, a character in the novella "Three Years" is really a portrait of his father. The narrator of this work recalls: "I remember my father starting to teach me, or to put it more simply beat me, before I was five years old. He flogged me with a birch rod, boxed my ears, and hit me round the head and every morning when I woke up the first thing I would think about would be: was I going to get beaten" (33). Much later, in a letter reproaching his older brother Alexander for reprehensible behavior to his wife and their cook, he wrote: "Despotism and lies also destroyed our own childhood, so much so that we become sick and fearful when we remember it."[2]

Despite such memories, Chekhov's behavior toward his father and mother (whom he supported in part and then in whole all through their lives) was exemplary; and he helped other family members as well in time of need. Moreover, there were other aspects of his upbringing and of his father that his son eventually learned to value. Typical for the merchant milieu was an intense religiosity; and this also formed part of the rigidly controlled background that Chekhov deplored. In "Three Years" he wrote that "we [he and the other children] had to go to matins and early mass, kiss the hands of priest and monks and read *akathists* [a series of prayers praising God]" (33). He and his brothers also sang in choirs that his father, who learned to play the violin and paint religious icons, loved to direct—to the exhaustion of all participants. Such activities provided him with a detailed and intimate knowledge of Russian Orthodoxy that surfaces again and again in his works, and perhaps only Nikolay Leskov among other Russian authors could match. It is not surprising that Chekhov called him "my favorite writer" in a letter after the two had met, and he describes the half-drunken Leskov as having said: "Thee I anoint with oil, even as Samuel anointed David.... You must write,"[3] evidently viewing the younger author as his successor.

Like so much else in Chekhov's work, his relation to religion is ambiguous and many-sided. There is no doubt that, as he wrote in a letter to Diaghilev just a year before his death: "I ... never fail to be puzzled by an intellectual who is also a believer."[4] But while intellectually he could not accept the faith of his fathers, he understood—and deeply sympathized with—the emotional importance of such faith for the Russian people. There can hardly be any doubt that the values it embodied also moved him very profoundly. A beautiful story, *The Student*, expresses sentiments that it is difficult to believe did not stir in him as well; and according to Bartlett, it was one of his works that he particularly cherished.

It depicts a young man, a seminary student, walking in a wood during a spring evening that had suddenly turned icily cold and gloomy. The change of weather had the effect of impelling him to think of the ter-

---

[2] *Anton Chekhov: A Life in Letters*, ed. Rosamund Bartlett, trans. Rosamund Bartlett and Anthony Phillips (New York: Penguin Books, 2004), 173.

[3] Ibid., 31.

[4] Michael Henry Heim and Simon Karlinsky, ed. and trans., *Letters of Anton Chekhov* (New York: Harper and Row, 1973), 453: July 12, 1903.

rible Russian past, and of a present filled with savage poverty and hunger, ignorance, anguish, and oppression. Nor would anything really improve, alas, in a thousand years. But then, noticing a fire fed by two peasant women, he approaches for warmth and tells them the story of St. Peter, also seeking relief from the cold on a bitter night. Deeply moved by his words, they break down and weep at Peter's denial of Christ, and at Peter's own tears because of his betrayal. Nineteen centuries had passed, but he now sees before his eyes that what had occurred in Palestine so long ago still had a relation to the present. It was not only the horror of Russia's bloodcurdling past that was still alive, and he realizes that "truth and beauty ... guided human life there in the garden and the high priest's palace ... [and] continued without a break till the present day, always as the most important element in man's life and in earthly life in general." As he leaves, filled with exaltation and a feeling of happiness, Chekhov notes that "he was only twenty-two."[5] This typical ironic touch does not really weaken the evocative power of the Christian affirmation, which relieves, even if momentarily, the sombreness of the initial thought; and Chekhov would refer to this story in countering the often-made charge of critics that his work offered nothing but pessimism and despair. The excellent critic Leonid Grossman once called him "a probing Darwinist with the love of St. Francis of Assisi for every living creature."[6]

Even before finishing the gymnasium at Taganrog, Chekhov began to write comic anecdotes and stories that he sent to his brothers living in Moscow, and a few years later he was publishing them, under the pseudonym of Antosha Chekhonte, in a humorous magazine called *The Alarm Clock*. On graduating from school he obtained a scholarship to study medicine at Moscow University and in 1879 went to join his family there; they had left three years earlier after the grocery failed and his father was threatened with debtor's prison. Chekhov had already begun to contribute whatever he could from his literary earnings, and even part of his scholarship, to relieve their gnawing poverty. His relation to Taganrog did not cease with his departure, however, and he returned there for several visits. What struck him in 1887 was the "Asiatic" aspect of this decaying port, with its leisurely way of life and the total unawareness of its inhabitants of anything beyond the primitive demands of existence; none of the relatives he was visiting read newspapers or books. "There are 60,000 inhabitants who just eat, drink and reproduce," he wrote, "but they have no other interests" (8). Later, he regularly sent shipments of books to the

---

[5] *The Oxford Chekhov*, vol. 7: *Stories 1893–1895*), trans. and ed. Ronald Hingley (London: Oxford University Press, 1978), 108.

[6] Leonid Grossman, "The Naturalism of Chekhov," in *Chekhov: A Collection of Critical Essays*, ed. Robert Louis Jackson (Englewood Cliffs, NJ: Prentice-Hall, 1967), 48.

Taganrog library and continued to do so up through his very last years. While living in Nice he provided all the French classics and participated in plans to build a museum in his birthplace.

Chekhov's time in Moscow for the next five years, during which he completed his medical degree, was divided between writing and medicine. While pursuing his medical studies, to supplement his scanty income he turned out a mass of comic anecdotes and brief stories for one or another journal in Moscow and Petersburg devoted to amusing the public. He acquired his medical degree in 1884 and practiced as a physician up to about 1888, treating hundreds of patients and writing in a letter that while literature was his mistress, medicine was his wife. These roles became reversed once he began to take himself seriously as a writer and ceased regarding his stories only as a profitable pastime. However, whenever he lived in the countryside during the summers and in later years, the moment his medical credentials became known to the neighboring peasants a long line would form in front of his dacha awaiting examination and treatment, always provided free of charge. During a cholera epidemic in 1892, he was enlisted by the district council to head the efforts to contain it and worked tirelessly between August and October under grueling conditions. "The peasants," he wrote in a letter, "are coarse, dirty and suspicious; but the thought that our efforts will not be completely in vain stops one noticing any of this" (218). This combination of clear-sighted truth combined with rectifying action, to which he would sometimes add a transforming visionary hope, provided the foundation of Chekhov's own sense of values and appears in some of his best work.

Chekhov's attitude to literature changed as a result of a letter from Dimitry Grigorovich, a minor writer enjoying some repute but chiefly famous as a survivor of the great literary generation of the 1860s. Grigorovich had shared a flat with Dostoevsky in 1845, when the latter was working on *Poor Folk*; and he was one of the two (the other was the important poet Nekrasov) who took the manuscript to the influential critic Belinsky, thus paving its way to fame. The incident had been recounted in Dostoevsky's *Diary of a Writer* (1873) and provided Grigorovich with the aureole of this glorious past. On a visit to Petersburg, Grigorovich and Chekhov met under the sponsorship of the important editor Aleksey Suvorin, another former intimate of Dostoevsky. A short time later, Chekhov received a letter from Grigorovich expressing admiration for his work and urging him to respect his talent and stop writing for deadlines.

Grigorovich had been much impressed with a story, little more than a sketch, called "The Huntsman." It depicts an accidental meeting in the countryside between a handsome peasant, raised a notch above his station by his prowess as a huntsman and fisherman supplying food for an aristocratic table, and the deserted wife to whom he had been married twelve years earlier. The marriage had been a forced one, performed while the huntsman was drunk and intended as a malicious humiliation by their patrician serf-owner. The wife pathetically implores him for a visit; but while he scorns any renewal of whatever relation they may have had, he turns back to press a ruble in her hand before vanishing into the landscape. The brief work is a little gem both of social commentary and of human feeling, and one can well understand Grigorovich's plea. "Your letter," Chekhov replied, "beloved bearer of good tidings, struck me like a bolt of lightning. I almost burst into tears." Although he possessed hundreds of acquaintances in Moscow, he continued, "I cannot remember a single one of them ... who has read me and saw me as an artist" (72).

It was during his last year in medical school that Chekhov began to cough up blood, although he refused to acknowledge that he was in the early stages of tuberculosis and spoke of it in a letter only as a ruptured blood vessel. Himself a doctor, one presumes that he knew the truth; but it remains unclear whether his refusal to admit openly the facts of his illness was genuine or feigned. Even when the true nature of his blood-producing coughs could no longer be concealed, either from himself or from others, his letters constantly downplay their effects as much as possible. It is worth noting that his younger brother Nikolay, a gifted artist and illustrator but a confirmed alcoholic, died of tuberculosis with Anton nursing him during his last days. Although it is difficult to gauge the effect of Chekhov's illness on the character of his work, one may well attribute some of its sense of fatalism, of the inevitable disappointment of most human hopes and ambitions, not only to his personal situation but to what he experienced day after day in his medical practice.

Chekhov was quite handsome and attractive and flirted with a good many women who hardly made a secret of their desire to become his wife; but his reluctance may well have been influenced by the constant sense of his own mortality and that of others, as well as by the more practical and financial reasons usually invoked. He was once engaged to a Russian-Jewish girl for a brief period of time, and certainly had love affairs as well as more casual brief encounters; one minor writer published a generally discredited book after Chekhov's death claiming to have been the object of a platonic grand passion. He was remarkably discreet and reclusive about his love life, aided by the prudishness of the various editors of his letters. Bartlett includes among them, for example, one detailing an encounter with a Japanese prostitute only recently made available in the latest complete edition. Three years before his death Chekhov married Olga Knipper, an actress in the Moscow Art Theater whom he met when she took a role in his play *The Seagull*. Even though he was deeply in love, perhaps for the first time in his life, it was only in response to her entreaties, and the fear of a definitive break, that he consented to a small wedding actually concealed from his family and friends until it was over.

Chekhov's intimates like Suvorin, familiar with the fragility of his health, were astonished at his decision in 1890 to undertake a journey to the Sakhalin Islands, a far-flung and godforsaken Russian penal colony in the Pacific. It was thousands of miles away from European Russia, and to reach it required a three-month's journey often under the most primitive and punishing traveling conditions. The prologue to Bartlett's book is entitled "Chekhov the Wanderer," and she views him, with a good deal of justification, as possessed by an irresistible wanderlust that he was rarely able to satisfy. At this point, however, his life had reached a crisis that impelled him to take action.

For one thing, his trip followed hard on the death of Nikolay, which he could not help viewing as a foreshadowing of his own fate; and his state of mind at this time is revealed in one of his gloomiest works, "A Dreary Story." Here he describes the life of a world-famous Russian scientific celebrity who, aged and dying, realizes that his life as a human being has been a failure and that he has emotionally alienated even those he loved and valued the most. The reason is that "all the thoughts and feelings, the conceptions which I form about everything something general—these things lack any common link capable of bonding them into a single entity." What he lacks is what is known as a "'general conception,' or the God of a live human being. And if one lacks that, one has nothing."[7] Chekhov always vehemently denied that any of the opinions uttered by his characters were really his own; but there is good reason to take such an utterance as reflecting some of his own dispirited ruminations at this moment. Another blow was the failure of his play, *The Wood Demon* (later revised as *Uncle Vanya*). Both these disasters combined to send him off on his journey halfway round the world.

But the question still arises: why Sakhalin? Part of the answer is certainly contained in an unusually impassioned letter to Aleksey Suvorin, who had claimed that nobody found Sakhalin interesting. In reply, Chekhov insisted that Russians should make pilgrimages to Sakhalin as the Turks go to Mecca. "It is quite clear from the books I have been reading ... that we have let *millions* of people rot in jail, and let them rot to no purpose, treating them with an indifference that is little short of barbaric. We have forced people to drag themselves in chains across tens of thousand of miles in freezing conditions, infected them with syphilis, debauched them, hugely increased the criminal population, and heaped the blame for the

---

[7] *The Oxford Chekhov*, vol. 5: *Stories 1889–1891*, trans. and ed. Ronald Hingley (London: Oxford University Press, 1970), 80.

whole thing on red-nosed prison supervisors" (166). Even though Chekhov enjoyed part of the trip, writing enthusiastic letters about the wonders of the Siberian landscape, what he encountered in Sakhalin surpassed his worst expectations. "It seemed to Chekhov," Bartlett writes, "that he had already arrived in Hell" (177).

Russian readers expected him to write a work detailing his impressions somewhat similar to Dostoevsky's *House of the Dead*; but instead he visited every prison habitation on the island, filling out, with the help of a native Buryat priest, over 8,179 questionnaires about prison conditions with the answers he received from the illiterate inmates. At a dinner with the governor-general of the region, he was assured that conditions were far from being intolerable; but what he found was quite the opposite—"prostitution, starvation and brutal corporal punishment" (177). Chekhov's book *The Island of Sakhalin*, published two years later, created a considerable stir with its unvarnished depiction of abominable prison conditions, and his exposé led to some minor reforms being made in the prison. He also castigated "our intelligentsia [who have] been saying for 20–30 years now that criminals are a product of society, but how indifferent it is to that product" (183). In general, this remark expresses his attitude toward the Russian intelligentsia as a whole, who argued endlessly about how to change the world but failed miserably, in his view, to lift a finger to help actual living people.

Bartlett's later chapters trace the course of Chekhov's life through his various peregrinations from place to place. He bought a little estate not far from Moscow called Melikhovo, where he could satisfy his passion for hunting, fishing, and gardening, and where he lived with his father and mother and his sister Masha, a schoolmistress who visited on weekends. Even in their days of poverty the Chekhovs' had always been hospitable, and numerous guests both personal and literary, as well as the families of his two older brothers, came down to enjoy what Chekhov had initially thought would be a country retreat. By the second summer, it was necessary to build a cottage in the garden for the overflow of visitors, and in which the master of the house wrote *The Seagull* and had his portrait painted by an artist commissioned by the Tretyakov Gallery. It was in Melikhovo too that Chekhov set up his already-mentioned impromptu clinic for the surrounding peasantry. He became a school examiner in addition, visited the fifty-seven schools of the district, and raised funds for the building of three more schools. Bartlett also provides an amusing excursus on the Russian enthusiasm for croquet, which was played at Melikhovo and continued to be played in Russia up through the 1920 and 1930s.

It is revelatory of Chekhov that, in the midst of all this charitable activity, he should have written one of his most devastating depictions of Russian life, "The Peasants." It was badly mutilated by the censorship because of its unsparing grimness, and one passage will illustrate why it aroused the wrath not only of the censors but of the left-wing Russian Populists who, like Dostoevsky and Tolstoy, tended to idealize the peasantry. It conveys the thoughts of a city-bred character come to live in the country and just about to leave. "Who keeps the pot-house and makes the peasants drunk? The peasant. Who squanders his village, school and church funds on drink? The peasant. Who steals from his neighbors, sets fire to their property, and perjures himself in court for a bottle of vodka? The peasant. Who is the first to run down the peasant at council and other meetings? The peasant. Yes, they were frightful people to live with. Still, they were men and women, they suffered and wept like men and women, and there was nothing in their lives for which an excuse could not be found."[8] This last sentence, well supported by the callous and brutal treatment the peasants suffered at the hands of visiting officials, strikes the customary Chekhovian note.

Melikhovo was abandoned after the death of Chekhov's father, but another reason for leaving was a massive hemorrhage of Chekhov's lungs during a meal with Suvorin at a restaurant in Moscow. It became clear that he could no longer continue to overlook his ailment, or to endure the winter climate of the Moscow region. From this time on he spent the winter months in a more clement location (twice in Nice) or in Yalta, where he eventually built a house in a Tatar village (few Russians chose to live there) overlooking the sea. His arrival in Nice was announced in a local newspaper, *The Franco-Russian Messenger*, owned and largely written by Mordechai Rozanov, the Russian-Jewish owner of a local bookstore with whom Chekhov became very friendly (shades of *Daniel Deronda*!). The newspapers at that time were full of stories about the Dreyfus case, and his contacts with Rozanov and others of his milieu no doubt aided his transformation into an ardent Dreyfusard, though probably his own inbred revulsion against injustice would have been quite enough. This led to a cooling of his relations for a number of years with the notoriously anti-Semitic Suvorin, whose newspaper had attacked Zola's *J'accuse!*. On leaving Nice in April 1879, Chekhov made a detour through Paris in order to meet the brother of Dreyfus. "He was the only major Russian writer," Bartlett notes, "to take an active stand in the affair" (234).

During the last five years of Chekhov's life he passed his winters in Yalta, whose history Bartlett fills in with her usual brio. He uses its locale as background for one of his most famous stories, "The Lady with the Little Dog," and one of its scenes—a conversation that takes place on a bench overlooking the bay—has led to this lowly accommodation being immor-

---

[8] *The Oxford Chekhov*, vol. 8: *Stories 1895–1897*, trans. and ed. Ronald Hingley (London: Oxford University Press, 1965), 221.

talized as the Chekhov Bench for the benefit of posterity. While Chekhov missed the cultural amenities of Moscow, there were charity concerts in the vicinity that he attended, and the Russian-Jewish pianist Semyon Samuelson became a personal friend who came to play on the writer's grand piano. Another friend was once again a Russian-Jewish bookstore owner Isaac Sinani, a member of the Karaite sect (the Karaites accept only the Old Testament and refuse the rabbinical tradition), and whose store on the seafront had become a gathering place for writers and artists in the community. Here Chekhov could meet the young Maxim Gorky, whose early stories he admired, and Ivan Bunin, with whom he became quite intimate and who left an uncompleted book about Chekhov among his papers. Although Chekhov shunned any public manifestation of political opinion, he resigned his membership in the Russian Academy of Sciences when Gorky's election was canceled because he was under police surveillance.

Tolstoy, with whom Chekhov was on the most cordial terms, came to Yalta occasionally for his health as well. The younger writer idolized Tolstoy as a human being, writing in a letter that "I have loved no man as I have loved him," adding that "when literature has a Tolstoy, it is easy and gratifying to be a writer." But while second to none in his admiration for *War and Peace* and *Anna Karenina*, and acknowledging that "there was a time when I was strongly affected by Tolstoy's philosophy," he found it impossible to accept the writer's later religious ideas. "But now something inside me protests ... : reason and justice tell me there is more love for mankind in electricity and steam than there is in chastity and abstaining from meat. It is true that war is evil and courts of law are evil, but that does not mean I have to go about in bast shoes and sleep on top of the stove."[9] Instead, appalled by the number of penniless consumptives flocking to Yalta for the same reason as himself, but living from hand to mouth and dying from neglect, Chekhov worked with local charities to raise money for a sanatorium that was finally established.

He wrote a number of first-rate stories during these last years, but most of his attention was devoted to his plays. Like the stories, which broke with reigning conventions and depended on mood (*nastroenie*) rather than on plot or character development, his plays too, with their lack of a central theme and disconnected dialogue, met with considerable resistance. The first performance of *The Seagull* was a disaster, not only because of the originality of the play's structure but because the actors were still using the conventional declamatory style of the Russian stage. Once Chekhov had persuaded Stanislavsky and Nemirovich-Danchenko to adopt a more casual acting style in their Moscow Art Theater, the plays were a huge suc-

---

[9] *Anton Chekhov*, ed. Bartlett, 324.

cess. By the time of Chekhov's death at the age of forty-four, just managing to complete *The Cherry Orchard* before his demise, he had become the dominant figure in the Russian literature of his time.

All through his lifetime, Chekhov was assailed by critics—even some who admired his work—urging him to use his talents to come forward with some clear-cut moral-social preachment. There could be no question that he was critical of many of the injustices and cruelties of Russian society, but it was impossible to align him, on the basis of his work, with any of the social-cultural and political movements agitating the intelligentsia and presumably pointing the way for the future of Russian society. When faced by such criticism even from an intimate like Suvorin, who remarked that, while posing the issue of pessimism Chekhov never resolved it, he replied: "It doesn't seem to me that it is the job of writers of fiction to decide questions like God, pessimism, etc. . . . The writer's task is only to describe those who have said or thought something about God and pessimism, how, and in what circumstances. The artist should not be a judge of his characters or what they say but an impartial witness."[10]

Chekhov's contemporaries were rather bewildered by his refusal to become what Vladimir Nabokov, a great Chekhov admirer, called a "special delivery" writer, eager to convey a message. But Bartlett remarks quite acutely, in her introduction to the letters, that this brings him closer to our own time. "Chekhov's themes of alienation and the absurdity and tragedy of human existence continue to have relevance, the random pathos and irony that we find in his work indeed making him as much a twentieth-century modernist as a nineteenth-century realist."[11] This is true enough. But one should add that, above all, it was his ability to feel and to convey what Wordsworth called "the still, sad music of humanity" that endeared him to his initial readers and will continue to do so for all who turn his pages or view his plays in the future.

[10] Ibid., 138.
[11] Ibid., xxxvii.

SIXTEEN

THE TRIUMPH OF ABRAM TERTZ

SO MUCH CHANGE has taken place in the ex-Soviet Union since the breakup of the empire that it is difficult now even to imagine the excitement produced by the arrest, trial, and sentencing of two young writers, Andrei Sinyavsky and Yuli Daniel, in February 1966. Their "crime" had been to smuggle out, and have printed in the West under the pseudonyms Abram Tertz and Nikolay Arzhak, various works of fiction and, in the case of Tertz-Sinyavsky, an essay, *On Socialist Realism*. Both were sent to work camps, Sinyavsky for seven years (though he was released after six) and Daniel for five. Already a noted scholar at the time of his arrest, Sinyavsky emigrated to France a year after obtaining his freedom and took up a post teaching Russian literature at the Sorbonne. Daniel remained in Russia and died in 1988.

Their case was not tried in public, but the proceedings were taken down secretly by several people admitted to the courtroom and published a year later both in Russian and English. The English volume, *On Trial*, also includes most of the other documents relating to the case—the press campaign launched against the defendants in advance of the trial, the protests of many Soviet Russian intellectuals, and the worldwide wave of petitions provoked by the arrests.[1] The reasons for this extraordinary outpouring would seem to have been twofold. Khrushchev's horrifying revelations about Stalin had badly shaken the faith in Soviet infallibility; and the grounds for the indictment itself erased whatever line still existed between literature and political propaganda. No law in the Soviet Union prohibited the publication of works abroad, and the authorities were thus forced to attempt to prove that the content of the works could be used as evidence of anti-Soviet activity. Many writers had of course been sent to prison camp in the Soviet Union, but never on the basis of evidence taken solely from their work; and the implications of such a charge called forth an unprecedented upsurge of public and international solidarity. Historians of the post-Stalin era date the rise of the Russian dissident movement, and

---

Originally published in a slightly different format in *The New York Review of Books* 38, 12. Copyright © 1991 *The New York Review of Books*. All rights reserved. Reprinted by permission.

[1] Leopold Labedz and Max Hayward, eds., *On Trial: The Case of Sinyavsky (Tertz) and Daniel (Arzhak)* (London: Collins and Harvill, 1967).

the large-scale establishment of a samizdat (underground) press, from the indignation aroused by the Sinyavsky-Daniel trial.

Two

Andrei Sinyavsky thus became universally known once his identity as the mysterious Abram Tertz was revealed; but Abram Tertz would not have been pursued so relentlessly, and finally unmasked, if he had not already become a world-famous figure. The appearance of *On Socialist Realism*, accompanied by a volume of stories (*Fantastic Stories*), two long novellas (*The Trial Begins* and *Liubimov*), and a series of aphorisms (*Unguarded Thoughts*), revealed a writer and critic of major stature, with a voice and sensibility unlike anything that had emerged from the Soviet Union in a very long time. Indeed, so sharply did these works stand out amid the drabness of standard socialist realist prose—involving, as Christopher Isherwood once remarked long ago, "the usual sex triangle between a girl with thick legs, a boy, and a tractor"[2] —that one party critic insisted they were the forgeries of a White Russian émigré being passed off as the genuine article. No writer educated and living in Communist Russia, he contended, could possibly have uttered such thoughts or created in such a style.

The thoughts in question, especially as they appeared in *On Socialist Realism*, told Western students of Soviet culture little that they did not already know.[3] The brochure was, however, written with a lapidary vehemence clearly stemming from a bitter disillusionment with the very foundations of the Soviet worldview—the belief, namely, that all the iniquities of Stalinism had been justified because Russia was well on its way to creating the perfect Communist society. Tertz-Sinyavsky thus offered one of the first glimpses of the rebellious sentiments seething, in the minds of a new generation, under the thick carapace of enforced surface unanimity. Even more, the style and technique of his own works could be seen as a response to the new situation created by the collapse of the revolutionary

---

[2] Christopher Isherwood, *Prater Violet*. (New York: Random House, 1945), 103.
[3] In 1958 Rufus W. Mathewson, Jr., published the first edition of his classic study *The Positive Hero in Russian Literature* (New York: Columbia University Press, 1958), which analyzes Socialist Realism in a much more extensive historical context than Sinyavsky provides and anticipates many of his conclusions. In the second edition of the book (Stanford: Stanford University Press, 1975), which includes an excellent new chapter on Sinyavsky, Mathewson remarks: "In Andrei Sinyavsky's brilliant essay 'On Socialist Realism' I have found heartening confirmation of many of my ideas, and I would be happy to think that if he has chanced upon my work ... he may have recognized affinities between his work and my own more pedestrian treatment of the same phenomena" (xiii–xiv).

idealism in which Sinyavsky's generation had been so assiduously educated. "Right now," he wrote, in a passage that has become classic, "I put my hope in a phantasmagoric art, with hypotheses instead of a purpose, an art in which the grotesque will replace realistic descriptions of ordinary life. May the fantastic imagery of Hoffmann and Dostoevsky, Chagall and Mayakovsky ... and of many other realists and nonrealists teach us how to be truthful with the aid of the absurd and the fantastic."[4]

Tertz-Sinyavsky's own works fully satisfy these prescriptions. Set in an unmistakable day-to-day Soviet reality, with all its depressing grimness and grinding deprivations, this recognizable world will suddenly be invaded by the fantastic, the grotesque, and even the supernatural. Sometimes, as in *The Trial Begins*, the distortions of the familiar are given in caricatural dream-visions, outrageous inversions of Marxist-Leninist clichés, and stylistic hyperbole. In *Liubimov* (regrettably translated as *The Makepeace Experiment*), the fantastic is built into the very conception of the work. A harmless and well-meaning bicycle mechanic, Leonid Tikhomirov, suddenly acquires a psychic power that enables him to hypnotize the inhabitants of his homely little provincial town into believing they are already living in the earthly paradise.

The short stories contain narrators whose contorted and confusing images of reality can be attributed to the paranoia and schizophrenia induced by the conditions of living in a police society. But the supernatural also intrudes in the form of one narrator miraculously able to foretell the future (the authorities immediately try to make use of his gifts for Russian foreign policy), and another narrator, who works for a local Housing Department, may well be a house-demon of Russian folklore (*domovoy*), who explains the burbling and gurgling sounds in the plumbing as the voices of the water nymphs (*rusalki*) come to take refuge in the city from the pollution of their native habitat.

Such examples give only a very inadequate notion of Tertz-Sinyavsky's exuberance and imaginative inventiveness, which mingle the sharpest satire, ideologically honed to the finest cutting edge, with a sense of profound oppression and loss. All these qualities are combined in the most moving of Tertz-Sinyavsky's short stories, "Pkhentz," one of the few contemporary works worthy to be placed beside Kafka's "The Metamorphosis." The narrator is the inhabitant of another planet, stranded on Earth as the result of some interstellar accident and living as a Soviet Russian citizen. He appears to be a hunchback because his body is more like a cactus plant than an earthly human form, and he must not only keep it concealed but also is forced to spend an inordinate amount of time in the communal bathroom

---

[4] Abram Tertz (Andrey Sinyavsky), *The Trial Begins and On Socialist Realism*, trans. Max Hayward and George Dennis; intro. Czeslaw Milosz (New York: Vintage, 1960), 218–19.

since he lives only on water. The piercing sense of alienation expressed in this story is made all the more poignant, as in Kafka, because of the withering banality of the circumstances in which he is forced to survive. Clarence Brown was perfectly right to have included "Pkhentz," as an undisputed masterpiece, in his Viking Portable Reader of twentieth-century Russian literature.

Since emerging from prison, Sinyavsky has published a number of important works that can only be mentioned here very briefly. His *A Voice from the Chorus* is largely a selection from the letters he wrote to his wife from the prison camp and hence first submitted to the censor. They deal mainly with reflections on art and religion, as well as reactions, raised to the level of philosophical generalizations, to the life going on around him. The book also includes extensive samples of the idiomatic speech of the other convicts, who came from all corners of the multilinguistic Soviet Empire.

Two other books, begun while Sinyavsky was still in prison, are scintillating critical studies of Gogol and Pushkin, which created a stir by their iconoclastic treatment of these two pillars of the Russian literary tradition.[5] In the case of the second, it created an outright scandal. Sinyavsky was attacked both inside and outside the Soviet Union for his supposed defamation of the writer whose work has become, in effect, the unofficial Bible of Russian moral-cultural mores. In fact, Sinyavsky was reacting against the Russian habit of treating writers as cultural and political mentors—he was sentenced to hard labor because of his presumed neglect of such a civic responsibility—and he stressed all the frivolous, lighthearted, and amiably amoral aspects of Pushkin (of which there are a good many, particularly in his early work).

What almost caused apoplexy was such a sentence as: "Pushkin ran into great poetry on thin erotic legs and created a commotion."[6] Sinyavsky then compares Pushkin's later attitude to life with that of Don Juan, who threw himself into each new adventure—as Pushkin into each subject—with perfect sincerity, becoming one with his theme "so that at any given moment our betrayer is truthful and sincere ... and ... for him impersonation is a way of life and subsistence."[7] This is not unlike what Keats said of Shakespeare's "negative capability" and is surely the secret of what, according to Dostoevsky, made Pushkin Russia's great national

---

[5] On Gogol, see Abram Tertz (André Siniavski), *Dans l'ombre de Gogol*, trans. Georges Nivat (Paris: Editions du Seuil).

[6] Abram Tertz (Andrei Sinyavsky), *Strolls with Pushkin*, trans. Catharine Theimer Nepomnyashchy and Slava Yastremski (New Haven: Yale University Press, 1992), 55. See also Abram Tertz (André Siniavski), *Promenades avec Pouchkine*, trans. Louis Martinez (Paris: Editions du Seuil).

[7] Tertz, *Strolls with Pushkin*, 83.

poet: his "panhumanism." But Sinyavsky provocatively couches this idea in a phraseology calculated to shock Russian literary pieties, and to offend those who believe that a writer—especially a great Russian one—should have firm ideological commitments.

Two other works illustrate Sinyavsky's strong affiliation with the Silver Age of Russian culture (the late nineteenth and early twentieth centuries), and he has spoken of the urgent need to reestablish the links between this period and the post-Marxist present. The Russian religious philosophy of this era, he has written, "is very interesting," and such writers as Berdyaev and Lev Shestov "tried, not to repeat but to rethink the very profound Church tradition in fresh terms, to think it anew, as it were, and very personally."[8]

In 1982 Sinyavsky published a compulsively readable lecture course given at the Sorbonne on V. V. Rozanov, one of the most original, eccentric, and, to tell the truth, morally questionable of these religious philosophers.[9] It is certainly exaggerated to say, as does the French critic Georges Nivat, that "in a sense all of Sinyavsky comes from Rozanov";[10] but he is powerfully attracted to certain aspects of Rozanov's thought, most of all, perhaps, to his deliberate cultivation of the most flagrant self-contradiction. Many of Rozanov's contemporaries considered him to be deceitful and treacherous precisely for this reason. He wrote both for and against Christianity, both for and against the Jews, both for and against social revolution; but Sinyavsky values such oscillations as a means of resistance to the pressure for ideological conformity. Rozanov's taste for an often demeaning self-exposure, conveyed in a style of unusual spontaneity and intimacy—many admire him simply for his prose—has led to him being called the *yurodivy* (holy fool) of Russian thought; but as Sinyavsky has recently written, "The holy fool acted on a profound religious assumption: the contempt for one's own person and dignity serves the glory of God"[11]—and this is how Sinyavsky justifies many of Rozanov's aberrations.

Sinyavsky's comment comes from *Ivan-Durak* (*Ivan the Fool*), an impressive study of Russian popular religion, which concentrates on the

---

[8] From an interview in *Knizhnoe Obozrenie*, January 13, 1989. I should like to thank my friend and colleague Lazar Fleishman, who keeps up with the Soviet press, for having generously placed his file of xeroxes and clippings of Sinyavsky material at my disposal.

[9] André Siniavski, "Opavshie Listya" V. V. Rozanova (Syntaxis).

[10] In an incisive article on Rozanov in *Histoire de La Littérature Russe, L'Age d'Argent*, ed. Efim Etkind, Georges Nivat, Ilya Serman, and Vittorio Strada (Paris: Fayard, 1987), 332. A very good introduction to Rozanov in English can be found in Renato Poggioli's book *Rozanov* (London: Bowes and Bowes, 1962).

[11] Andrei Sinyavsky, *Ivan the Fool: Russian Folk Belief: A Cultural History*, trans. Joanne Turnbull and Nikolai Formozov (Chicago: Northwestern University Press, 2007), 260. See also Andrei Sinyavski, *Ivan le simple: Paganisme, magic et religion du peuple russe*, trans. Antonina Robichou-Stretz (Paris: Albin Michel).

peculiar intertwining of Orthodox Christianity with magic and paganism and reveals Sinyavsky's deep fascination with these persistent elements of the Russian folk tradition that neither the Church nor the Soviet state has been able to stamp out. Part of this tradition is also embodied in the *Raskol* (Old Believers) and other Russian sectarians, many of whom Sinyavsky met in prison camp. He writes about them with great respect and concludes his book by describing a secret meeting at night in the boiler room of his camp in order to read the *Apocalypse*: each convict had been assigned a chapter and recited it from memory. "This was culture," Sinyavsky writes, "in its continuity, in its primordial essence, continuing to exist at the lowest, most primitive, underground level.... But this was culture in perhaps one of its purest and noblest forms. If not for people and traditions like that, man's life on earth would lose all meaning."[12]

Three

The book *Goodnight!*, whose enigmatic title may contain a satirical allusion (this is only a guess) to a popular Soviet television program of the same name for children, is called a "novel"; but this designation, as so often in Russian literature, is more misleading than helpful.[13] There is nothing conventionally "novelistic" about the book, which is squarely based on various incidents in Sinyavsky's life and, in the last section, contains an incriminating confession that was no doubt very painful to make. The first-person narrator is Sinyavsky himself, who calls up events of his past, starting with his arrest, with all the imaginative and stylistic brilliance, all the play of literary, artistic, and ideological allusion, all the sarcasm and the (often self-mocking) irony familiar from his fiction.

The book also includes entirely imaginary or at least not directly autobiographical sections—a brief play in an Expressionist, Brechtian style, a short excursus on mice, extracts from a presumably eyewitness account of the torture and carnage surrounding the murder of Dimitry the tsarevich by Boris Godunov, and a cynical yet wholly reverent dialogue in heaven between Jesus Christ and His Mother that might have come from Bulgakov's masterpiece *The Master and Margarita*. All these, as Sinyavsky explains, because "sometimes a writer is free to disregard the facts in order to elucidate them more fully and lend them greater power" (4). The book is thus a bewilderingly rich mix of memories and reflections that ebb and flow in no apparent order except that of one incident recalling another, or

---

[12] Ibid., 388.

[13] Abram Tertz (Andrei Sinyavsky), *Goodnight!:A Novel*, trans. Richard Lourie (New York: Viking, 1989). Page references to this work are hereafter cited in parentheses in the text.

a phrase or expression setting off a particular memory-related response. But through all this nonetheless weaves the narrative of how the "believing Komsomol member" that Andrei Sinyavsky still was in the 1950s became the literary outlaw Abram Tertz (the Jewish name comes from a thieves' ballad popular among students); and it is this narrative thread, to the regrettable neglect of much else, that we shall try to follow.

The first chapter, called "The Turncoat," begins at a point when Sinyavsky had long been Abram Tertz in secret without quite realizing what this assumed identity really involved; but he learned very quickly after his arrest. "A ridiculous intellectual," whose "only thought was to behave with as much decency and dignity as possible" (3), he passively allowed himself to be taken into custody on the street without fuss and was pushed into a limousine and driven to Lubyanka prison. At first he denied knowing anything about "Abram Tertz," to the great amusement of his interrogators, but soon realized that by doing so he was playing into their hands. "The more I denied I was Abram Tertz, the more guilt I would experience" (8); by his denial he accepted the implicit assumption that what he had done was a criminal offense. But once he confessed to being Tertz, openly accepting his fictitious identity, his entire situation changed—not practically, of course, but psychically and morally.

For who and what was Abram Tertz? "I can see him as if it were just yesterday," Sinyavsky writes with pride, "a crook, a cardshark, a real son of a bitch, his hands in his pants pockets, his mustache stringy, his cap snapped down over his eyes, walking with a light step.... He'll steal, but he'll croak before he'll squeal" (9). Once having become Abram Tertz, he accepted the outlaw code of his alter ego and stood firm against all attempts to make him "squeal" by pleading guilty. The jazzy playlet, which contains some extremely funny (Groucho) Marxist exchanges ("The Three Sisters are calling upon the fraternal peoples of New Guinea—to Moscow, to Moscow!" [55], etc.) dramatizes the unsuccessful efforts to make him admit that some of his works were slanders on Russian life and culture and thus anti-Soviet propaganda. As he realized later, the Sinyavsky-Daniel case had been intended "to be a present to the party from the KGB on the occasion of the 23rd Congress. A model trial served up with an eye to the West on a crisp snow-white napkin" (68). Sinyavsky's stubborn refusal to accept any guilt (Daniel expressed a partial repentance but withdrew it later in an open letter) sabotaged the whole arrangement. "Like blowing up a long-awaited new building ... or a factory" (68).

By becoming Abram Tertz, Sinyavsky thus foiled the KGB; but his real triumph came in the train taking him to the prison camp. He had been warned to be wary of the nonpolitical prisoners, the real Abram Tertzes, who were notorious for their ruthless cruelty to the others; and Sinyavsky was genuinely frightened, as well he might have been. Unexpectedly, to his amazement the prototypes of Abram Tertz greeted their fictional spokesman with friendship and even deference. "Each of them hurried to express his respect for me, to put it mildly. They had read about it in the papers!" (78). Abram Tertz had been catapulted into fame; but even more, "the abuse heaped on me by the radio, at meetings and in the press was an honor—I'd been honored! And the fact that I had smuggled my manuscripts out to the West, had not confessed, and remained unbowed at the trial conferred on me an exaggerated stature" (79). The criminals, who had also never bowed before Soviet law, clamorously greeted Abram Tertz as one of their own; and the chapter ends with the triumphant exclamation: "You've lost the argument with me—you've lost, Pakhomov [the name of his KGB investigator]!" (80).

A year later, Mariya Sinyavskaya comes to visit her husband in "The Public House" (as the second chapter is called), a phrase that can also mean "brothel." This is a building at the entrance to the camp in which convicts are allowed to spend three days each year with their wives or members of their family. There is a heartfelt invocation to Mariya and all the other wives ("Oh, Russian women, draft horses of the nation!" who "all come to the public house from every corner of the land" [84]), and what the Sinyavskys tell each other when they meet alternates with dialogues taking place in the adjoining rooms. (There is the mother, come to visit her son who had been tricked into returning to Russia by a letter to which her signature was forged. Also, an ex-German collaborator who urges his lieutenant son to renounce his father publicly for the sake of his career.)

There are also stories of fabulous escape attempts that sound like, but presumably are not, excellent examples of the Sinyavskian "fantastic" (one convict has constructed a plastic submarine with paddles made of tin cans and might have reached the safety of Mother Volga if he had not run up against an underwater barrier). Most important, though, is the news brought by Mariya of events surrounding the trial. But since the Sinyavskys knew the rooms were bugged (the whir of the listening devices at night sounded like the scratching of mice, hence the small "treatise" about them), they spoke innocently of past vacation trips to the North while Mariya wrote in her notebook and "cut the paper into strips like herbs and tossed pinches of paper macaroni into the saucepan" (93).

These strips contained a "soup of celebrities," the names of those who had spoken up in Sinyavsky's defense and of less well-known friends, those who had stood fast as well as others that had failed to pass the test of loyalty. Also, an unknown benefactor had left a chicken in front of the door after Sinyavsky's arrest, and a debate had broken out. Should it be cooked, or was it a poisoned gift from the KGB? It was eaten by Mariya and her friends with great enjoyment, never forgotten, and taken as a good augury.

Such news slides into recollections of the days when information about Abram Tertz began to filter back—first at a session at the Gorky Institute, when the assembled scholars were told in strictest confidence about the interest his works were arousing in the West, and "with each new reference to Tertz, my ears, like a vampire, distended with new, claret-colored flesh" (96). Sinyavsky felt like H. G. Wells's Invisible Man, everywhere present but never seen, transparent, and hoping to leave no footprints in the snow.

But, after a while, his trail was picked up, nobody still knows quite how. One rumor making the rounds was that the CIA gave him to the KGB in return for information about a new Soviet submarine—just a business deal between competing firms. "Mariya and I were immediately enraged at this. Cut the price! A little humility, please!" The Russian ambassador in Paris tried to do a little fishing for Tertz's identity at a reception, "casting his line with virtuosity at the person who was my impresario at the time" (105), but was told with French aplomb that the manuscripts published in Paris had arrived in the mail.

Warning signals, however, began to accumulate—the janitor in the Sinyavskys' building was asked if they had many foreign visitors; Sinyavsky's withdrawal records in the Lenin Library were commandeered; when walking at night he became aware he was being shadowed. He had once intended "to check out a mass of books that had nothing to do with me" so as to dissolve his identity in the vast reaches of the Lenin Library (Borges would have loved the idea), and he fantasizes amusingly about how this might be done. He would withdraw, say, Sherlock Holmes, Nat Pinkerton, "if I knew English I'd ask for Agatha Christie! ... or the *Count of Monte Cristo*—what better literary patron for a convict on the lam?" (113–14). But somehow he had never gotten around to covering his tracks in this way, and "while we were making jokes they were excavating" (112). Indeed, he had known it all in advance—in *The Trial Begins*, a sieve is placed over the sewage pipe in the author's apartment house, and the rejected drafts he flushes down the drain, carefully retrieved, send him to prison camp.

Four

A deep strain of piety and reverence for the family, and for the moral and human values that it embodies, runs through the "public house" chapter and softens the bleak treatment of sexual relations that some critics had noticed in the earlier Sinyavsky. It is thus only fitting that the next chapter, "My Father," should be a loving evocation of his own family, especially of his father, whom he obviously adored and who fits very well into the classic Russian category of "repentant nobleman." Of gentry origin, he joined the ranks of the revolution after reading *Crime and Punishment* ("I'm afraid that it wasn't Raskolnikov who drew him to the revolution but Sonya Marmeladova" [180]), and he became an agitator and member of the Left Socialist Revolutionary Party, which continued the traditions of the Populists of the 1870s. Historians have noted an "ecstatic cult of the revolution" in the Left Socialist Revolutionaries,[14] who also believed in the spontaneity of the masses and opposed the Bolsheviks' assumption of dictatorial powers. They were severely suppressed in 1922, and Sinyavsky's father suffered all his life because of this ill-fated affiliation. His past "hung over him like an indictment, creating an atmosphere of heroism and long years of hopeless poverty." His mother, a teacher and librarian from a peasant family, could never understand his father's "cold disdain for bourgeois vulgarity. A revolutionary nobleman knows how to lead the simple life" (168–69).

It is one of the ironies of Russian culture that such people believed themselves to be "materialists" and "egotists." Sinyavsky's father thought of himself as a rationalist and materialist through and through. Widely knowledgeable about science, "after reading a few books on modern power engineering, he worked out a scheme in which nothing was lost but everything went into outer space as a cloud of will power" (166) (is this not one of the sources of *Liubimov*?). But Andrei, brought up in his father's cult of revolutionary idealism and personal self-sacrifice, is not deceived. In a passage that Dostoevsky would have admired, he speaks of his father in words that reveal much about himself as well. "Which way were you Christians looking when humanity was abducted by atheism from under your noses? The revolutionaries were drawn to the heights. What match were all those petty officers who thought only about themselves and their estates.... Who could have known back then at the beginning how it would all turn out?" (185). Well, if his father had paid a little more attention to Raskolnikov ....

The senior Sinyavsky had been accused of being an American spy in 1922 because he had distributed gifts to schools and kindergartens donated by the American (Hoover) famine-relief society. Exculpated then, he was rearrested in 1951, when Stalin was making a clean sweep of "the last Mohicans of the revolution" (188), and purged them along with the Jews. The house search made at that time was a traumatic experience; it lasted twenty-one hours, turned everything topsy-turvy, and, to prove pro-Americanism, unearthed a perfectly legal magazine called *Amerika*

---

[14] See Sergei Hackel, *The Poet and the Revolution* (Oxford: Oxford University Press / Clarendon Press, 1975), 46 n1. The poet is Aleksandr Blok, and the book is a study of "The Twelve," a work of great importance for Sinyavsky.

that Andrei had bought the day before for some reproductions of Picasso. Looking through Andrei's notebooks, the KGB man pointed out that he spoke of the "official definition of socialist realism" and asked menacingly if this meant there was an "unofficial" one. "I'll say here that this incident, along with the overall tone of the search, undoubtedly served as the seed of Abram Tertz's scandalous essay that would be cooked up some five years later" (195).

The climax of this chapter occurs as father and son tramp through the woods in silence, shortly after the father's release from prison, the older man abruptly cutting short all attempt at conversation. Finally, cocking his head to one side as if listening for a signal, he tells Andrei that scientific experiments of some sort had been performed on him, and that his brain waves could now be read back in Moscow except at certain times when his control was not functioning. He speaks lucidly and calmly, describes the apparatus that had been placed in his head—some loot from Nazi Germany—and concedes that, while he might be having hallucinations, he does not believe so; nor can Andrei detect any signs of mental disturbance.

What, Andrei asks himself, was he to make of all this? Even more, why should he have become enraged by the simple scientific hypothesis that his [father's] brain had been tapped and was now under surveillance? "And that was me—me!—who accepted every last fantasy, fable, and faith! Who believed in devils, in magic, in a God in Heaven, whatever you like!" (211). After a few years, his father's brain surveillance appeared to cease, but "the reality of what happened to him," his son writes, "remains a mystery to me" (214). On their way home, Andrei himself underwent some sort of mystical experience when, looking at a cluster of trees agitated by the wind, he felt that "spirits were at work, and I could not break free of them, for I too was raised into the air by a feeling of what could be called reverential terror." Reality "seethes, as you and I do, like the universe in an abyss of hypotheses and hyperboles" (215). The mystery of his father's thought-control thus only reaffirmed his own belief in the mystery of the universe and the invisible dimensions of "reality."

This sense of mystery is transferred to the political plane in the next section, "Dangerous Liaisons," in which Sinyavsky recounts his fascination with an actress presumably endowed with clairvoyant powers. His "liaisons" with her are sexual, and also links between empirical reality and the paranormal and supernatural. The time is the short period of Stalin's last illness and his death; on the night he dies, "The Mustache" appears to the actress-medium, then living on the outskirts of a prison camp in the Far North, as "a weighty column" made of "pure coldness, of something like methane or nitrogen reduced to absolute zero" (228). This Stalin-vision asks forgiveness for his sins and, when she refuses, tries to argue her into complying with his wishes in a superbly sarcastic parody of various ideological strategies, including the Russian Orthodox ("he had of course been trained in a famous seminary" [234]).

She finally forgives him for herself, but not for all the others; he must seek them out one by one, "beseech them in the name of our Lord," and with these words the column vanishes as the Devil traditionally does at the sight of the cross. For Sinyavsky, the grip of Stalin was itself something magical, supernatural, extraordinary, and he evokes with a certain shudder of terror, and yet of perverse pleasure, those years "of mature, late-flowering Stalinism ... all those bits and pieces of madness and horror that I describe here, all the witches and vampires that charged daily life with the electricity of an imminent end of the world" (266).

During Stalin's last days, and when his death is announced, Sinyavsky immerses himself in reading old accounts of the murder by Boris Godunov of Dimitry the tsarevich, whose death the people refused to believe just as they desired not to believe that of Stalin. And he sketches a hallucinatory scenario, recalling what occurred during the Time of Troubles in the seventeenth century, in which a Stalin-Pretender arises claiming never to have died and begins to march on Moscow from the Caucasus. The delirious details of this putsch, which come straight from the pages of Russian history (all the leaders of peasant rebellions always claimed to be the true tsar, not dead but returned from hiding), furnish a remarkable example of Sinyavsky's gift for satirical political fantasy; one does not know whether to laugh or weep at the pompous communiqué, with its deadly pastiche of Stalinist-Marxist rhetoric. This gloomy celebration of the bewitched and diabolical world of late Stalinism, ending in a nighttime bacchanalia of people trampling each other to death to view the corpse, contains some of the most powerful and haunting pages in contemporary Russian prose.

Sinyavsky himself is a child of these years of Stalinism, and his final chapter, "In the Belly of the Whale," concentrates on one of its predominant features—denunciation of others in the name of socialist virtue, the pathological hunt for spies, traitors, and enemies of the people inculcated from childhood. The mythical hero of this period, in whose cult all Soviet children were educated, was Pavlik Morozov, a young Pioneer who turned in his own father for selling false papers to kulaks in exile and who testified against him at his trial; he was later murdered by the kulaks and became a martyr. "The blessed Pavlik Morozov walked among us, as if alive," Sinyavsky writes, "like the incorporeal youth in Nesterov's visionary painting.... A wanton little smile of holiness weeps, curdling on the martyr's lips." His example inspired many, and "we knew idealists of the highest purity and caliber, people who were kind by nature and who were proud of their denunciations, made without any intent of personal gain" (291). All this is a preparation for the portrait of a childhood friend called only

Sergei or Seryozha, who was much more sophisticated than the youthful Sinyavsky, and who introduced him to the Impressionists, Cézanne, Gauguin, and some of the newer Russian poets, while Andrei was still stuck in admiration of the utilitarian essayist Pisarev.

In a series of anecdotes and recollections, Sinyavsky builds up a portrait at once pseudo-admiring and venomous of Sergei/Seryozha as unscrupulous, sadistic, cowardly, treacherous, and ultimately a provocateur and KGB informer. Two of Sergei's friends and fellow classmates, Kabo and Breghel, disappeared in the camps, and Sinyavsky knew that Sergei had been responsible for their arrest (he admitted it, after the returning pair boldly denounced him at his doctoral examination). This admission was volunteered because Sinyavsky told Sergei that he too had been approached to become an informer, and that they were both in the same boat.

One of Sinyavsky's classmates at the university, who soon became an intimate of his circle that included Sergei, was Hélène Peltier, later Peltier-Zamoyska, the daughter of the French naval attaché in Moscow who was to become (and still is) an eminent French Slavist.[15] She had learned Russian in France during the Second War and as a special diplomatic favor was admitted to Moscow University just as the Iron Curtain was being banged shut. Hélène Peltier was a revelation for Sinyavsky and his friends, bringing with her a culture and an intellectual world wholly new to them (she was a believing Catholic, steeped in contemporary French literature, and astonished everybody, after getting an A in the course in Marxism-Leninism, by announcing that she was still an Idealist). She firmly defended her completely alien convictions in the impassioned conversations to which young Russian intellectuals are so prone; and while they initiated her into their cult of Mayakovsky, whose heretical Futurist past allowed them to look into all sorts of then-forbidden poets and artists, she argued in favor of Christianity and brought her friends art books on Picasso and Van Gogh, whose reproductions dazzled them. "I had never seen anything more beautiful in my life" (324).

One day Sinyavsky was called to his draft board, taken into a separate room, and found that the KGB was interested in this friendship. He was told to continue it, even deepen it, and summoned two more times; at the last meeting he was ordered to propose marriage. The purpose seemed to be to compromise Hélène in some way so that she could be used for KGB purposes; but this was too much for Sinyavsky to stomach. He confessed to Hélène at their next meeting and speaks of this moment as "the most serious crisis in my life, after which it was emotionally impossible for me

---

[15] An invaluable source for understanding the early Sinyavsky is her article "Sinyavsky, the Man and the Writer," in *On Trial*, 46–49.

to return to the ranks of moral and political unity with the Soviet people and Soviet society, placing my hopes in the initial purity of the revolution" (339). It was at this instant, one can say, that Abram Tertz was born; and it is poetic justice that Hélène Peltier, in a few years, was to become Tertz's courier to the West, who smuggled out his works and arranged for their publication. But it was necessary for self-protection to make the KGB believe that the marriage plan had fallen through because of a quarrel caused by Hélène's outraged feelings. For this they used the known informer Sergei, concocting a scenario and acting it out for him so that he could report it.[16]

The plan worked, though the KGB did not give up entirely; and when Sinyavsky's father was under arrest, Andrei was ordered to write Hélène that he was going to be in Vienna (on the way home from a supposed uni-

[16] After the publication of *Goodnight!*, in a development worthy of John le Carré, Sergei (who is of Jewish origin, and whose family name is Khmelnitsky) resurfaced with an apologia *pro vita sua* sent from (then) West Berlin to a Russian-language journal in Israel, *Dvadsat Dva* (22). Some former intimates of the Sinyavsky-Daniel circle (actually closer to Daniel) edit this journal, and on the twentieth anniversary of the trial printed a roundtable conversation between them reminiscing about the events: "Dvadtsat Let Spustya" ("Twenty Years Later"), no. 46 (1986). Two issues later another article appeared about the same events, "Pravo Bit Usishlannim" ("The Right to be Heard"), no. 48 (1986), which contained Khmelnitsky's attempt to excuse his past and charge Sinyavsky with defamation. He admitted publicly, for the first time, that he had indeed betrayed Kabo and Breghel, attributing this misdeed to his youth and the pressure of the times; but he charged Sinyavsky with having been as much of an informer as himself, and now attempting to cover up the depth of his own involvement. No new facts are adduced, however, and the article is just a skillfully written tissue of slanderous insinuations and innuendoes.

The printing of this article called forth a flood of letters and commentary in the émigré press that cannot be gone into further here. Of most importance is Sinyavsky's letter in the next issue (no. 49) of *Dvzadsat Dva*, also containing two others, one by Hélène Zamoyska and the other by Yuri Breghel. Zamoyska confirmed everything that Sinyavsky had said and expressed her unending gratitude to him; Breghel, now an émigré himself, retold his story and added further information about Sergei's perfidy. Another Russian-language Israeli journal published a letter from Breghel's sister, Olga Levenson, straight out of Conrad's *Under Western Eyes*. Sergei had come to visit her in Tashkent, spent a few days in her flat, and spoken of her brother as a dear friend; on this basis she had confided in him very freely. After the arrest, he visited her Moscow flat to break the news and tell her how disturbed and upset he was. Sinyavsky had placed the Tashkent visit after the arrest, but it had occurred a month or so before; as his sister remarks, morally this makes very little difference since he had been reporting on his friend to "the organs" for about a year anyway. See *Vremia i My*, no. 91 (1986): 229–30.

Sinyavsky charges, in his letter, that Khmelnitsky is still working for the KGB, and engaged in his usual task of provocation and disinformation. His aim is to discredit Sinyavsky as much as possible, with whom the KGB has an old score to settle, and copies of Khmelnitsky's article turned up in Paris almost immediately in considerable quantities and were circulated among the émigré colony. Questions have also been raised about the motives of *Dvadsat Dva*, but I have seen nothing that throws light on this issue one way or the other.

versity assignment in Prague) and would like to meet her there. The KGB took pictures of her dining with Sinyavsky and a "friend" (a worldly KGB colonel), but no attempt was ever made to use this photograph. The book ends as Sinyavsky is on the way back to Russia in a train filled with returning officers and soldiers, listening to the crash of empty bottles thrown out of the windows along the way, and reminded by the whistle of the locomotive of the days when, as a child, he had slept out of doors in the country and "your conscience is clean as you hear a train passing on the far side of the ancient woods, the locomotive whistling at the Batraki landing, out past Syrzan" (363). Such details help one to understand better a poignant passage just a few pages back, addressed rhetorically to Hélène Peltier, but penetrated by that deep nostalgia for a lost paradise that is one of the most pervasive motifs in Sinyavsky's work: "Even though they say I called Russia a bitch, Russia is my mother, Lenka, and it was so beautiful and just in my eyes when I was starting out in life" (340).

Five

Soviet Civilization is subtitled "a cultural history," and it is important to keep this qualification in mind. Sinyavsky is not writing history per se, that is, a recital of specific events through which something called "Soviet civilization" came into being, but rather an outline of its fundamental principles seen primarily through the literary examples that express its dominating values.[17] As was the case with *On Socialist Realism*, there is little here not already familiar, to anyone who has dipped into the flood of literature about Soviet life and culture. What makes it so valuable, however, is that these principles are defined by someone who has lived them from the inside, who often illustrates their workings with incidents from his own life, and who has felt both their seductive power and all the inhuman consequences of their practical realization. And who, in addition, is also one of the most perceptive connoisseurs of the literature that responded to the revolution, both positively and negatively, and sometimes in both ways at the same time.[18] Sinyavsky's book is unrivaled in the sensitivity of its penetration into the inner workings of the Soviet cultural psyche; and

---

[17] Andrei Sinyavsky, *Soviet Civilization: A Cultural History*, trans. Joanne Turnbull and Nikolai Formozov (New York: Arcade, 1988). Subsequent references to this work are cited in parentheses in the text.

[18] Sinyavsky's reputation inside Russia was made by his first book, written in collaboration with A. Menshutin and dealing with Russian poetry during the early years of the revolution: A. Menshutin and A. Sinyavsky, *Poeziya Pervikh Let Revolutsii, 1917–1920* (Moscow: Nakra, 1964). The *Times Literary Supplement* picked this work as one of the best critical studies published that year in a language other than English.

precisely for this reason he has no easy answers or consoling panaceas. What he does, however, is to affirm certain moral values, whose denial or suppression he believes responsible for the worst excesses of the Soviet system.

Sinyavsky joins many others in viewing the Russian Revolution, despite all its Marxist slogans and its claim to be the realization of a "scientific" historical law, as ultimately religious in inspiration, an attempt to realize the Kingdom of Heaven on Earth, "a marriage of the most exact historical science (Marxism, by its own definition) and man's religious strivings from time immemorial" (5). Dostoevsky was the first to realize this perverted religious nature of Russian radical aims, and Sinyavsky quotes both Mayakovsky and Aleksandr Blok to support the validity of Dostoevsky's intuitions.

Blok's great poem "The Twelve," in which a detachment of Red Guards marches through a howling snowstorm while "crowned with a crown of snow-flake pearls / a flowery diadem of frost / ahead of them goes Jesus Christ" (16), is the poetic incarnation of the apocalyptically religious significance of the revolutionary upheaval. It released an elemental force whose imagery was always that of a natural catastrophe, but which was felt to provide the basis for a renewal of the world and hence not to be judged according to ordinary moral standards. The same conception can still be found as late as *Doctor Zhivago*, but Sinyavsky also notes another aspect of such release in the unbridled behavior of the Cossacks in Babel's *Red Cavalry*. When the Cossack leader Pavlichenko tramples on the corpse of his old *barin* for an hour, he is expressing this elemental force in its most terrible form. "The idea of power here is vital. For power is the principal product of the revolution and the class struggle" (27).

The triumph of power was then channeled by the Bolshevik Party into what Sinyavsky calls the notion of a "real-life utopia," the belief that all the age-old dreams of mankind were to find their fulfillment in the Soviet state. This state and its system were being created in defiance of all the socialist dogmas the Bolsheviks had nominally accepted, the dogma, namely, that the revolution could only occur in an advanced industrial economy; but instead of material existence dominating ideas, as Marxists were supposed to believe, "in practice, the idea forms everything, dominates everything" (31). The Soviet state is the first completely ideological state in history; and emerging as it did after the chaos of the First World War, which shook Western civilization to its foundations, it gave life a new meaning and purpose. "For many people, for many years [and here Sinyavsky is by no means talking only for or about Russians], this was undoubtedly the attraction of the revolution and the civilization that it forged" (36). This civilization, as Sinyavsky sees it, was a strange combination of the fantastic and the rational, and he links some of the grandiose artistic projects of the

Russian Futurists to this dream of a complete transformation of the world and of mankind. Even though they at first limited themselves to art, the Futurists were expressing "the utopian spirit that the revolution partly adopted and encouraged and then destroyed" (43).

What dealt the death blow to the early utopian energy of the revolution was the competing spirit of revolutionary utilitarianism, which came straight from the Russian 1860s and required the sacrifice of everything for the social good. The Futurists, who had begun as artists, threw themselves into the service of the revolution, heaped scorn on the bourgeois art of the past, and were trapped when "the revolution introduced a spirit of cruel expediency that went so far as ascetic intolerance of anything that seemed useless in the moment" (48). To illustrate the point, Sinyavsky tells the story of the hapless Mayakovsky who experimented with verse forms all his life, and who was asked at a public reading whether he would write in iambic verse if ordered to do so "for the good of the revolution" (49). Since this good was the ultimate criterion of value, he could only answer "Yes"; a short time later he committed suicide. This utilitarian spirit distorted all aspects of the life of the new society, and "man's every move was now judged by the good or harm it did vis-à-vis communism's supreme goal.... Superutilitarianism became perhaps the essence of Bolshevik psychology" (49).

Two chapters are devoted to Lenin and Stalin, the first of whom Sinyavsky sees as having founded a "state of scholars," that is, a state governed by those who were entitled to rule because of their superior knowledge, "state-of-the-art specialists in the application of Marxism to present-day policy" (70). Lenin himself was a "rather kind person whose cruelty was stipulated by science and incontrovertible historical laws" (56). Sinyavsky finds him even more difficult to understand than Stalin because of this "all-consuming intellectuality—the fact that from his calculations, from his neat pen, flowed seas of blood, whereas by nature this was not an evil person" (56). By concentrating all power in his hands, however, and setting up the mechanisms of a police state with the most careful attention to details, Lenin paved the way for Stalin, who erected a "state church" on Lenin's foundations, and for whom the most important thing "was to imbue his power with an impenetrable mystery, a supreme irrationality" (99). He was, Sinyavsky writes, "a kind of hypnotist who managed to convince the people that he was their god by shrouding his cult in the mystery he knew power required" (103). It is in Bulgakov's great novel *The Master and Margarita*, rather than in anything written by historians, that Sinyavsky thinks one finds the best sense of the "mass psychosis" that overcame Soviet society during Stalin's reign.

The aim of all this was to create a new human type, Soviet man, whose main characteristic would be the suppression within himself of any trace of "egoism or individualism, the desire to live for oneself as opposed to the common good" (116). Morality was redefined according to the "super-utilitarianism" already mentioned and became subordinate, according to the dictates of Lenin, to the class struggle of the proletariat. This had not been the case earlier, as Camus also long ago noted in *L'homme revolté* and his play *Les Justes*, because the Populist terrorists had continued to believe revolutionary violence to be a terrible evil even if a necessary one. As one of them wrote, "You don't have to think that by lying you are sacrificing yourself, that by killing you are saving your soul" (121).

But this is exactly what the Communists did think, or at least taught, and they set out to construct a new human personality whose moral and emotive reflexes would work according to the commands of such a code. The hero of this new ethos then became the head of the secret police (*Cheka*), Feliks Dzherzhinsky. Otherwise an exemplary human being, devoutly religious when young, who loved nature, flowers, and children, he lived the life of an ascetic and became a cruel and pitiless executioner in order to fulfill the highest demands of revolutionary duty. Sinyavsky cites a number of poems (including one by Mayakovsky) celebrating Dzerzhinsky and holding him up as a "knight of the revolution" whose example Soviet youth would do well to follow.

In writing of the dissident movement, Sinyavsky stresses its essentially moral, apolitical character; the dissidents had seen and felt all too well what resulted from taking politics as the be-all and end-all of human existence. The dissident movement, Sinyavsky says, fights "not for material privileges. Not even for democracy. It fights for the individual. After a hiatus of fifty years, Soviet man suddenly discovered that he was a person, not an impersonal sociopolitical category" (239). These are words that might well be taken to heart by all those in whatever country who insist that "persons" can only be defined (or should be defined) in terms of "race, class, and gender." Sinyavsky's pages might help them to see what occurs when impersonal social-political categories take precedence over individuals and are used as unquestioned guides to social action.

So far as the future of Russia is concerned, Sinyavsky fully appreciates the relative freedoms granted in recent years; but he is properly skeptical of the depth and durability of the changes. "For now," he wrote in 1988, "we have no reason to doubt the sincerity of Mikhail Gorbachev and of his noble efforts and intentions. However, once again, Soviet liberalism and the sovereignty of the Russian people are ultimately contingent on the goodwill of the father-tsar and his loyal courtiers" (271). He compares Soviet civilization with a pyramid, the most stable and enduring of architectural forms, and wonders whether a pyramid can really be restructured; at the moment the question still remains open. Drawing on his own encounters in prison with various nationalities, he illustrates the intractable hatred of the conquering Great Russians that he found among all of them. But what bothers him most is the growth of anti-Semitism, which has now become accepted even by an influential fraction of the intelligentsia and openly advocated by a mathematician of international renown, Igor Shafarevich, whom Sinyavsky sees as only "developing one of Solzhenitsyn's ideas" (273). Sinyavsky and his wife, who is an art historian, edited a Russian language journal in Paris, *Sintaxis*, which has carried on an unremitting campaign against advocates of anti-Semitism and those who reject the possibility (or desirability) of a Western-style "pluralist" democracy in Russia.[19]

The roots of anti-Semitism in Russia, as everywhere else, go back a long way, but Sinyavsky interprets it in the Soviet era as a transference from the now invisible class enemy to an easily identifiable group of foreign origin. He notes that official anti-Semitism only began to be encouraged after the state "had liquidated the last class enemies, the kulaks, or prosperous peasants" (262). Also, he acutely points out that the Jews played the role of the Russian nobility in Soviet history. After the revolution they occupied many posts in literature, art, and science; but it is absurd to want to chastise them for having assumed this positive role of the intelligentsia. Nonetheless, in what he calls a "glimpse of the future" (264), he foresees the possibility of a resurgent Russian nationalism turning into a kind of fascism under Orthodox auspices and allying itself with a more or less intact Soviet state. Anti-Semitism and charges of Russophobia (Sinyavsky himself has been called a Russophobe), thrown out in such an atmosphere, are like playing with matches in a room with gasoline fumes; and if an explosion occurs, "May Christ forgive us for once again linking his name with the urge to launch massacres and pogroms" (276).

Do we not here come full circle back to *The Trial Begins*? In its last scene, an old dagger with a handle in the shape of the cross is found by a Jewish doctor-convict digging in a Siberian trench, and he holds it up for the admiration of two fellow diggers: "A nice place they found for God—the handle of a deadly weapon. God was the end and they turned him into the means—a handle. And the dagger was the means and became the end."[20]

---

[19] An anthology of texts from this journal has been published in French, *Syntaxis: Reflexion sur le sort de la Russie* (Paris: Albin Michel, 1981). See especially, on the question of anti-Semitism, Sinyavsky's "Commentaire de l'interview de N. N.," 21–39. These are comments made on the text of an interview with a well-known Russian writer, not an émigré, who agreed to explain his anti-Semitic opinions so long as his anonymity was guaranteed. Sinyavsky's criticism of the anti-Semitic views in Igor Shafarevich's *Russophobia* was published in *Granta* 30 (Winter 1990).

[20] Tertz (Sinyavsky), *The Trial Begins and On Socialist Realism*, 127.

SEVENTEEN

D. S. MIRSKY

VERY FEW even of well-informed present-day readers will be familiar with the name of Prince Dimitri Svyatopolk-Mirsky; but anyone who took a course in Russian literature either in England or the United States between the mid-1920s and the present probably ran across its shortened, plebeian variant, D. S. Mirsky. Indeed, starting in 1920 and ending in 1932, this name would have been immediately recognized by all perusers of serious literary journals in English, French, Italian, German, and Russian (to be sure, only those published in that language in Europe). Mirsky's native tongue was Russian, but he possessed a mastery of the others as well; and during these years he became an internationally known literary critic and commentator on the rapidly changing cultural events taking place behind what was not yet called the Iron Curtain. His chief claim to fame, however, lay in a two-volume *History of Russian Literature* (1926), written directly in English and later (1949) abridged to one volume by the American Slavist Francis J. Whitfield. This book, universally recognized as a classic in its field, has never been out of print.[1]

Even those who read and admired Mirsky though can hardly be acquainted with the remarkable and quite tragic story of his life, which has now been thoroughly explored for the first time in Smith's wide-ranging biography. For here was a man who swung from one extreme to another in relation to the revolutionary upheavals in his homeland. After a twelve-year stay in the West, during which he gained access to the highest reaches of European culture, he finally rejected them as doomed to extinction and returned from exile—a choice that led fatally to his own extinction in the Gulag. His trajectory of prolonged expatriation and tormentingly rationalized return not only is noteworthy in itself, as exemplifying the dilemmas of Russians cut off from their community and their culture, but also illuminates as well a whole stretch of recent history in which not only

---

Originally published in a slightly different form as "The Tragedy of Prince Mirsky," *New York Review of Books* 50, 10:64–67. Copyright © 2003 *The New York Review of Books*. All rights reserved. Reprinted by permission.

[1] The authoritative *Handbook of Russian Literature* (1958), 457, calls Mirsky's work "perhaps the most readable of all histories ... characterized by a refined taste and replete with perceptive and provocative insights."

Russian exiles wrestled with the issues posed by communism and the Russian Revolution.

At the time that Mirsky's books were being abridged, his American publisher wrote Vladimir Nabokov asking for a blurb. The supercilious Nabokov, so scornful of most critical opinion, expressed his admiration for the work ("I consider it the best history of Russian literature in any language, including the Russian"), but regretfully refused this politically naïve request. To the innocent American publisher, he explained that " I must deprive myself of the pleasure of writing a blurb ... since the poor fellow is now in Russia and compliments from such an anti-Soviet as I am known to be might cause him considerable unpleasantness."[2] Nabokov's sense of the precariousness of Mirsky's status was all too justified, and in fact he had already been dead for ten years when this remark was made—which merely illustrates how people could vanish in Stalinist Russia without a trace. The critic had been swept up in the hecatomb of intellectuals, not to mention other social categories, in the late 1930s and breathed his last in a prison camp in June 1939 under conditions that have only been clarified since the end of the Soviet Union.

Mirsky's return to Russia in 1932 created something of a stir because, by this time, he had acquired a considerable stature not only in England but in France and Germany as well as in Russian émigré circles. Indeed, he felt it incumbent to explain the reasons for his decision in public; and he published an article in the *Nouvelle Revue Francaise* (1931) entitled "The Story of a Liberation" to elucidate what had motivated his surprising reversal.[3] But Mirsky's choice to return from exile was not only unexpected; it was greeted with perplexity because his family background and personal history would make him, as it were, a marked man in the new Russian order.

In one of her letters, Virginia Woolf sets down her acute, merciless, but all too prophetic impression of Mirsky, who moved freely in Bloomsbury circles. "Has been in England ... in boarding houses, for 12 years; now returning to Russia 'for ever.' I thought as I watched his eye brighten and fade—soon there'll be a bullet through your head" (209). The enigma posed by Mirsky's action crops up all through the book (there is even a subsection entitled "Why Mirsky Went Back"), and various temperamental reasons have been proffered by those who knew him personally. Smith locates the answer in broader and rather more convincing social-cultural

[2] G. S. Smith, *D. S. Mirsky: A Russian-English Life, 1890–1939* (Oxford: Oxford University Press, 2000), 295. Page references to this work are hereafter cited in parentheses in the text.

[3] A translation of this article into English by the editor is contained in D. S. Mirsky, *Uncollected Writings on Russian Literature*, ed. G. E. Smith (Berkeley: Berkeley Slavic Specialties, 1989), 358–67.

terms: "He was born a Russian and brought up with the idea of service to his country, and his extraordinarily cosmopolitan education and his exposure to non-Russian societies reinforced rather than weakened his sense of national identity" (212).

Two

Prince Dimitri Svyatopolk-Mirsky was not an ordinary run-of-the-mill Russian exile. He was an offspring of that small group of Russian aristocratic families known as the *Ryurikovichi*—those claiming descent from the Varangian prince Ryurik who founded the Russian state in the ninth century. They constitute the very peak of the Russian social order, and as Smith notes, in one of many such incidental observations that enliven and enrich his book, "even after the seventy years of Soviet effort to erase their memory, many of these clans still have instant name recognition and inherent glamour among ordinary Russians" (8). The distinguished history of the Mirsky family, whose male members zealously served the Russian state in various high offices, is traced in the early pages of Smith's carefully researched work. Mirsky's father rose from an army career to various important posts (at one time he was governor-general of what is now Lithuania and parts of Belarus and exhibited "a sympathetic attitude toward the Jews") (14). When appointed minister of the interior under Nicholas II in 1904, he was known as a "liberal" who tried, without much success, to ease some of the repressive policies leading the country to disaster. He ordered, for example, the release of many dissidents from prison or exile, one of them being Maksim Gorky. Years later, Gorky would play a crucial role in the life of his eldest son, partly prompting his return to Russia and protecting him there as far as he could.

Educated at home by private tutors and governesses, from whom he acquired a mastery of English, French, and German, Mirsky entered the Imperial Lycée in Moscow at the age of fifteen. This school was reserved for the sons of the highest privileged classes, and its status might be compared to that of Eton in England. The results of this education were described by Maurice Baring, a minor Victorian man of letters who visited the estate of the Mirskys in 1907 (he was one of the few Englishmen at the time who spoke Russian fluently), and he published a well-informed book, *Landmarks in Russian Literature*, in 1910. There he mentions having been a house guest on an estate known to be that of the Mirskys, where the seventeen-year-old son "was familiar with the literature of seven languages" (33). There is ample evidence of Mirsky's wide-ranging mastery not only of five modern languages and their literatures (Russian, English, French, German, Italian) but also of Latin and ancient Greek. Such family friendships were to play a significant role in the young Mirsky's later life. On arriving in London as an exile, it was Baring who first provided him with an entrée into the English literary scene.

Mirsky's first appearance in print was in a journal published by a group of students in a famous gymnasium, known for its literary orientation, to which he transferred from the Lycée (Osip Mandelstam and Vladimir Nabokov were also graduates, but not classmates). This group produced two issues of a miscellany called *Zvenya* (*Links*) in 1906 and 1907, and these contained Mirsky's translation of a sonnet on Keats by Dante Gabriel Rossetti, along with what Smith severely labels "an extraordinary piece of rhetorical prose, the like of which—fortunately—Mirsky was never to attempt again" (37). Such disparaging judgment is made of a rhapsodical prose-poem proclaiming the death of the old world based on "Reason" and "Utility" and awaiting a new revelation from "an eternal unfading kingdom of unlimited freedom and divine Beauty"—presumably to be created by "Art" (37). Smith downgrades this vision as merely an adolescent effusion because Mirsky later showed little sympathy for the eschatological and messianic tendencies typical of Russian Modernism. Perhaps so; but it also indicates how early the search for some new, positive ideal, which later became identified with Marxism, had taken root in his sensibility.

This group also intended to stage Alexander Blok's play, *Balaganchik* (*The Clown*, or *Jester*) and received the poet's permission to do so; but this plan never came to fruition. Music to accompany the play had been composed by Mikhail Kuzmin, also a highly gifted poet, playwright, and critic as well as composer, less well-known outside Russia but notorious for his overt homosexuality; his novel *Wings* (1907) "is the earliest work in Russian high literature that is explicitly homoerotic" (40). Visits of Mirsky and his schoolmates are noted in Kuzmin's diary, parts of which became available only after the demise of the Soviet Union. Kuzmin unabashedly listed the names of his conquests, and Mirsky, designated coyly as *il principino*, is not among them; but the association of himself and his group with Kuzmin raises the whole obscure issue of the critic's sexuality.

He was considered homosexual by many who knew him in England, but even the indefatigable Smith could not turn up evidence of any affairs. Wounded during the war, Mirsky married one of his nurses but divorced after two weeks; and a woman to whom he proposed marriage in 1930, the much younger ex-wife of a friend, told Smith that she had refused not because of the age difference but because he was sexually impotent. Smith speculates that perhaps Mirsky, an impassioned gastronome who did not hesitate to take a train in order to visit famous French restaurants, satisfied his sensuality "by oral gratification for the purpose of filling his stomach" (44).

Although he attended St. Petersburg University for three years, studying Asian languages, very little trace of their effect can be found in his criticism. He also took part in the famous Pushkin seminar of Professor S. Vengerov, which eventually produced a monumental edition of the poet's work. In his excellent English book on Pushkin (1926), Mirsky called the edition "a monster ... everything can be found there except understanding of Pushkin" (328). He then oscillated between the academy and the army, becoming an officer in a fashionable regiment of the Life Guards but taking military leave and studying in the classics department of the university in 1913. Prof. Rostovtsev, the greatest Russian classical historian, asked him to remain; and if not for the outbreak of war, he would probably have been destined for an academic career.

During these years Mirsky published a volume of poetry that was treated quite condescendingly by the young but influential critic Nicholas Gumilyov; later it was never listed by the author among his publications. Influenced by the dominant Symbolist style of the time, but already showing the effect of the Acmeist movement that broke with the mistiness of Symbolist imagery, the book also reveals Mirsky's impressive erudition, even containing an epigraph in Sanskrit. One poem is a lament for the lost splendors of the past, with imagery drawn both from the Mongol conquest and from the glory that was Greece ("*Iliads* we write no longer"):

> I do regret—the Throne once lofty
> We neither dread nor worship now,
> That Earth possesses no Great Mogul,
> That shallowness has won the day.

This was written before the Russian Revolution, but Mirsky had already become thoroughly disillusioned ("Our fathers' course is risible / Our grandsires have no path to show"). "The young poet," as Smith perceptively notes, "is plaintively looking for something big enough to be worth serving. Eventually, he found it; and paid the price" (51).

Mirsky went back to his regiment at the outbreak of the war, rising to the rank of captain and serving on both the Crimean and Caucasian fronts. Returning to the family estate in the Ukraine after the defeat, he then took a degree in history at Kharkov University; but in March 1919 he joined the army of General Denikin, one of the several generals who had come south to organize resistance against the Bolshevik Revolution. Serving as an adjutant on Denikin's divisional staff, he took part in numerous battles that he later carefully enumerated for the benefit of his NKVD interrogators. "The [Russian] civil war," he wrote in 1925, "was a much more terrible business than the war with Germany. On all sides—White, Red and Green—it was accompanied by nameless cruelty" (66). Writing of Mikhail Sholokov's *The Quiet Don* in 1934, a novel in which the Red Army comes off little better than the White, he praised it as the best portrayal of the Civil War in Soviet literature. He was also among the first to call attention in England to the finely chiseled savagery of Isaac Babel's *Red Cavalry*.

Interned in a Polish camp, Mirsky easily escaped to Warsaw, where a relative helped get him to Austria and finally Greece. A letter from there to Baring in September 1920 expresses his desire to emigrate to England or France, where he hoped to support himself "by literary work." The same letter also refers to the "dreadful losses" he has suffered in the past several years (a brother killed, along with all except two of his friends), and of course, what he does not mention, the loss of the family estate and most of their fortune. He also comments bitterly on the politics of the period, which brought nothing but "disillusions ... Russia came first with Rasputin, Kerensky, the bolsheviks and all, and Europe followed close behind with the infamous treaty of Versailles, that damned humbug Wilson, that despicable coward Lloyd George and those traitors the French" (70–71) Whatever his grievances against his own country, he could not help regarding Europe (which included the United States) as equally guilty and perhaps even worse because more hypocritical. Although seeking shelter in Europe, there is no sense that he was choosing a better or more preferable world than the one he had been forced to abandon.

Three

On arriving in London, thanks to Baring's recommendation he immediately obtained a post as book reviewer for the *London Mercury,* writing on novels, literary history, and criticism published in the various languages he commanded. Another family friend, Bernard (later Sir Bernard) Pares, the author of a standard history of Russia (1926) and a confirmed anti-Bolshevik, had also been a pioneer in the establishment of Russian studies in England even before the war. He managed in 1919 to set up a School of Slavonic Studies in the University of London and hired Mirsky, "who became the first and only full-time academic specialist in Russian literature in the country" (94). The school still issues a journal, *The Slavonic Review,* to which Mirsky became one of the chief contributors. Thus began Mirsky's twelve-year stay in Europe, which provided him with a small if steady income and a certain security as a refugee with no national identity.

Five hours a week, on Tuesdays and Thursdays, were occupied by his courses in Russian literature; the remainder of his time was spent in writing, though he was also required to do some language teaching. These language classes often included army officers, and he was later accused of having trained intelligence operatives to work against the Soviet Union. His lectures on Russian literature were very sparsely attended (he speaks in one letter of a class of five students) but became the basis of his famous *History*. To supplement his income he also lectured to private audiences and, as already remarked, turned out a steady stream of articles in various languages on Russian literary and cultural topics that brought his name into prominence.

Allusion has also already been made to Mirsky's frequentation of the Bloomsbury circle centered around Virginia and Leonard Woolf. He had met them, not in London but in Paris (where his mother and sisters lived) in the spring of 1924, introduced by the classical scholar turned anthropologist Jane Ellen Harrison. Her work on the history of religion exercised a wide literary influence, and she had also written on the Russian language, arguing for its acceptance in the university curriculum on the same basis as ancient Greek. Her friendship with Mirsky was very close, and she edited the English of three of his books; it was to her that he dedicated his *History*.

Through Harrison he also came into contact with the very top echelon of the French literary scene, taking tea at her apartment (only tea?; Mirsky was a heavy drinker) with such luminaries as Jacques Riviere and Jean Schlumberger (both important in the *Nouvelle Revue Francaise*) and Charles du Bos, a penetrating critic who ranged over several literatures. As a result, Mirsky was invited to participate in the famous summer colloquies organized in the former Cistercian abbey at Pontigny. These gatherings of European intellectuals from various countries (Malraux indelibly depicted one such session in his too-little-read novel, *The Walnut Trees of Altenburg*), represented the very apex of European cultural life in those years; to be invited was to be recognized as having attained international stature. Mirsky attended three of these prestigious meetings, to which very few Russians were ever summoned—the only others being the philosophers Lev Shestov and Nikolay Berdyaev and the historian of philosophy and science, Alexandre Koyré.

Roger Fry, the eminent English art critic and Bloomsbury habitué, had also been at a Pontigny assemblage in 1925. Meeting Mirsky accidentally in a hotel in Chablis soon after, the two dined together; and Fry recorded their impassioned conversation, perhaps struck by the intemperance of his companion's predictions and rejections. Probably "well-oiled" by this time, as Smith idiomatically puts it, Mirsky declares very frankly that "Europeans now face a period of violent convulsions." When Fry asks whether Mirsky anticipates "a new Dark Ages," an idea popularized by Berdyaev, Mirsky agrees, adding that "I'm impatient to see them." Fry expresses astonishment that his interlocutor is willing to contemplate the disappearance of "all the slowly piled up achievements of European thought," and Mirsky's answer is blunt: "I'm not interested in Europe, it's done for. I'm interested in Russia." Fry objects that, after all, Russia "has surely come into the orbit of European thought," but Mirsky snaps back: "No, never really, and it is freeing itself and is going to create a new conception of life and that's what I care for" (102). Mirsky also offhandedly confesses that while "violence to others is repugnant to my nerves," he can find no moral objections to violence and even to cruelty." Such statements may have been meant to shock Fry, who stoutly defended the value of reason and science, prompted by what Mirsky probably considered his bourgeois complacency; but the battle-hardened feelings they express may also, as Smith suggests, have helped to pave the way for Mirsky's later acceptance of Stalinism.

One of Mirsky's ambitions, evident as early as 1922, was to found a Russian-language journal that would close the gap between the literature being produced in exile and that being written in his ex-homeland. In addition, he wished to acquaint Russians with the best that was being published outside their borders. He finally succeeded in launching a journal called *Vyorsts* (*Mileposts*) in 1926, whose title duplicated that of an earlier volume by the émigré poet he much admired, Marina Tsvetaeva. *Vyorsts* lasted for three issues, printing works by Tsvetaeva and another émigré, the novelist Aleksey Remizov, as well as essays by French critics such as Ramon Fernandez and one by E. M. Forster, whose English original has been lost. There was also a substantial article by Mirsky on T. S. Eliot, whom he knew personally, in which he declared *The Hollow Men* to be "a work of genius in terms of the concentration of its feeling for the death and impotence of post-war Europe" (158).

In the same year, Mirsky also gave a lecture in Paris, "The Ambience of Death in Pre-Revolutionary Russian Literature," that scandalized the émigré community and led, as it were, to a second exile, this time from their ranks. Without dwelling on individual writers, he insisted that the "entire literature of the last reign [which included the works of a number of writers in his audience, such as Ivan Bunin], is shot through with a spirit of death and decay" (151). The revolution had put an end to the world from which this literature had sprung, and he spoke of its effects as being similar to a surgical operation. "Thus the Revolution itself was a crisis that could have been followed by either death or recovery, but without it recovery is impossible" (151). The oscillation evident in this article, with its justification of the revolution as paving the way for any possible future, indicates to what extent Mirsky was coming round to adopting a pro-Soviet position.

Vyorsts was considered to be the mouthpiece of a faction among the exiles known as the Eurasians; when that publication ended, Mirsky became the editor of a newspaper, *Eurasia,* voicing the views of this group more overtly.[4] The Eurasians, whose original inspirer was the important linguist N. S. Trubetskoy, argued that Russia was neither Asian or European but part of another ethnic grouping spanning the two, and whose outstanding attribute, according to the philosopher Leo Karsavin, was "a symphonic personality" immune to any extreme individualism. In an English article of 1927, Mirsky described the Eurasian political position as being an acceptance of "the great Revolution as a historical necessity," and even an admiration of the Bolsheviks for "their organizing genius and their contempt for the paraphernalia of liberal democracy"; but they were "unduly and detrimentally influenced by Marxian theory and Socialist prejudice."[5] It was, clearly, only the materialist philosophy of Marxism that the Eurasians could not accept; and Mirsky, with a good deal of intellectual ingenuity, strains himself to work out a basis for reconciliation. Both the Eurasians and the Marxists, as he sees it, accept "materialism"—the first in a metaphysical-religious sense ("the transfiguration of the flesh"), the second in a more practical one ("Lenin's schemes for electrification"[6]). The aim of both is the transformation of matter, and Mirsky suggests that in this respect there is no absolute opposition between them.

Mirsky had by this time become a "left Eurasian," and in the Christmas vacation of 1927–28 he went to visit Maksim Gorky in Sorrento. Although living abroad, Gorky was on the best of terms with the Soviet authorities, who were trying (and finally succeeded) to persuade him to return to Russia. Writing to Gorky in February, Mirsky tells him that "I feel that I was not in Sorrento but in Russia, and this time I spent in Russia really *straightened me out*" (166; italics in text). A week later he writes to a fellow-Eurasian: "I keep asking myself what divides me (us) from the Communists. Only first principles" (166). These "first principles" finally vanished during the next year, a period when Mirsky devoted the majority of his spare time not to literature but to social and political history.

---

[4] The Eurasian movement began as a perfectly respectable creation of a few intellectuals, and at the start was financed by a wealthy English retired civil servant, H. N. Spalding, who also endowed Oxford University with a chair of Eastern religions and ethics. But later some rather suspicious characters became associated with it, and the conjecture arose that it might have been taken over by "the Trust," that is, "a fictional anti-Soviet organization on Soviet territory invented by the GPU to smoke out, draw in, and eventually control anti-Soviet activity abroad" (172). An important and rather mysterious figure in the Eurasian inner circle was Pyotr Arapov, another ex–White Guard officer who was also a close friend of Mirsky's; he is now considered by Russian scholars to have been a Soviet courier. None of this has been conclusively established, but it raises serious and disturbing questions. (Those who had the good fortune to view the excellent television series *Reilly, Ace of Spies* will be familiar with "the Trust.")

[5] Mirsky, *Uncollected Writings on Russian Literature*, 244–45.

[6] Ibid., 242.

He was working on what Smith considers his "unduly neglected" book, *Russia: A Social History* and on a translation of the two-volume work of the Marxist historian Pokrovsky, *A Brief(?) History of Russia*; and he began to do the reading for a study of Lenin. Mirsky describes these works, particularly the latter two, as having cleared his mind of "a good deal of idealist refuse" (163). He had spoken favorably of Lenin as far back as 1926 ("he had a gift of irony, and a genius for formulating his ideas ... in pithy and memorable form"),[7] and now he called his immersion in his works "the most important and fruitful of my life."[8] Nor should one overlook the context in which he places these remarks. He was reading them "during decisive months in the history of the world," a period when American capitalism was collapsing and a world economic crisis had begun, months which, at the same time, "saw the triumphant completion of the first year of the five-year plan and the great agrarian revolution in the Russian countryside."[9] Mirsky had always believed that Europe would be unable to solve its dilemmas, and the proof now seemed to be before his very eyes, as he accepted at face value the totally false Soviet self-glorification that seemed to justify Lenin in every respect. Like so many others, Mirsky was completely taken in; at least he had the excuse, unlike his Western counterparts, of having always nourished in his heart a nostalgia for Russian grandeur and a belief in its restoration.

Four

Mirsky joined the British Communist Party in 1931 and began to speak at Communist meetings as well as contribute to their publications. This created difficulties for the School of Slavonic Studies and led to a break with his old patron Pares, who had to certify each year that Mirsky's residence in England would not involve any disturbance of the peace. In 1932 he thus decided to return to Russia and arranged to do so, regaining his citizenship with the help of Gorky. Smith gives a very full and fascinating account of these Moscow years during which Mirsky managed to keep afloat with the help of a few surviving friends and an old classmate like Victor Zhirmunsky, a distinguished literary scholar and professor. His living conditions, however, were such as he could have scarcely imagined before, and he constantly moved from place to place. He wrote to Dorothy Galton, secretary of his old school who supplied him with English

---

[7] Ibid., 193.
[8] Ibid., 366.
[9] Ibid., 367.

books and other commodities hard to obtain, that he was living in a room under which the Moscow subway was being built, and "a stone-breaking machine stands under my very window & works 24 hours a day" (220). Malcolm Muggeridge, a one-time fellow traveler and soon thoroughly disillusioned correspondent in Moscow for the *Manchester Guardian*, reports Mirsky asking if he could take a bath in his apartment (the request was granted) because there was no such facility in his own.

Mirsky continued to be extremely productive nonetheless, installing himself every morning at the café of the National Hotel in Moscow with a bottle of mineral water and working away. He soon became a fixture on the Moscow literary scene, and a group would gather around him at midday. Among them was Yuri Olyesha, whose novel *Envy* (1928)—apparently upbeat and forward-looking, but with an underlying ironic ambiguity—Mirsky had unerringly praised in 1926 as one of the masterpieces of Soviet literature. At first Mirsky was officially employed in the English translation of Lenin's works, but he also produced his last book, *The Intelligentsia of Great Britain*, a no-holds-barred onslaught on the country and the people that had given him shelter. When translated in 1935, it was greeted with disdain and contempt as a base act of unpardonable ingratitude. But Edmund Wilson, who had been stimulated to learn Russian by Mirsky's book on Pushkin, and who sought him out in Russia shortly before his arrest (Wilson wrote a famous article about this meeting called "Comrade Prince"), considered it "an able and intelligent book," which, even if "ill-inspired," contained "very good things" (238).

The Russian literary scene to which Mirsky returned was racked by its own internal conflicts, and his blunt outspokenness soon aroused a great deal of hostility—especially since, as he was constantly being reminded, such judgments were hardly to be tolerated from a former White Guard officer who had taken up arms against the revolution. Thanks to Gorky, who once intervened on his behalf with a letter to Stalin, Mirsky's enemies could be fended off; but after Gorky's death in June 1936 he was left unprotected. As one notable after another, both political and literary, were denounced as traitors, Mirsky's innocent association previously with some of them (such as the once-powerful head of a writer's association, Leopold Averbakh) made him vulnerable to attack.

He also found it impossible to contain his reactions when, for example, he was enlisted as a participant in the literary celebration of the completion of the White Sea canal. Built by convict labor with little or no machinery, it was denounced by Solzhenitsyn as one of the worst atrocities of the labor-camp regime (the death rate was ten thousand a month). Mirsky posed questions at the time that made everyone uncomfortable and attracted unfavorable attention; he spoke recklessly to a younger writer of what had been "hidden" about the project, ending with the request not to tell any of the others that "this former prince is tempting you away from the straight and narrow" (248). Vera Traill, the woman he had once wanted to marry, was now in Moscow and had become an ardent Communist. They saw each other frequently, and when she spoke to him rapturously about the new Russian Constitution, "his face was completely distorted, and he said: 'Surely you understand that it's a *diabolical* lie!'" (286).

It is sad to read of the formerly independent and intransigent Mirsky, as he felt the noose tightening, writing an article vituperating the victims of the Stalinist show trials, and letters not only condemning his "mistakes" but soliciting the help of the Union of Soviet Writers "to liquidate the negative results both of my connection with Averbakhism and with my previous biography" (291). All this was to no avail, and he was taken into custody on the night of June 2, 1937. His disappearance was never explained, and many legends arose about what had occurred; nobody knew where he was and whether he were alive or dead. Only now has it been established that he died two years later, having been assigned to work at what was practically a death camp in the Far East, first at logging and then, as his health weakened, as a watchman. The prison report, incidentally, is critical of his failure to participate in "mass-cultural work." The records of his questioning have now become available as well, and one can apply to them the words that Smith uses about the interrogation of Sergey Efron, another Eurasian and the husband of Marina Tsvetaeva: they "are grotesque to a degree that makes *Darkness at Noon* seem infantile" (171).

Mirsky wrote a number of solid and important literary-historical articles in these final years, excellent introductions to various translations of English novels, worked on an English-Russian dictionary with a collaborator, and edited an anthology of modern English poetry in Russian translation (some by himself) that still has no rival. It was about to be published when he was arrested and his name was removed. When Joseph Brodsky first came across the poetry of Auden in its pages twenty years later, he had no inkling to whom he should be grateful for the discovery.

In 1967, during the Khrushchev thaw, Mirsky's name was mentioned again for the first time in a literary encyclopedia, which stated that he had been "posthumously rehabilitated." A later (1997) volume on Russian criticism of the 1930s contains a somewhat heavy-footed but respectful chapter on Prince Dimitri Svyatopolk-Mirsky, who is credited with having helped to raise the aesthetic consciousness of Russian society for the independent value of poetry and the creative freedom of the artist.[10]

---

[10] V. V. Perkhin, *Russkaya Literaturnaya Kritika 1930-x godov* (Petersburg, 1997), 228.

EIGHTEEN

VLADIMIR NABOKOV:
LECTURES ON LITERATURE

BETWEEN 1941 AND 1948 Vladimir Nabokov taught courses in Russian and European literature at Wellesley College, and from 1948 to 1958 he was a professor of Russian literature at Cornell University. One of his courses at Cornell was devoted to "selected English, Russian, French, and German novels and short stories of the nineteenth and twentieth centuries." All works were read in English translation, and the catalog note added that "special attention will be paid to individual genius and questions of structure."[1] Among the non-Russian novels included in the course were *Madame Bovary*, *Mansfield Park*, *Bleak House*, *The Strange Case of Dr. Jekyll and Mr. Hyde*, *Swann's Way*, Kafka's "The Metamorphosis," and *Ulysses*. The volume, entitled *Lectures on Literature*, is composed of a reconstruction of both the handwritten and typewritten notes made for these lectures by Nabokov the university professor, who intended eventually to turn them into a book; but he never managed to put them into a more polished and accessible form. Nonetheless, the work undertaken by the editor Fredson Bowers, with the help of Vera Nabokov, has resulted in a book that communicates the considerable charm of Nabokov's puckish classroom personality, as well as providing invaluable glimpses into his views on important novelists and the art of the novel.

Nabokov of course drew on his own experience as a novelist in communicating what he felt was most important about all the works he discussed—not their content as such, or as it might be expressed in one or another generalization about the book, but that content as it was developed concretely in and through the form and structure, the manipulations used by the author to obtain his effects. In an introductory lecture entitled "Good Readers and Good Writers," he warned his young American listeners not to come to books with preconceived notions (such as that *Madame Bovary*, for example, is a "denunciation of the bourgeoisie"), but rather

---

Originally published in a slightly different form as "Lectures on Literature." Reprinted with permission from Vladimir Alexandrov, ed., *The Garland Companion to Vladimir Nabokov* (New York: Garland, 1995), 234–58

[1] Vladimir Nabokov, *Lectures on Literature*, ed. Fredson Bowers (New York: Harcourt Brace Jovanovich, 1980), vii. Subsequent references to this work are cited in parentheses in the text.

to look on each book as the creation of an entirely new world "having no obvious connection with the worlds we already know" (1). What is important is to immerse oneself in this new world and to understand its indigenous features; only after this is done should one "examine its links with other worlds, other branches of knowledge" (1). There are, Nabokov says, three kinds of novelists—storytellers, teachers, and enchanters. A major writer combines all three, but "it is the enchanter in him that predominates, and makes him a major writer" (5). It is the "enchanter" who ultimately creates a new fictional universe, and Nabokov's chief aim was to introduce his students into the architecture of these universes.

Just as he warns against approaching a novel with ready-made ideas of what it contains, so he warns against what he calls "emotional reading." A particular work causes readers to daydream about one particular experience in their own life; or readers identify with one or another character so completely that they lose themselves in this vicarious substitute for their own personality. This is not to say that imagination should not be used in reading; but "the reader must know when and where to curb his imagination" (4) by focusing on the specific world created by the author in all its details. Nabokov himself—probably because it amused him to do so but also as a pedagogic technique—was in the habit of drawing detailed maps on the blackboard (a number are reproduced in the book) of all the localities in which the action took place. For *Bleak House*, he produced an entire map of England to follow the movement of the characters. This certainly helped to counter the tendency to "emotional" reading; and in general he stressed the importance of such matters as "the rooms, the clothes, the manners of an author's people" (4) rather than their feelings or their ideas and values stated in more general terms. Such a stress on the objective and the impersonal may seem rather limiting but is in fact exaggerated to counter the bad reading habits he knew he would encounter. In discussing the texts, he does not hesitate to offer his own estimations and moral judgments; but these always emerge from an extremely concrete and detailed description of whatever is taking place on the level of language and of narrative movement and arrangement.

For Nabokov, who was not only a novelist but a lepidopterist engaged in making very precise observations about butterflies, the ideal reader would be someone capable of using an "impersonal [i.e., scientific] imagination" to attain the experience of "artistic delight" (and he stressed the importance of such a feeling with great emphasis) (4). But this delight should arise primarily from an appreciation of the artistry of the author; what the reader ought to "keenly enjoy—passionately enjoy with tears and shivers—[is] the inner weave of a given masterpiece" (4). This appeal to the sensuous and physical thrill imparted by artistic perception recurs several times (elsewhere he calls it "the telltale tingle between the shoulder blades" [64]); and one suspects here the influence of A. E. Housman, who said much the same thing about poetry. That Nabokov was a reader of Housman is indicated by a casual citation of a line of his poetry in the lecture on Dickens (65–68).

To conclude with Nabokov's preliminary observations on reading, one should note his insistence that "a good reader, a major reader, an active and creative reader, is a rereader" (3). Contrary to theorists like Stanley Fish, J. Hillis Miller, and Wolfgang Iser, who have argued that the temporality of a novel's perusal is crucial to its proper understanding, Nabokov sees such temporality more as an obstacle than an aid. Unlike a painting, which can be apprehended as a whole at a glance, a book is read in time and thus "one must have time to acquaint ourselves with it." This requires rereading, and it is only "at a second, or third, or fourth re-reading" that "we do, in a sense, behave towards a book as we do towards a painting" (3). Nabokov thus sees the form of novels as primarily spatial, or synchronic rather than diachronic, and his belief that "aesthetic delight" is communicated by "the inner weave of masterpieces" expresses the same idea in a more figurative form.

Nabokov's course began with Jane Austen, whom he included on the advice of Edmund Wilson and apparently against his own initial inclinations. He wrote Wilson that "could never see anything in *Pride and Prejudice*" and admitted to being "prejudiced, in fact, against all women writers"; but he finally yielded to Wilson's prodding, and his suggestion that "you [Nabokov] ought to read *Mansfield Park*" (xxi). Nabokov did, and six months later he thanked Wilson for putting him on to the text. He also enjoyed reading some of the works alluded to by Jane Austen (assigning them to the students as well) and was particularly amused by August von Kotzebue's *Lover's Vows* (1798), a play quite important for the novel's plot, which he read "in Mrs. Inchbald's inimitable translation (a scream)" (xxii).

By the time he came around to lecturing on *Mansfield Park*, Nabokov's opinion about Jane Austen had considerably changed, and he does his best to overcome what he senses would be the resistance of his students to her world, which to them may appear "old-fashioned, stilted, unreal" (10). But he reminds them that "in a book, the reality of a person, or object, or a circumstance depends exclusively on the world of that particular work," and that we can only appreciate *Mansfield Park* if "we adopt its conventions, its rules, its enchanting make-believe." The book is "not a violently vivid masterpiece" like *Madame Bovary* or *Anna Karenin* (Nabokov always refused to include the usual "a" ending), but it is "the work of a lady and the game of a child." Nonetheless, from the workbasket of the lady comes "exquisite needlework art," and there "is a streak of marvelous genius in the child" (10).

One of the conventions that Nabokov points out immediately is the status of Austen's heroine, Fanny Price, who is a ward of the aristocratic family to whom she is related (and he notes that her mother's maiden name is Ward). Nabokov explains that such a heroine, popular in the eighteenth- and nineteenth-century novel, was useful for a variety of narratological purposes. Her alien status evokes pathos, she can enter into a love affair with the son of the family, and she can be used as a surrogate for the author as "detached observer and participant in the daily life of the family." Dickens, Dostoevsky, and Tolstoy all used the same convention, and Nabokov remarks that the prototype of these "quiet maidens is, of course, Cinderella. Dependent, helpless, friendless, neglected, forgotten—and then marrying the hero" (10).

Most of the lecture is given over, as will invariably be the case, to a close and careful survey of what goes on in the text; but these are never plot summaries and are filled with insight into thematic relationships and interconnections as well as craft and technique. Defining the "four methods of characterization" (13) that Jane Austen uses (direct ironic description, directly quoted speech, reported speech, imitative speech of one character by another), Nabokov provides examples of each. And though he had insisted that we cannot "learn anything about the past" from novels (1), he admiringly goes into the details of the education that young girls received in that period and carefully explains what it meant to possess an ecclesiastical "living" (a parish, with an income from taxes) in the England of the time. The question of coming into a "living" is important for the action of the plot.

Nabokov also pays a good deal of attention to what is now called "intertextuality," the interweaving by Austen of other texts into her own. He appreciatively cites a poem of Cowper that Fanny refers to and quotes Scott's "Lay of the Last Minstrel" to clarify one of Fanny's allusions. He reminds his students that "in Fanny's time the reading and knowledge of poetry was much more natural, more usual, more widespread than today" (24). And he delivers a broadside against "the vulgarities of the radio, video, or the incredible, trite women's magazines" that have replaced "Fanny's immersion in poetry" (24). Nabokov also spots what he calls "reminiscence," that is, not a direct quotation but "an unconscious imitation on the author's part of some earlier author" (26).

There are a number of admiring comments on the skill with which Jane Austen organizes the structure of her action, and the manner in which "characterization ... often grades into structure," so that the personal qualities of a character involve a type of behavior necessary for proper arrangement of the action. Lady Bertram's indolence keeps her in the country and thus allows Fanny to remain there as well "without complicating the situation by journeys to London" (16). When Fanny leaves Mansfield

Park to stay with her slovenly family in Portsmouth, whose depiction reminds Nabokov of Dickens, much of what occurs is conveyed by letters; and Nabokov disparagingly remarks on this lapse into "the easy epistolary form. This is a sure sign of a certain weariness on the part of the author when he takes recourse in such an easy form" (49). Nabokov does not clarify his dislike of the epistolary novel but suggests only that it leads to "too much ... [happening] behind the scenes and that the letter-writing business is a shortcut of no very great artistic merit" (52).

Nabokov comments more favorably on what he calls Austen's use of *"stream-of-consciousness* or *interior monologue* to be used so wonderfully a hundred and fifty years later by James Joyce" (50). In fact, Austen's interior monologues are hardly stream-of-consciousness, a term now used for a more radical disruption of syntactical patterns than anything to be found in her work. Nabokov also singles out various other narrative and stylistic devices used by Austen and taken over by Dickens, not because of a direct influence of the first on the second but because both derived from the comedy of manners. These include the point already made about the use of a "Cinderella type" for what Nabokov now calls "the sifting agent," that is, the focus of consciousness "through whom and by whom the other characters are seen." To this he now adds the use, for "dislikable, or less likable characters," of "some little trick of demeanor, or manner, or attitude, and bringing it up every time the character appears" (56). E. M. Forster had made the same point in general, many years earlier, about what he had called "flat" characters in the novel.[2]

Nabokov concludes with some observations on Austen's style, whose imagery he finds "subdued," and he speaks of her quite traditionally as painting "graceful word pictures with her delicate brush on a little bit of ivory" (56). He notes the probable influence of Samuel Johnson on her use of parenthetical expressions and on "the oblique rendering of the construction and intonation of a speech in descriptive form." With a term taken both from chess and Russian criticism ("the knight's move," the title of a book by Viktor Shklovsky), he describes "a sudden swerve to one or the other side of the board of Fanny's chequered emotions" (57). He also refers, in what is not one of his happiest coinages, to the "special dimple" of her style, which means the insertion of "a bit of delicate irony between the components of a plain informative statement" (58).

Finally, there is an admiring comment about the "epigrammatic intonation" of her language, "a certain terse rhythm in the witty expression of a slightly paradoxical thought." Nabokov clearly savors this quality of Austen's style and speaks of her tone of voice as "terse and tender, dry and yet musical, pithy but limpid and light." But this style is not her invention

---

[2] E. M. Forster, *Aspects of the Novel* (New York: Harcourt, Brace, 1927).

alone, and he suggests that "it really comes from French literature," where it is found throughout the eighteenth and early nineteenth centuries. Austen "handles it to perfection," and Nabokov then concludes by remarking that style is not something external to a writer. It is far from being only a "tool" involving "a choice of works"; it is rather the very essence of the writer's personality (59).

Nabokov has done his best for Jane Austen, and there is little doubt that he became a qualified admirer of her talent. In beginning his lectures on Dickens, however, he leaves no doubt that his esteem was hardly spontaneous. "Personally," he confesses, "I dislike porcelain and the minor arts, but I have often forced myself to see some bit of precious translucent china through the eyes of an expert and have discovered a vicarious bliss in the process." This is manifestly what he did with Jane Austen; but he still finds her fiction to be "a charming rearrangement of old-fashioned values" (63) that required some effort to elicit his sympathy. In a footnote not included in the main lecture text, he remarks: "No doubt can exist that there is in Jane Austen a slight streak of the philistine" (12). For Nabokov, nothing of the sort exists in Dickens, for whom he has the greatest admiration and whose talent he celebrates in rapturous terms.

Nabokov's first order of business is to sweep away the usual sociological or political approaches to *Bleak House,* which of course contains a ferocious attack on various abuses and injustices of the English legal system. The book is therefore a "satire," but Nabokov insists that a satire not possessing any aesthetic value cannot attain its object; and if it is "a satire permeated by artistic genius" (which is the case with *Bleak House*), then "its object is of little importance and vanishes with its times while the dazzling satire remains, for all time, as a work of art" (64). A bit later, summarizing various aspects of the book, Nabokov writes: "The sociological side, brilliantly stressed for example by Edmund Wilson in his collection of essays, *The Wound and the Bow,* is neither interesting nor important" (68). What is important is Dickens, the great enchanter, whose imagery and mastery of language Nabokov cannot praise too highly, and whose wordplay seems to inspire some of his own penchant for verbal puns. Telling his listeners not to pay too much attention to the book as "an indictment of the aristocracy" represented by the Dedlock family, he remarks that "as artistic achievements the Dedlocks, I am sorry to say, are as dead as doornails or door locks (the Dead locks are dead)" (65).

Nabokov breaks down the huge cast of characters into two groups, the evil and the good. The world of the Chancery, where the lawsuit of Jarndyce versus Jarndyce has been going on interminably, is "a kind of Hell" (68), with a whole host of devils as its emissaries. The good characters are those who escape this world, or those who, though tempted and erring, are finally redeemed because they are essentially good. "Lady Dedlock is redeemed by suffering, and Dostoevski is wildly gesticulating in the background" (68). Nabokov cuts his way through the profusion of the book by distinguishing three main themes: (1) the Chancery suit, "emblemized by London's foul fog," and all the characters entangled in its web; (2) "the theme of the miserable children and their relationships with those they help and with their parents, most of whom are frauds and freaks," and (3) "the mystery theme," involving Esther Summerson, who narrates a good part of the book and turns out to be the illegitimate daughter of Lady Dedlock (69).

Nabokov dwells at length on the opening passage, with its superbly eloquent depiction of the fog, rain, and mud of a London day in November, and points out how Dickens verbally slides from the external scene to the courtroom. "Sitting in the midst of the mist and the mud and the muddle, the Lord Chancellor is addressed by Mr. Tangle as Mlud," which becomes "Mud if we reduce the lawyer's slight lisp." Other examples are given of such wordplay, in which "inanimate words not only live but perform tricks transcending their immediate sense" (72). Nabokov then discusses other Chancery-theme characters such as the crazed Miss Flite, whose room is filled with caged birds that she intends to set free when the Chancery suit is settled; but whole generations of them have already died. Ever on the lookout for thematic linkages, Nabokov notes that when Esther left for school in her teens, "her only companion [was] a bird in a cage" (74).

Another character in this group on whom Nabokov expatiates is Krook, the junk dealer who collects and sells anything and everything and whose shop, with all its detritus, is linked verbally as well as materially with the "mad muddle and poisonous visions of the Chancery inheritance that will never come" (77). The gnarled, wizened, and gin-sodden Krook makes his appearance, to quote Dickens, with "breath issuing in visible smoke from his mouth, as if he were on fire within" (77)—and indeed he was! Krook, Nabokov remarks, "seems to carry with him wherever he goes a kind of portable Hell," and he likes this last phrase—"portable Hell"—so much that he reminds the class: "this is Mr. Nabokov, not Mr. Dickens" (78).

In a famous scene that Nabokov surely read aloud with great delectation, Krook disintegrates because of "spontaneous combustion"—"the gin and the sin catching fire," Nabokov explains, "and the man burning to the ground" (81). Nabokov savors the poetic appropriateness of such a death for Krook, and it "matters not a jot whether or not a man burning down that way from the saturated gin inside him is a scientific possibility" (80). Of more importance, Nabokov insists, is the contrast between the two styles in the death scene—the "rapid, colloquial style" of the two characters who horrifiedly discover the disintegration, and the eloquent "apostrophic style" of Dickens himself as the scene concludes. Where does this second style come from, Nabokov asks, and locates the source in Thomas Carlyle's *History of the French Revolution* (1837). A few samples are quoted from Carlyle's "magnificent work," which Nabokov assures the class "it is fun to dip into" (81).

Turning to the child theme in *Bleak House*, Nabokov begins with a discussion of the "false childishness" of Harold Skimpole (83), a character in whom Dickens satirizes the selfishness and moral irresponsibility of a purely "aesthetic" approach to life. Nabokov does not mention that Skimpole is usually taken as a harsh caricature of the English Romantic man of letters Leigh Hunt; what interests him is Skimpole's claim that, since he is really a child, he is released from any duties and obligations to anyone, even to his own children. The good John Jarndyce is taken in, but the course of the book reveals Skimpole's "essential cruelty and coarseness and the utter dishonesty of the man. As a parody of the child, he serves, moreover, the purpose of bringing out in beautiful relief the real children in the book, who are little helpers, who assume the responsibilities of grown-up people, children who are pathetic imitations of guardians and providers" (91).

Nabokov is obviously moved by Dickens's portrayal of such children and rejects the usual "charge of sentimentality made against this strain that runs through *Bleak House*" (86). At this point, Nabokov throws out a general comparison between the literature of the past ("the world of Homer ... or Cervantes") and the present, much to the advantage of the present. Neither Homer nor Cervantes, he argues, knew "the divine throb of pity," and he emphatically asserts that "modern man is on the whole a better man than Homer's man.... In the imaginary battle americus versus homericus, the first wins humanity's prize." As for Cervantes, Don Quixote "is a madman ... and there is always a belly laugh just around the corner of the least pity." Not so for Dickens, where "it is the real thing, keen, subtle, specialized compassion ... with the very accent of profound pity in the words uttered" (87). As for the crime-mystery theme involving Lady Dedlock, "structurally it is the most important of the themes of mystery and misery, Chancery and chance" (94). But Nabokov goes through its intricacies conscientiously without any comment of particular interest; he merely observes that "the plot of the mystery theme does not quite live up to the poetry of the book" (97).

He then shifts to some general observations about narrative technique, citing Flaubert's dictum that an author should be like God, "nowhere and everywhere, invisible and omnipresent." Actually, Flaubert "did not attain that ideal in *Madame Bovary*" (the work Nabokov will be taking up next), and Dickens had no such ambition at all; he is one of those authors who are not "supreme deities, diffuse and aloof, but puttering, amiable, sympathetic demigods, who descend into their books under various disguises" and in the shape of a whole variety of characters (97). This leads Nabokov into a classification of three types of such authorial representatives. One is the first-person narrator, either the author himself or a character, or an invented author like the Arabic chronicler in *Don Quixote*, or a mixture of first- and third-person narrators. There is also the type of character already mentioned, "the sifting agent," a third-person character like Fanny Price who acts as the consciousness through which the action is seen and felt. A third type of character is christened a "perry" by Nabokov, a term derived from "periscope" and invented by him in a not very inspired moment. The term designates what he calls the "lowest kind of authorial minion," a character invented for the author's convenience and who can be used and moved around at will to meet the needs of the text—"a peregrinating perry" (98). (One wonders if the term was not invented to allow for this pleasing alliterative combination.) Henry James called this type of character a "ficelle" (a piece of string), necessary to tie up and hold the book together; and James's term seems a more apt one, since the notion of "periscope" suggests a function too close to that of a "sifting agent."

After disposing of his three main thematic complexes, Nabokov then moves on to discuss eight structural features of *Bleak House*. One is the usage of Esther as first-person narrator in half of the book, which Nabokov considers "a little mistake for which he [Dickens] will have to pay dearly." The problem is that Esther's "bubbling baby talk" (100) is much too limited, and that Dickens finds it necessary very soon, and quite inconsistently, to endow her with much of his own "incantatory eloquence" (101). Nabokov thinks that it was "a main mistake ... to let Esther tell part of the story. I would not have let the girl near!" (102). Another problem arises from Esther's looks, which are ruined when she catches smallpox and is left with a scarred and pitted face. But since it is necessary that she marry the young doctor Allan Woodcourt at the end, Dickens is very vague about what she looked like, and she seems, as time goes on, to have regained some of her attractiveness. Nabokov wonders whether the scars have not vanished after seven years and notes Dickens's efforts to cope with this problem.

Nabokov singles out Dickens's use of Allan Woodcourt as a "perry," who turns up whenever he is necessary, and excuses the plethora of coincidences arising from his use because it leads to some first-rate scenes (such as the death of the desolate young streetsweeper Jo). He also points out an interesting anomaly: Esther as narrator recounts incidents involving Woodcourt at which she was not present. Only Woodcourt could have told her about them, and such knowledge thus foreshadows their future marriage long before it takes place. There are many more shrewd notations of this kind about *Bleak House* that are too numerous to mention in detail, and the lectures conclude with several pages of comments on some traits of Dickens's style.

Nabokov celebrates the exactitude and precision of Dickens's gift for vivid evocation and calls the first description of the Dedlock estate, Chesney Wold, "a passage of sheer genius" (114). Of a description of the sea, he points out some details of color that Dickens "noted for the very first time with the innocent and sensuous eye of the true artist ... and immediately put into words" (116). What literature consists of is precisely such observations, which may seem like trifles but are in fact the heart of the matter; it is not "general ideas" but "particular revelations" that are important, "not ... schools of thought but ... individuals of genius" (116).

One such individual was certainly Flaubert, and Nabokov begins his lectures on *Madame Bovary* with the remark that "of all the fairy tales in this series, Flaubert's novel ... is the most romantic. Stylistically, it is prose doing what poetry is supposed to do" (125). The novel is concerned with adultery, and Nabokov, then at work on what became *Lolita*, fills in the historical background of Flaubert's indictment and trial for obscenity. "As if the work of an artist could ever be obscene," he says in passing. Flaubert won his case a hundred years ago, he goes on, but "in our days, in our times ... " (125). The sentence trails off in this fashion, and one surmises that he may have been thinking of the possible destiny awaiting his own novel.

Just as the socially satirical aspects of *Bleak House* had been swept aside, so he warns the class not to regard Emma's life as a product of objective social conditions. "Flaubert's novel deals with the delicate calculus of human fate, not with the arithmetic of social conditioning" (126). Emma and most of the other characters are described as "bourgeois," but by this word Flaubert is not describing a politico-economic class; what he means is a "philistine, preoccupied with the material side of life and believing only in conventional values" (126). In this sense, all of "Soviet literature, Soviet art, Soviet music, Soviet aspirations are fundamentally and smugly bourgeois. It is the lace curtain behind the iron one" (127). The essence of the bourgeois can be found in Flaubert's smugly epical pharmacist Monsieur Homais, and both Flaubert and Marx were bourgeois each in his own way—the well-to-do Flaubert in an economic sense, Marx in a spiritual one.

Nabokov then begins to explore the various thematic lines that he distinguishes in the novel, and which are very far from being the usual ones. The first is "the layers or layer-cake theme" (128), which he illustrates by the absurdly ridiculous shako that Charles Bovary wears on his first day in school. This is carefully described as composed of various layers that Flaubert methodically goes through, and Nabokov cites other examples (such as the wedding cake, or the description of the Bovary house at Tostes, or Charles's directions for Emma's funeral) in which the same layering arrangement of details is used. These passages echo each other for Nabokov and provide a certain structural framework, but it may well be doubted whether such a purely external feature will take on the same significance for other readers, who Nabokov assumes (?) will recall all instances of this kind "with the utmost lucidity." (132)

Emma Bovary is a "romantic" person, which means someone "mentally or emotionally living in the unreal"; and such people can be profound or shallow, "depending on the quality of his or her mind." Nabokov finds Emma to be shallow, despite her "charm, beauty, and refinement" (132), and he exhibits no sympathy whatever for her plight. "Her exotic daydreams do not prevent her from being a small-town bourgeois at heart," and her way of rising above the conventional was to commit adultery— which is "a most conventional way to rise above the conventional" (133). On the other hand, though Charles Bovary is a philistine, "he is also a pathetic human being," and Nabokov considers his love for Emma to be "a real feeling, deep and true, in absolute contrast to the brutal or frivolous emotions paradoxically experienced by ... her smug and vulgar lovers." Nabokov thus paradoxically finds that the "dullest and most inept person in the book" is the only one "who is redeemed by a divine something"— that is, "the all-powerful, forgiving, and unswerving love that he bears Emma, alive or dead" (133).

Nabokov illustrates how Flaubert indirectly communicates Emma's sensuous charms through carefully chosen details seen through the enraptured eyes of her future husband (correcting various mistranslations as he goes along) and then compares the wedding procession with that of Emma's funeral to bring out certain similarities. With reference to the "daydream theme," Emma's romantic reveries nourished by her reading of Romantic literature, he links this up with his earlier advice on how to read properly. Emma "is a bad reader. She reads books emotionally, in a shallow juvenile manner, putting herself in this or that female character's place" (136–37). But Flaubert's listing of "all the romantic clichés dear to Emma's heart" is done with such skill that "they produce an effect of harmony and art" (138). The same occurs in the case of Homais's vulgarities. Even though "the subject may be cruel and repulsive.... Its expression is artistically modulated and balanced" (138).

In addition to the daydream theme, there is also that of deceit, which impels Emma to hoodwink Charles so as to move from Tostes to Yonville even before committing adultery. Nabokov sees Emma as being "deceitful by nature," and as not really differing in essence from Homais. But he thinks that the resemblance is "veiled by her grace, her cunning, her beauty, her meandering intelligence, her power of idealization, her moments of tenderness and understanding, and by the fact that her brief bird life ends in human tragedy" (142). All the same, there are qualities in this list that can hardly be attributed to Homais, against whom Nabokov releases the full force of his invective. Homais is called a "traitor, a cad, a toad ... a coward ... a pompous ass, a smug humbug, a gorgeous philistine." Noting that Homais gets his coveted government decoration in 1856, Nabokov insists that "this kind of thing is not peculiar to any given government régime," and that "philistinism is more in evidence during revolutions and in police states than under more traditional régimes" (143).

Nabokov had a deep-rooted dislike of literary labels of all kinds, and he disposes of those usually attached to Flaubert very briefly. "Can we call *Madame Bovary* realistic or naturalistic" he asks (146)? His answer is to list some of the implausibilities that abound in the book (such as the unbelievable blindness of Charles Bovary to his wife's infidelities) so as to indicate how little "realism" the book contains. Besides, as he goes on to explain, terms like realism and naturalism "are only comparative notions. What a given generation feels as naturalism in a writer seems to an older generation an exaggeration of drab detail, and to a younger generation not enough drab detail" (146–47). The Russian Formalist critic Boris Eikhenbaum, in a well-known book on *The Young Tolstoy*, had made the same point many years before, and the relative nature of "realism" had also been pointed out in an essay of Roman Jakobson's.[3] One assumes that Nabokov was familiar with these Russian works and was outlining their results for his American students.

Interweaving his observations with citations from Flaubert's letters, Nabokov illustrates what he calls Flaubert's "counterpoint method" of linking "two or more conversations or trains of thought" in the same scene (147). The best-known instance of this is the country-fair ("comices agricoles") episode, during which the hardened landowner and man-of-the-world Rodolphe seduces Emma while speeches are being made and prizes handed out for prize crops and animals; the contrast between "the stale journalese" of the speeches and "the stale romantese" of the courtship exchanges leads to some brilliantly ironic effects (147). Nabokov points out other examples of the same cross-cutting technique, which exercised an enormous influence, and he also speaks of Flaubert's skill in motivating changes of scene in the course of a chapter rather than waiting for the end of chapters, as in *Bleak House*. Flaubert's grouping of characters in certain scenes, so as to suggest and anticipate their thematic relationships, also comes in for approving notice.

By way of conclusion, Nabokov returns to his opening remarks that Flaubert's novel is prose doing the work of poetry and mentions that

---

[3] Eikhenbaum, *Molodoi Tolstoy*, Jakobson, "O khudozhestvennom realizme" ("On Artistic Realism"). Jakobson's article was first published in Czech translation in 1921 and in Ukrainian in 1927; its first Russian publication was in 1962.

Gogol called *Dead Souls* "a prose poem" (171). The same is true for *Madame Bovary*, and this book is even "composed better, with a closer, finer texture." Nabokov then lists and illustrates some of the features of Flaubert's style, such as the habit of rounding off a paragraph with "and, and a semi-colon"; this introduces "a culminating image, or a vivid detail, descriptive, poetic, melancholy, or amusing" (171). Another feature of the style is "what may be called the unfolding method, the successive development of visual details, one thing after another" (172); this would seem to be related to the "layering" arrangement noted earlier, but Nabokov fails to link them up specifically. He does point out, however, Flaubert's use of the French imperfect tense, referring to Proust's famous article on the subject, whose effect is to render "something that has been happening in an habitual way" and to display, as Proust said, Flaubert's "mastery of time, of flowing time" (173).

Nabokov's general view of Flaubert is conveyed by what he asks his class to "ponder most carefully, namely," that "a master of Flaubert's artistic power manages to transform what he has conceived as a sordid world inhabited by frauds and philistines" into "one of the most perfect pieces of poetical fiction known" (147). It is through "the inner force of style," and by "all such devices as the counterpoint of transition from one theme to another, of foreshadowing and echoes," that such a feat has been accomplished—one that has affected the entire future of the novel. "Without Flaubert there would have been no Marcel Proust in France, no James Joyce in Ireland. Chekhov in Russia would not have been quite Chekhov" (147).

The same certainly cannot be claimed for Robert Louis Stevenson, whose *The Strange Case of Dr. Jekyll and Mr. Hyde* Nabokov insisted on including in his course over the objections of Edmund Wilson. Stevenson, in Wilson's opinion, was "second-rate. I don't know why you admire him so much," he wrote Nabokov (xxi). Nabokov hardly explains this admiration in his careful account of the book, but perhaps one of his quotations may provide a clue. Dr. Jekyll speaks of his chemical transformation from one personality to another as a challenge to the power of the material over the human spirit, a denial of the omnipotence of the body. "I began to perceive more deeply than it has ever been stated, the trembling immateriality, the mist-like transience, of this seemingly so solid body in which we are all attired.... Certain agents I found to have the power to shake and pluck back that fleshly vestment, even as a wind might toss back the curtains of a pavilion" (181). Commentators have noted the strong influence of Gnostic philosophy on Nabokov, which views the body as trapped in a lower world of materiality from which it longs to escape; and this metaphysical strain in Stevenson's book, usually neglected in favor of its moral theme, could well have had a special appeal for Nabokov.

"Three important points," according to Nabokov, are usually overlooked in "the popular notions of this seldom read book" (182). One is that Dr. Jekyll is "a mixture of good and bad" and thus not entirely good at all; the second is that Jekyll does not simply become Hyde, but Hyde represents "a concentrate of pure evil" (182) that is mixed in Jekyll with the good; the third is that when Hyde dominates the personality, "a Jekyll residue" remains that is "horrified at his worser half's iniquity" (184). Nabokov sees these relations as "typified by Jekyll's house" (184), and as usual describes the structure very carefully, with a diagram to match. The imposing entrance is on a fashionable street, but the back part is dingy and disreputable.

Stevenson's artistic problem, as Nabokov sees it, was to convey his "fantastic story" through the medium of two "matter-of-fact persons," Dr. Jekyll's lawyer Utterson and his friend, the young businessman Enfield, "in an atmosphere familiar to the readers of Dickens, in the setting of London's bleak fog" (188). But if he made them too stolid and matter of fact, "they will not be able to express even the vague discomfort Hyde causes them" (193). What happens is that "Hyde's presence brings out the hidden artist in Enfield and the hidden artist in Utterson"; they react in a way that "can only be explained by the abrupt intrusion of the author with his own set of artistic values and his own diction and intonation" (193). Whether Nabokov thinks this a defect remains unclear.

There is also another problem that Nabokov points to and specifically labels as a weakness; this is the vagueness and unspecificity of the evil pleasures in which Dr. Jekyll is supposed to have indulged. Victorian restrictions of course held Stevenson in check; but even if he had wished to make the doctor a libertine like Tolstoy's Stiva Oblonsky in *Anna Karenin*, "the pleasures of a gay blade" would have clashed with "the medieval rising as a black scarecrow against a livid sky in the guise of Hyde." Women hardly appear in the book at all, and Nabokov raises the possibility that this "may suggest ... that Jekyll's secret adventures were homosexual practices so common in London behind the Victorian veil" (194). Utterson suspects that Dr. Jekyll is being blackmailed by Hyde, who is named as Jekyll's inheritor in his will, and this raises a spectre that could well be homosexuality. As for Hyde, all we learn of his "pleasures is that they are sadistic—he enjoys the infliction of pain" (196). Stevenson hated cruelty above all else and thus depicted Hyde as an "inhuman brute" who lusts to kill, not as someone indulging in "beastly lusts" (196).

Even before reaching Proust, Nabokov had remarked that his vast opus was "the greatest novel of the first half of our century" (139), and he turns to *Swann's Way* (which he translates literally as *The Way to Swann's Place*) with eager enthusiasm. In fact, however, he ranges over the entire work in his comments, and he calls "the whole ... a treasure hunt where the treasure is time and the hiding place the past" (207). Noting that Proust "had studied the philosophy of Henri Bergson," he attributes to this influence "Proust's fundamental ideas regarding the flow of time ... the constant evolution of personality in terms of duration, the unsuspected riches of our subliminal minds which we can retrieve only by an act of memory, of individual association; also the subordination of mere reason to the genius of inner inspiration and the consideration of art as the only reality in the world" (208).

Nabokov immediately discards the notion that the book is an autobiography and stresses that "the narrator is not Proust the person, and the characters never existed except in the author's mind." To speak of Proust's life would "only cloud the issue" (208), especially since there is a resemblance between the narrator and author, and they live in the same environment; in other words, the question of distinguishing between them is too difficult to tackle. Nabokov also refuses to enter into the social-historical context of Proust's world and lays down the highly contestable dictum that "the inhabitants of that world are of no social or historical importance whatever" (208). This is of course a wild exaggeration, but perhaps Nabokov felt it necessary so as to focus on the chief thematic nexus. Otherwise, it might seem as if the book were nothing but a series of parties narrated at enormous length, and that "the narrator's main concern was to explore the ramifications and alliances which link together various houses of the nobility" (210). On the contrary, the book is really about the process of its own creation, though the work we read is not the ideal novel that the narrator sets out to write at the conclusion of the last volume. "Proust's work is only a copy of that ideal novel—but what a copy!" (211).

Nabokov justly sees the center of the book as defined by Proust's famous sentence: "What we call reality is a certain relationship between sensations and memories which surround us at the same time, the only true relationship, which the writer must recapture so that he may forever link together in his phrase its two distinct elements" (211). He then goes on to speak of the two walks taken by the narrator in his youth, one toward Swann's place and the other toward the Guermantes estate, and explains that "all its [the novel's] fifteen volumes in the French edition is an investigation of the people related in one way or another to the two walks of his young life." The depiction of the narrator's boyhood agony on failing to receive his mother's goodnight kiss in *Swann's Way* foreshadows "Swann's distress and love, just as the child's love for Gilberte and then the main love affair with a girl called Albertine are amplifications of the affair that Swann has with Odette" (211). Both walks are united at the end in the figure of Swann's granddaughter, who is herself a Guermantes.

Proust's style comes in for extensive discussion, and Nabokov stresses its wealth of metaphorical imagery as well as Proust's "tendency to fill in and stretch out a sentence to its utmost breadth and length, to crowd into the stocking of the sentence a miraculous number of clauses, parenthetic phrases, subordinate clauses, sub-subordinate clauses. Indeed, in verbal generosity he is a veritable Santa" (212–14). Comparing Proust and Gogol, he says that Proust's imagery "differs from Gogol's rambling comparisons by its logic and poetry. Gogol's comparison is always grotesque, a parody of Homer, and his metaphors are nightmares, whereas Proust's are dreams" (214). As he continues his survey, Nabokov also singles out the relativity of perception in Proust, "the various ways in which a person is seen by various eyes." The example cited is how Swann is seen by Marcel's family, who can "think of him only as the son of their old friend, the stockbroker" (217).

This observation leads Nabokov into a comparison "between the Proustian and Joycean methods of approaching their characters." What Joyce does is to take "a complete and absolute character ... then breaks it up into fragments and scatters these fragments over the space-time of his book." Proust, on the other hand, "contends that a character, a personality, is never known as an absolute but always as a comparative one. He does not chop it up but shows it as it exists through the notions about it of other characters" (217). Each ultimately depends on the reader to put the characters together into a unity. Another comparison is also made between Proust, Gogol, and Tolstoy in relation to a scene in which Proust dwells on the effects of moonlight in Marcel's room. Gogol "would also have used rich imagery" in describing a moonlit garden, "but his rambling comparisons would have turned the way of grotesque exaggerations and some beautiful bit of irrational nonsense" (220). Nabokov thinks, however, that there is a resemblance between the vision of moonlight in Proust and the scene in *War and Peace* where Prince Andrey and Natasha both look out at a moonlight-filled night from separate windows, and he hears her singing in the room above.

Nabokov then comes to the episode involving the madeleine, the first of those moments when the narrator suddenly gains access to his buried memories, and which is called here "The Miracle of the Linden Blossom Tea." The narrator does not understand the meaning of this recovery of the past through the sudden and haphazard shock provoked by some insignificant sensation, and it is only in the last volume, when he "received in rapid succession three shocks, three revelations (what present-day critics would call an epiphany)—the combined sensations of the present and recollections of the past"—that he understands their "artistic importance" (222). Up until that time, though he knew that these experiences filled him with happiness, he did not know what they meant—that in them he had found the secret to the recovery of "lost time," the secret that would lead him to his creation.

Nabokov sees the figure of Marcel's invalid Aunt Léonie in Combray as "a kind of parody, a grotesque shadow of Marcel himself in his capacity of sick author spinning his web and catching up into that web the life buzzing around him" (228). Turning to Marcel's grandmother, "the most noble and pathetic character in the book" (216), whose gifts to her grandson were always works of art of one kind or another, Nabokov observes that Proust's imagery was often taken from the same realm. He explains this in two ways: one is that "for Proust art was the essential reality of life," and thus he tends to view everything in its terms; another is that "in describing young men he disguised his keen appreciation of male beauty under the masks of recognizable paintings," while "in describing young females he disguised ... his sexual indifference to women and his inability to describe their charm" (228).

Proust's depiction of what are now called same-sex relationships is also exemplified by the scene involving the daughter of Vinteuil, the musician and composer, whose lesbian friend desecrates the picture of the dead Vinteuil before the two women make love. Nabokov thinks this scene "a little lame" without explaining why, though he pinpoints the use of eavesdropping as "enhancing its awkwardness.... Its purpose, however, is to start the long series of homosexual revelations and revaluations of characters that occupy so many pages in the later volumes and produce such changes in the aspects of the various characters" (232). According to Nabokov, "the first homosexuals in modern literature" (231) were described by Tolstoy in *Anna Karenin* (part 2, chap. 19), where he depicts two officers of Vronsky's regiment breakfasting in the mess room and leaves no doubt about their relationship. Just as he mentions Proust's own homosexuality, so Nabokov provides the information that Proust was half-Jewish on his mother's side; and despite his denial that Proust's characters possessed any "social or historical importance," he makes an exception for Marcel's Jewish friend Bloch and for Swann, also of Jewish origin. Proust was "greatly concerned with the anti-Semitic trends in the bourgeois and noble circles of his day," and in fact, "the Dreyfus affair [is] the main political event discussed in the later volumes" (230).

Describing Marcel's bewilderment at not being able to find a philosophic theme for some great literary work and wondering at the impression made on him by "some material object devoid of any intellectual value, and suggesting no abstract truth" (237, a quotation from Proust), Nabokov brings out the implications of this passage in a manner revelatory of his own conception of art and of the strong Proustian influence he had assimilated. "Contrasted here are the literature of the senses, true art, and the literature of ideas, which does not produce true art unless it stems from the senses. To this profound connection Marcel is blind. He wrongly thinks he had to write about things of intellectual value when in reality it was that system of sensations he was experiencing that without his knowledge was slowly making an authentic writer of him" (237). Nabokov's own insistence on the importance of "sensations" throughout his analyses, his distrust of generalizations and abstractions, are obviously related to this Proustian process of Marcel's self-discovery as an artist.

Nabokov loved to bring his specialized knowledge to bear on a literary work, and he regaled the class with information about the orchid, *Cattleya labiata*, so essential in the love affair between Swann and Odette. He drew a picture of it and explained that its name came from William Cattley, "a solemn British botanist," and that its color—"rose-purple mauve, a pinkish lilac, a violet flush"—"is linked in European literature with certain sophistications of the artistic temperament." In the United States, alas, it "regularly adorns the bosoms of matrons at club festivities." For Nabokov, the "mauve color" of the orchid, "the violet tint ... runs through the whole book, is the very color of time" (241). By this he probably means that pinkish colors show up in the hawthorns of the Combray chapters, in the pink dress worn by Odette years earlier, and then a pinkish light, "the color of heliotrope" (241) is associated with Marcel's recollections of Gilberte. The concluding pages of these Proust lectures, which quote extensively from *The Past Recaptured*, were inserted by the editor to fill out Nabokov's notes.

One can hardly imagine two artistic worlds more different than those of Proust and Kafka, but Nabokov moves blithely from one to the other without drawing any comparisons. He opens his lectures on Kafka, however, by stressing the importance of being able to respond to a work of art intuitively, without waiting even for the best analysis to furnish some sort of explanation of why a "poor fellow is turned into a beetle." What is necessary is "to have in you some cell, some gene, some germ that will vibrate in answer to sensations that you can neither define, nor dismiss." Such reflections lead Nabokov to what he calls "the closest we can get to a definition of art"—which turns out to be "*beauty plus pity*" (italics in text). This definition is then given a metaphysical twist by the further statement: "Where there is beauty there is pity for the simple reason that beauty must die: beauty always dies, the manner dies with the matter, the world dies with the individual" (251). Pity is thus primarily a mourning over human temporality, though Nabokov, as we have seen, also sympathizes intensely with all those characters who suffer unduly in the world of temporality as well.

Since Kafka's story involves a "fantastic" event, Nabokov discusses the general question of the relation between reality and fantasy. Imagining the perceptions of several kinds of people (a vacationer in the country, a botanist, a local farmer), he vividly illustrates how different the response of each would be to the same environment; but if we mix them all together and pick a fragment of the mixture at any moment of time, we get what is called "*objective reality*" (italics in text). The term means "an average sample of a mixture of a million individual realities" (253), and this is how Nabokov distinguishes it from worlds which are "specific fantasies."

Nabokov then compares "The Metamorphosis" with Gogol's "The Overcoat" (which for some reason he calls "The Carrick" [?]), and with Dr. Jekyll and Mr. Hyde as examples of fantasies. The first two belong together because each contains a central figure "endowed with a certain amount of human pathos among grotesque heartless characters" (253–54). Even more, "their central human characters belong to the same private fantastic world as the inhuman characters around them, but the central one tries to get out of that world, to cast off the mask, to transcend the cloak or the carapace" (254). This striving would also seem to be true of Dr. Jekyll; but Nabokov disparagingly notes that he is surrounded by a second-hand Dickensian world, which has not been sufficiently transformed to become part of the imaginative fantasy. Stevenson's novel thus possesses only "conventional pathos" (255), though Nabokov insists that it is very far from being a failure.

Providing some elementary information about Kafka, Nabokov declares him to be "the greatest German writer of our time," in comparison to whom Rilke and Thomas Mann "are dwarfs and plaster saints" (255). Well, this merely reveals the limitations of Nabokov's own taste, as well as his delight in startling his listeners by such iconoclastic and peremptory judgments. He also dismisses the opinion of Max Brod "that the category of sainthood, not that of literature" (255) should be applied to Kafka, and ridicules the Freudian commentators who focus on Kafka's relation to his father; these interpret "the bug" as characterizing "his own sense of worthlessness before his father" (256). Kafka himself, he points out, was "extremely critical of Freudian ideas," and as for himself, Nabokov declares that "I am interested in bugs, not in humbugs, and I reject this nonsense." What he wishes to do is to "concentrate ... upon the artistic moment." Nabokov believed that the greatest literary influence on Kafka was Flaubert; and whether this is true or not, he perceptively notes that Kafka's style has "a kind of ironic precision, with no intrusions of the author's private sentiments," that was "exactly Flaubert's method" (256).

Nabokov is very methodical in his discussion of "The Metamorphosis," breaking it up into three parts, the first of which is divided into seven scenes, the second nine, and the third ten. What occurs in each scene is carefully outlined, and the economic situation of the family at the beginning is described as particularly noticeable in "the canned music or plugged-in music of today" (278).

The lectures conclude with a summing up that singles out the importance of the number "three" in the story, which repeatedly turns up in one guise or another. Nabokov repeats his warning against reading any deep meaning into this fact "for once you detach a symbol from the artistic core of the book, you lose all sense of enjoyment" (283). He excoriates the search for "such inept symbols in the psychoanalytic and mythological approach to Kafka's work, in the fashionable mixture of sex and myth that is so appealing to mediocre minds." For him, the symbolism of three is both aesthetic and logical: "the trinity, the triplet, and triad and triptych are obvious forms" for the expression of the stages of human life and the movement of the mind. Nothing else is necessary to understand Kafka's masterpiece, in which "the limpidity of his style stresses the dark richness of his fantasy" (283).

Joyce's *Ulysses* was the final novel taken up in Nabokov's course, and it was a work that he had long admired (with some reservations). The two writers had met briefly at a dinner party in Paris in 1939, and Joyce presented Nabokov with a copy of *Haveth Childers Everywhere*, a fragment of *Finnegan's Wake*. Nabokov calls the complete work "one of the greatest failures in literature" (349), but he did not cease to admire *Ulysses* and submits it to a very thorough analysis. In doing so, he exhibits a detailed knowledge of Dublin topography whose source he did not try to conceal. Like Joyce himself, he relied "on data from Thorn's Dublin Directory, whither professors of literature ... secretly wing their way in order to astound their students" (285). Joyce also used a copy of the Dublin newspaper *The Evening Telegraph* for Thursday, June 16, 1904, the day whose events are depicted, or rather refracted, through the prism of Joyce's literary imagination. It was the day, apparently, on which Joyce had met his wife Nora Barnacle. "So much for human interest," Nabokov remarks wryly (286).

He then goes on to furnish some information about the three major characters—Leopold Bloom, his wife Molly Bloom, and Stephen Dedalus. Most attention is given to Stephen, whom Nabokov calls "an abstract young man, a dogmatist even when drunk, a freethinker imprisoned in his own self, a brilliant pronouncer of aphoristic sayings" (286). But he is "a bitter and a brittle young fellow," who is "a projection of the author's mind rather than a warm new being created by an artist's imagination." Nabokov thinks it "neither here nor there" that critics tend to identify Stephen with Joyce himself. Also, noting that all three characters have "artistic sides" (Molly Bloom is a concert singer), Nabokov thinks that this aspect of Stephen "is almost too good to be true—one never meets anybody in 'real life' approaching such a perfect artistic control over his casual and everyday speeches as Stephen is supposed to have" (286). It is rather odd to see Nabokov, in view of his own novels, applying such a criterion of verisimilitude to Joyce.

Nabokov is generally sympathetic to Leopold Bloom, whom he sees as the type of the exile, the Wandering Jew, and whose qualities of kindliness and humanity he stresses appreciatively. But he is bothered by the fact that, while Joyce pretended to portray him as an "ordinary citizen," it is clear (at least to Nabokov) "that in the sexual department Bloom is, if not on the verge of insanity, at least a good clinical example of extreme sexual preoccupation and perversity with all kinds of curious complications" (287). What Nabokov means is that "in Bloom's mind and in Joyce's book the theme of sex is continually mixed and intertwined with that of the latrine." Nabokov explains that he has no objection to "frankness in novels," indeed he favors it, but he is upset by Joyce's inconsistency. For it is simply not true "that the mind of an ordinary citizen continuously dwells on physiological things. I object to the continuously, not the disgusting" (287).

Nabokov also believes that *Ulysses* has been "slightly overrated" by critics who are "more interested in ideas and generalities and human aspects than in the work of art itself" (287). This seems a highly unsatisfactory way of dismissing those critics who think that Joyce's parallelism with Homer is important for the book; to be concerned with such a parallel is scarcely to abandon the work of art for "ideas and generalities." But Nabokov thinks it important to "warn against seeing in Leopold Bloom's humdrum wanderings and minor adventures ... a close parody of the *Odyssey*" (288). To focus on the "very general Homeric echo" in the book would turn it into a "protracted and sustained allegory based on a well-worn myth," and nothing could be more tedious. Nabokov points out that Joyce himself eliminated the pseudo-Homeric chapter, or, rather, episode heads of the magazine publication, and assumes that this was done "when he saw what scholarly and pseudo-scholarly bores were up to." He singles out Stuart Gilbert for special condemnation, and, exhibiting his command of American local color, compares such allegorization with turning "a thousand and one nights into a convention of Shriners" (288).

For Nabokov, the book is really about Bloom's never-ending despair over his dead son, Bloom's love for Molly—who he knows is on the point of having an affair with her manager Blazes Boylan—and the Fate that brings him together with Stephen Dedalus, whom he would much prefer to Boylan as a lover for Molly. Pointing out that each episode is written in a different predominating style, Nabokov thinks, unlike most critics, that "there is no special reason why this should be" (288), though he has some kind words for the effect created. He compares it to bending over, looking between one's outspread legs, and suddenly seeing the world in a new perspective; "this trick of changing the vista, of changing the prism and the viewpoint," is similar to Joyce's constant shift of stylistic tonality, which "conveys a more varied knowledge, fresh vivid glimpses from this or that side" (289).

Joyce writes in three main styles, which Nabokov labels as "the original Joyce: straightforward, lucid and logical"; stream-of-consciousness, which is now defined as "incomplete, rapid, broken wording ... the stepping stones of consciousness"; and parodies of all kinds of other styles, both literary and "nonnovelistic" (289). While admiring Joyce's inexhaustible verbal ingenuity ("puns, transposition of words, verbal echoes, monstrous twinning of verbs, or the imitation of sounds"), Nabokov thinks that these, along with "the overweight of local allusions and foreign expressions," may create "a needless obscurity" of detail (290). These styles are employed to depict the characters as they come and go "during their peregrinations through a Dublin day" in what Nabokov calls "a slow dance of fate." The whole of *Ulysses*, he says, "is a deliberate pattern of recurrent themes and synchronization of trivial events" (289).

Most of the Joyce lectures are given over to a careful précis of what goes on in each episode of the book, numbered by part and chapter, and preceded by information about the time and place of the action and the characters involved. It is obviously impossible to summarize Nabokov's own summary of the book, but Nabokov makes evaluative and explanatory comments both on the characters themselves or the style of the section; and a few may be singled out as typical. One such is a reference to the scene culminating in Buck Mulligan wiping his razor blade on Stephen's snot-green handkerchief. "This links up," Nabokov says, "the snotgreen sea with Stephen's filthy handkerchief and the green bile in the bowl; and the bowl of the bile and the shaving bowl and the bowl of the sea, bitter tears and salty mucous, all fuse for a second in one image. This is Joyce at his best" (297).

Nabokov notes with approval Stephen's rebuke to the anti-Semitism of Mr. Deasy, the headmaster of the school in which he teaches, and he returns to the issue later to stress that "vicious or conventional prejudice animates most of the people whom Bloom meets in the course of his dangerous day" (316). Stephen Dedalus himself offends Bloom when he sings a song "which is a parody of the sixteenth-century ballad about young Hugh of Lincoln, believed in early times to have been crucified by the Jews in the twelfth century" (316). Nabokov particularly likes the scene in which Bloom brings Molly her breakfast in bed; he calls this "one of the greatest passages in all literature" (306). He is also fascinated by an unnamed character, who is referred to eleven times and only identified as wearing a brown mackintosh. Nabokov conducts an elaborate inquiry in order to establish, at least to his own satisfaction, that the Man in the Mackintosh is really Joyce himself.

The famous journalism chapter (part 2, epis. 4), whose sections "bear humorous titles in a parody of newspaper headlines," is not to Nabokov's taste; he declares it "poorly balanced" (320). But he is lavish in praise of the Gerty McDowell chapter (part 2, epis. 10), where he savors the parody of the feminine magazine style and notes how Joyce somehow managed to reconvert "bits of dead prose and rotting poetry" into genuinely moving expressiveness that is "tender and beautiful" (346). He is also touched by the contrast between Gerty's clichéd preoccupation with beautiful and elegant clothing and the disclosure that she is hopelessly lame. By this means "Joyce manages to build up something real—pathos, pity, compassion—out of the dead formulas which he parodies" (347).

Nabokov himself, so preoccupied with mysterious patterns determining the fate of characters in his novels, is also impressed with the various types of synchronization that Joyce uses to indicate the simultaneity of what is occurring. He carefully follows the course of a printed scrap of paper, containing a sermon about the coming of Elijah, that Bloom crumples up and throws into the Liffey River. It appears and reappears in various places, just like characters "who walk through several chapters as one of the many synchronizing agents in the book" (323). One episode (part 2, epis. 7), which contains fifty characters, is analyzed in detail to bring out how they "cross and recross each other's trails in a most intricate counterpoint." He rightly considers this technique "a monstrous development of Flaubert's counterpoint themes, as in the agricultural show scene in *Madame Bovary*" (330).

As usual, Nabokov dismisses any attempt to interpret the great Nighttown scene, where the characters undergo all kinds of hallucinatory metamorphoses, in psychoanalytic terms. For Nabokov, it is "an hallucination on the author's part, an amusing distortion of his various themes." The style is described as "a nightmare comedy," and Nabokov detects in it an "acknowledgement to the visions in a piece by Flaubert, *The Temptation of St. Anthony*, written some fifty years earlier" (350). Nabokov focuses particularly here on the relations between Stephen and Bloom and contrasts them very eloquently. "Bloom is the kindly, diffident, humane materialist; Stephen the ascetic, hard, brilliant, egotist who in rejecting God has also rejected mankind" (355). Joyce makes Stephen physically disgusting, but Nabokov is obviously attracted to "his lofty, soaring mind ... and fantastically rich and subtle frame of reference" as well as the proud integrity and moral courage of "his independence carried to the point of obstinacy" (355).

The final pages are devoted to the memorable, forty-page soliloquy of Molly Bloom just before falling asleep; and this leads Nabokov to some further comments on the stream-of-consciousness technique. He believes that readers are "unduly impressed" by this type of narration, which is not more "realistic" or "scientific" than more familiar narrative means. He repeats the point that we think in images as well as words, and this stylistic convention thus unrealistically eliminates description; it also results in a "blurring of the time element," since reflections often slow and stop and do not really proceed in an uninterrupted flow. Nabokov warns against considering "the stream-of-consciousness as rendered by Joyce a natural event;" it is just a literary convention like any other (363). It of course has had a tremendous influence, and "in the typographical broth many a poet has been generated: the typesetter of the great James Joyce is the godfather of tiny Mr. Cummings." Nabokov also adds that "if punctuation marks be inserted" into the text, "Molly's musings would not really become less amusing or less musical" (363). This last sentence indicates Nabokov's aesthetic enjoyment of Molly's recollections, whatever his reservations about the more extravagant claims made for its narrative mode, and he ends by quoting substantial extracts of its stylistically epoch-making pages. These culminate in Molly remembering how she had embraced Bloom during their courtship and led him on to propose, responding with a yes. Nabokov echoes her last word in his final sentence: "Yes: Bloom next morning will get his breakfast in bed" (370).

Lectures on Literature also includes a talk entitled "The Art of Literature and Commonsense," not part of the Cornell series but written earlier, in 1940—41 and given as part of a creative writing course at Stanford University. It deals, very allusively and charmingly, with the question of the artist's relation to reality and what his obligations are to respond to this reality in terms of his art. Written in a light tone of irreverent mockery, it is still one of Nabokov's most important statements of his ideological beliefs, and sets up a clear-cut antithesis between "commonsense"—which might be defined as the dominance of the mass-mind—and the art of literature. Individuality of all kinds is crushed by "commonsense," and "the meek prophet, the enchanter in his cave, the indignant artist, the nonconforming little schoolboy all share in the same sacred danger" (372). The artist should thus have no truck with "commonsense," and "I never could admit that a writer's job was to improve the morals of his country, and point out lofty ideals from the tremendous heights of a soapbox, and administer first aid by dashing off second-rate books" (376).

This does not mean that the artist has no concern with morality, but only that this concern should take into account that a "commonsensical majority in a righteous rage" is perfectly capable of putting to death anyone because of "the color of one's creed, neckties, eyes, thoughts, manners, speech" (372). Nabokov himself cherished "an irrational belief in the goodness of man (to which the farcical and fraudulent characters called Facts are so solemnly opposed)" (373); and it is precisely because nothing in the world of "commonsense" can justify such a belief (quite the opposite!) that it is so valuable, precious, and indestructible. The same is true for a belief in personal immortality: "That human life is but a first installment of the serial soul and that one's individual secret is not lost in the process of earthly dissolution, becomes something more than an optimistic conjecture, and even more than a matter of religious faith, when we remember that only commonsense rules immortality out" (377).

There is much more in this essay of first importance for understanding Nabokov's convictions and worldview, but this is not the topic of the present article. He finishes, however, with an evocation of literary inspiration that may be cited as a finale. What he says is very similar to what T. S. Eliot and Ezra Pound also wrote about poetic inspiration as the grasping, "in an instant of time," of a whole complex of impressions and sensations that fuse together in a hitherto unperceived unity. "It is," Nabokov writes, "the past and the present and the future (your book) that come together in a sudden flash; then the entire circle of time is perceived, which is another way of saying that time ceases to exist" (378). This is the initial revelation of inspiration, "and the pages are still blank, but there is a miraculous feeling of the words all being there, written in invisible ink and clamoring to become visible" (379). Moreover, as the writer settles down to put these words on paper, most important of all is that he forget "the monster of grim commonsense that is lumbering up the steps to whine that the book is not for the general public, that the book will never never—And right then, just before it blurts out the word, s, e, double-l, false commonsense must be shot dead" (380).

INDEX

Acis and Galatea (Lorrain), 58
Adam Bede (Eliot), 2
Akhmatova, Anna, 101, 103, 104, 130
Alarm Clock, The, 222
Alexander I, 109, 112, 113, 146, 150, 151; death of, 114
Alexander II, 73, 152–53, 168, 187, 189 >
Alexander III, 153
"Ambience of Death in Pre-Revolutionary Russian Literature, The" (Mirsky), 256
Andrei Rublev (1966), 104
Anna Karenina (Tolstoy), 139n7, 263, 274, 277; Konstantin Levin in, 3
Annenkov, P. V., 12
Ansky, S. R., 187
Antiquities of the Russian State, 93
Apocalypse, The, 5, 235
Apology of a Madman (Chaadaev), 151–52
Around the Golden Calf (A. Kovner), 193–94
"Art of Literature and Commonsense" (Nabokov), 284–85
Asakov, Ivan, 152
atheism, 43, 47, 140, 239
Atheism (Dostoevsky), 47–48
Auerbach, Erich, 3, 135n5
Austen, Jane, 3, 263–66; language and style of, 265–66; use of characterization, 264–65; use of interior monologue, 265
Averbakh, Leopold, 259

Babel, Isaac, 245, 254
Bakhtin, Mikhail, 4, 138, 141, 191
Bakst, Leon, 95
Bakunin, Mikhail, 49, 61, 131; correspondence with Belinsky, 132
Balaganchik (*The Clown* [Blok]), 252
Balakirev, Mily, 93
Balanchine, George, 105
Ballets Russes, 95–96, 105
Balzac, Honoré de, 11, 59, 62, 129
Barchester Towers (Trollope), 3
Baring, Maurice, 251, 252, 254
Bartlett, Rosamund, 219–20, 229
Batyushkov, Konstantin, 109

Beckett, Samuel, 43, 119
Behrs, Sofya, 72
Belinsky, Vissarion, 12, 13, 50, 122, 129, 133–34, 161, 178, 223; correspondence with Bakunin, 132; on individual moral responsibility, 134; opinion of Gogol, 151
Bely, Andrei, 101
Benois, Alexander, 95
Berdyaev, Nikolay, 255
Bergson, Henri, 275
Berlin, 104
Berlin, Isaiah, 80, 141
Bezhin Meadow (Turgenev), 102
Binyon, T. J., 107, 108, 109, 113, 115; on Pushkin's poetry, 111
Blackamoor of Peter the Great, The (Pushkin), 108
Bleak House (Dickens), 59, 262, 272; Allan Woodcourt in, 269; breakdown of the cast of characters in, 266–67; Krook in, 267–68; major themes of, 267; Miss Flite in, 267; presentation of children in, 268; as a satire, 266; structural features of, 269
Blok, Alexander, 101, 130, 245, 252
Boborykin, P. D., 82
Bolshevik Party, 245
Bolshevik Revolution, 89, 129, 253
Bolsheviks, 9, 93, 101, 239, 245, 254, 257; and "superutilitarianism," 246, 247
Bonald, Louis, 151
Booth, Wayne, 139, 141
Boris Godunov (Pushkin), 11, 103, 108, 113; Nicholas I's opinion of, 114
Borodin, Alexsandr, 93
Bos, Charles du, 255
Bouquet of Flowers, A (A. Kovner), 188
Boyhood (Tolstoy), 68
Brafman, Yakob, 169
Brief History of Russia (Pokrovsky), 258
Brod, Max, 279
Brodsky, Joseph, 260
Bronze Horseman, The (Pushkin), 90, 92, 116
Brooks, Peter, 191

Brothers Karamazov, The (Dostoevsky), 2, 9, 48, 59, 96, 165, 180, 200, 213; anti-Semitism in, 170–71; criticism of, 154; equating of Stavrogin with Dostoevsky in, 201; Father Zosima in, 57, 97, 98, 99, 213, 214; Ivan Karamazov in, 59, 213–14; Liza Kokhlakova in, 170–71
Bulgakov, Sergei, 102, 246
Bunin, Ivan, 95, 175
byliny (epic oral poetry), 100
Byzantium, 96, 148, 151

Camus, Albert, 247
Cancer Ward (Solzhenitsyn), 99
Captain's Daughter, The (Pushkin), 69, 116
Carlyle, Thomas, 268
Catechism of a Revolutionary (Nechaev), 49–50
Catherine the Great, 149–50
censorship, in Russia, 4, 120–21
Cervantes, 268
Chaadaev, Pyotr, 111, 151–52
Chagall, Marc, 101
Chaplin, Charlie, 102
Chechneya, 68
Chekhov, Alexander, 221
Chekhov, Anton, 4–5, 95, 98, 219–20, 228–29; admiration for Tolstoy, 228; anecdotes and humorous stories written under the pseudonym Antosha Chekhonte, 222; attitude toward the Russian intelligentsia, 226; charitable activities of, 226; country estate (Melikhovo) of, 226, 227; detailed knowledge of Russian Orthodoxy, 221; financial support of his parents and family members by, 221; influence of Dimitry Grigorovich on, 223–24; journey to the Sakhalin Islands, 225–26; love life of, 224; marriage of, 224–25; merchant background of, 220–21; in Moscow, 223; in Nice, 227; poor health of, 224, 225, 227; relationship of with his birthplace (Taganrog), 220, 222–23; restlessness of, 225; in Yalta, 227–28
Chekhov, Nikolay, 225, 226
Chekhov, Pavel Egorovich, 220
Chekhov: Scenes from A Life (Bartlett), 219–20
Chenier, André, 114

Chernyshevsky, Nikolay G., 47, 50, 94, 164; attack on by Herzen, 51
Cherry Orchard, The (Chekhov), 229
Childhood (Tolstoy), 66, 68; critical praise for, 69
Christian, R. F., 82
Christian morality, 2–3; among prison camp inmates, 23
Christian social romanticism, 11
Christianity, 39, 148, 151, 164, 194, 234; and faith, 32; heritage of in Russian culture, 96–99; of the peasants in Russia, 97–98; Russian Christianity as ritualistic in nature, 96; and the Russian "holy fool" motif, 100; Utopian Socialist Christianity, 208
cinema, 102
Citizen, The, 168, 189
Coetzee, J. M., 196, 204, 205–6
Cohen, Norman, 167
Common Story, A (Goncharov), 122
"Comrade Prince" (Wilson), 259
Confession (Tolstoy), 140
Confessions (Rousseau), 129, 135–36
Constant, Benjamin, 129
Contaminated Family, The (Tolstoy), 73
Contemporary, The, 164
Cossacks, 100, 161, 245
Cossacks, The (Tolstoy), 67, 73, 100
"Country, The" (Pushkin), 111
Courage (Akhmatova), 103
Craft, Robert, 106
Craft of Fiction, The (Lubbock), 75
Crime and Punishment (Dostoevsky), 9, 24, 29, 47, 165, 173, 180, 207; beginnings of as a novella, 32; Raskolnikov in, 47, 132–33, 160, 190, 212–13
Crimean War, 70, 92, 152
Critique of Practical Reason (Kant), 146
Custine (Marquis de), 100

Daniel, Yuli (aka Nikolay Arzhak), 230
d'Anthés, George, 117; duel of with Pushkin, 117; infatuation of with Pushkin's wife, 117; marriage of to Ekaterina Goncharova, 117; relationship of with Baron van Heeckeren, 117
Day, 163, 164
Dead Christ, The (Holbein the Younger), 31; reference to in *The Idiot*, 31–32
Dead Souls (Gogol), 2, 12, 64, 97, 273

Death of Ivan Ilich, The (Tolstoy), 98–99
Decembrists, The (Tolstoy), 73–74
Decembrists/Decembrist revolt, 73–74, 91, 94, 109, 110, 114, 151
Deconstruction, 142n9
Delvig, Anton, 109
Demons (Dostoevsky), 4, 9, 46, 57, 61, 63, 94, 187–88, 189, 190, 196; "birthday party" at the Virginskys in, 61; boredom of Stavrogin in, 54, 55; clash of generations theme in, 54–55, 58; ego and power of Stavrogin, Pyotr, and Kirillov in, 60; *Envy* section of, 51, 53; Golubov in, 54; Governor-General von Lembke in, 60; hostility toward radicalism in, 60; Kirillov in, 55–56; Lyamshin in, 166–67, 180; murder (of a student by a revolutionary group) as the inspiration for, 48–49; as a "pamphlet-novel," 54; plans in Dostoevsky's notebooks concerning, 51, 56–57; the Prince (Stavrogin) in, 32, 51, 53–54, 55, 57, 58, 123; Pyotr Verkhovensky in, 49, 50, 56–57, 58, 60, 62, 160, 166, 200; quarrel between Pyotr and his father in, 50–51, 54–55; revisions of, 56–58; Shatov in, 54, 55–56, 62; Shigalyov in, 61; Stepan Trofimovich in, 33, 51–52, 58, 59; the Ward in, 51, 53, 54
Derzhavin, Gavrila, 110
determinism. *See* scientific determinism
Devils, The. See Demons
Diaghilev, Sergei, 95
Diary (Grigoryevna), 31, 176
Diary of a Superfluous Man, The (Turgenev), 123
Diary of a Writer (Dostoevsky), 166, 167, 168, 185, 189, 190, 210, 223; attacks on Jews in, 192–93
Dickens, Charles, 2, 264, 265, 266–70
Dobrolyubov, Nikolay, 47, 123, 128
Doctor Zhivago (Pasternak), 103, 245
Don Quixote (Cervantes), 268, 269
Dostoevsky, Feodor, 1, 4, 91, 120, 122–23, 134, 138–39, 138n7, 146, 183, 185–86, 219, 227, 264; addiction of to roulette, 29–30; admiration of for Gogol, 12; admiration of for Pushkin, 10, 107; arrest of, 18; atheism of, 25; Christian faith of, 25–26; as a Christian socialist, 18, 22; on the clash between generations, 50–51; correspondence with Kovner, 190, 191, 192–93; death of his son Aleksei, 97; defense of his "fantastic realism," 47; desire to write for the stage, 11, 12; despair of over the death of his daughter, 30–31; "dialogism" of his novels, 4; epilepsy of, 38, 56; in Europe, 29, 46–47, 196–97; as a father, 30; financial problems of, 29, 47; hatred of serfdom, 18, 27; imprisonment of, 19; influence of Hugo and Balzac on, 11; influence of Karamzin on, 13; intellectual sophistication of, 58; involvement of in a revolutionary conspiracy, 62; as a member of the Petrashevsky circle, 18–19; mock execution of and its effects on, 19, 25, 29, 37–38; novels of as "novel-tragedies," 4; opinion of Goncharov, 122; opinion of marriage, 42; parody of Turgenev's prose-poems by, 59; poor standing of among Russian progressives, 61–62; populist ideology of, 94, 95; preoccupation of Jewish scholars with, 160–61; in prison camp, 4, 19, 21, 22–23; prolific imagination of, 34; quarrel with Turgenev, 50, 174; radicalism of, 152–53; on the redemptive quality of the Russian peasant soul, 97–98; religious convictions of, 41–42, 211; religious sensibility of, 59, 60; as a satirical humorist, 44, 58; "sentimental Naturalism" of, 208, 210; socialism of, 97; themes of in his writing, 9–10; transformation of his beliefs concerning the educated versus the peasant classes, 21–24, 27–28; use of Gothic devices in his writing and others' criticism of, 63. *See also* Dostoevsky, Feodor, anti-Semitism of; Dostoevsky, Feodor, and evil
Dostoevsky, Feodor, anti-Semitism of, 159, 171–72, 180, 184, 185, 192–93; and the blood libel, 171; challenge of, 159–60; conflict of with his Christian ideals, 165; evidence of in his work, 161–62, 166–67, 168, 169, 170–71; failure to recognize the rights of Jews, 192; and his portrait of Isai Fomich Bumstein, 161–63; roots of in his millenarianism, 167–68; and the "Rothschild idea," 165–66, 169, 170

Dostoevsky, Feodor, and evil: depictions of evil at work in his writing, 212–13; experience of evil during his time in prison camp, 209, 210–11; preoccupation of with violent crime, 207–8; protagonists of his major novels are criminals, 207; and the struggle of moral conscience, 212
Dostoevsky, Mikhail, 10, 20, 46, 163
Dostoevsky, Sofya, 30–31
Dostoevsky and the Jews (Goldstein), 159
Dostoevsky and the Legend of the Grand Inquisitor (Rozanov), 194
Double, The (Dostoevsky), 208
"Dreary Story, A" (Chekhov), 225
Dreyfus affair, 227
Dubnow, Simon, 169
Dzherzhinsky, Feliks, 247

Eastern Orthodox Church, 208
Efron, Sergey, 260
Eikhenbaum, Boris, 129, 272
Eisenstein, Sergei, 102, 103
Eliot, George, 2
Eliot, T. S., 256, 285
Elizabeth Costello (Coetzee), 204, 205, 206–7, 214–15; and Paul West, 207, 214–15
Engels, Friedrich, 61
English novels, religion in, 2–3
Envy (Olyesha), 259
Eternal Husband, The (Dostoevsky), 48, 57
Eugénie Grandet (Balzac), 161
Eugeny Onegin (Pushkin), 3, 55, 112, 113, 116, 123; as the first great Russian novel, 3; Lensky in, 109; Tatiana's rejection of St. Petersburg's glamour in, 91–92
Eurasian movement, 257, 257n4
European culture: hegemony of, 91; idealization of by Russians, 91
Evenings on a Farm near Dikanka (Gogol), 92

Family Happiness (Tolstoy), 71
"fantastic realism," 47, 60
Fantastic Stories (Sinyavsky), 231
Fathers and Sons (Turgenev), 50; Bazarov in, 50, 53
Feast of the Goat, The (Vargas Llosa), 206
Fernandez, Ramon, 256
Feuer, Kathryn, 75

Figes, Orlando, 87, 92, 100, 106
Finnegan's Wake (Joyce), 280
Fish, Stanley, 263
Flaubert, Gustave, 2, 69, 129, 270–73, 283; "counterpoint method" of, 272
Fleishman, Lazar, 234n8
Foe (Coetzee), 196
Forster, E. M., 256, 265
"Fountain of Bakhchisaraym, The" (Pushkin), 112
Fourier, Charles, 165–66
Franco-Russian Messenger, The, 227
French Naturalism, 2
French Revolution, the, 91, 114, 146, 149, 153
French Romanticism, 11–12
French Utopian socialism, 12, 18
Friend of the Family, A (Dostoevsky), 10
Frigate Pallas, The (Goncharov), 120
From the Notes of a Jew (Kovner), 186
Frost, Robert, 219
Fry, Roger, 255–56
Futurists, 246

"Gabrieliad, The" (Pushkin), 112, 115
Galton, Dorothy, 258–59
Gambler, The (Dostoevsky), 30
Gannibal, Abram, 113
Gastev, Alexei, 102
German Romantic Idealism, 120, 133, 138
German Romanticism, 11
Gilbert, Stuart, 281
Ginzburg, Lydia Iakovlevna, 129, 130n2, 131n4, 142, 191; circle of her friends, 129–30
God, man's relationship to, 59
Goethe, Johann Wolfgang von, 179, 181
Gogol, Nikolay, 2, 92, 96–97, 107, 151, 197, 208, 233; compared to Proust, 276; on *Dead Souls* as a "prose poem," 273; death of by starvation, 97
Goldstein, David, 159, 162, 165
Goncharov, Ivan, 118, 178; charges of that Turgenev stole his ideas, 121–22; criticism of for his position on the censorship bureau, 120–21; Dostoevsky's opinion of, 122; education and early career of, 118–20; realism of, 122–23; as secretary to Admiral Putyatin, 120; semihumoristic style of, 120

Goncharova, Ekaterina, 117
Goncharova, Natalya, 115; flirtatious nature of, 116–17
"Good Readers and Good Writers" (Nabokov), 261–63
Goodnight! (Sinyavsky), 235–37; "Dangerous Liaisons" chapter, 240–41; "In the Belly of the Whale" chapter, 241–42; "My Father" chapter, 238–40; "Public House" chapter, 237–38
Gorbachev, Mikhail, 247
Gorky, Maxim, 105, 228, 251, 257, 258, 259
Grandet, Eugénie, 11
Granovsky, T. N., 52
Grigorovich, Dimitry V., 12, 13, 223–24
Grigoryevna, Anna, 29, 49, 174, 176, 179
Grossman, Leonid, 63, 168, 176, 191; opinion of Chekhov, 222
Grossman, Vasily, 103
Guggenheim, Peggy, 118
Gulag Archipelago (Solzhenitsyn), 9, 162
Gumilyov, Nicholas, 253
Gypsies, The (Pushkin), 113

Hadji Murad (Tolstoy), 68
Harrison, Jane Ellen, 255
Hasidism, 186
Haskalah, 186
Haveth Childers Everywhere (Joyce), 280
Hedgehog and the Fox, The (Berlin), 80, 141
Heine, Heinrich, 166
Hero of Our Time, A (Lermontov), 53, 100
Herzen, Alexander, 51, 61, 72, 90, 91, 94, 123, 129, 131, 135; dedication of to revolutionary action, 140; importance of his work as a step toward historical self-awareness in the Russian novel, 136–37; memoirs of, 132, 166; praise for Dostoevsky's *Poor Folk*, 134
History of Russian Literature (Mirsky), 249, 249n1, 255
History of the French Revolution (Carlyle), 268
History of the Russian State (Karamzin), 146
History of Yesterday, A (Tolstoy), 68
Hitler, Adolf, 93, 103
Hobbes, Thomas, 147
Hoffman, E.T.A., 11

Holbein the Younger, 31, 32
Hollow Men, The (T. S. Eliot), 256
Homer, 268, 281
Honest Thief, An (Dostoevsky), 208
House of the Dead, The (Dostoevsky), 9, 10, 19–20, 64, 97, 180, 189, 209; apparent simplicity of, 20; concept of time in, 26; as a memoir, 27; presentation of peasant life in, 21, 210–11; structure of, 210
Houseman, A. E., 263
Hugo, Victor, 11, 59
Hunt, Leigh, 59
"Huntsman, The" (Chekhov), 223–24

Identity Theft: The Jew in Imperial Russia and the Case of Avraam Kovner (Murav), 185
Idiot, The (Dostoevsky), 3, 29, 46–47, 57, 160, 165–66; Adelaida Epanchin in, 37–38; Aglaia Epanchin in, 38, 40–41; autobiographical nature of, 37–38; Dostoevsky's conception of "the idiot," 33–34; Dostoevsky's conception of "the idiot" as a prince, 35; Dostoevsky's difficulties in planning of, 39–40; Dostoevsky's notebooks concerning, 33, 38; Dostoevsky's opinion of, 44–45; epilepsy in, 38; General Ivolgin in, 44; goal of to "portray a perfectly beautiful man," 35–36, 41, 46; humor in, 44; the idiot as a Christ figure, 29, 34, 41; Ippolit in, 31, 32, 43; Ippolit's "Necessary Explanation" in, 43; Lebedev in, 43; love theme in, 41–42; Marie in, 38; minor characters as the opposites of Myshkin in, 43; moral extremism in, 44; narratives of minor characters in, 42–43; Nastasya Filippovna in, 36–37, 38, 40, 42; Prince Myshkin in, 31, 37–38, 46–47; Prince Myshkin's involvement with Aglaia in, 40–41; Radomsky in, 40; revisions to, 32–33; Rogozhin in, 37, 38, 40, 42
Ilarionov, Andrei, 155
Inquiry, The (A. Kovner), 188
Intelligentsia of Great Britain, The (Mirsky), 259
Iser, Wolfgang, 263
Island of Sakhalin, The (Chekhov), 226
Ivan IV (the Terrible), 148, 149
Ivan-Durak (*Ivan the Fool*), 234–35

Ivan the Terrible (Prokofiev), 103
Ivanov, Vyacheslav, 4

J'accuse! (Zola), 227
Jackson, Henry, 143
Jakobson, Roman, 116, 272
Jesus Christ, 3, 29, 31, 41, 42, 213; as perpetual eternal ideal, 211, 212
Jew Yankel, The (Dostoevsky), 12, 161
"Jewish Question, The" (Dostoevsky), 163, 169, 183
Jews, 152, 192; Karaite sect, 228; Orthodox Polish Jews, 144; place of in Russian society, 167; the Russian Jewish Pale (western provinces), 186. *See also* Dostoevsky, Feodor, anti-Semitism of; Hasidism; Haskalah
Johnson, Barbara, 142n9
Joseph of Volokolmansk, 148
Journey to Ezerum (Pushkin), 115
Joyce, James, 265, 276, 280–84

Kafka, Franz, 232, 233, 278–80; Flaubert's influence on, 279; Freudian interpretations of, 279
Kahler, Erich, 130
Kandinsky, Wassily, 93, 99, 101
Kant, Immanuel, 146
Karamzin, Nikolay, 31, 91, 109, 112, 146, 147, 149, 151
Karsavin, Leo, 257
Karyakin, Yury, 61–62
Katchaturian, Aram, 103
Katov, Mikhail, 29, 49, 56, 152, 153
Keaton, Buster, 102
Kelly, Aileen, 167, 172
Kennan, George, 144–45
Ketscher, Nikolai, 136
Khrushchev, Nikita, 61, 260; revelations of concerning Stalin, 230
Kireevsky, Ivan, 96
Kovner, Arkady, 168, 169, 183, 185, 195; admiration for Rabbi Hillel, 194–95; arrest and trial of for bank swindling, 185–86, 190; correspondence with Dostoevsky, 190, 191, 192–93; Dostoevsky's acceptance of Kovner's explanation for his crime, 191–92; exile to Siberia, 190, 193; as an imposter, 190; Jewish studies of, 186–87; marriage of, 187; reasons for his crime, 190, 191

Kovner, Savelii, 187
Koyre, Alexandre, 255
Kuchelbecker, Wilhelm, 109
Kukolnik, Nestor, 163
Kuleshov, Lev, 102
Kunitz, Joshua, 163, 167
Kurbsky, Andrei, 149
Kuzmin, Mikhail, 252

La Dame aux Camelias (Dumas), 36
La Guerre et la Paix (Proudhon), 72
La Traviata (Verdi), 36
Lady Macbeth from Mstensk (Shostakovitch), 102
"Lady with the Little Dog, The" (Chekhov), 227–28
Lamartine, Alphonse de, 69
"Landlady, The" (Dostoevsky), 197, 208
Landmarks in Russian Literature (Baring), 251
Language of Facts, The: About the Isolation of the Jews (A. Kovner), 193
Le dernier jour d'un condamne (*The Last Day of a Condemned Man*), 11
"Legend of the Grand Inquisitor" (Dostoevsky), 17, 165, 200, 213
Lenin, Vladimir I., 66, 102, 105, 154, 246, 247
Leontiev, Konstantin: contempt of for modernity, 153; criticism of *The Brothers Karamazov*, 154
Lermontov, Mikhail, 53, 100, 129; description of Simbirsk, 118–19
Les Illusions perdues (Balzac), 62
Les Justes (Camus), 247
Les Misérables (Hugo), 36
Leskov, Nikolay, 221
Letters of a Russian Traveller (Karamzin), 31, 91
L'homme revolté (Camus), 247
"Liberty: An Ode" (Pushkin), 111, 112
Life and Fate (V. Grossman), 103
Life and Times of Michael K. (Coetzee), 202
Life for the Tsar, A (Glinka), 92
Life of a Great Sinner, The (Dostoevsky), 48, 57
Life of the Elder Leonid, 97
Likhachev, Dimitry, 100
"Literary and Social Curiosities" (A. Kovner), 189

Little Tragedies (Pushkin), 116
Liubimov (Sinyavsky), 231
Lorrain, Claude, 58
Louis XVI, 153
Lover's Vows (Kotzebue), 263
Lubbock, Percy, 75
Lurie, Sofya, 169–70

Machiavelli, 147
Machiavellianism, 49, 60
Madame Bovary (Flaubert), 261, 263, 268, 270–73; Charles Bovary in, 271; "daydream" theme of, 271; deceit in, 271–72; Emma Bovary in, 270, 271; "layering" theme of, 270–71; as a prose poem, 272–73; realism and naturalism in, 272
Mahomet II, 148
Maikov, Apollon, 30, 47, 48
Maikov, Valerian, 35
Maistre, Joseph de, 151
Makepeace Experiment, The. See *Liubimov* (Sinyavsky)
Malevich, Kazimir, 93, 101
Man, Paul de, 142n9
Mandelstam, Osip, 102, 130, 252
Mann, Thomas, 89, 279
Mansfield Park (Austen), 263–64; importance of the setting of, 264; and "intertexuality," 264
Marquis de Sade, 206
Mary Stuart, 11
Marx, Karl, 61
Marxism, 245, 246, 252, 257; in Russia, 154–55; in Scandinavia, 154
Master and Margarita, The (Bulgakov), 235, 246
Master of Petersburg, The (Coetzee), 196, 202–3, 215; Dostoevsky's defense of Pasha against Maximov in, 198–99; Dostoevsky's obsession with Pasha's death in, 197–98; involvement of Dostoevsky with Nechaev in, 199–200; mixture of fact and fiction concerning Dostoevsky's life in, 196–97
Maxim the Greek, 148
May Night (Rimsky-Korsakov), 92
Mayakovsky, Vladimir, 93, 102, 130, 245, 246
Mediator, The, 188
Mendelssohn, Moses, 186

"Metamorphosis, The" (Kafka), 232, 278–80; importance of the number "three" in, 279–80
Meyerhold, Vsevolod, 102
Mikhailovsky, N. K., 94
Miller, J. Hillis, 263
Mimesis (Auerbach), 3, 135n5
Mirsky, D. S. (Prince Dimitri Svyatopolk-Mirsky), 249; association with the Bloomsbury circle, 255–56; bitterness of toward the politics of the time, 254; as book reviewer for the *London Mercury*, 254; death of, 260; decision to return to Russia and consequences of, 249–51; early publications of, 252, 253; as editor of *Eurasia*, 256–57; education of, 251, 253; founding of a Russian-language journal (*Vyorsts*), 256; as lecturer on Russian literature, 254–55; as a "left Eurasian," 257; literary career in Moscow, 258–60; mastery of several languages by, 251; as member of the Communist Party, 258; as member of the *Ryurikovichi* aristocracy, 251; military service of, 253; opinion of the Russian civil war, 253–54; opinion of the White Sea canal, 259–60; personal losses of, 254; in prison camp, 260; sexual orientation of, 252; time spent living in Europe, 254–58; visit with Gorky, 257
Miscellany (Tolstoy), 67
modernism, 141
Moll Flanders (Defoe), 65
Moscow, 72; contrast of with Petersburg, 92–93
Moscow Art Theater, 93, 228
Moscow Opera, 93
Muggeridge, Malcolm, 259
Murav, Harriet, 185, 187, 188, 191, 192; reasons for studying A. Kovner, 195
Muraviev, N. M., 190, 193
Mussorgsky, Modest Petrovich, 92, 93, 94
My Past and Thoughts (Herzen), 72, 166; description of the 1840s in, 133
Mystery-Bouffe (Mayakovsky), 102

Nabokov, Vladimir, 1, 63, 104–5, 229, 250, 252, 284–85; on Austen, 263–66; criticism of Stuart Gilbert, 281; definition of art as "beauty plus pity," 278; on Dickens, 266–70; on Flaubert, 270–73;

Nabokov, Vladimir (*cont'd*)
  on the ideal reader, 262–63; influence of Proust on his own conception of art, 277–78; on Joyce, 280–84; on Kafka, 278–80; on narrative technique, 268–69; as professor of Russian literature at Wellesley and Cornell, 261–62; on Proust, 274–78
Napoleon, 72, 110, 146, 151; and the "great man" theory of history, 81
Napoleon, Louis, 117
Natasha's Dance: A Cultural History of Russia (Figes), 88–106 passim. *See* Russian culture for detailed analysis of
Natural School, 2
Nazism, 144
Nechaev, Sergei, 48, 49, 54, 61; as an advocate of Machiavellianism, 49
Nekrasov, Nikolay A., 12, 178, 211, 223
Nemirovich-Danchenko, Vladimir, 228
Nest of Gentlefolk, A (Turgenev), 121
New Times, 194, 195
Nicholas I, 18, 37, 73, 91, 114, 151, 166
Nicholas II, 98, 154, 251
Niebuhr, Reinhold, 39
Nietzsche, Friedrich, 27–28, 143, 144, 210
Night on Bald Mountain (Mussorgsky), 92
Norma (Bellini), 126
Notes from Underground (Dostoevsky), 140
Notes of a Hunter (Turgenev), 27
Notes of the Fatherland, 12
Notre Dame de Paris (Hugo), 60
Nouvelle Revue Francaise, 255
Novikov, Nicholas, 149–50
Nussbaum, Martha, 141, 142n9

Oblomov (Goncharov), 118, 120, 121; childhood dream sequence in, 122, 124–25; literary ancestry of Oblomov in, 127–28; Matveyevna in, 127; Olga and Oblomov's relationship in, 126–27; Penkin in, 124; problems in interpretation of, 125–26; Stoltz in, 124, 125, 126, 127–28; symbolic role of Oblomov's dressing gown in, 123–24; topicality of, 128; Zakhar and Oblomov's relationship in, 124
Obryv (*The Precipice* [Goncharov]), 121, 122
Observations on Property Management (Tolstoy), 67
Oedipus Rex (Stravinsky), 105
Ogarev, Nikolai, 49
Old Believers, 54, 96, 136, 235
Olyesha, Yuri, 259
On Psychological Prose (Ginzburg), 129; on the "conception of man," 133; on Dostoevsky, 138–39, 139n7; on Flaubert's *L'Education Sentimentale*, 137–38; on "ordinary social life," 133–34; on realism, 137; on Rousseau's *Confessions*, 136; as a study of "social psychology," 130–31; on Tolstoy, 137, 138, 139–41; on Tolstoy as founding father of the modern novel, 139; on Tolstoy's pursuit of causality, 139n7; on writing that arises directly from social experience, 131–32
On Socialist Realism (Sinyavsky), 230, 231–32, 231n3, 244
On the Eve (Goncharov), 121
On the History of Religion and Philosophy in Germany (Heine), 166
On the Literary Hero (Ginzburg), 142
On the Lyric (Ginzburg), 129
On Trial: The Case of Sinyavsky (Tertz) and Daniel (Arzhak) (Labedz and Hayward), 230
Optina Pustyn monastery, 96; visits of Gogol and Dostoevsky to, 97; visits of Tolstoy to, 98
Ostromir Evangel of Novgorod, 2
Ostrovsky, A. N., 220
Overcoat, The (Gogol), 2, 12, 13–14, 279; Akaky Akakievich in, 14

Pale Fire (Nabokov), 104–5
Pares, Bernard, 254
Past Recaptured, The (Proust), 278
Pasternak, Boris, 93, 103
Peasant Wedding, The (Stravinsky), 95–96
Peasants, The (Chekhov), 95, 226–27
Peltier, Hélène (later Peltier-Zamoyska), 242–44, 243n16
Peresvetov, Ivan, 148
Pestel, Pavel, 110
Peter the Great, 89–90, 108
Petersburg, 36, 89, 90; contrast of with Moscow, 92–93
Petersburg (Bely), 101
Petersburg Tales (Gogol), 12
Petrashevsky circle, the, 18, 37, 166, 207

Phillips, Anthony, 220
Pilnyak, Boris, 102
Pinkerton Agency, The (Ginzburg), 130
Pipes, Richard, 143–44, 150; hard-line views of Russian communism, 145; on the sanctity of private property, 147–48; on Soviet Russia as a "multinational empire," 145
Pisarev, Dimitry, 47, 187–88
"Pkhentz" (Sinyavsky), 232–33
Plato, 206
Pnin (Nabokov), 105
Pobedonostev, Konstantin, 153
Poe, Edgar Allen, 11
Pokrovsky, Mikhail, 258
Poor Folk (Dostoevsky), 2, 9, 10, 19, 134–35, 161, 178, 189, 223; Anna Feodorovna in, 15; depiction of God's will in, 17–18; depiction of poverty in, 15–16; depiction of the young intellectual (*raznochinets*) in, 15; "different view of God's world" in, 15; evolution of Devushkin's character in, 16–17; form of as a sentimental epistolary novel, 14–15; Makar Devushkin in, 13, 14; narrative of the Gorshkov family in, 15; parodies of Romantic historical novels in, 13; plot of, 14–15; Pokrovsky in, 15; relationship of Pokrovsky to his father in, 15; social realism of, 12–13; use of anticlimax in, 16; Varvara Dobreselova in, 14–15, 17–18
Poor Liza (Karamzin), 13
Pound, Ezra, 285
Pride and Prejudice (Austen), 263
"Prisoner of the Caucasus, The" (Pushkin), 113
Prokofiev, Sergei, 103, 105
Property and Freedom (Pipes), 147
"Prophet, The" (Pushkin), 61
Protocols of the Elders of Zion, 152
Proudhon, P. J., 72
Proust, Marcel, 129, 274–78; belief in art as the essential reality of life, 277; compared to Gogol, 276; concern of with anti-Semitism, 277; influence of Bergson on, 275; style of, 275–76
Pudovkin, Vsevolod, 102
Pugachev uprising, 116
Pursuit of the Millennium (Cohen), 167–68

Pushkin, Aleksandr, 3, 10, 11, 55, 90, 107–8, 151, 163, 175, 233–34, 253; addiction to gambling, 111; atheism of, 112, 113; attempts to escape his banishment to the Mikhailovskoe estate, 113; bravado of, 110–11; chauvinism of, 115; "conservative liberalism" of, 111; cultured childhood of, 108–9; death of from wounds suffered in a duel, 117; education of, 109; exile of, 112; flirtatiousness of his wife, 116–17; friends of among the Decembrists, 110, 114; life of in St. Petersburg, 111; love affairs of, 112–13; marriage of, 115; as member of the *Arzamas* literary group, 110; placement of under the supervision of the tsar Nicholas I, 114–15; productivity of at his country estate, 115–16; productivity of at the Mikhailovskoe estate, 113; reputation of as a duelist, 111–12; reputation of in Russia, 107; sexuality of, 109; social life of at court, 116
Putin, Vladimir, 155

Queen of Spades, The (Pushkin), 116
Quiet Don, The (Sholokov), 253

Rachmaninov, Sergei, 104
Radcliffe, Ann, 62
radicalism, 47, 60, 63
"Raid, The" (Tolstoy), 67
Raskol. *See* Old Believers
rationalism, 56, 60
Raw Youth, A (Dostoevsky), 48, 58, 170, 185; Arkady Dolgoruky in, 170
"Recollections in Tsarakoe Selo" (Pushkin), 109–10
Red Cavalry (Babel), 245, 254
Reflections of a Russian Statesman (Pobedonostev), 153
Reminiscences (Grigoryevna), 31, 176
Remizov, Aleksey, 256
Repin, Ilia, 94
Revisor (Gogol), 56
Rhetoric of Fiction (Booth), 139
Rilke, Rainer Maria, 89, 279
Rimsky-Korsakov, Nikolay, 92, 93
Rite of Spring (Stravinsky), 95, 100, 106
Riviere, Jacques, 255
Rodionovna, Arina, 113
Roerich, Nicholas, 100

Roman Catholicism, 96, 208
Roman-Uprezhdenie—"A Novel of Warning," 61
Rosengrant, Judson, 129
Rostov, Nikolai, 141
Rothschild, James, 166, 168
Rousseau, Jean-Jacques, 129, 131, 135–36
Rozanov, Mordechai, 227
Rozanov, V. V., 194
Russia, 133; acceptance and implementation of Western ideas in, 4; artistic energy given over to the idea of Russian nationality in, 89; beginnings of political controversy in, 148; conquest of by the Mongols, 99–100, 147; deification and autocracy of the tsar in, 148–49; destiny of, 61; dilemma of "historical myth" versus actual Russian history in, 88–89; emergence of political theory in, 149; European Russians' "split-identity," 90–91; faith of the peasants in, 97–98; Finno-Ugrian people of, 99; folksongs and folktales of, 92; invasion of by Napoleon, 146; myths concerning peasant life in, 93–96; peasant life in, 94–95; pre-Christian Scythian civilization of, 100–101; revolutions of 1905 and 1917 in, 95, 245; Russia as the Third Rome, 148; Russian society as "patrimonial," 147. *See also* Soviet Russia
Russia: A Social History (Mirsky), 258
Russia under the Old Regime (Pipes), 146
Russian Conservatism and Its Critics (Pipes), 143, 146, 147
Russian culture, 55–56, 58, 62, 87–88, 168; "The Children of 1812" phase of, 91; Christian heritage of, 96–99; cultural myth of the "Russian soul," 89, 96–97; in exile after the Russian Revolution, 104–5; the "going to the people" movement, 94–95; "neo-Byzantine" architecture of, 92; and the revival of neoclassicism, 105; role of Eastern and Asiatic cultures in the development of, 99–101; during the Soviet period, 101–4
Russian literature, 64, 94, 136–37, 187; and anti-Semitism, 163; conflict between educated elites and the religious sensibility of the peasant class in, 3–4
Russian Messenger, The, 29
Russian Modernism, 252

Russian Nihilism, 44, 49, 51, 52, 128, 187
Russian novels: distinctiveness of, 1; English novels comparable to, 2; history of, 3; "ideological" nature of, 4; literary realism of, 3; narrative traditions of historical and epic novels in, 65; science/rationality versus Christian morality in, 2–3, 4–5
Russo-Turkish War, 167

Sadko (Rimsky-Korsakov), 100
Said, Edward, 100
Saint-Simon, Claude Henri, 131; memoirs of, 135, 135n5
Samarin, Iury, 152
Schiller, Friedrich, 179, 181
Schlumberger, Jean, 255
scientific determinism, 133, 140
Scirabin, Aleksandr, 93
Scott, Walter, 65, 114, 125, 163
Seagull, The (Chekhov), 224, 226, 228
Selected Passages from Correspondence with Friends (Gogol), 97, 151
Sevastopol Sketches (Tolstoy), 27, 70, 92, 220
Seventh Symphony (Shostakovitch), 103
Shestov, Lev, 255
Shklovsky, Viktor, 265
Sholokov, Mikhail, 253
Shostakovitch, Dmitri, 102, 103, 105, 106
Silas Marner (Eliot), 2
Sinani, Isaac, 228
Sinyavsky, Andrey (aka Abram Tertz), 5, 230, 243n16, 244n17; as Abram Tertz, 236–37, 243; attraction of to the work of V. V. Rozanov, 234; belief in the fantastic and the grotesque in art, 232; on utopian society/civilization, 245–46
Sketches from a Hunter's Album (Turgenev), 94
Slavonic Review, The, 254
Slavophiles, 55, 91, 92, 94, 96, 152; journal of (*Day*), 163, 164
Smith, G. S., 249, 250–51, 252, 258, 260
Smoke (Turgenev), 49, 179
Snitkin, Ivan, 49
Socialist Realism, 231n3
Soirees de St. Petersbourg (de Maistre), 151
Solaris (1972), 104
Solovyev, Vladimir, 172

Solzhenitsyn, Aleksandr, 9, 99, 162, 175
"Some Words about the Book *War and Peace*" (Tolstoy), 64
Sontag, Susan, 174
Sorrows of Young Werther, The (Goethe), 131
Sorsky, Nil, 148
Soviet Civilization (Sinyavsky), 244–45
Soviet Russia, 144–45; conservatism of, 145–46; deficiencies of, 145; future of, 247–48; growth of anti-Semitism in, 248, 248n19; as a "multinational empire," 145; Soviet-style communism and the creation of the "Soviet man," 246–47
Spalding, H. N., 257n4
Speak, Memory! (Nabokov), 104
Speransky, Michael, 150–51
Speshnev, Nikolai, 62
Spirit of the Law (Montesquieu), 149
St. Tikhon Zadonsky, 57, 97
Stalin, Joseph, 61, 102, 103, 105, 130, 230, 241, 246
Stalinism, 231, 241
Stalker (1979), 104
Stanislavsky, Konstantin, 93, 228
Stankevich, Nikolai, 129
Stasov, Vladimir, 100
Stationmaster, The (Pushkin), 13
Stendhal (Marie-Henri Beyle), 129
Stevenson, Robert Louis, 273, 274
Stolypin, Peter, 154
"Story of a Liberation, The" (Mirsky), 250
Strakhov, N. N., 47, 51
Strange Case of Dr. Jekyll and Mr. Hyde, The (Stevenson), 273
Stravinsky, Igor, 95–96, 105–6
Student, The (Chekhov), 4–5, 221–22
Summer in Baden-Baden, A (Tsypkin), 160–61, 173–74; cinematic nature of, 174–75; evocation of Anna Grigoryevna's *Diary* in, 176–78, 179; evocation of Dostoevsky's *House of the Dead* in, 177–78; the narrator's identification with Dostoevsky in, 182–83; parade of characters from Dostoevsky's novels in, 180–81; portrayal of Dostoevsky's gambling in, 178–79; transformation of Dostoevsky into a Jewish character in, 181–82; Turgenev in, 179

Superfluous and the Bilious, The (Herzen), 51
Suvorin, Alexsey, 223, 225, 227, 229
Swann's Way (Proust), 274–78; Aunt Léonie in, 277; as an autobiography, 275; depiction of same-sex relationships in, 277; Marcel's grandmother in, 277; and the orchid *Cattleya labiata* in, 278; thematic center of, 275

Taganrog, 220
Tales of Belkin (Pushkin), 116
Taras Bulba (Gogol), 12; the Jew Yankel in, 161, 162
Tarkovsky, Andrei, 104
Taylor, F. W., 102
Temptation of St. Anthony, The (Flaubert), 283
Thompson, Lawrence, 219
Thought, A (Poem), Theme Called "The Emperor" (from Dostoevsky's notebooks), 34–35
"Three Years" (Chekhov), 220–21
"To the Slanderers of Russia" (Pushkin), 115
Tolstoy, Alexei, 104, 105
Tolstoy, Leo, 2, 9, 64–65, 65–66, 94, 95, 113, 120, 122, 129, 132, 139–42, 209, 220, 227, 264, 276; admiration of for Pushkin, 69; admiration of for Rousseau, 67; ambition of, 66, 67; artistic credo of, 70; bluntness of, 72; childhood of, 66; early writings of, 68–69; education of, 66; erudition and sophisticated reading materials of, 66–67; establishment of a free school by, 71–72; fascination of with the motivation of men to go to war, 80; gambling of, 67, 72; hostility toward in literary circles, 72–73; as an inventor of the interior monologue, 66; marriage of, 72; and modernism, 141; obsession of with death, 98; preference of for character study over narrative, 69–70; relationship of with Turgenev, 72–73; restless nature of, 67; "Rules of Life" set down in his diary, 66; struggle of between different aspects of his worldview, 140–41; tenacity of in revising his writings, 69; trips to Europe, 72; uniting of narrative traditions (the epic/myth and the historical novel) by, 65, 88–89; visits

Tolstoy, Leo (*cont'd*)
of to the Optina Pustyn monastery, 98; Yasnaya Polyana ("clear glade") estate of, 66, 71, 71–72, 94. *See also* Tolstoy, Leo, military career of
Tolstoy, Leo, military career of, 67; bravery of as a volunteer, 68; commendations of for bravery, 70; dissatisfaction of with service in the border regions, 70; retirement from the army, 71; transfer of to Sevastopol during the Crimean War, 70
Tolstoy, Nikolay, 67
Tolstoy and the Genesis of War and Peace (Feuer), 75
Tom Jones (Fielding), 65
Traill, Vera, 260
Trial Begins, The (Sinyavsky), 231, 232
Trollope, Anthony, 3
Trotsky, Leon, 101
Trubetskoy, N. S., 101
Tsvetaeva, Marina, 104, 105, 175, 256, 260
Tsypkin, Leonid, 160, 173, 182
Turgenev, Ivan, 1, 9, 13, 27, 46, 69, 99, 102, 120, 123, 129, 138, 162, 175, 178; caricature of by Dostoevsky, 59; quarrel with Dostoevsky, 50, 174; quarrel with Goncharov, 121, 122; relationship of with Tolstoy, 72–73; and the "superfluous man," 132
"Twelve, The" (Blok), 245
Tynianov, Yuri, 129

Ulyanov, V. I., 66
Ulysses (Joyce), 280–84; Gerty McDowell in, 283; "journalism" chapter in, 282–83; Leopold Bloom in, 280–81; Molly Bloom in, 280, 282; Molly Bloom's soliloquy in, 283–84; Nighttown scene in, 283; rebuke of anti-Semitism in, 282; relationship of Dedalus and Leopold Bloom in, 283; as "slightly overrated" according to Nabokov, 281; Stephan Dedalus in, 280, 282; stylistic shifts of tone in, 281–82; synchronization in, 283
Uncle Vanya (Chekhov), 225
Uncle's Dream (Dostoevsky), 10
Unguarded Thoughts (Sinyavsky), 231
utilitarianism, 47; "superutilitarianism," 246, 247

Utopian socialists, 245–46; anti-Semitism of, 165–66; idealism of, 47

Vargas Llosa, Mario, 206, 207
Vengerov, S., 253
Verdi, Giuseppe, 36
Viardot, Pauline, 46
Village, The (Bunin), 95
Virgin Mary (Mother of God), 60
Vixi: Memoirs of a Non-Belonger (Pipes), 143
"Vlas" (Nekrasov), 211–12
Vogüé, Eugene Melchior du, 1–2, 80, 219
Voice, The, 168, 189, 190
Voice from the Chorus, A (Sinyavsky), 233
Volga Barge Haulers, The (Repin), 94
Vremya (Time) 20, 163, 164
Vyorsts (*Mileposts*), 256

Waiting for Godot (Beckett), 118
Walnut Trees of Altenburg, The (Malraux), 255
War and Peace (Tolstoy), 82–83, 92, 139–40; Anatole Kuragin in, 70, 75, 78–79; Andrey Bolkonsky in, 70, 75, 76–77, 79, 81, 150; Andrey Bolkonsky's retreat from the world in, 78; contrast of the Rostov family to the Kuragin family in, 79; critical reaction to, 64; Denisov in, 79; depiction of Napoleon in, 78; depiction of the occupation of Moscow in, 81; Dolohov in, 76; Ellen Kuragin in, 75, 76; issue of morale in, 81; Marshal Kutuzov in, 80–81; Marya in, 77, 79; massiveness of the original manuscripts for, 74; Natasha Rostova in, 70, 71, 75, 79, 82; Natasha's dance in, 87–88; Nikolay Bolkonsky in, 74, 77; Nikolay Rostov in, 68, 79–80; opening scene of, 74–75; origins of, 73–75; patriotism in, 81–82; Pierre Bezuhov in, 3, 74, 75, 76, 132; Pierre Bezuhov's craving for moral purification in, 76–77, 78; Platon Karataev in, 3, 77, 132; portrayal of military life in, 80–82; prefaces to, 74; return of Andry Bolkonsky to the army in, 78; revisions to, 74–75; satirical war scenes in, 80–81; Speransky in, 78; Tolstoy's view of, 64–65, 82–83; Tushin in, 81; Vasily Kuragin in, 75, 76; view of Petersburg society in, 75–76

Wasiolek, Edward, 33, 34
We (Zamyatin), 102
Weber, Max, 147
Weidlé, Wladimir, 165
Wells, H. G., 238
Westernizers, 55
"What I Believe" (A. Kovner), 194–95
What Is Art? (Tolstoy), 64
What Is Needed for the Welfare of Russia? (Tolstoy), 67
"What Is Oblomovschina?" (Dobrolyubov), 123
What Is To Be Done? (Chernyshevsky), 47
Whitfield, Francis J., 249
Who Is Happy in Russia? (Nekrasov), 94
Widening Gyre, The (Frank), 142
Will to Power, The (Nietzsche), 27, 143
Wilson, Edmund, 259, 266, 273
Wings (Kuzmin), 252

"Winter Landscape" (Pushkin), 113
Without a Label (A. Kovner), 189
Woe from Wit (Griboedov), 90
Wood Demon, The (Chekhov), 225
"Wood Felling, The" (Tolstoy), 67
Woolf, Leonard, 255
Woolf, Virginia, 89, 250, 255
Wound and the Bow, The (Wilson), 266

Young Tolstoy, The (Eikhenbaum), 272
Youth (Tolstoy), 68, 73

Zamyatin, Yevgeny, 102
Zhdanov, Andrei, 103, 105
Zhirmunsky, Victor, 258
Zhukovsky, Vasily, 109, 110
Zola, Emile, 2
Zoschenko, Mikhail, 102, 103
Zvenya (*Links*), 252

GPSR Authorized Representative: Easy Access System Europe - Mustamäe tee 50, 10621 Tallinn, Estonia, gpsr.requests@easproject.com